AMERICAN PROPHETS

AMERICAN PROPHETS

★ ★ ★

The Religious Roots of
Progressive Politics
and the
Ongoing Fight for
the Soul of the Country

JACK JENKINS

HarperOne
An Imprint of HarperCollinsPublishers

HarperOne

HarperCollins books may be purchased for educational, business, or sales promotional use. For information, please email the Special Markets Department at SPsales@harpercollins.com.

FIRST EDITION

Designed by THE COSMIC LION

Library of Congress Cataloging-in-Publication Data
Names: Jenkins, Jack (Journalist), author.
Title: American prophets : the religious roots of progressive politics and the ongoing fight for the soul of the country / Jack Jenkins.
Description: First edition. | New York, NY : HarperCollins Publishers, 2020. | Includes bibliographical references.
Identifiers: LCCN 2019056140 | ISBN 9780062935984 (print) | ISBN 9780062936004 (digital edition)
Subjects: LCSH: Christianity and politics—United States—History—21st century. | Progressivism (United States politics)—Religious aspects— Christianity. | Liberalism—Religious aspects—Christianity. | Liberalism— United States. | United States—Church history—History—21st century. | United States—Politics and government—2009-2017. | United States Politics and government—2017
Classification: LCC BR526 .J45 2020 | DDC 261.70973—dc23
LC record available at https://lccn.loc.gov/2019056140

20 21 22 23 24   LSC   10 9 8 7 6 5 4 3 2 1

For Dad

Contents

Introduction

I fiddled with my camera as I emerged from the Park Street T station in downtown Boston, ignoring the bluster of wind that swept across my face. I adjusted and readjusted the lens before turning the DSLR over, crossing the street as I flipped through an endless litany of settings crammed into its minuscule screen. I tinkered aimlessly while walking southeast from Boston Common toward the city's financial district, barely looking up as I sped past fellow pedestrians, clogged shopping centers, and the offices of Bank of America.

I was nervous.

My neurotic state was one well known to many reporters. It was 2011, and I was working on my first freelance assignment for *Religion News Service*, tasked with chasing down a religion angle in the Occupy Wall Street movement. As a native southerner, I never fully adjusted to the infamously frigid winters in Boston, where I was attending divinity school at the time. The ice and snow hadn't arrived yet, but I forgot my gloves that day, which was a problem: I was worried that any religious presence I found would be fleeting, and that I probably wouldn't be nimble enough to set up my camera in a crucial moment with my clumsy, frozen digits.

I was still anxious when I arrived at Dewey Square, home to Occupy Boston, the local branch of the rapidly expanding Occupy movement. I paused across the street from the encampment to take in

the sight and catch my breath, bouncing on my toes and hugging myself to keep blood flowing. Feeling slightly warmer, I raised my camera to snap a photo of the sea of multicolored tents sprawled across
a patch of green in the shadow a nearby office building. Through my
viewfinder I could see a hastily constructed protest camp bustling
with activity: men and women, most of whom looked to be in their
twenties, meandered a tangled web of walkways that snaked through
the tent city. Some of them wore shirts or gripped signs of protest
that championed "The 99%," a phrase I had heard chanted over and
over at Occupy demonstrations across the country.

But as I lined up my shot, I didn't hear chants.

I heard hymns.

Dumbstruck, I shoved my camera back into its new case and wandered across the street and into the expanse of temporary structures,
following the music until I found its source: a makeshift A-frame
tent fashioned from wrinkly, weather-beaten blue tarps patched over
with duct tape. Inside, a group of worshippers sat in a tight circle,
belting out the last notes of an impassioned spiritual. I made moves
to join them, but one looked up at me, pointed at my muddy feet,
and gestured toward a list of rules scrawled in barely legible marker
on a cardboard sign: *Sacred Space Guidelines*, it read. And below it:
Rule No. 2: Remove shoes.

I stared at the sign, which appeared to have led a very active past
life as a FedEx box. My mind reeled; removing shoes is a common
practice in many religious communities, but usually only when entering a venerated place of worship. In some traditions, the command
to do so occurs when God asks an important religious figure to approach holy ground. Even then, it is a request most often reserved
for one very specific group of people: prophets.

I looked back at the group, which had already launched into the
next song. I was in the presence of prophets.

Not that many of the interfaith activists in that tent would have
used that phrase to describe themselves, of course. Prophet means
different things in different faith traditions, and some don't have a
concept of it at all. But it was one of my early introductions to what

many activists call the *prophetic tradition* of social justice activism, a spiritual lineage that comprises a myriad of movements and an even greater number of faiths. It's a phenomenon I would later come to associate with the Religious Left, an amorphous, ever-changing group of progressive, faith-based advocates, strategists, and political operatives. I was surprised to find representatives of this movement at Occupy, but I shouldn't have been—and not just because I was tipped off that the tent existed before I got there. As I would learn over the next several years of reporting on the Religious Left for *ThinkProgress* and *Religion News Service*, these activists and others like them have been a core component of progressive social movements throughout American history, often rising to meet moral crises in times of need. Far from being a historical relic, the Religious Left I have come to know exerts growing influence on modern Democratic politics—be it by staging massive protests, leading legislative fights, training future candidates, or pressuring political leaders. The Religious Left is the beating heart of modern progressivism; although rarely acknowledged by members of either major political party, it is one of the Left's most secret of weapons and has the potential to impact US politics for years to come.

This book is an attempt to unearth some pieces of that secret. Such a task requires digging into the history, theology, and strategy used by Religious Left leaders to exert influence on their fellow progressives. My intention is not to tell an exhaustive history of this coalition of coalitions and its historical progenitors. (For those seeking such a history, see historian Albert J. Raboteau's similarly named *American Prophets: Seven Religious Radicals and Their Struggle for Social and Political Justice*). Rather, my aim is to home in on the iterations that are having the greatest impact in modern politics—and explain where they came from. The result (I hope) is the story of a movement that is fundamentally different from the similarly named Religious Right, one that makes sense only when examined through the overlapping lenses of protest, policy, and politics.

But first, a quick note about terms. I use the phrase *Religious Left* a lot in this book, but many people who may fall under that category—including leaders I profile in these pages—actively reject the term. A running joke I've had with editors for years is that one of the hallmarks of a Religious Left leader is vehement opposition to the phrase *Religious Left*. (Look: I'm a journalist, not a comedian.)

Still, readers should not assume—unless otherwise noted—that people who fall into that category necessarily embrace the term. When appropriate, I do my best to list most of their objections to the epithet. Some see it as too limiting, and others don't like the association with the Religious Right, whose tactics and approach to politicized faith they hold in contempt. Still others quibble over the finer definitions of the words themselves—a political moderate's *left* is often not the same as a democratic socialist's or, for that matter, a hard-charging conservative's. Political scientists also spar over the exact borders of these ideological camps, some of which have morphed in profound ways in just the past three years.

Nevertheless, I use *liberal*, *progressive*, and *left* relatively interchangeably in this book when referring to those who mostly (but not always) fall in and around the Democratic Party, if for no other reason than that is how the terms are used in popular political discourse—the water in which these activists and operatives swim.

Moreover, as any number of scholars have made clear to me in classrooms and over the course of my career, the category of religion is hotly contested. Different thinkers use different criteria to classify what is or isn't a faith community, and many reject the idea that such a thing can ever be fully defined in the first place. I have my own thoughts on this matter, but I strive to rely on the terms that faith communities use to describe themselves (thus, Native American *spirituality* instead of religion), acknowledging that preferences can differ even among individual believers within the same tradition.

And as this is a larger-than-average journalistic work about religion and politics, some deeper-than-average disclosures are in order. While I have voted for both Republicans and Democrats in my life, I worked for Democratic campaigns in general and Barack Obama's 2008 presidential campaign in particular (primarily by doing field work, such as the glamorous act of trudging through the snow to knock on doors) prior to becoming a full-time journalist. In addition, my transition to working as the religion reporter at *ThinkProgress* occurred only after the Center for American Progress (CAP) hired me as a writer for its Faith and Progressive Policy Initiative. Although that job was already legally forbidden from engaging in electoral-style political advocacy (CAP is beholden to traditional nonprofit regulations), I still preferred a more journalistic approach and freelanced for *ThinkProgress* (which operated under the CAP Action Fund) until the politics-savvy site invited me to become its first and only full-time religion reporter. I consider my prereporter time in these circles to be an enhancement to my dedication to journalistic fairness when covering the Religious Left, not a detriment. All reporters must extend themselves beyond personal biases, but I have the added benefit of being able to call on my experiences while doing so—in fact, it is through these experiences that I was able to track down many of the stories in this book.

More to the point, I do not consider this book to be an advertisement for the Religious Left. If I am an advocate, it is only because I engage in the kind of advocacy that virtually all reporters practice daily: I believe the subjects of my stories are important and worth your time. Whether those subjects constitute something "good," "bad," or anything in-between is entirely up to you.

With these parameters in mind, this book seeks to understand the Religious Left through one of its favorite mediums—namely, through storytelling. These stories often recount specific times, places, and movements, but if you pay close attention, you'll notice a recurring cast of characters.

We begin with a series of chapters that delve into the more overtly political elements of the Religious Left. First is the fight over the Affordable Care Act, which focuses on how a small band of Washington, DC-based advocates worked to create a temporary bridge between inside-the-Beltway politicos and faith-based activists to pass one of the most important pieces of liberal legislation in a century. Then we provide context for this legislative victory by explaining why Barack Obama had such a vested interest in faith groups in the first place—and why Religious Left activists consider him one of their own. And since no discussion of the Religious Left is complete without a treatment of its political opposite, we move on to highlight how an unexpected transformation within the Religious Right—namely, the rise of Christian nationalism and the influence of Donald Trump—triggered a dramatic spike in progressive faith activism.

With that broader political context in mind, we then crisscross the country, tracing the development of some of the most influential progressive faith leaders and grassroots movements of the past twenty years. Beginning with the sizable impact of Rev. William Barber and the Moral Monday movement in North Carolina, we examine the complicated relationship between the Religious Left activists and racial justice movements—from Ferguson to Charlottesville. We travel to the border to learn how a small Tucson, Arizona, church helped make the New Sanctuary movement a central pillar of the #Resistance to Donald Trump, and make stops in Hawaii and North Dakota to better understand the influence of Indigenous spirituality on the global campaign for climate justice. We march through the streets of New York to observe the intersection of spirituality and socialism, process through the echoing halls of the Washington National Cathedral to trace the development of the faith-based LGBTQ rights struggle, double back to Manhattan to unpack the importance of the interfaith movement, and return to the conference rooms of the capital city to see how Democrats did—or, in many cases, did not—capitalize on these movements during the 2016 election.

We end our journey with a trip to another camp, this time in the rural hinterlands of western North Carolina, to see how this swirling torrent of activists—and the prophetic leaders who guide them—will influence the future of faith itself.

Even with all those stories, it should be acknowledged that this book, by its very nature, is incomplete. Attempting to sum up the collective histories and happenings of progressive faith activism in the United States is a laughably impossible task, which is why this book does not seek to achieve that goal. Rather, this book tackles a more targeted, though still challenging task. My hope is to lift up the untold (or simply ignored) stories of how various progressive faith communities shape modern American politics in this historical moment and look ahead at what that might mean.

I freely admit that there is simply not enough room in a chapter (or several chapters) to include all the voices necessary to expose the full truth of these efforts. Wiser writers than I have argued the media's perception of the Religious Left is often disproportionately Christian-centric, and while this book is more concerned with tracing the influence of the Religious Left than painting a complete picture of its boundaries, it's worth acknowledging the importance of such critiques.[1] What's more, my hope is that this book will be seen as a *beginning* to a much longer process of storytelling—one in which I am by no means the primary storyteller—that will explain, add to, or even correct the narratives I've uncovered in this book. Virtually every group, leader, or movement mentioned in these pages could constitute a tome (or two, or twelve) unto itself, and I leave the daunting challenge of offering a proper, full treatment of their efforts to others.

Put another way: If you read this book and think there are more stories to tell, good. Tell them. Write them. Preach them.

But in the meantime sit back, take off your shoes, and listen to what these heirs to the prophetic tradition have to say.

CHAPTER ONE

★ ★ ★

Faith in Public Life

John Podesta half walked, half stumbled his way into the hotel bar, tottering about on shaky legs. He wasn't drunk, at least not yet. Rather, Podesta, the former chief of staff to President Bill Clinton, had just completed the 2010 Rome marathon in Italy at the tender age of sixty-one and was feeling every bit of it. On the short list of places he wanted to be at that moment, a bar was a distant second behind his own bed.

But the prominent progressive strategist had promised to grab a drink with his friend Sister Carol Keehan, a Daughters of Charity nun, after running into her at the Rome airport earlier that week. So with the help of his wife and a couple of friends, he dragged his lanky, exhausted frame to a hotel near the Eternal City's famous Villa Borghese gardens to meet up.

It turned out to be an anticlimactic trip. According to Podesta, Keehan, who was in town for a Vatican conference as head of the Catholic Health Association, proved a poor drinking buddy that day. As he attempted to regale her with stories of the marathon, she spent most of her time on her phone frantically calling members of the US House of Representatives. The pivotal vote on the Affordable Care Act (ACA) was about to happen that same day back home, and she was lobbying every representative she could to back the bill—especially her fellow Catholics.

Podesta wasn't offended by her antisocial manner, however. He was delighted and found the whole situation kind of hilarious.

"We were trying to have a good time in Rome overlooking the city, but she's just on her flip phone talking to [House] members," Podesta told me as he recalled the moment, pausing several times to descend into fits of laughter. "She couldn't enjoy any of that!"[1]

The moment was a window into one of the great, untold stories of the ACA, the landmark piece of liberal legislation often derisively (or lovingly) referred to as Obamacare. Conservatives and liberals alike have long argued that an organized Religious Left is either hopelessly anemic or simply doesn't exist and thus can never claim the kind of power in Washington, DC, ostensibly held by the Religious Right. But Democratic insiders who fought to pass Obamacare tell a very different story. Although the ACA was a victory for many different progressive movements, the legacy-defining achievement of Barack Obama's presidency also represented the triumphant culmination of a long-term collaboration between grassroots faith groups and a religion-savvy advocacy infrastructure in Washington backed by prominent institutional progressives.

Put another way: if it weren't for the Religious Left, the ACA probably wouldn't exist.

Unpacking the origins of this inexact, inconsistent, but unmistakably powerful system of influence is crucial to understanding how the modern Religious Left's decentralized nature can be wielded to great effect. It may not have the same laser-focused legislative agenda as the Religious Right's inside-the-Beltway power brokers, but the Religious Left's passion—combined with an admittedly ephemeral, and sometimes heavily Catholic religion-and-politics apparatus that helps grassroots activists influence the influential—has proven strong enough to force laws through Congress, stoke the ire of the Vatican, and stare down Donald Trump.

THE SEARCH FOR GOD INSIDE THE BELTWAY

John Podesta may be able to laugh about it all now, but back in 2003 he was, well, pretty mad.

In his defense, there were a lot of things for liberals to be mad about in 2003. George W. Bush was president, thanks to an election so tight and contentious it required the Supreme Court to step in and spare the country the horrors of a Florida recount. His administration thrust the United States into a wildly unpopular war in Iraq that March—despite waves of protests at home and abroad—only to have Bush declare "Mission Accomplished" (spoiler alert: it wasn't) from the deck of an aircraft carrier little more than a month later. Unemployment hit 6.4 percent that June,[2] and right-wing pundit Ann Coulter released a new book that sold half a million copies in three weeks.

Much of that probably ate at Podesta, a bespectacled, smoky-voiced veteran of Bill Clinton's administration, who would go on to serve in Barack Obama's White House and chair Hillary Clinton's 2016 campaign for president. But he was particularly peeved about something else: he believed Republicans had co-opted the perception of religion in the public square to the point where, as he put it, "to be religious was to be conservative."[3]

The raw electoral power of conservative God talk was obvious during Bush's reelection bid. As the Democratic primary season progressed, it became increasingly clear that the incumbent Texas Republican, a United Methodist often described as a born-again Christian, would be pitted against Massachusetts senator John Kerry, who, despite being a Catholic Democrat and war veteran, somehow managed to come across to voters as an elitist WASP and whose Boston archbishop threatened to deny him communion because of his support for abortion.[4] Kerry's campaign would mostly avoid discussing faith (more on that later), but Bush's potential road to victory was paved with the ecstatic prayers of what were often described as "values voters"—primarily conservative Christians who opposed abortion and same-sex marriage and who typically cast their ballots for Republicans.[5]

Podesta kept this God differential in mind when, in October

2003, he used his hard-earned prominence among Washington liberals to found the Center for American Progress (CAP), a massive, sweeping policy think tank geared toward counterbalancing such DC-area conservative intellectual havens as the Heritage Foundation and the Cato Institute. Initially bankrolled by prominent donors that included George Soros, CAP and its sister organization—the Center for American Progress Action Fund (CAPAF), which could legally flex more explicit political muscles—would exert broad influence over liberal politics for years to come.[6]

CAP would also play a role in the realm of faith. Podesta has long insisted that his interest in the subject was first and foremost personal: a liberal Catholic, he spoke regularly in the mid-2000s of how religion informed his politics, once declaring that his faith was "really what makes me a progressive."[7] He found a kindred spirit in Melody Barnes, a former aide and chief counsel to Sen. Edward M. Kennedy, whom Podesta brought on board to help build out CAP's influence. The two collaborated on making faith a key part—albeit often unsung—of CAP's work, and in June 2004, they convened a gathering of four hundred clergy, advocates, and scholars for a faith and policy conference. Attendees included prominent faith voices that ranged from stalwart religious progressives such as Rev. Jim Wallis, of Sojourners, to more issue-specific leaders such as Sister Carol Keehan.[8]

"There was a need to organize a different group of voices from across faith traditions," Podesta said. "We got them all together and that gave rise to a bunch of work that went on through the course of the summer."

Part of that work included drafting a report on the future of the progressive faith movement, penned by a group known as Res Publica. The organization was relatively obscure in Washington circles, but Podesta had connected with some the group's young founders at the CAP faith conference: Ricken Patel, Tom Pravda, and Tom Perriello, a Catholic who would later be elected to Congress, serve in the State Department, and run CAPAF. Res Publica described itself as "a group of young public sector professionals dedicated to promoting good governance, virtuous civic cultures, and deliberative public discourse globally," and its now-defunct website boasted that the organization was working with CAP in 2004 to "catalyz[e] a resurgence of the progressive religious community." To that end, Res Publica claimed that faith leaders asked its team to prepare a report after seeing "a resurgence of the spirit of a progressive and prophetic faith movement."[9]

"There was a strong sense that the policies of greed, othering, and militarism demanded a moral response beyond partisanship, that it was a moment to breathe fresh life into that prophetic coalition," Perriello told me in 2019.[10]

As it turned out, that coalition was in need of full-on refurb. The more than forty-page document Perriello, Patel, and Pravda ultimately delivered to CAP—aptly titled "The Future of the Progressive Faith Movement"—was a candid and sometimes scathing assessment of the strengths and weaknesses of an atomized, divided Religious Left. CAP officials were impressed with the report and set about scheduling a closed-door gathering with prominent liberal religious leaders to allow Res Publica to present its findings a month after Bush clinched his reelection.[11]

According to multiple people in the room that day, it was not a happy meeting.

"It was a somewhat uncomfortable conversation," Podesta said, recalling that some faith leaders in the room were visibly disquieted by the report's critiques.[12]

The report did list *some* positive attributes of progressive religious activism. But it also claimed that the movement was plagued by a dearth of media training, struggled to articulate a uniform vision, lacked a firm connection between grassroots efforts and national actors, and "suffer[ed] from deep challenges of leadership, turf-battling, personality-conflict and ego-competition, and incompetence."[13]

To solve these problems, the report's authors proposed several new initiatives. Among them was a progressive faith resource center to facilitate "open-source" communication; two pastoral leadership centers to cultivate progressive faith leaders; a role for a progressive faith voice at a left-leaning think tank; a progressive faith congress for late 2005; monthly luncheons that would bring together faith leaders and politicians using a method pioneered by conservative crusader Grover Norquist; and a blue ribbon movement commission to guide these projects into the foreseeable future.

Some of these suggestions fizzled out before they were ever implemented. But others had legs, especially CAP's attempt to address the movement's structural issues. Dubbing their project Faith in Public Life (FPL), CAP leaders envisioned it as a sort of organizational anchor for the Religious Left, a strategy hub that would coordinate disparate groups and develop overarching media strategies for campaigns.

There was no obvious person to lead such a complicated, experimental project, which required a mix of religious fluency and high-level political savvy. That's why Rev. Jennifer Butler—a southern, curly-haired Presbyterian minister—was pretty sure she wouldn't get the job when she applied. She assumed they wanted a "Washington insider," something she absolutely was not, thank you very much. She was a pastor, although an unusual one: she spent her days wrangling international dignitaries at the United Nations office of the Presbyterian Church (USA), her denomination, and her nights hammering out a book on the Religious Right.

Butler did, however, share Podesta's exasperation with the Religious Right's grip on the public perception of faith. And she mirrored his simmering discontent with the failures of progressive religious organizing. When she got called up for an interview, she saw it as an opportunity to vent.

"I said to my husband Glenn, 'I'm going to go give [Podesta] a piece of my mind. I'll be back. Nothing will come of this,'" she told me. "I was just mad. I was like, 'We're so lame, and we need to get our act together.'"[14]

Something did, in fact, come of it. CAP promptly hired Butler, and incubated FPL at the think tank before spinning it off as an independent organization in 2008. Far from rejecting her as an outsider, Podesta and other CAP staffers were effusive about Butler's work.

"[Podesta] was personally very passionate about the project," Butler told me years later while sitting in FPL's glossy offices—where she still serves as CEO—near DC's Dupont Circle. "He's a man of few words, but the few things he said to me were, 'Go be visionary, don't listen to the polls, don't get close to the DNC.'"

It was around this same time that the Religious Left's fledgling DC-based apparatus developed a sort of spiritual community unto itself. This was thanks in part to a weekend excursion hosted by Perriello: In the spring of 2005, the thirty-one-year-old Catholic invited around twenty of his fellow Washington-based religious progressives to join him for a three-day retreat in Grassmere, the name of the area surrounding his family's estate near Charlottesville, Virginia. It was the closest thing the fledgling institutional Religious Left had to a strategy summit, and those who attended still talk about it with an air of nostalgia.

"It was frickin' awesome," said Mara Vanderslice Kelly, a former faith outreach staffer for Kerry's presidential campaign who attended the outing. She grew increasingly emotional as she recalled the event, struggling to hold back tears: "It was this mix of deeply spiritual conversations, times of prayer, really emotional, personal storytelling, and people talking about their faith journey."[15]

It was also, by all accounts, a pretty great time. Kelly said attendees stayed up until three in the morning joking, drinking bourbon, and playing poker before collapsing onto couches and sleeping bags strewn across the floor. Some knew each other beforehand, but many were new to the DC progressive faith fold, which made the gathering a sort of community-building-exercise-meets-pastoral-retreat.

But these were Washington operatives, and Washington operatives are nothing if not elite champions of work-hard/play-hard culture. As such, the revelry was mixed with intense three-hour-long planning sessions. Kelly said the conversations revolved around hashing out a collective strategy for their movement and determining how various organizations and leaders would use their resources to influence Democratic politics. It was a threshold moment: their band of like minds, which would thereafter be referred to as the Grassmere group, finally had enough people in places of power to start pushing their own progressive, faith-fueled agenda.

"It was the first time we all felt like we had enough status, and more collectively that they might actually be able to move the needle,"

Kelly said. "We were in places in our lives where we could commit our lives to this work for a while—and we were becoming friends."

The era that followed was something of an organizational renaissance for the Washington-based wing of the Religious Left, spawning several faith-related groups geared toward aiding progressive legislative battles. Among them was Catholics in Alliance for the Common Good (CACG), founded in 2005 by Perriello and Alexia Kelley.[16] Around the same time, Chris Korzen and James Salt created Catholics United, a similar group. The two men were seasoned activists who steered the organization toward a bolder, more brazenly political approach than that of CACG, such as sending out mass emails to blast political opponents and filming prickly confrontations with lawmakers.

Meanwhile, Res Publica coordinated with the National Council of Churches to create FaithfulAmerica.org, a website founded with the dream of "us[ing] the internet to connect up faith communities and individuals and enable a 'viral' form of activism that allows ideas and actions to spread rapidly." The site eventually transformed into something resembling a progressive Christian version of the left-leaning digital activism powerhouse MoveOn.org.

The rapid development of these groups happened alongside a separate but no less significant shift that occurred within an existing California-based organization known as PICO National Network, later renamed Faith in Action. Faith in Action defies tidy descriptors: it has ties to Washington-based Religious Left organizations but fancies itself something of a consummate outsider. Although its campaigns often skew toward liberal interests, leaders at the organization vehemently reject the Religious Left label, arguing that the moniker is too narrow and pointing out that they work with people who are theologically or even politically conservative. They also do not always coordinate with Washington-based Religious Left organizations, even when their goals appear to overlap. Faith in Action leaders describe their categorical aloofness as a strength, even if leaves others in the Beltway vexed. (To wit, several DC-based progressive religious advocates described Faith in Action to me as a group that sometimes "does not play well with others.")

Yet aversion to political labels did little to diminish Faith in Action's importance among the rapidly expanding pantheon of progressive-leaning religious groups in the first half of the decade. According to Faith in Action senior adviser Gordon Whitman, it was faith leaders who shoved them onto the national stage: the group spent years hosting trainings for local clergy on how to use community organizing techniques to influence local governments, but beginning around 2002, their trainees began to ask for more.

"They said, 'We make changes in our cities and in our states, but we've never worked together on a national level. If we can meet with our mayor and governor, why can't we meet with our congressperson?'" Whitman told me.[17]

Faith in Action took the advice to heart and relaunched after the 2004 election as a national network of congregations and interfaith coalitions. The change instantly transformed the group into the single largest bloc of (mostly) progressive-leaning, faith-based activists in the country. Organizers wasted little time before stress-testing their power by working to protect something deemed crucial to their members: access to health care, particularly Medicaid, which was subject to potential cuts.

But while grassroots groups like Faith in Action had long pushed Washington from the outside, they now had faith-based allies on the inside—especially on the topic of health care. In January 2005, CAP sponsored a faith-themed forum about health care at the National Press Club featuring Podesta along with Frank Griswold, then presiding bishop of the Episcopal Church; Laurie Zoloth, a professor of Jewish studies and bioethics at Northwestern University; and Ann Neale, a bioethicist at Georgetown University. They championed health care as a moral concern, with Zoloth going so far as to suggest that the issue could become a rallying cry for religious progressives in the same way that opposition to abortion and same-sex marriage galvanized conservative Christians.[18]

The National Press Club event was tied to CAP's rollout of its first universal health care plan, one that would be credited with laying the groundwork for what became the Affordable Care Act.[19] According to Podesta, the presser was designed to "put the commitment to health care for every person living in America in a profoundly moral context" and was an intentional, strategic attempt to stitch religious language into conversations about health care policy.[20]

"We were explicitly trying to put that into the bloodstream," he said. "This was the next stage in what was truly a movement of spiritual solidarity with everyone. To lift everyone up, you had to have health care be seen as something that was a basic right and stem from people's humanity. I think that was a powerful argument."

He added: "At the end of the day, the push for health care as a basic human right was something I think that connected very strongly to people who saw their obligation not just as citizens, but as believers to try to extend that support to their brothers and sisters."[21]

But Podesta and CAP didn't invent a connection between faith and health care. More than a few religious leaders argue that tie was established centuries if not millennia before by the founders of their respective faiths, which is why so many religious groups have been working in the health care business for so long—and why Podesta's message found such a captive audience.

THE CATHOLIC CONNECTION

Sister Carol Keehan sat among the crowd in Las Vegas, listening attentively to Barack Obama speak. She wasn't impressed.

It wasn't that she didn't recognize then-candidate Obama's famous way with words or ability to captivate a crowd at the March 2007 event. It was just that the forum, convened at the University of Nevada by the Service Employees International Union and CAPAF, was about health care, an issue Keehan knew a bit about. In addition to her not-inconsequential commitment to being a nun, she had a background in nursing and a master's in health care finance, and she served as head of the Catholic Health Association of the United States (CHA), which comprises roughly six hundred hospitals and sixteen hundred long-term care and other health facilities in all fifty states.[22] Her bar for a candidate's health care policy expertise was also a bit higher than most: she and CHA had ironed out an internal list of preferences for health care policies in 2006 and were assessing presidential candidates based on those specific criteria.

And when it came to health care, Obama had very little to say.

"They asked him about health and he literally had no answer," Keehan recalled, noting that Obama had yet to put forward a health care plan at the time. "He wasn't stellar."[23]

Indeed, the famously unflappable Obama appeared very much flapped in the face of pointed inquiries from attendees at the event. It would be remembered as an awkward low point for his upstart campaign; Ezra Klein, writing for the *American Prospect*, described then Illinois senator Obama as "unprepared and overwhelmed" at the forum,[24] and a headline from the Associated Press account of the event asked, "Is Obama All Style and Little Substance?"[25] Democratic presidential hopefuls Hillary Clinton and John Edwards, on the other hand, garnered high marks for their comparatively detailed health care proposals.

But if Obama's opening argument on fixing the United States health care system was a dud, Keehan nonetheless appreciated his apparent support for the idea that health care wasn't a privilege, but a right. She also had a knack for recognizing political savvy—a skill she knew would be needed to pass any substantive health care bill—and believed Obama, a rising star in the Democratic Party, had the ability to "pull on a lot of very talented people" as he developed a plan. So Keehan and CHA stayed in touch with the Obama campaign over the course of what turned out to be a lengthy election season. It was a prescient play: when Obama claimed his historic victory in November 2008, the nun and her team were brought in to help craft what would become the Affordable Care Act.

Keehan became a fixture at endless meetings in stuffy congressional offices and White House conference rooms throughout 2009, lending her expertise as lawmakers and policy wonks hashed out the finer details of the bill. All the while, she insisted that her CHA team stay true to distinctly Catholic ideals.

"One of our principles was health care is a human right and everybody needs to be in it," she said. "We were not getting everybody health care with the Affordable Care Act. [But] it didn't violate our principles, because it said, 'We can take a giant step forward or we can take no steps.' On the other hand, there is the principle of no federal funding of abortion, of euthanasia. And we were very satisfied with that [in the bill]."[26]

There were other Catholics who were decidedly *not* satisfied with the evolving bill, however. Whereas Keehan and CHA were, as she put it, constantly trying to "get to a yes" in support of the bill, the US Conference of Catholic Bishops (USCCB)—widely seen as the most powerful organization in the American Catholic Church—took a decidedly different approach. The USCCB did not respond to my multiple requests to discuss its ACA lobbying efforts, but according to Keehan, the Catholic group didn't so much engage with the bill as try to find a way to hold a middle ground that was "not endorsing but not opposing." The potential repercussions of the USCCB refusing to endorse the ACA were significant, as an outright rejection could scare away Catholic Democrats wary of suffering the same theological thumping John Kerry had endured in 2004.

The bishops' posture maddened Keehan. It just didn't make sense; she believed that many bishops were already quietly supportive of the proposal: chief among them was Cardinal Francis George, the archbishop of Chicago, who served as president of the USCCB at the time. Keehan was convinced that George, who began a battle with cancer in 2006 that would ultimately claim his life in 2015, was someone who "wanted health care for everyone really badly."

Ever the problem solver, Keehan pulled George aside at a meeting unrelated to health care and asked if they could find a time to discuss the bill at length. The archbishop agreed and invited her to his lavish residence in Chicago for a meeting. Keehan said they met there over lunch for two hours, during which she outlined a scenario in which they would both sign a letter expressing support for the ACA. George allegedly told Keehan he liked her draft of the letter but wanted to tweak some of the language, adding that he would get back to her in a day or two.

When Keehan reached out days later, the archbishop didn't respond. Nor did he respond the second time, or the third, or to any of her repeated inquiries from then on. She eventually resorted to faxing copies of the letter to his office, but even that proved fruitless.

"I believe that the staff at the bishops' conference was giving the bishops very bad advice," she told me, her voice still tinged with frustration nearly a decade later.[27]

*   *   *

Back in Washington, Butler and Faith in Public Life were in active negotiations with the USCCB, serving as a sort of diplomatic attaché between clerics and abortion-rights organizations such as Planned Parenthood. The goal was to revise the ACA bill in ways amenable to both sides of the abortion debate, ultimately securing something resembling a consensus.

"Everybody said they wanted to be 'abortion neutral,' but what does that look like?" Butler said.[28] She, like Keehan, wasn't sure the USCCB was operating in good faith.

"I remember at one point we're sitting at the USCCB with a table of their staff and a couple of us religious leaders, and they are walking us through this portion of the bill that we thought had resolved the conflict [about abortion]," she said. "And they're explaining how it can be misappropriated, misused. We digested that and argued it to some degree, being like, 'Is your goal to remain neutral or are you trying to tip the scales here?'"

Despite their misgivings, Butler and her FPL staff forged ahead, sharing the USCCB's concerns with Podesta's old confidante Melody Barnes, who had become assistant to President Obama and director of the White House Domestic Policy Council.

The Obama administration was already well aware of the USCCB's seemingly questionable approach to negotiations. In the lead up to a major vote on the ACA, White House officials hosted a conference call with representatives from the USCCB to hash out ways to garner the clerics' support—one of many similar calls they would host during the debate over the bill. But as the bishops moved to end the call that day, things took an awkward turn. According to a person in the room who preferred to remain anonymous, USCCB representatives inadvertently failed to terminate the call on their end, leaving them on the line with White House officials able to overhear them. The clerics then initiated a separate conference call with conservative opponents of the bill, including organizations such as Concerned Women for America and the Family Research Council. As Obama staffers listened in, USCCB officials allegedly began discussing strategies for how to mobilize to stop the ACA.

Meanwhile, the ACA was facing fierce public scrutiny. The summer of 2009 saw the meteoric rise of the conservative Tea Party movement, which quickly morphed into a media nightmare for many Democrats poised to support the bill. In addition to constant attacks from right-wing pundits on outlets like FOX News, lawmakers endured heated town hall meetings at which constituents adorned in tricorn hats shouted, waved signs, and demanded that elected officials vote against health care reform.

Sometimes, things turned biblical. In one passionate exchange, a man stood up at a health care town hall in Lebanon, Pennsylvania, and got in the face of Democratic senator Arlen Specter. After initially accusing the lawmaker of stuffing his pockets with lobbyist money, the man's rant took a dark eschatological turn.

"One day God is going to stand before you, and he's going to judge you and the rest of your damn cronies up on the Hill, and then you can get your just deserts," the man shouted before storming out of the assembly.[29]

But as the Tea Party promulgated an end-times theology to defame the bill, Religious Left groups crafted a more expansive moral argument to defend health care reform. In August of that year, Faith in Action, FPL, Faithful America, Sojourners, and CACG announced they were collaborating on a "40 Days for Health Reform" campaign in support of a health care overhaul. The effort included fifty prayer vigils and rallies in forty-five cities in eighteen states, as well as cable advertisements featuring evangelical, Catholic, and mainline Protestant pastors voicing religious support for health care reform.[30]

"Millions of people of faith are supporting health care reform," an Indiana pastor declared in one ad. As the screen cut to a text-heavy slide filled with information about how to contact Congress, a disembodied voice asked, "Members of Congress, will you?"[31]

A few days later, FPL, Faith in Action, and others helped organize a massive educational call-in webinar about the bill. Roughly 140,000 people of faith dialed in to listen to President Obama and grassroots leaders—including several affiliated with Faith in Action—discuss the merits of the universal health care plan. The call included representatives from evangelical Christian, Jewish, Muslim, and other traditions, who spoke about the issue in moral terms.

Obama also echoed the moral message, saying that attacks on the ACA were designed to "discourage people from meeting what I consider to be a core ethical and moral obligation, and that is that we look out for one another, that I am my brother's keeper and my sister's keeper."[32]

But the real push for FPL, Faith in Action, Sojourners, and others was a multistate organizing strategy focused on congressional delegations that Butler described as "more moderate," such as Nebraska and Pennsylvania. According to Butler, a complicated and overlapping division of labor emerged: Faith in Action's vast network of congregations would function as a sizable chunk (but not all) of the effort's ground game; FPL would oversee much of broader media strategy (but not exclusively); and Sojourners, Catholics United, and CACG would lend additional visibility to the entire campaign (with some efforts more targeted than others).

The idea was to leverage the religious voice in these states to make it easier for lawmakers to embrace health care reform.

"Faith can play a role of creating common ground," Faith in Action's Whitman said. "Just practically providing politicians with cover for supporting things they know are right, but are afraid they're going to pay a penalty for. If you have the major religious leadership in a community and a state standing there, it's easier for you to stand there [with them] if you're an elected official."[33]

The strategy was crucial in Nebraska, where Ben Nelson served as senator. Nelson, a Democrat, worked as a lay preacher for several Protestant Christian congregations before running for governor of Nebraska and later US Senate, and he had earned endorsements from conservative groups for preaching an ardently antiabortion stance.[34] As a consistently conservative voice in the Democratic Party, he was also vocally skeptical of the ACA throughout 2009. This was a significant problem for Democrats, whose sixty-vote supermajority in the senate provided zero margin for error.

Faith groups detected the importance of Nelson's vote early on. Faith in Action, Catholics United, the African Methodist Episcopal Church, and others had already organized a prayer vigil outside the US Capitol in October 2009, at which clergy from moderate states made the moral case for a health care overhaul and advocated for low-wage workers. Among them was a Nebraska delegation, which announced plans to meet with Nelson's staff and demand "lower premiums and stronger caps on out-of-pocket costs for working families in Nebraska."[35]

Fast-forward to December of that year, and Nelson was still waffling on whether or not to support the bill. Out of options, the White House scrambled to find a way to appease the anti-abortion Democrat. After a marathon thirteen-hour negotiation session, they ultimately brokered a compromise that allowed states to ban federal funding of abortions in insurance plans purchased through their exchanges.[36]

It still wasn't enough: Nelson initially rejected the compromise. But as the Senate vote approached, FPL helped coordinate a sign-on letter on December 18, with two dozen Nebraska faith leaders—both those who described themselves as pro-life and those that preferred the term pro-choice—urging Nelson to support it.

"We are Nebraskan religious leaders, guided by the core of our faith traditions that teach the principles of justice, human dignity, and the common good," the letter read in part. "We appeal to you today to support the compromise on abortion coverage and funding, proposed in the manager's amendment to the Senate bill."[37]

The letter also suggested signers would defend Nelson if he voted for the ACA, noting that the abortion compromise would "strengthen our ability to gather religious support for those members who take tough votes in favor of reform, even in the face of opposition from both sides of the debate."

The next day, as the Senate gathered amidst blizzard-like conditions in Washington, Nelson announced he would support the ACA.

"Change is never easy, but change is what's necessary in America," Nelson said at a press conference that morning. "And that's why I intend to vote for . . . health care reform."[38]

As with any vote, a number of factors informed Nelson's decision. Many would later attribute his ultimate support for the ACA to the so-called Cornhusker Kickback, a carve-out he negotiated in the Senate version of the bill that would force the federal government, not the state, to cover the cost of expanding Medicaid in Nebraska.[39]

But when the state Democratic Party produced a television advertisement in January 2010 to defend Nelson's vote, it selected five Nebraskan voices to speak alongside the senator: a businessman, a doctor, a nurse, a senior citizen, and a Catholic priest.

The priest was Father Jack McCaslin, one of the signers of FPL's letter.

"[Nelson] really listened to Nebraska and made the plan better," he said, facing directly into the camera, his clerical collar in full view.[40]

★ ★ ★

Several months and more than a few negotiations later, it was spring 2010, and the pivotal House vote on the ACA was fast approaching. Sister Keehan had a decision to make: she and her CHA staff were convinced the bill did not provide federal funding for abortions, but the USCCB did not appear to agree, and Cardinal George still wasn't responding to her messages. If she was going to step out in favor of the bill without the bishops, the moment had arrived.

So on March 13—a Friday—she published a short, 350-word column in *Catholic Health World*, the CHA's newspaper, declaring that while the ACA was not "perfect," it was still "a major first step." She titled her column "The Time Is Now for Health Reform."[41]

Keehan didn't think much of it at the time. After all, her support for the bill was hardly a secret. She wasn't sure people would even *see* her statement in CHA's small trade newspaper.

"Did I think that was going to make a big difference? Not on your life," she told me. "I don't think you can find anybody who sits and waits to see when the CHA paper comes out."[42]

But someone did see it—specifically, Joshua DuBois, the director of the White House Office of Faith-based and Neighborhood Partnerships and eventual member of the Grassmere group. He called her that evening, breathless with excitement.

"You endorsed it," DuBois said.

"Of course I endorsed it," Keehan replied. "That's what I've been working for."

The news set off a flurry of activity in Catholic circles as well, including at the offices of Network, a social justice lobby run by Sister Simone Campbell of the Sisters of Social Service. Campbell fired off an email to Keehan thanking her for the endorsement and saying that Network would stand with CHA if she got pushback from the bishops. Campbell then began pulling together a sign-on letter of her fellow nuns in the Leadership Conference of Women Religious (LCWR)— the umbrella organization of most American nuns—to back Keehan.

But the following Monday, Campbell got a call from a White House staffer.

"I think I'm a Buddhist," the staffer allegedly told Campbell. (She did not name the contact, but said he was Catholic.)

"What?" Campbell replied. "Why do you think you're a Buddhist? What's going on?"[43]

The staffer explained that Cardinal George had come out against the ACA. The cleric had insisted that the bill must be opposed because it did not do enough to ban federal funding of abortion.[44] The nuns and the bishops were now on opposite sides of the issue.

"I burst into tears," Campbell said.

She didn't wallow in despondency for long, however. The next day, Campbell took a redeye flight back to Washington, DC, from California, where she had been staying with other nuns. By Wednesday morning her sign-on letter boasted the names of fifty-nine nuns, most of whom were leaders of major orders of women religious— including the president of the LCWR. Collectively, they represented nearly sixty thousand nuns nationwide.

"Despite false claims to the contrary, the Senate bill will not provide taxpayer funding for elective abortions," the letter read in part. "It will uphold longstanding conscience protections, and it will make historic new investments—$250 million—in support of pregnant women. This is the REAL pro-life stance, and we as Catholics are all for it."

It closed with an unambiguous endorsement: "We urge you to vote 'yes' for life by voting yes for health care reform in [the ACA]."[45]

After posting the letter online, Campbell and Network marched over to Capitol Hill and hand-delivered the letter to Catholic Democrats.

It was a staggering power move in direct defiance of the bishops, and it likely didn't hurt that nuns in recent years have typically enjoyed significantly higher approval ratings in opinion polls than male leaders of the Catholic hierarchy, sullied as they were by the Church's sex abuse scandal.[46] The sisters' popularity extended to Capitol Hill: one of the Catholic Democrats who received their letter was Tom Perriello, the onetime Grassmere organizer who had since become the freshman Democratic congressman from Virginia's 5th District. He told me he was livid with the Catholic bishops at the time, whom he accused of "putting partisanship over theology."

But things were complicated on Capitol Hill. Perriello was also one of sixty-four Democrats—thirty-six of them Catholic—who voted for a "Stupak-Pitts amendment" to an early version of the House health care bill. Like the Nelson deal, the amendment—initiated by Rep. Bart Stupak, a Michigan Catholic Democrat—was designed to placate anti-abortion lawmakers by prohibiting federal funding for abortion coverage in the government-subsidized insurance plans under the ACA.[47] Perriello, who has a long history of supporting abortion rights, later said he regretted the vote.[48]

Meanwhile, Campbell and women religious had ample backup thanks to the Washington progressive religious apparatus Perriello helped build: Faith in Public Life began managing media operations for the nuns, pushing both Keehan's statement and Network's sign-on letter out to reporters.

Butler explained that many journalists simply didn't know what the CHA was, but that was a fixable problem for a nimble shop like FPL. They hosted press conferences and media conference calls featuring Campbell and pro-life Catholic Democratic House members, such as Rep. Dale Kildee of Michigan—who spent six years in a Catholic seminary before entering politics—explaining their support for the bill.[49] Meanwhile, Catholics United blasted its email lists with messages encouraging supporters to call Cardinal George and "let him know that Catholics in the pews want the bishops to get their facts straight and support health care reform."[50]

Just a few days later, on March 21, the House passed the Senate version of the ACA bill with a 219 to 212 vote. It included ample support from Catholic Democrats who opposed abortion.

Obama signed the bill into law two days after the House vote in a highly anticipated White House ceremony. After the president scribbled his final left-handed stroke onto the parchment, he handed out the pens he used to a bevy of assembled dignitaries, which included lawmakers, cabinet members, White House officials, Vice President Joe Biden, and Ted Kennedy's widow.

But he made sure to set aside one for Sister Carol Keehan, the nun who once doubted his health care acumen. She was still in Rome and unable to attend the ceremony, but her fellow nun Simone Campbell was there and snagged a moment with the president. When he walked by, she told him, "I'm the troublemaking nun who wrote the nun's letter.'" According to Campbell, Obama responded by embracing her and kissing her cheek, saying "[We're] so grateful. Thank you so much.'"[51]

Keehan, for her part, would hold her pen aloft from the stage of CHA's annual convention later that year, which also featured a video address from Obama thanking the nun for her "extraordinary leadership."[52] He was even more effusive five years later, when he attended the 2015 convention personally to deliver an address.

"I don't know if it's appropriate, but I just told Sister Carol I love her," he told the CHA convention crowd. "It is true, though, I do! . . . We would not have gotten the Affordable Care Act done had it not been for her."[53]

THE LONG GAME

The passage of the ACA was a monumental win for progressives and the Religious Left, but it came at a cost—especially for American Catholic nuns. The Catholic hierarchy, stung by the nuns' rejection of their position, struck back in ways large and small.

Shortly after the vote, the USCCB issued a statement deriding the efforts of Keehan, Campbell, and Catholics United as "a wound to Catholic unity."[54] In April 2010, the bishop of the Diocese of Greensburg banned nuns in nearby Baden, Pennsylvania, from promoting their order in his diocese because they "publicly repudiated" the USCCB on health care.[55]

The real smackdown came in April 2012, however, when the Vatican—which had already initiated two investigations of American women religious in 2008—unexpectedly issued a scathing critique of the LCWR and Network. Among other things, the Vatican accused American nuns of promoting "radical feminist themes incompatible with the Catholic faith" and reprimanded them for issuing public statements that "disagree with or challenge the bishops, who are the church's authentic teachers of faith and morals."[56]

Keehan was quick to note that some form of rebuke was bound to happen irrespective of the health care fight, arguing that Catholic hierarchy under Pope Benedict XVI—a conservative pope who had previously served as the Church's formal disciplinarian—were already "on a roll" to investigate American nuns in general. But she acknowledged that the battle over the ACA gave bishops ammunition to step up their efforts, and the timing and intensity of the Vatican rebuke was widely seen as a response to the nuns' public support for the ACA.

Campbell agreed, saying that the Vatican name-checked her group "just because the bishops were mad at us for winning on health care," explaining the delay between the vote and the reprimand was because "they're just slow."[57]

Campbell added that the formal reproach did little to break the resolve of her fellow nuns: "It made them angry that we won, and they lost," she told me, barely suppressing a grin. "Well, we got twenty-three million people health care. I thought that was worth it."

In fact, if the goal of the bishops was to silence women religious into dutiful complacency, their strategy backfired spectacularly. If anything, the pushback *raised* the public profile of Campbell and Network, setting a wind at their backs and steering the organization into more visibly political waters.

In 2012, when Network launched its first cross-country, nine-state Nuns on the Bus tour to oppose the GOP's proposed budget—which suggested cuts to federal programs that help the poor—it garnered widespread media attention. But while the USCCB itself criticized the Ryan budget—a reference to Wisconsin congressman and then vice presidential candidate Paul Ryan—some bishops forbade Campbell from speaking in their dioceses. According to Campbell, that only inspired larger crowds, even when organizers were forced to make last-minute venue changes.

"It was the notoriety [from the ACA fight] that got us the bus," she told me in 2017.[58]

That attention eventually catapulted Campbell to the main stage of the 2012 Democratic National Convention. As a euphoric crowd cheered her mention of the Affordable Care Act, Campbell delivered a primetime address that implored her fellow Americans to pay attention to the plight of the poor and the sick.

Other fixtures in Washington's progressive faith apparatus haven't been so lucky. As of 2019, Res Publica no longer exists, Catholics United has languished into obscurity, and Catholics in Alliance for the Common Good has "essentially folded," according to John Podesta.[59]

Bad blood also remains between veterans of the ACA debate and the Catholic hierarchy.

"I have refused to take communion on US soil since the ACA fight," Perriello told me. "I take communion when I'm overseas, but I largely avoid taking it under the auspices of the USCCB."

The progressive faith community has maintained its dedication to health care all the same. At Obama's urging, leaders at mosques, churches, synagogues, temples, and other houses of worship across the country literally preached the value of health insurance enrollment, and in 2014 Faith in Action launched a Bring Health Care Home initiative that encouraged religious communities to host education or enrollment events for uninsured people. The White House promoted its own Faith and Community ACA Days of Action campaign as well, and nonprofit groups such as Enroll America—staffed by Obama campaign veterans and a former DNC faith outreach director—partnered with religious communities and groups such as the National Council of Jewish Women, American Muslim Health Professionals, and Network.[60]

Granted, the ACA also faced significant pushback from conservative faith groups, particularly over the law's so-called contraceptive mandate—its provision that requires employers to cover certain female contraceptive costs for employees. Catholic bishops, the conservative Christian owners of the craft store giant Hobby Lobby, and others raised ethical and legal challenges to the provision, with Hobby Lobby securing a Supreme Court victory granting it a religious exemption in 2014.[61]

But progressive faith groups defended the ACA in many of those instances, filing amicus briefs that sided with the government's position.[62] And when the GOP-led Congress that rode into power with Donald Trump pushed to repeal and replace the ACA, it was religious groups that banded together to march at the front of protests on Capitol Hill and elsewhere to save the law.

During that same fight, Campbell joined other groups in personally lobbying potential swing votes such as Sen. Lisa Murkowski, a moderate Alaska Republican who also happens to identify as Catholic (she voted against the repeal). FPL's Butler was among those who stormed the Capitol to pray and protest outside the office of Senate Majority Leader Mitch McConnell until police arrived (Butler was among those arrested during the demonstration).[63] In addition, Campbell and Network teamed up with other left-leaning religious groups—including the Friends Committee on National Legislation (Quakers), Bread for the World, the Religious Action Center of Reform Judaism, and FPL—to host a twenty-four-hour prayer vigil opposing the repeal bill. It featured speeches from faith leaders such as Campbell as well as politicians such as Sen. Cory Booker, Sen. Tim Kaine, Rep. Jan Schakowsky, and Rep. Nancy Pelosi.[64]

Progressive faith voices were even heard in the Senate gallery during the final late-night vote on the Republican health care plan in July 2017. Earlier that day, Jane Adams, a policy analyst with Bread for the World and one of the organizers of the twenty-four-hour prayer vigil, told *ThinkProgress* she was entering the Senate gallery to pray for the GOP bill's defeat because "as Christians [and] as people of faith, [we] feel called to protect the poor and vulnerable."[65]

When Republican senator John McCain gave his famous thumbs-down gesture hours later to signal his no vote—effectively killing the GOP repeal-and-replace effort—Adams realized her prayers were answered. Overwhelmed, she let out a "gasp of joy" before immediately breaking down into tears. Her outburst, paired with a spate of applause, spurred Sen. Chuck Schumer to turn around and angrily shush her and others in the gallery.

The moment garnered Adams a moment of internet fame, as many pundits noted her gasp in the widely distributed (and endlessly dissected) footage of the incident. But for Adams, the experience proved to be powerful in more ways than one: that day, combined with the three years she spent as a lobbyist for Bread for the World, inspired her to move her family back to Arkansas, where she plans to run for mayor.[66]

That transition into the world of electoral politics for a progressive faith activist is more complicated than it sounds, however. While the Religious Left's power in the world of liberal policy making is considerable in an ad hoc sort of way, its role in the realm of Democratic Party politics is far more complex and arguably even less consistent.

But if Adams needed an example of a progressive faith-based organizer who successfully ran for office as a Democrat and took faith seriously, she need only look at the signature painstakingly scrawled across the bottom of the ACA: *Barack Obama*.

CHAPTER TWO

★ ★ ★

The Personal Is
Political—and Spiritual

J oshua DuBois was a twenty-something graduate student who liked government and didn't know what he wanted to do with his life. So, like a lot of twenty-something graduate students who like government and don't know what to do with their lives, he got a summer internship on Capitol Hill. That's why he found himself on July 27, 2004, doing the most quintessentially twenty-something-Hill-intern thing one could do: bellying up to a Washington bar, drinking a beer, eating a burger, and watching the Democratic National Convention.

DuBois, a fast-talking man with a big smile and an even bigger laugh, remembers glancing up at the bar's flickering television when a guy he'd never heard of, Illinois state senator and US Senate candidate Barack Obama, strutted onstage to deliver the convention's keynote address. Obama's ability to wrap human stories around policy and offer a hopeful vision for America resonated with a political junkie like DuBois, then a student at Princeton University's Woodrow Wilson School of Public and International Affairs. But it was when the self-described "skinny kid with a funny name" referenced religion that DuBois's ears really perked up. "Out of nowhere, he started talking about the 'awesome God' that we serve in the blue states," said DuBois, who had worked as an associate pastor at a small Pentecostal church while in undergrad.[1] "I immediately was thinking back to my childhood going to Fellowship of Christian Athletes camp in the Shenandoah Valley, singing 'Our God Is an Awesome God' with our hands raised. There was a moment of spiritual and cultural connection there, and I thought, 'That is the guy I need to try to work for.'"

DuBois promptly sent several letters asking for work to Obama's staff, receiving only stale form letters in response. But his dream refused to die. When Obama won his Senate race several months later, DuBois made a last-ditch play straight out of an Aaron Sorkin script: he marched over to the senator's transition office, knocked on the door, and demanded they take him seriously. The move garnered surprisingly Sorkinesque results: Obama hired DuBois in 2005 to work on labor, trade, commerce, transportation, and immigration policy.

That was already enough to delight DuBois, but roughly a year later he got an even bigger break. That was when Obama announced to his staff that he was working on two religion-related projects: a book chapter about faith and a speech for a conference organized by progressive Christians. He needed help.

"He asked if there's anyone at the office that wanted to work with him on this who thought a lot about faith in public life," DuBois recalled. "I raised my hand."

DuBois sometimes tells another version of this story that is slightly less dramatic, but arguably more nerve-racking. When DuBois spoke at the Newseum in 2015, he said that Obama and his then chief of staff, Pete Rouse, had called him into the senator's office in 2006 to discuss Obama's faith speech, essentially putting him on the spot. DuBois rose to the challenge and suddenly found himself among Obama's inner circle.[2]

Regardless of how it started, it was the beginning of a professional and spiritual relationship that would add another booster rocket to Obama's already ascendant career and define for an entire political generation what the intersection of religion and politics could look like for a Democrat. The connection between Obama, whose own faith was formed by religion-rooted grassroots activism, and DuBois, who would later become the president's in-house pastor, would lay the foundation for one of the most robust religious outreach efforts of any Democratic campaign in modern political history, allowing Obama to lean on religion to enhance his hopeful message and survive political turmoil.

This kind of partnership was, in a word, unusual. Most Democrats still profess a belief in a higher power, but religious progressives who try to court their fellow faithful for a living often find themselves ignored by the media, undervalued by other liberals, or both. Half the challenge of their work is convincing campaign operatives that faith outreach matters at all, a dynamic they find both infuriating and ironic. When it comes to winning elections, they say, the success of Obama's 2008 campaign is blinding evidence that faith outreach *not only works but is arguably necessary for progressive politics.*

Examining the religious outreach program DuBois, Obama, and others created highlights this complex relationship between today's Religious Left activists and the highest levels of political power. To analyze the 2008 campaign is to expose why so many progressive faith leaders see Obama as not just one of their own, but also as a *product* of the left-leaning religious heritage they claim—and why some still yearn to replicate the successes of a man once dubbed America's "theologian-in-chief."

OF ZEALOTS AND CONVERTS

By the time Obama met DuBois, the newly elected senator was already something of a savant when it came to God talk. Although rarely framed as such, the future president's religious and political consciousness was, by his own admission, sculpted by progressive faith organizing, and he gained his hard-earned fluency in religious verbiage from an array of experiences rarely found among Washington's elite.

Obama's religious heritage is, to put it mildly, complex. In interviews, he described his father as a Muslim turned agnostic and his mother as a Methodist who, while a "deeply spiritual person," was "not someone who wore her religion on her sleeve." Further complicating this curious spiritual pedigree were grandparents who were not adamantly religious and a childhood that included attending Catholic school in Muslim-majority Indonesia. "I was studying the Bible and catechisms by day, and at night you'd hear the [Muslim] prayer call," he told religion reporter Cathleen Falsani in 2004.[3]

Obama's mother, an anthropologist, reportedly made a habit of teaching her son about several religions at once, dragging young "Barry" along on field trips to Christian churches as well as Buddhist temples, Shinto shrines, and ancient Hawaiian burial sites.[4] None of these were expected to be conversion experiences, but Obama still carried them with him years later after he graduated from Columbia University in 1983, when he espoused what he called "more of an intellectual view of religion."[5]

His spiritual perspective began to evolve in his midtwenties, however, when he took a job as a community organizer in Chicago's South Side with the Developing Communities Project (DCP), a group originally founded as a faith-based entity that organized people primarily through religious congregations. Like Faith in Action and other organizing groups, DCP was rooted in both the progressive legacy of the civil rights movement and the writings of organizer Saul Alinsky (although some now quibble over which legacy offers a superior organizing model). It was also unapologetically religious: in addition to organizing through houses of worship, the advertised position listed duties such as "serve as consultant to local parishes" and spend time in "theological reflection" with clergy.[6] The job would also land Obama a side gig as a consultant and instructor for the Gamaliel Foundation—another congregation-based organizing group.

The experience of working with Chicago congregations had a profound impact on Obama, who went on to champion the value of faith-rooted activism in an obscure 1988 essay he wrote entitled "Why Organize? Problems and Promise in the Inner City." While extolling the virtues of organizing as a method for social change, Obama lamented that the community groups he worked with in Chicago lacked the "high-powered direct-mail and video approaches successfully used by conservative organizations like the Moral Majority." He went on to say that "nowhere is the promise of organizing more apparent than in the traditional black churches," but he cautioned that "a fierce independence among black pastors and a preference for more traditional approaches to social involvement"—doing outreach through soup kitchens and backing certain political candidates—kept the black faith community from bringing its "full weight to bear." As an alternative, he put forth DCP as one of several organizations that could serve as "a powerful tool for living the social gospel, one which can educate and empower entire congregations and not just serve as a platform for a few prophetic leaders."[7]

Obama wrote these words with the confidence of a believer, because by that time he was one. Gone was his understanding of faith as merely an academic curiosity because, according to his interview with Falsani, the experience of working at DCP helped lead him to Jesus. Obama referred to spending "an enormous amount of time with church ladies" in Chicago—largely because they made up a healthy percentage of his volunteer base—and would later explain in political speeches that it was in the streets of the Windy City where he "witnessed the power of faith."[8] That power eventually guided him to find a spiritual home in Trinity United Church of Christ on Chicago's South Side, where he walked down the red-carpeted aisle and committed himself to Christ in response to an altar call from pastor Rev. Jeremiah Wright Jr.[9]

(Obama never lost his pluralistic bent, however. He also expressed an affinity for Judaism, and as president he would carry around a hodgepodge of religious symbols in his pocket: a rosary that Pope Francis gave him or a tiny Buddha statue handed to him by a monk. Not all the objects were faith-related: he also kept a "lucky poker chip" given to him by a tattooed biker.)[10]

After marrying Michelle Robinson and settling down in the Windy City in 1992, Obama, now an aspiring politician, cultivated friendships with a variety of faith leaders in Chicago and across the country. Among them was Sojourners president and CEO Jim Wallis, a titan in progressive evangelical circles who got to know Obama when they were both invited to join an elite group assembled by author and Harvard political science professor Robert Putnam. In preparation for his landmark book *Bowling Alone*, Putnam took to gathering dozens of high-profile participants every three months from 1997 to 2000 for what he dubbed the Saguaro Seminar—a group tasked with helping him better understand "social capital." The brain trust convened for bus tours and intellectual debate, mixing Obama and Wallis in with such prominent thinkers as George Stephanopoulos, former White House aide to Bill Clinton; E. J. Dionne, author and *Washington Post* columnist; Kirbyjon Caldwell, Houston megapastor and counselor to President George W. Bush; and Ralph Reed, former head of the Christian Coalition.[11]

"Obama was one of the least-known people in the group," Wallis recalled with a laugh.[12]

But most of Putnam's think tank eventually warmed to Obama, with Dionne jokingly referring to the then state senator as "the governor," predicting his political future. (Dionne told me that after one especially engaging seminar session, he returned home and gushed about Obama to his wife, saying, "I think this guy might be president."[13]) Wallis also had extended dialogues with Obama about theology during seminar bus rides, including pointed conversations about what it meant to be a progressive Christian.[14] The connections were lasting: when Obama was mulling his run for the White House a decade or so later, one of the people he called for counsel was Wallis.[15]

DuBois kept this spiritual legacy in mind as he worked with Obama on his June 2006 faith speech, easing into his new role as the senator's faith adviser. The aide used the speechwriting process as a way to set up meetings with a stream of religious figures to mine their collective wisdom: DuBois sat down with officials from the Religious Action Center for Reformed Judaism, the Islamic Society of North America, the National Association of Evangelicals, and others, steeping himself in different schools of thought regarding the proper role of religion in politics.

Obama delivered the final product at the Building a Covenant for a New America conference cosponsored by Sojourners and its faith-based antipoverty initiative, Call to Renewal. Rarely discussed outside of progressive faith circles, the speech is today eclipsed by other Obama oratorical triumphs, such as "Yes, We Can!" or "A More Perfect Union." But looking back, the then senator's faith address—which stretched beyond four thousand words and took around forty minutes to deliver—brimmed with foreshadowing about the kind of campaign he would launch less than a year later. Delivered in what would become Obama's famously professorial-meets-pastoral style, it issued a rallying cry for a resurgent Religious Left, fusing an unapologetic rejection of the Religious Right's dominance in American politics with a clarion call for Democrats to embrace faith.

"At best, [Democrats] may try to avoid the conversation about religious values altogether, fearful of offending anyone and claiming that—regardless of our personal beliefs—constitutional principles tie our hands," Obama said as he stood at the pulpit of National City Christian Church, a towering stone building that sits along Thomas Circle Park in Washington. "At worst, there are some liberals who dismiss religion in the public square as inherently irrational or intolerant, insisting on a caricature of religious Americans that paints them as fanatical, or thinking that the very word *Christian* describes one's political opponents, not people of faith."[16]

He went on: "But over the long haul, I think we make a mistake when we fail to acknowledge the power of faith in people's lives—in the lives of the American people—and I think it's time that we join a serious debate about how to reconcile faith with our modern, pluralistic democracy. . . . If we truly hope to speak to people where they're at—to communicate our hopes and values in a way that's relevant to their own—then as progressives, we cannot abandon the field of religious discourse."

The liberal-leaning crowd that packed the church that day could not have agreed more. Fellow Saguaro Seminar alum E. J. Dionne, writing in *The Washington Post*, gleefully declared Obama's address "the most important pronouncement by a Democrat on faith and politics since John F. Kennedy's Houston speech in 1960 declaring his independence from the Vatican."[17] (Dionne later referenced Obama's address a second time in his 2008 book, *Souled Out*.)[18]

DuBois capitalized on the good press, using it as a way to introduce influential faith leaders across the country to his boss. "I remember mailing it to every pastor and rabbi and imam that I could find," he said, noting that large sections of the address were also reworked (or in some cases cribbed wholesale) for the "Faith" chapter of Obama's book published later that year.[19] And just in case anyone doubted the importance of faith in Obama's life, that book's title—*The Audacity of Hope: Thoughts on Reclaiming the American Dream*—was a direct reference to a line from one of Rev. Wright's sermons.[20]

"Senator Obama realized that the intersection of faith in public life could be a unique thing for him," DuBois said.

Eight months later, on a cold February morning, Obama strutted onto another stage—this time in Springfield, Illinois—waited just long enough for the ethereal riffs of U2's "City of Blinding Lights" to fade, and told the crowd of thousands that he was "giving all praise and honor to God for bringing us here today." He then announced his candidacy for the presidency of the United States, making sure to mention that it was in "Chicago's poorest neighborhoods" that he "learned the meaning of my Christian faith."[21]

To oversee his campaign's faith outreach efforts, Obama tapped DuBois, giving him ample resources to assemble a robust team. "Senator Obama said, 'We want to make faith outreach a centerpiece of what we do,'" DuBois recalled. "We had the first full-on faith outreach department in a [Democratic] presidential campaign."

MAINSTREAMING PROGRESSIVE FAITH-SPEAK

Faith outreach, like most elements of the famously data-driven 2008 Obama campaign, was part of a larger strategy that was ultimately all about votes. DuBois crafted a meticulous strategy memo, pulling cross tabs from the Association of Religion Data Archives—one of the few granular-level datasets of US religious groups—to map out potential Obama voters in early primary states.

"I remember the memo of how we laid all of this out: 'Here are the number of progressive Catholics in New Hampshire, and black churchgoers in South Carolina, and United Church of Christ, United Methodist, and Evangelical Lutheran Church in America folks in Iowa,'" he said.[22] His strategy revolved around a simple notion: "If we have a message that resonates with progressives of faith, that will be an advantage over others who are not speaking to the faith community."

Luckily for DuBois, he wasn't starting from scratch. Mara Vanderslice Kelly, a founding member of the Grassmere group, had—through seemingly herculean efforts several years before—managed to carve out a faith space for Democrats. Her first attempt involved finagling a faith outreach spot on Howard Dean's short-lived 2004 presidential run, during which she worked in Iowa before the candidate infamously screamed his way into electoral oblivion. Unlike DuBois, however, Kelly struggled to sell her vision for reaching religious voters to the Dean campaign, which did not receive it—or her—well. Once, when Kelly introduced herself to a national-level Dean staffer as the Iowa faith outreach director, he replied, "How the fuck did you get hired?"

Just twenty-nine at the time, Kelly painstakingly explained just why faith outreach matters.

"I pulled myself together enough to make the case I'd made before: a lot of these faith communities are against the war in Iraq and with us on progressive issues, so we're going to reach out to them—there's votes to be had," she told me. "I made my pitch in a minute and a half and shut the guy up."[23]

Dean's implosion as a candidate meant that Kelly eventually ended up on John Kerry's campaign, where the pattern of pushback continued, albeit with (relatively) less cursing. She wasn't short on ideas. She suggested booking the senator to speak at the same Sojourners conference that Obama would address two years later, and she lined up a chance for Kerry to give a faith-related speech at a Catholic school in the Diocese of Cleveland.

Neither appearance happened, according to Kelly, because she faced a myriad of roadblocks from senior-level campaign staff—most of which are documented in Amy Sullivan's 2008 book, *The Party Faithful: How and Why Democrats Are Closing the God Gap*. Staffers roundly ignored her advice, especially after the Massachusetts senator was beset with intense scrutiny from Catholic leaders over his support for abortion rights. The situation escalated when Cardinal Raymond Burke threatened to deny communion to Roman Catholic politicians who held positions like Kerry's. Burke was in the minority among his fellow bishops, but the warning led to reporters camping out in the back pews of parishes Kerry visited, craning their necks above congregations to see whether or not he would be denied the host by a priest. The spiritual scandal even got its own name: Wafer Watch.[24]

Instead of drawing on Kelly's expertise to confront the controversy head-on, however, staffers used her work to avoid it. Kelly said that despite her pleas, campaign leaders used her network of Catholic allies primarily to map out where Kerry could take communion without risk of divine humiliation.

"Almost every idea I came up with was shot down," Kelly said. "At the end of the day, they ended up feeling [faith] was something to run away from, to hide from, to try to draw the least amount of attention to. . . . They wanted to just stay away from it completely instead of embracing the language around it."

Years later, Kelly summed up her time on the 2004 Kerry campaign in bleak tones.

"I cried a lot, to be honest," she told me. "I probably cried every week, if not most days."

Granted, the campaign did do *some* faith work. Kelly noted that a Jewish outreach director worked independently of her, and the person tasked with African American outreach also intersected with faith. In addition, the campaign eventually brought on Mike McCurry, the former press secretary for President Bill Clinton. He shared Kelly's passion for faith outreach and had already become a mentor to her, making regular visits to her office to consult on the topic—something Kelly saw as public expressions of support for her work.[25] His hiring was a late-in-the-game move (he was brought on in September 2004), but it appeared to either kick-start religion-related work or increase the visibility of previous plans. Shortly after McCurry became involved, Kerry delivered a speech at the National Baptist Convention that framed George W. Bush as one of the villains in the biblical parable of the Good Samaritan, describing the Republican president as someone who has "seen people in need, but . . . crossed over to the other side of the street."[26]

Kelly, meanwhile, was able to actualize her vision for faith outreach only in the twilight days of the campaign, when her bosses sent her to Michigan during the last two months before the election. She and the state's sympathetic campaign director ran a targeted, Catholic-focused operation that included direct-mail campaigns and nuns phoning undecided Catholic voters. She would spend years touting the results as an example of effective faith outreach: Kerry was the first Democrat presidential candidate in recent history to lose the Catholic vote nationwide, but exit polls showed him narrowly edging out Bush among Catholics in Michigan. By contrast, Bush gained among Catholics in Ohio, Wisconsin, and Pennsylvania compared to his 2000 election.[27]

"We got a bigger share of Catholic voters for Kerry than any of the comparable neighboring states, where these programs were not run," Kelly told me.

At the request of prominent Democrats, including Leah Daughtry (Howard Dean's chief of staff at the DNC) and US Representatives James Clyburn and Nancy Pelosi, Kelly used that data to compile an election postmortem with Alexia Kelley. They parlayed their work into a consulting firm known as Common Good Strategies to help Democratic candidates push faith messages to evangelicals and Catholics. In the 2006 midterms, their slate of clients did 10 percentage points or so better than Democrats nationally among those targeted voters.[28]

Compared to Kelly's fledgling attempts, Obama's faith outreach machine in the 2008 campaign—officially, the Religious Affairs Department—was a leviathan. For starters, it had significantly more staff; Michael Wear, one of DuBois's interns at the time, told me that in addition to DuBois, deputy director Paul Monteiro, and a gaggle of interns based in Chicago, the campaign claimed several staffers dedicated to specific religious constituencies. Rev. E. Terri LaVelle, Obama's senior adviser for Religious Affairs, took point on many outreach efforts to black churches. Shaun Casey, then a professor of Christian ethics at Wesley Theological Seminary, targeted white evangelicals. Mark Linton worked with Catholics. Jewish outreach was handled outside of the Religious Affairs team, but the campaign had two Muslim outreach directors at different times—Mazen Asbahi and Minha Husaini.

"We had at least six paid staff over the course of the campaign. In [Kerry's] campaign, you had Mara and an intern shoved into a closet with one landline phone," said Wear, who would go on to work in Obama's White House.[29]

Kelly later clarified that she and an intern had "a third of a table" during the Kerry campaign, which is *technically* superior to a closet. But she agreed the scale of Obama's faith operation was undeniably immense by comparison, and she bolstered its work by operating her own independent PAC, the Matthew 25 Network, which produced pro-Obama faith-related advertisements for television, radio, and print. One ad featured Christian author Brian McLaren—who would go on to be a prominent progressive faith activist—and Saguaro Seminar alum Kirbyjon Caldwell discussing Obama's faith and his dedication to family.[30]

Within the campaign itself, DuBois and his team took pains to match their quantity with quality. In South Carolina, staff launched a 40 Days of Faith and Family initiative, from late September through October 2007. The effort organized gospel concerts and tapped into existing Bible study programs to help inform voters about "how Obama's faith informs how he thinks about the issues of our time." Obama was already stumping at churches across South Carolina, a common tactic for candidates in a state where Democrats were overwhelmingly religious and roughly 50 percent black. But the religious push also allowed him to talk about his faith at length at Redemption World Outreach Center, a multiracial megachurch in Greenville,

South Carolina. The sanctuary was near its 4,200-seat capacity when Obama told the crowd that faith "plays every role" in his life.

"It's what keeps me grounded. It's what keeps my eyes set on the greatest of heights," said Obama, who was often likened to a preacher on the campaign trail. He added that faith is "what propels me to do what I do, and when I am down it's what lifts me up."[31]

Obama also spoke at preacher's conferences in 2007 because, DuBois told me, "Every religious convention in the country wanted [Obama] to speak that year."[32] The faith team chose the General Synod of United Church of Christ (UCC)—Obama's chosen denomination after joining Trinity Church—as the venue for a speech entitled "A Politics of Conscience." The senator structured part of his address around the UCC tagline, "God is still speaking," repeating the axiom several times as he outlined what he saw as hopeful trends among people of faith.[33] He addressed the AME conference the following year (an event that produced a photo of bishops laying hands on Obama in prayer) as well, and Michelle Obama gave a rousing talk at the National Baptist Convention.

Meanwhile, DuBois and his staff orchestrated a weekly prayer call for pastors, with clerics offering up telephonic orisons for the senator (who would not be on the call) every Friday morning. Linton, the Catholic outreach director, would sometimes lead the main call (he once simply read the Peace Prayer of St. Francis),[34] but there were separate weekly prayer-and-strategy calls for Catholics, African American Christians, evangelicals, and Jews.[35]

The team augmented its spiritual work with more traditional campaign tactics, such as shipping out stacks of glossy, faith-focused campaign literature for the seemingly infinite army of Obama field organizers to distribute. The pamphlets—or, as staff called them, faith lit—might feature Obama standing in front of an illuminated cross or bowed in prayer, juxtaposed next to imposing phrases such as Committed Christian or the all-caps descriptor ANSWERING THE CALL. The converted could even acquire a series of faith-related buttons and stickers handed out at events or sold via the campaign's online store, each adorned with a slogan such as Believers for Barack, People of

Faith for Obama,[36] Catholics for Obama, and one that spelled out his name phonetically in Hebrew as ברק אובמה.[37]

Come October 2007, the religion website *Beliefnet* declared that Obama invoked his faith more than any other Democratic candidate, and as he clinched the nomination in 2008, the competition—by that point, mainly ardent Methodist Hillary Clinton—wasn't even close.[38] His team was already producing for supporters a weekly *American Values Report* newsletter, each of which featured lengthy discussions of religion and values. Most made a direct connection between faith and the ideals embodied by the senator and his new running mate, then Delaware senator Joe Biden.[39]

"As with Senator Obama, Biden views faith as an 'active, palpable agent'; you can't just talk about values, you have to 'do something' to realize those values," read one newsletter.[40] It drew heavily from the campaign's website, which had an entire section dedicated to religion under the URL faith.barackobama.com. The account, written by Alyssa Martin, also name-dropped Alexia Kelley, then director of Catholics in Alliance for the Common Good—the organization that would later aid Obama in his bid to pass the Affordable Care Act.

"The trick was trying to do it in a way that wasn't like the Religious Right—co-opting pulpits," DuBois said. "Helpfully for us and for the churches, UCCers, United Methodists, ELCAs [the Evangelical Lutheran Church in America], and others would never respond to that anyway."

DIVINE DEFENSE

Obama's religion work was not without its troubles. His 2007 speech at the UCC General Synod, for instance, triggered an investigation by the IRS the following February. Officials argued that the denomination might have jeopardized its tax-exempt status by hosting the political speech, an allegation UCC leaders rebuked, calling it "disturbing."[41] (The IRS dropped the investigation three months later.)[42]

Indeed, even as Obama's God talk played well with many audiences, religion itself proved to be a liability for his campaign. His candidacy was haunted from day one by a right-wing whisper campaign that claimed he was secretly a Muslim. (Note: Obama was and remains a Christian, but being Muslim doesn't disqualify someone from public office anyway, as the US Constitution explicitly forbids religious tests for public office.)[43] He was also beset with criticism from Rep. Keith Ellison, the nation's first Muslim congressman, and other members of the Islamic faith, who claimed Obama was keeping Muslim supporters at arm's length. Although Obama met privately with Islamic leaders and spoke inclusively about the faith, he never publicly visited a Muslim house of worship on the trail, and campaign officials reportedly asked Ellison to cancel a trip to speak at an Iowa mosque on Obama's behalf.[44]

The campaign's Muslim outreach directors, Asbahi and Husaini, also suffered minor controversies that highlighted the intense scrutiny American Islamic leaders faced at the time. Asbahi resigned after just over a week on the job, when he was linked to an old business connection with a controversial imam,[45] and Husaini was blasted for going to a meeting with the Council on American-Islamic Relations[46]—a group that, ironically, would later meet with Obama administration[47] *and* Trump administration officials at different levels.[48]

Then there were the two largest controversies of the election cycle, the first of which erupted after years-old video emerged in March 2008 of Obama's pastor, Rev. Jeremiah Wright, preaching firebrand sermons that discussed the September 11 terrorist attacks and the Japanese assault on Pearl Harbor. Many found his remarks offensive, and Obama quickly distanced himself from Wright in an address, "A More Perfect Union," also known as his "race speech," that many analysts would deem one of his best. Obama condemned Wright's comments (but not his person) and explained that his "faith in God and my faith in the American people" grounded his belief that the country could move beyond "racial wounds."[49] It was enough to quiet some of the uproar, but not enough to quiet Wright: the pastor reignited the controversy the following month by making some even more inflammatory comments. Obama resigned his membership from the church soon after.

As if that weren't enough religious drama, Obama again waded into God trouble a month later, when he was caught on tape at a San Francisco fundraiser describing Rust Belt voters in Pennsylvania and elsewhere in the Midwest in less-than-flattering terms. Specifically, he said that in the wake of decades of economic stagnation in the region, many "get bitter . . . cling to guns or religion or antipathy to people who aren't like them or anti-immigrant sentiment or antitrade sentiment as a way to explain their frustrations." Obama's opponent, Hillary Clinton, wasted little time in turning the gaffe against him, framing the former university lecturer as an elitist who doesn't understand faith.

"I grew up in a church-going family, a family that believed in the importance of living out and expressing our faith," she said at a rally in Indianapolis. "The people of faith I know don't 'cling to' religion because they're bitter. People embrace faith not because they are materially poor, but because they are spiritually rich."[50]

The media covered Obama's faith *faux pas*, combined with the Wright controversy, as a potential candidacy killer. But the end result was arguably a case example of just how valuable faith outreach can be for Democrats. Unlike Kerry four years prior, Obama tackled the issue head-on: In his first speech addressing the "guns or religion" remarks, Obama led with the line, "I'm a person of deep faith, and my religion has sustained me through a lot in my life." He then made an overt reference to his 2006 religion speech, pointing to a line in which he exclaimed that Democrats "make a mistake when we fail to acknowledge the power of faith in people's lives."[51]

The faith team redoubled its outreach efforts and even made a play for conservative Christian voters—a tricky group for any Democrat to win over. Obama met with thirty evangelical leaders in Chicago in June 2008, and while he impressed some in the room, he was reportedly peppered with questions from Rev. Franklin Graham about his father's Muslim heritage.[52] The senator was more successful at winning praise from California megapastor Rick Warren, who hosted him and his general election opponent, Sen. John McCain, at his church for a Civil Forum on the Presidency.[53]

Faith outreach did not *erase* Obama's controversies, of course. But it softened the impact of scandals that could have halted his journey to the Oval Office, helping him build up what Wear called a "reservoir of trust" with religious voters that could be siphoned out and used to douse the political flames of problematic news cycles.[54]

Faith outreach also paid electoral dividends over the course of the campaign, especially in early primary states. DuBois pointed to deeply religious South Carolina, where Obama trailed behind Clinton in public opinion polls throughout 2007. Outreach to black pastors, however, helped tip the scales in Obama's favor by election day.

"The voices of black pastors who supported him in South Carolina were essential," DuBois said. "Those voices would not have been mobilized if it were not for a concerted outreach operation."

DuBois said they made similar strides in Iowa, where the campaign conducted dozens of faith forums across the state, and in New Hampshire.[55] He rattled off gains among Methodists, progressive Catholics, and UCC members in places such as Davenport, Iowa, where Obama won nearly 48 percent of caucus-goers in the surrounding county compared to Clinton's 29 percent.

According to exit polls, Obama also shaved off a sector of the evangelical vote in the general election. Although he improved upon Kerry's numbers with white evangelicals by only 3 percentage points overall (24 percent versus 21 percent), Obama doubled Kerry's 2004 numbers among *young* white evangelicals and made similar gains among those aged thirty to forty-four. The improvements were far more dramatic in swing states: Obama did better than Kerry with the group in Michigan, Florida, Indiana, Pennsylvania, and Virginia, and did *10 points* better in Colorado, the home of conservative Christian groups such as Focus on the Family.[56]

One study showed that Obama made gains with people of faith across the board nationally, including those who attend worship weekly (+8 percent), Catholics overall (+7 percent), and Jews (+4 percent). The only exceptions were mainline Christians (no change) and the catchall category "Other faiths" (-1 percent), which is arguably too broad to draw many firm conclusions.[57]

To fans of faith outreach, it was all the proof they needed. Roughly a month after Obama delivered his soaring victory speech to a sprawling crowd in Chicago, Mike McCurry penned an article in *The Daily Beast* under the headline "How My Party Found God." He raved about the impact of Obama's Religious Affairs operation, saying, "Where Democrats organized real outreach to mainstream Protestant and Catholic congregations, the share of Obama's vote went up compared to the percentage John Kerry won in 2004."

Perhaps the most telling excerpt was the article's subhead, which echoed Obama's own words from his 2006 faith speech: "Liberals have practiced secular politics since the 1960s, but with the ascent of Barack Obama, the Left discovered it can actually keep the faith."[58]

But as Obama cautioned, keeping the faith—especially one that is, as he once put it, grounded in struggle[59]—is never easy, in private or in politics. It takes persistence and dedication, and as Democrats— and more than a few Republicans—would learn eight years later, failure to understand it or take it seriously can sometimes mean having to endure dark nights of the soul.

CHAPTER THREE

★ ★ ★

When God Chooses a Leader

I t wasn't even 9:00 a.m., but Russell Moore was already fuming. This was, admittedly, a bit odd. Southern Baptist ministers are known for delivering red-faced lectures on the evils of sin while in the pulpit, but Moore isn't exactly a fire-and-brimstone kind of guy. The typically urbane, mild-mannered pastor is better known for wearing immaculately pressed suits and heading up the Ethics and Religious Liberty Commission (ERLC) of the Southern Baptist Convention (SBC), the largest Protestant Christian denomination in the United States.

But a fire had been stoked within Moore that Monday morning in January 2016, heating his otherwise slow-simmering anger to a boiling point. The evangelical Christian thinker, who just a month before had outed himself as a stalwart opponent of then Republican presidential candidate Donald Trump, was watching the businessman's appearance at Liberty University, a prominent evangelical Christian school in Lynchburg, Virginia. And there on his screen, Liberty president Jerry Falwell Jr.—son of the school's late founder and famous cultural crusader, Jerry Falwell Sr.—was invoking holy scripture while introducing "The Donald."

"'By their fruits ye shall know them.' Donald's Trump's life has borne fruit," said Falwell, who would endorse Trump later that month.[1]

Moore was having none of it. Naturally, he turned to the medium best suited for venting frustration to the masses: Twitter.

"Absolutely unbelievable," he wrote above a quote-tweet of Falwell's words.[2] He then proceeded to live-critique Trump's entire speech, irately tapping out theological zingers on his iPhone, such as "This would be hilarious if it weren't so counter to the mission of the gospel of Jesus Christ"[3] and "Evangelicals can love a golden calf, as long as Aaron promises to make Mexico pay for it."[4]

And tucked within his digital diatribe was a subtweet heard round the evangelical world: "Trading in the gospel of Jesus Christ for political power is not liberty but slavery."[5]

To outsiders, that line sounded strange coming from Moore, whose ERLC operates as the political face of the SBC and, by extension, is sometimes considered part of the conglomeration of conservative religious groups described as the Religious Right. Although bolstered by conservative Catholics, mainline Protestants, Jews, and Mormons, the Religious Right locates its most loyal supporters among evangelical Protestants, particularly *white* evangelical Protestants who have spent decades fusing faith and politics in their tenacious pursuit of a conservative legislative agenda.

But to Moore, Trump represented something very different. As the businessman sparked nervous laughter among the crowd by mistakenly referring to a Bible chapter as "two Corinthians" (instead of the more common phrasing "Second Corinthians"), Moore punctuated his Twitter polemic by posting an image that featured a portion of his book *Onward: Engaging the Culture Without Losing the Gospel.*[6]

"If politics drives the gospel, rather than the other way around, we end up with a public witness in which Mormon talk-show hosts and serially monogamous casino magnates and prosperity-gospel preachers are welcomed into our ranks, regardless of what violence they do to the gospel," read a section illuminated in hastily applied yellow highlighter. "They are, after all, 'right on the issues.'"

Moore would articulate versions of this sentiment throughout Trump's campaign. He published multiple editorials in the *New York*

Times and the *Washington Post*, pleading with his fellow evangelicals to "count the cost of following Donald Trump," describing their growing support for him as "illogical," and arguing that "to back Mr. Trump, these voters must repudiate everything they believe."[7] When Trump began to make gains among white, self-described born-again Christians—a broad group of primarily evangelicals—Moore claimed that support for the candidate by so-called evangelicals was damaging to the faith itself and "will take longer to recover from than the '80s TV evangelist scandals."[8]

"I was more concerned with evangelical Christianity itself than with whatever was happening in the political campaign," Moore would tell me in 2019, insistent that his efforts were narrowly focused on rescuing his faith tradition.[9] "What I was concerned about, and am concerned about, and always have been concerned about, is what J. Gresham Machen called *liberalism*—which is sort of an unfortunate word because people identify it politically either with classical liberalism or progressivism. But in the usage there [Machen] was seeing Christianity as a means to an end, whether that end is spreading Wilsonian democracy or something else."

Put another way, Moore worried that Falwell and other evangelicals were fawning over Trump because despite the twice-divorced businessman's questionable behavior, he tapped into longstanding self-serving political tendencies of the Religious Right—ones that some evangelical Protestant elites like Moore had railed against for years. Trump, in his own way, spoke directly to the evangelical quest for power and influence, building on decades of efforts by conservative Christian activists to secure a robust, reliable voting bloc, even if that bloc didn't necessarily embody the values it professed.

It was a smart political play on Trump's part. If exit polls are any indication, pandering to the evangelical vote with lofty promises and Christian nationalist fusions of God, country, and money was a successful campaign strategy. But the short-term gain for Trump may have important long-term side effects for evangelicalism itself: it may have fractured part of the GOP's evangelical base by creating a vacuum of moral authority for anyone who didn't resonate with Trump's nationalistic politics, giving the modern Religious Left the opportunity of a generation.

THE RELIGIOUS RIGHT, TRUMP-STYLE

In fairness to Moore, changes in the conservative religious landscape manifested during Trump's rise in ways that surprised even veteran observers of religion and politics. Yet the pastor's vexations with certain subsets of the Religious Right are hardly new and are rooted in two older religious trends that Trump simply remixed and set to repeat during his campaign: Christian nationalism and the prosperity gospel.

Both phenomena have bubbled up repeatedly at points in American history, but scholars such as Princeton University's Kevin Kruse argue that their modern iterations were born out of a 1930s-era campaign by conservative Christians and big businesses to push back against the Religious Left of their day. In the early twentieth century it was liberal Christianity that was ascendant in American politics, not conservative religious fervor. The period saw the explosive growth of the Social Gospel movement (see chapter 8), which described the various unsavory aspects of the Industrial Revolution—child labor, a destitute working class, and more—as forms of larger structural or "social" sin instead of personal moral failings. President Franklin Delano Roosevelt's own secretary of labor embraced the Social Gospel and the phenomenon is credited with helping fuel the labor movement, the broader progressive movement, and the passage of the New Deal.[10]

Naturally, the Social Gospel's biggest detractors were the heads of corporations who stood to lose the most from its reforms. As such, a coalition of business leaders responded by fielding their own God squad, known as the Spiritual Mobilization movement, which preached a combination of nationalist fervor, faith, and a strong belief that money can be a spiritual good. By the late 1940s, this group—led by Congregationalist minister Rev. James W. Fifield Jr., one of America's early megapastors—had grown to boast more than seventeen thousand member ministers preaching opposition to the

New Deal, the Social Gospel, and liberalism in general. When the anti-Communist Red Scare took hold in the 1950s, these Spiritual Mobilization pastors wedded their existing message of Christian libertarianism with a form of Christian nationalism, convening Freedom Under God rallies across the country to champion the idea that America is a Christian nation.

You can still hear echoes of Spiritual Mobilization's quasi-libertarian theology in the rhetoric of Trump, who once attended a church led by pastor Norman Vincent Peale, a man Kruse told me was once asked to lead the Spiritual Mobilization movement (he turned it down). One line often repeated at Trump's rallies could have come straight from the movement's workbooks: "In America, we don't worship government, we worship God."[11]

In addition to this early form of Christian nationalism, Spiritual Mobilization set in motion what would eventually become the prosperity gospel movement. It rose alongside the more political Religious Right in the 1970s and '80s, when televangelists such as Creflo Dollar and Jim Bakker mixed conservative Christian theology with self-help tactics and an insistence that money is evidence of faithfulness and God's favor (and for some, *especially* when that money is given to the pastor). The ideology reached a crescendo around the year 2000 with the rise of Joel Osteen, a best-selling author and prosperity preacher who grew Lakewood Church in Houston, Texas, into the single largest church in the United States, cramming thousands of worshippers into a former basketball arena every Sunday.[12]

Figures from all across the Christian theological spectrum, including prominent conservatives like Rick Warren,[13] Albert Mohler,[14] and Jerry Falwell Sr., penned scathing criticism of the prosperity gospel's theology.[15] So did Russell Moore: when Dollar asked his followers to buy him a $65 million jet in 2015, Moore decried his theology as a "full-deal heresy."[16] The critiques were intense, but theological sniping at the prosperity movement was a low-cost political move—because unlike Religious Right cultural crusaders, prosperity gospel preachers largely avoided political debates.

At least, that *was* the case—until Trump.

It's not hard to see where the mutual appreciation between Trump and prosperity gospel preachers comes from; both have a long history of courting fame and money. With a few exceptions (most notably, Jerry Falwell Jr.), Trump's vocal faith-rooted supporters and advisers in the early stages of his campaign were not rank-and-file members of the Religious Right. Instead, many were leaders of the prosperity gospel movement, such as Paula White, pastor of a church in Orlando, Florida; Kenneth and Gloria Copeland, televangelists and head of the Texas-based Kenneth Copeland Ministries; and Mark Burns, a relatively unknown pastor from South Carolina. All preached versions of prosperity theology in ways that transitioned smoothly into support for a billionaire-turned-presidential candidate. Several already had relationships with Trump before he ran: White, who is sometimes called Trump's "God whisperer" and was later tapped for a White House post, has known him since 2011.[17] And while Osteen did not officially endorse Trump, the businessman did help the pastor launch his Sirius XM radio channel in 2014.[18]

Moore and other relatively moderate evangelicals have made it clear since 2016 that they see Trump's glad-handing with prosperity gospel preachers to be a scandalous amalgamation of God and mammon. Moore, for example, decried Burns and White as "heretical prosperity gospel hucksters" when they spoke on Trump's behalf at the Republican National Convention.[19]

But the presence of prosperity preachers has done little to diminish Trump's clout among white evangelicals. On the contrary, Trump and the prosperity pastors stumping for him have kept conservative Christians in the fold through a new form of Christian nationalism predicated on the belief that America was established as a Christian nation and that its religious heritage must be preserved at all costs.

"[Trump] is authentically, whether people like it or not . . . raised up by God," White said on televangelist Jim Bakker's show in August 2017.[20] She went on to argue that resisting Trump is akin to "fighting against the hand of God," that early European settlers founded American colonies as Christian mission fields, and that Christians have a responsibility to "take back our school systems, take back our families, take back our homes, [and] take back our nation."

White would later tell me and other journalists that she regretted making those remarks, explaining that she believes *all* leaders are uplifted by God. But her words nonetheless expressed a modern, Trumpified brand of Christian nationalism that represents a mutation of what the Religious Right has preached for decades.[21] Rooted in the same America-centric theology trumpeted by Spiritual Mobilization in the 1930s, Christian nationalism's contemporary flavor was a crucial part of how conservative Christian leaders rallied so-called values voters to the polls in the 1980s, '90s, and in recent decades. Jerry Falwell Sr., for instance, was chastised (and praised) for referring to the United States as a Christian nation in 2004,[22] and Alabama chief justice Roy Moore became a folk hero that same year when he was pulled from the bench for refusing to remove a monument of the Ten Commandments in the state judicial building.[23]

Christian nationalism was especially *in vogue* in the Bush era among a core group of primarily white evangelical Christians, and it often manifested in what some journalists described as "dominionism," a reference to a biblical passage in the book of Genesis in which God declares to Adam and Eve that they have dominion over the earth. So-called dominionists (who rarely use the term to describe themselves) interpret this to mean that Christians have a God-given right to rule the United States and, by extension, should run it in ways that are often unapologetically theocratic. The foundational tenets of this hypothetical theocracy have generally orbited around a small cluster of beliefs: support for "religious liberty," and opposition to abortion and same-sex marriage.[24]

The evangelical elite has long dismissed the most brazen iterations of this sentiment as extreme, but the beliefs nevertheless remain popular among many everyday evangelicals and leaders of the Religious Right—and have achieved a new life under Trump. He made regular appeals to them during his presidential campaign, insisting that America will "say Merry Christmas again" (as opposed to the more religiously inclusive "Happy Holidays") and tapping as his running mate then Indiana governor Mike Pence, whom religion journalist Jeff Sharlet and *New York Times* columnist Michelle Goldberg have linked to Christian nationalism.[25]

It was Trump's nationalistic and seemingly self-involved approach to faith that Russell Moore tried to combat throughout 2016. When Moore referred to Trump and his Democratic opponent, Hillary Clinton, as "reality television moral sewage" during an interview with CBS News, Trump lashed out on Twitter.

"Russell Moore is truly a terrible representative of Evangelicals and all of the good they stand for," Trump tweeted, making sure to tag Moore's username. "A nasty guy with no heart!"[26]

Moore responded by quote-tweeting the president and adding "Sad!"—a sarcastic reference to Trump's oft-mocked Twitter catchphrase. He then published an Instagram post of Trump's quip alongside a reference to 1 Kings 18:17–19, a Bible passage in which the prophet Elijah accuses a king of abandoning the Lord's commands.[27] By evangelical standards, it was a pretty epic Bible Burn.

The SBC leader and a small cadre of the evangelical elite were also appalled shortly before the election, when an old *Access Hollywood* clip emerged featuring Trump bragging openly about sexually assaulting women. Moore and the others were no fans of Clinton or the Democrats, but they still saw Trump as a man devoid of personal integrity, if not personal faith. Along with many nonevangelicals, they were outraged that anyone in their flock would support a man they saw as fundamentally unfit for the presidency, much less deserving of support from conservative values voters. But Moore and other white evangelical "Never Trumpers" failed to convert their fellow conservative faithful to their cause: come Election Day, Trump cleaned up among white evangelicals, garnering at least 80 percent of the group's vote—the highest margin for any presidential candidate in decades.[28]

Moore insists the concern he showed throughout the 2016 campaign season is also why the election results did not shock him. He had correctly predicted to a reporter that if Trump became the nominee, "He'll get 80 percent of the white evangelical vote."[29] Yet Trump's electoral victory stunned many others, and it was arguably an expression, not a cause, of what some see as the slow-motion moral collapse of politicized conservative Christianity, in which politicians and their religious backers effectively deem adherence to Christian nationalism and victory in the culture wars to be more important than theological consistency in one's personal life. As shown by Trump's upset victory—partly thanks to white evangelicals and Catholics—this strategy offered significant political gains for the Religious Right and finally gifted them many of their long sought-after goals.

In fact, Trump and his religious backers became even more brazen in their use of Christian nationalist language after his election. On Inauguration Day, Texas pastor Rev. Robert Jeffress—one of the president's most loyal defenders and a regular fixture on FOX News—delivered a private sermon to the soon-to-be president entitled "When God Chooses a Leader," in which he breathlessly interlaced God and country with Trump. Trump echoed a similar sentiment during his inaugural address later that morning, when he referred to his fellow Americans as "God's people" and insisted that citizens should have "no fear" because the Almighty would now protect the nation.[30]

Since moving into the Oval Office, Trump has continued to ratchet up the religious rhetoric. When he spoke at the National Prayer Breakfast in February 2017, he proclaimed to attendees, "That is what our people want: one beautiful nation, under God."[31] When he offered the commencement address at Liberty University in May of that year—a first for a sitting president—he told the graduating class that America is a "nation of true believers."[32] And when he delivered a foreign policy speech in July to a crowd in Warsaw, Poland, he argued that a yearning for the divine was a central part of western culture, declaring, "The people of Poland, the people of America, and the people of Europe still cry out, 'We want God.'"[33]

In addition to the rhetoric, Trump continued to deliver on campaign promises pulled straight from the Christian nationalist playbook. He championed religious liberty, appointed conservative justices to the Supreme Court, and signed executive orders that chipped away at laws that prohibit churches from endorsing political candidates.

But perhaps the most prominent embrace of Trumpian Christian nationalism took place in 2017 during an Independence Day–themed celebration in Washington, DC. As the president sat nearby, Jeffress—standing before a deeply evangelical crowd assembled at the Kennedy Center—directed his own church choir to belt out an original hymnlike ballad prepared for the occasion.

The title and refrain? "Make America Great Again."

Trump, unsurprisingly, was delighted by the ode, which the black-and-blue-clad choir singers performed while standing in front of a massive American flag. He posted footage of the moment to his Twitter page—high praise from the famously social media savvy president.[34] Some observers were shocked by the display, but Christian conservatives who flocked to Trump's rallies seemed to like it just fine.

THE NEW EVANGELICAL BASE

Trump's success is counterintuitive for many. There has been much hand-wringing—including among evangelicals—about his consistently sky-high approval ratings among white evangelicals despite his various theological flubs, gaffes, and personal encounters with sin. Progressive political pundits have also wondered aloud how Trump managed to rally a supposedly values-conscious religious base around such wildly controversial proposals as building a wall along the US-Mexico border, separating migrant families, or banning Muslims from entering the country.

The answer may lie in Christian nationalism. In 2017, a group of social scientists led by Clemson University professor Andrew Whitehead mined data from the Baylor Religion Survey. Participants were asked a series of questions regarding Christian nationalism, such as how they feel about prayer in public schools, displaying religious symbols in public spaces, and the separation of church and state. The results revealed that those who scored high on the survey's Christian nationalism index were significantly more likely to vote for Trump regardless of their religious tradition or worship attendance habits. They were also more likely to embrace the more unsavory hallmarks of Trumpism: negative views of immigrants, refugees, and Muslims.[35]

"There wasn't a really religious vote [in 2016], but there was a Christian nationalist narrative that can unite these religious groups," Whitehead told me in 2017.[36]

This discovery led Whitehead and his colleagues to conclude that Christian nationalism isn't a religious term defined by nuanced theological structures; it isn't even tied exclusively to white evangelicalism. Instead, it functions primarily as an *identity* that largely exists *outside* of a specific religious moral code. Although rooted in historical and theological arguments, it operates less like a rigid litany of ethical rules and more as a vague set of ideas and symbols that can easily trigger the demonization of others.

As White and his colleagues wrote in their paper: "This brand of religious nationalism appears to be unmoored from traditional Christian ideals and morality, and also inclined toward authoritarian figures."

Indeed, Trump has made deference to American symbols a hallmark of his presidency, be it by hugging American flags or by verbally attacking National Football League players who knelt during the national anthem to protest racism and police brutality. Many of the kneelers—football players and performers alike—have cited their faith as inspiring their activism, but here, too, White and his colleagues saw a connection between Christian nationalism and those who derided the protests. In a follow-up paper, researchers observed that adherents to Christian nationalism are more likely to believe not only that police treat African Americans the same as whites but also that police shoot black people more often because blacks are supposedly more violent than whites.[37]

The passionate preaching of Christian nationalism by leaders of the Religious Right and the group's seemingly unbreakable bond with the Republican Party have been a boon to Trump in particular and the GOP in general. When I asked Greg Smith, associate director of research at Pew Research Center, about the conservative Christian embrace of the GOP, he pointed out that white evangelicals have shifted dramatically in their political affiliation over the past twenty years. "In 2000, 58 percent of white evangelical Protestants who were registered voters identified or leaned toward the Republican Party, but last year that number stood at 77 percent," he said. "They have grown 20 points more Republican over the last couple of decades."[38]

During that same period, Smith noted, white Catholics have also drifted toward the GOP, responding in much the same way that evangelicals did to the appeal by Trump (and the party) to Christian nationalism and opposition to same-sex marriage and abortion. Although he fell short of Obama's commanding win among Catholics as a whole in 2008 (Obama won 54 percent versus Trump's 52 percent), Trump won 60 percent of white Catholics, the highest margin of any presidential contender since at least 2000.

Like white evangelical Protestants, a significant number of white Catholics relate to Christian nationalism, including the version preached by Trump campaign adviser and proud Catholic Steve Bannon.[39] The former executive chairman of Breitbart News is well known for his love affair with nationalism, but one can see the religious dimensions of his populist ideology in a 2014 speech to a Vatican assembly, in which he insisted that his fellow Catholics should protect the "Judeo-Christian West" in its "struggle against Islam."[40] These views would prove influential several years later: Bannon is credited with helping craft not only Trump's God-heavy inauguration speech but his Warsaw address as well.

Granted, Catholics who outwardly celebrate this ideology are sometimes dismissed as marginal by more liberal Catholics. But margins make the difference in politics: white Catholics, along with a healthy number of Trump-supporting white mainline Protestants and evangelicals, are heavily represented in Rust Belt states such as Wisconsin, Michigan, and Pennsylvania—the three states most responsible for Trump's Electoral College victory. And they're not moving away anytime soon.

FROM RESPECTABLE RETICENCE . . .

If going all-in on Christian nationalism elevated Trump to the White House, it also shifted the tectonic plates of political evangelicalism, exposing fissures in a right-wing religious coalition that had sat undisturbed for decades. His efforts to energize his base provided the perfect target for his religious critics, even among evangelicals who railed against what some called a "toxic" version of their faith.

A few, like Russell Moore, had voiced dissent early. A couple of months after Jerry Falwell Jr. publicly backed Trump in 2016, Liberty University board member Mark Demoss spoke out, questioning the appropriateness of Falwell's endorsement and saying that Trump's "bullying tactics of personal insult have no defense . . . certainly not for anyone who claims to be a follower of Christ." Two months later, Demoss, who served as chief of staff to the senior Falwell for several years and reportedly considered him a second father, was asked by his fellow board members to resign.[41]

The small diaspora of Trump-averse evangelicals expanded rapidly after the 2016 election, but the spectrum of spiritual discontent was broad. On the more moderate end were those described by CNN's Daniel Burke as "institutional" and "arm's-length" evangelicals.[42] These were leaders closely tied to elite universities and institutions within conservative Christianity who can be quick to offer a biblical exegesis to address everyday spiritual concerns, but who distance themselves from electoral politics. Moore is said to belong to this group, and others share many of his qualities, such as an attachment to conservative theological principles but a disdain for opportunism and immoral behavior.

Moore wasn't one of Trump's main evangelical critics after the election, however, at least not as fervently as during the 2016 campaign. The SBC leader still criticized the Trump administration at points throughout the president's first term, but he largely dialed back his Twitter rants. He even apologized to his fellow Baptists for using words on social media that were "overly broad or unnecessarily harsh" when he criticized Trump and his supporters.[43] The reason for his shift is murky: some implied that Moore was interested in keeping his job at the SBC, but officials in the denomination remained largely supportive of him after the election, suggesting that his change in demeanor was an adherence to religious principles of candor and deference to power.

Other institutional evangelicals shared Moore's relative reticence after Trump took the oath of office, as the group generally declined to challenge the president publicly during his first year. The one exception was when Trump blamed "both sides" for the deadly violence in Charlottesville, Virginia, which left a woman dead at the hands of a white supremacist. Several prominent evangelical voices responded to the incident by condemning racists, though most stopped short of condemning Trump or his comments.

There was, however, a brief moment in April 2018 when observers thought this group might break its collective silence. With little warning, several institutional evangelicals announced they were meeting at Wheaton College, a private Christian school outside Chicago renowned as an academic powerhouse of conservative Protestantism. Early reports described the gathering as an occasion for open dialogue, where attendees could commiserate over their concerns about the state of evangelicalism, which many saw as increasingly tied to the president's image. As conference organizer Doug Birdsall put it: "When you Google evangelicals, you get Trump."[44]

The plan was for the conference to produce a statement, a potentially groundbreaking development, given that the guest list was a veritable who's who of the evangelical cognoscenti. Attendees included Tim Keller, pastor at New York City's Redeemer Presbyterian Church; Harold Smith, then president and CEO of the historic evangelical magazine *Christianity Today*; Jenny Yang, vice president of World Relief, an evangelical refugee-resettlement group and international development agency; and A. R. Bernard, a black pastor of a forty-thousand-member church in Brooklyn, who was the only faith leader to resign from Trump's evangelical advisory board after the president's Charlottesville comments.

The conference wasn't touted as anti-Trump per se, and organizers insisted it was designed to address a "series of challenges approaching us from both the right and the left."[45] But an invitation to participants described it as "prompted by the challenges of distortions to evangelicalism that have permeated both the media and culture since the 2016 election," noting that "support of 'eighty-one percent of self-identifying white evangelicals' for Donald Trump is a call to self-reflection on the current condition of evangelicalism."[46]

As Yang later told the *Religion News Service*: "All of us in the room know that's the context in which we're operating."[47]

If you tilted your head and squinted just right, you could almost make out a streak of liberalism at the gathering. It included such left-leaning evangelical voices as Jim Wallis of Sojourners and Gabriel Salguero, the often liberal-leaning president of the National Latino Evangelical Coalition. But perhaps the most telling invite was Ohio governor John Kasich, a Republican moderate and former presidential candidate who was deeply critical of Trump before being bested by him in the 2016 primaries. Kasich, an Anglican, ultimately did not attend the conference, yet the invitation sent a none-too-subtle signal to conservative Christians about the particular brand of polite, moderate politician the Wheaton group preferred as a dialogue partner.

In the end, the gathering produced more cognitive dissonance than critique. Journalist and former *Christianity Today* editor Katelyn Beaty, who attended, said the assembly eventually took a tense turn, with younger evangelicals pushing for the group to denounce racism and sexism and older attendees being skittish to address topics that donors might see as "too political."[48]

Ultimately, the group of teachers and preachers fell back on a newfound tradition of respectable reticence. The gathering kept no public records, and when Beaty began tweeting from what were originally touted as on-the-record sessions, Birdsall pulled her aside and asked her to stop. No collective statement was ever released.

Beaty later told me she found this silence frustrating, and that it resembled a quietude over political matters that she saw in both Russell Moore and the pages of *Christianity Today* after Trump's election. She acknowledged that these "evangelical thought leaders" might be keeping a low profile for fear that critiquing Trump would invite a backlash among their fellow evangelicals. But she argued that the alternative only allowed leaders like Falwell and Jeffress (who were not at the conference) to soak up all the media attention and turn off a "younger generation that really does want to talk about, say, what is happening at the [US-Mexico] border."[49]

. . . TO RIGHTEOUS RESISTANCE

In the age of Trump, there is ample evidence that the Religious Right may finally be encountering the political equivalent of Newton's third law. It is well established that the GOP relies heavily on the loyal voting habits of conservative white Christians. But Democrats, as Greg Smith of the Pew Research Center pointed out to me, benefit from the support of voters with no religious affiliation—sometimes called "nones"—and nonwhite religious voters. The two demographics have their differences, but appear to be mutually agitated by the same group: conservative Christians.

To be sure, nones—which now make up more than a quarter of the Democratic Party, according to a 2017 study by the Public Religion Research Institute (PRRI)[50]—constitute a broad and often perplexing group that defy tidy categorization and express a range of opinions about faith. While their ranks include many atheists and agnostics, a 2018 Pew survey found that most still concede they believe in a higher power.[51] But the same survey also revealed the nones' clear frustration with politicized churches and hint at a revolt against the Religious Right: roughly half of the religiously unaffiliated said they don't belong to a religious tradition because they "don't like the positions churches take on social/political issues." When coupled with the fact that nones support same-sex marriage and abortion rights more than almost any other US demographic,[52] it's hard to ignore the possibility that their flight from faith is at least partly a rejection of the Religious Right.[53]

This broad-based repudiation of conservative Christianity is especially apparent in the *exvangelical* movement, which features voices such as religion scholar and activist Chrissy Stroop and podcaster Blake Chastain that are unapologetically critical of evangelicalism. When discussing their movement, which saw an explosion of interest after Trump's election, both often condemn evangelicalism as abusive or toxic, saying they and others like them left the fold to either join another faith community or join the ranks of the nones by abandoning religion altogether.

Even more worrisome for the Religious Right is another trend buried in that 2017 PRRI study: white evangelicals made up 26 percent of Americans aged sixty-five or older in 2016, but represented only 8 percent of Americans age eighteen to twenty-nine—one of the largest percentage drop-offs across generations of any major religious group polled. By comparison, nones constituted a whooping 38 percent of eighteen-to-twenty-nine-year-olds that year compared to only 12 percent of those sixty-five or older.[54]

And then there is the other three quarters of the Democratic Party, who remain religious and often take cues from Religious Left leaders who, like the nones, typically embrace LGBTQ identities and relationships, are at least tolerant of abortion, and reject Christian nationalism. Unlike religious Republicans, who tend to be overwhelmingly white, religious Democrats are racially diverse, and researchers now believe that nonwhite faith voters may be crucial for Democrats hoping to flip red states. According to other Pew research data presented to journalists in 2018, states with higher religious attendance and expression leaned Republican, but nonwhite populations in those same states skewed highly religious and deeply Democratic.[55]

The electoral implications of southern, religious nonwhite voters were on full display during the special US Senate election in 2017 in Alabama, a pivotal moment for modern Democrats and a critical example of the emerging political power of progressive religious coalitions. The lefty faithful were a vote to be courted, however imperfectly: Doug Jones, the Democratic challenger, visited black churches ahead of election day with the famously theologically salient senator Cory Booker, while progressive faith leaders like Rev. William Barber held rallies encouraging black churchgoers and others to show up at the polls to oppose the Christian nationalist judge Roy Moore (no relation to Russell Moore).[56]

"[Judge] Moore's political agenda presents a credible threat to millions of vulnerable people in America—and children—yet Moore claims to be the moral and Christian candidate," Barber said during an event in Alabama. He was flanked by dozens of ministers, many who signed a letter explicitly condemning Judge Moore's Christian nationalism.[57]

It goes without saying that Moore lost the election for many reasons, including numerous allegations that he sexually abused minors. But several political analysts readily acknowledged that it was African American voters—many spurred to the polls by their churches—who played a key role in electing the first Democratic senator in Alabama since 1992.[58]

Even if modern Religious Right leaders wanted to stem the tide and muster bipartisan support for their cause, those dreams may be dashed for the foreseeable future. When the polling firm Morning Consult asked Americans in 2018 about individuals whose endorsements would make them more likely to support a candidate, not a single faith leader cracked the top ten, even among *Republicans*, let alone Democrats or Independents. But when people were asked whose endorsements they believed would make them *less* likely to support a candidate, one faith voice did place tenth among Democratic respondents: Liberty's Jerry Falwell Jr., just behind Senate Majority Leader Mitch McConnell.[59]

Falwell in particular has proven polarizing even among his fellow white evangelicals—especially the tradition's emerging progressive wing—and the pushback he has faced offers a hint as to what drives not only disaffected conservative Christians but also many in the emerging Religious Left. More than a few evangelicals—including deeply conservative voices—spent much of 2016 and 2017 chiding Falwell for his unflinching support of Trump. When the Liberty president defended Trump in the wake of the *Access Hollywood* tape, for instance, right-wing Christian commentator Erick Erickson agreed that he should step down,[60] as did author Ben Howe on Erickson's *Red State* blog.[61] And an increasingly vocal band of Liberty students and alumni issued statements signed by more than three thousand people rejecting his Trump endorsement.[62]

Falwell, for his part, seemed either incapable of or uninterested in stifling the dissent, and he even inadvertently managed to give his critics' ire national exposure. When he personally censored a Liberty student newspaper's attempt to run an op-ed critical of Trump's rhetoric regarding women, the piece was promptly republished in *The Daily Beast*.[63]

The backlash only escalated in August 2017, when Falwell, like many of Trump's evangelical advisers, defended the president in the wake of his controversial Charlottesville response, describing it as "bold" and "truthful."[64] He later went on television to express his support for Trump, a move that appeared to be at least partially coordinated by the White House: Martha Raddatz, hosting ABC's *This Week* Sunday talk show, said that when her staff asked administration officials to appear on the show to discuss the Charlottesville comments, they were directed to Falwell instead.[65]

Beaty told me Falwell's seemingly unconditional support for Trump is one of several things that make younger self-identified evangelicals uncomfortable to the point where many are "definitely attracted to leaders of the Religious Left, people who are very politically engaged." She noted that disillusioned evangelicals "wouldn't necessarily toe the Democratic Party line," but the Religious Left could still have a potential impact on their political leanings.

"At least someone's responding" to issues they care about, she said.[66]

This same spiritual discontent is what drove evangelical author Jonathan Martin to fire off a series of tweets in October 2017 calling for a prayerful protest of Liberty University, asking students and faculty to join him in standing "against the idolatry of nationalism and the politics of demonization in the name of Jesus Christ" and "for the oppressed."[67] When Martin attended a concert at Liberty at the invitation of the band four days later, police forcibly removed him from campus. Falwell subsequently announced a series of new

campus security reforms and had police officers observe students as
they prayed at a small gathering that was originally scheduled to
include Martin.[68]

Martin's ordeal set in motion a series of events that would ultimately culminate in the Red Letter Revival, whose name was a reference to the teachings of Jesus, which are highlighted in red in some
Bibles. Organized by the similarly named Red Letter Christians—a
progressive-leaning group headed by Tony Campolo, a well-known
liberal-leaning evangelical voice, and Shane Claiborne, a pastor, author, and activist based in Philadelphia—the gathering took place
in Lynchburg, Virginia, right down the street from Liberty in April
2018. It assembled speakers to preach proudly what some in Wheaton allegedly preferred to keep quiet: opposition to racism, bigotry,
Christian nationalism, toxic evangelicalism, and, of course, Donald
Trump.

"Some evangelicals are more committed to the amendments than
the commandments," Maryland pastor David Anderson declared
to the gathered crowd at the E. C. Glass Auditorium.[69] Anderson
was one of several nonwhite speakers at the event, a move organizers said was an intentional effort to push back against the idea that
evangelicals are exclusively white. Other preachers of color included
Brenda G. Brown-Grooms, a pastor in Charlottesville, and Lisa Sharon Harper, a Sojourners alum who had joined other faith leaders the
year before to stare down white supremacists in that same city.

Speakers decried Christian nationalism as an "apostasy," and the
program included altar calls—albeit ones that sounded a bit different
from what you might find in a more conservative church.

"Are you ready to say, 'I'm going to commit myself to Jesus'?"
Campolo prayed aloud during one session, as several people closed
their eyes and raised their hands in supplication.[70] "'I'm going to be
committed to the poor'? 'I'm going to stand up for the refugee'? 'I'm
going to speak for those who feel oppressed by our society'?"

Despite their religious zeal, the gathering garnered a relatively
small crowd of 300 to 350 people, a tangible reminder of the uphill
battle progressive evangelicals face in their effort to crack the armor

of loyalty created by the Religious Right. Indeed, if the Religious Right's power is measured in electoral might, it's still unclear what, if any, impact Red Letter Christians and other progressive evangelicals have had thus far. Election Day exit polls from the 2018 midterms detected that white evangelical support for the GOP (75 percent) was down compared to what Trump had garnered two years before (nearly 81 percent),[71] but Smith at Pew said those numbers roughly correspond to how white evangelicals voted in previous midterm elections and shouldn't be compared to a presidential race. What's more, he noted that Trump's approval rating among white evangelicals has remained largely intact over the course of his presidency, beginning at 78 percent before dipping to 67 percent in late 2017, only to rebound to 71 percent at the end of 2018.

"I'm not seeing any evidence that white evangelical voters are turning away from President Trump," Smith told me two weeks after the midterms.[72]

But left-leaning evangelicals are playing the long game. They remain hopeful that they can eventually change the hearts of their spiritual siblings, even as the divide between them seems to widen by the day. In November 2018, Claiborne and Campolo hosted another Red Letter Revival in Dallas, this time near Robert Jeffress's church. Despite their fierce criticism of Jeffress, Claiborne told me they offered to pray with him about the future of evangelicalism, just as they had asked Falwell in Lynchburg. (According to Claiborne, Falwell never responded, and Jeffress demanded a background check first.)

Even if progressives struggle to win converts among Christian conservatives, the combination of nones and a newly revitalized Religious Left is already countering Trump's religious coalition in other ways. To truly appreciate the nascent spiritual power that has risen to counter the new Religious Right, however, one must look to another self-identified evangelical—one who, in addition to regularly keynoting at Red Letter Revivals, has emerged as one of the most important progressive strategists of the modern era: Rev. William Barber II.

CHAPTER FOUR

★ ★ ★

Revolutionary Love

The day the Reverend Dr. William J. Barber II won a Mac-Arthur "genius grant," he was in handcuffs.

It's not clear if that was how he intended things to go down when news broke on October 4, 2018, that he had been awarded the illustrious grant, which included a $625,000 check. Journalists who cover religion and politics dropped everything that morning and scrambled to pen a story that essentially wrote itself: Barber, a small-town, southern, African American minister turned social justice advocate, who walks with a hunch but preaches with a bellow, was being given one of the nation's most prestigious awards.

The news was widely seen as a major moment for the Religious Left, which by autumn 2018 had adopted the enigmatic Barber as its champion. Barber, whose broad frame and dulcet tones were fixtures at progressive podiums and pulpits across the country, came by his liberal religious street cred honestly: Since 2013, he had led a massive progressive protest movement in North Carolina, which was credited with unseating a Republican governor; he had captured national attention in 2016 by delivering an electric, sermonlike prime-time address at the Democratic National Convention; and he had emerged during the Trump era as a dynamic and headline-grabbing critic of the president, his policies, and the evangelical leaders who supported him.

I was one of many journalists that day who saw their in-boxes fill with invitations from communications firms offering to connect reporters to Barber. But when my North Carolina–based *Religion News Service* colleague Yonat Shimron reached out to snag the coveted interview, she, along with many other journalists, was unexpectedly rebuffed. A representative sheepishly informed her that Barber was now unavailable[1] because he was, well, a smidge busy: he had been arrested outside of McDonald's headquarters in Chicago, protesting the company's refusal to raise its minimum wage for workers to fifteen dollars an hour.[2]

It was a serendipitously on-brand moment for Barber, whose relentless activism has inspired thinkers such as Cornel West to describe him as "the closest person we have to Martin Luther King Jr. in our midst."[3] But it was also evidence as to why the MacArthur Foundation tapped him for distinction and how he catapulted a fledgling Religious Left into relevance: his knack for pairing dramatic civil disobedience with what he calls moral fusion organizing—a strategy that assembles disparate religious and secular advocacy groups into massive political coalitions, usually with faith leaders at the helm.

It's a recipe for social change that evades simplistic categorization and looks very different from the right-wing Christian political machines that analysts have spent years dissecting. Instead of standing alone as an isolated voting bloc, *à la* the Religious Right, the vast and complex faith-rooted organizing apparatus Barber helped create often functions as a particularly vocal element *within* broader progressive campaigns—a sort of coalition among coalitions. And in the era of "Resistance," Barber and his faith-fueled fusion model of organizing have taken on a *leading* role, winning victories in legislatures and at the ballot box, and laying the foundation for a new political structure that could alter the future of liberal activism and the Democratic Party.

*   *   *

The phenomenon Barber helped bring about has a thousand branches, but one of its most important roots began to grow in 1993 in the small military town of Goldsboro, North Carolina, about an hour outside of Raleigh. That's where Barber pastors Greenleaf Christian Church, a Disciples of Christ (DOC) community founded by formerly enslaved people in 1886.[4] It's an unlikely place to incubate a national celebrity: while its four-hundred-member congregation is larger than many small-town churches, only about two hundred worship each Sunday, a far cry from the teaming crowds that once packed megachurches for that *other* famous North Carolina evangelist Billy Graham.

Even so, the congregation knew they were taking on an ambitious leader when they called Barber, a scion of a successful preacher, to be their pastor. Shortly after assuming his post, Barber told church leaders that he believed the congregation was called to help revitalize neighborhoods within three miles of the church, some of the poorest parts of Goldsboro. The decision rankled some who thought money should be spent on the aging sanctuary and not to set up an untested nonprofit and build homes for low-income families. But Barber pressed on, pushing the church to rally around goodwill ventures such as converting an abandoned supermarket into a thriving daycare center.[5]

This kind of activist work takes a toll on anyone, but it was especially painful for Barber, who in 1993 was diagnosed with ankylosing spondylitis, a vicious form of arthritis that fuses bones together, including spinal vertebrae. The crippling disease has ravaged his form, forcing him to walk stiffly, hunched over, sometimes with a walker or a cane battered from use. Therapy and treatments can help but there is no cure, and while Barber's mobility has improved in many ways since the trying months following his original diagnosis, health care remains an important issue for him and his family (his daughter was born with a brain disorder).

And yet Barber, guided by a supportive congregation and a theology that demands holy practice as well prophetic preaching, refused to let the illness defeat him and insisted there was more work to do in the state. In 2005, he was elected head of the North Carolina NAACP, sailing to victory on a platform that argued the organization should shift "from banquets to battle,"[6] focusing on pressing issues of social justice rather than the general concerns of social clubs. And by 2007, he had already assembled what was called the "Historic Thousands on Jones Street" coalition (HKonJ for short) outside the North Carolina State Legislative Building, with representatives from various organizations calling for action on issues ranging from affordable housing to environmental concerns to ending the Bush administration's War on Terror.[7]

Assembling the HKonJ coalition was a formative learning experience for Barber. It was his first major experiment at what he calls moral fusion or fusionist organizing—a reference to the fusion coalition of Black Republicans and Populist Party members that came together in North Carolina in the nineteenth century to enhance voting rights and increase taxes for education in the state, among other things.[8] Barber envisioned his project as a modern expression of this legacy, theorizing that while not everyone in his coalition was passionate about the same issues, they did recognize the same systems of power holding them back. Thus, they shared a common cause.

The true test of this method emerged in 2012, when the Tar Heel State experienced a sudden political shock. Despite the state's history of being relatively moderate in the South, a slate of hard-right conservative Republicans swept the 2012 election and took control of North Carolina's governorship and legislature. The shift gave the state its most conservative government in more than century,[9] making national news and leaving political analysts stunned. And while the newly elected governor, Pat McCrory, was initially seen as a moderate, many of his fellow Republicans were tied to the increasingly influential Tea Party movement. Within months, the legislature was pushing one of the most conservative agendas in the country: it passed or voted on legislation cutting unemployment benefits,[10] instituted restrictive voter ID laws,[11] and blocked Medicaid coverage to as many as five hundred thousand people,[12] among other draconian proposals.

Barber and his HKonJ partners immediately protested these measures, but their demonstrations did little to alter the legislature's policy stratagems. So on April 29, 2013, Barber addressed a crowd of about fifty people at Davie Street Presbyterian Church in Raleigh, just a few blocks away from the state legislature.

"There must be a witness in the face of extremism and regressive public policy," Barber said to the assembled group that Monday afternoon. He added: "There must be an act that dramatizes the shameful."

He wasn't being figurative. Shortly thereafter, Barber and a racially diverse group of sixteen other activists—primarily clergy but also academics, students, community organizers, and at least one woman in a wheelchair[13]—gathered in front of the two towering golden doors of the North Carolina State Legislative Building. The group prayed, sang, and chanted as they were approached by police, who demanded that they leave or risk arrest. The activists refused, and a short time later police escorted them out, most with their hands zip-tied behind their backs.

A few supporters rushed to the back of the building, gathering near the bus that would whisk the detainees away for processing.

As it departed, they chanted after it: "Revolutionary love!"[14]

A THEORY (AND THEOLOGY) OF CHANGE

In retrospect, news coverage of what would become known as the first Moral Monday protest was relatively understated. Raleigh's *News and Observer* devoted fewer than four hundred words to the demonstration; many newspapers didn't cover the protest at all.[15] But word of the arrests quickly rippled through the activist community, and next week Barber returned with eighty demonstrators gathered at Davie Street. Police ultimately led thirty of them—again, mostly clergy but also lawyers, doctors, and elderly grandmothers—away from government buildings in handcuffs.

That's when things really took off. The third protest saw fifty-seven arrests. The number of arrests increased every week, at one point ballooning to 155. By the time the legislative session ended in August, the arrest tally for 2013 Moral Monday demonstrations had hit eight to nine hundred.[16]

Perhaps even more affecting were the throngs that gathered to support Barber and the other protesters. Crowds swelled into the thousands each week, with the masses fanning out across Harris Mall outside the state legislature to cheer and listen to speakers. Gov. McCrory attempted to dismiss the protesters as outsiders, but researchers from University of North Carolina–Chapel Hill polled the crowd and found that they were overwhelmingly of local stock.[17] And if there was any question about the level of progressive support for the movement in North Carolina, Barber capped off the season of demonstrations in August with a massive Mountain Moral Monday rally in unabashedly liberal Asheville, where an estimated ten thousand people flooded the city's central park to hear the pastor speak.[18]

The Moral Monday movement's synthesis of arrests and sheer mass eventually piqued the interest of such national media outlets as *The Atlantic*,[19] *The Washington Post*,[20] and the *New York Times*[21] as well as progressive-leaning publications such as *Slate*[22] and *Think-Progress*, the latter of which dubbed the movement "the biggest liberal protest of 2013."[23] Several journalists noted how Moral Monday effortlessly reimagined older forms of religious progressivism in a modern secular liberal context.

"The Rev. William Barber . . . doesn't put himself in the place of the Rev. Martin Luther King Jr.; but he does set his cause in the tradition of King and the civil-rights movement," North Carolina columnist Mary C. Curtis wrote in the *Post*. "It's a heartfelt comparison, and it's smart, especially when some folks on the other side fall so predictably into a script written fifty or more years ago."

Moral Monday participants could be spotted holding signs that spoke to a number of modern progressive causes, including women's health and abortion rights, police brutality, voting rights, and Medicaid expansion.[24] But more secular protesters stood alongside clergy from various faith traditions who supported the same ideals, some waving their own signs emblazoned with scripture references or faith-themed slogans such as "Now this is what we call church!"[25]

Among the crowd at the second demonstration was Jonathan Wilson-Hartgrove, a Baptist preacher and longtime collaborator of Barber's. The tall, gangly author and activist with a short buzz cut and a long southern drawl was arguably one of Barber's earliest converts: Wilson-Hartgrove, who grew up evangelical Christian, steeped in the teachings of the Religious Right, once worked as a page for Sen. Strom Thurmond, the prominent South Carolina Republican best known for his long life and unabashed support for segregation. A chance encounter with Barber in February 1998, three months after Wilson-Hartgrove had left Thurmond's office, began a life-altering journey that was equal parts political and theological.

"It was meeting Rev. Barber at that point that opened my eyes to the fact that there was a whole 'nother way of reading scripture and imagining Christian social engagement,"[26] said Wilson-Hartgrove, who now directs the School for Conversion in Durham. He said he first saw Barber speak at an event put on by then North Carolina governor Jim Hunt—a Democrat—when Barber was serving on the state's human relations commission.

"I recognized that he was a preacher, and it created a kind of a spiritual crisis for me, realizing that the moral framework I had for practicing my faith in public was bankrupt," he explained. He noted that Barber exposed him to a theology that permeates many black churches—namely, a version of the social gospel interwoven with black liberation theology.

That same theology—rooted in a belief that God is on the side of the poor and the oppressed—is a constant of Barber's rhetoric. His spiritual beliefs are something of a fusion unto themselves, lashing together ideas from several different Christian thinkers to build a makeshift political theology that is more than the sum of its parts. For instance, Barber found deep resonance in the debate between theologians Stanley Hauerwas and Reinhold Niebuhr over Christian realism, a political theology popular among twentieth-century politicians, but which Hauerwas criticized as leading to a quest for political influence instead of the teachings of the gospel. Barber contends that Hauerwas's critique, while a valuable corrective, prevents Christians from recognizing the holy outside their own churches. Or, as Barber put it, it is "often folk outside the church who inspired us the most, standing as examples of what the church can be."[27]

It's a vision that contrasts sharply with conservative religious communities that cast other faiths or the secular world as insidious, demonic forces bent on threatening the purity of their beliefs. So it is with conservative thought leaders such Rod Dreher, author of *The Benedict Option: A Strategy for Christians in a Post-Christian Nation*, who achieved acclaim in recent years for proposing a retreat from society to protect conservative Christians from the influence of other worldviews, especially the inclusive vision of the LGBTQ rights movement. Barber would never dream of retreating from society, nor would he see that as an option afforded to many marginalized communities. (Wilson-Hartgrove, himself a "new monastic," agreed, and would later describe Dreher's proposal as "essentially an effort to hold onto white culture as the demographics of American democracy trend blacker and browner.")[28] In his book, Barber argued that citizenship in Jesus Christ's "city upon a hill" in the Bible wasn't limited to "good church folk," explaining that he had come to believe that "the church didn't have a monopoly on God's dream."[29]

This helps explain why Barber was so comfortable standing next to secular leaders at the second Moral Monday protest while infusing his speech on economic and health care policy with references to the biblical book of Matthew. ("When I was hungry, did you feed me? When I was sick, did you heal me? In prison, did you visit me? When I was naked, did you clothe me?") Or why, when the bus of detainees drove away from the state legislature that day, it was Barber who led the crowd in singing "We Shall Overcome"—a slave spiritual and the anthem of the civil rights movement. His is a form of public religious expression that not only accepts secular partners but actively seeks them out as moral exemplars.[30]

Jim Bazán, a local North Carolina activist who got involved with the Moral Monday movement in 2013 after spending years advocating for immigrant rights, told me how Barber and other faith leaders won him over despite Bazán's skepticism about organized religion. Although he describes himself as a person of faith, Bazán, like many progressives, does not affiliate with a religious tradition.

"I had to learn how to be comfortable in that profoundly religious setting," he said, referring to Moral Monday gatherings.[31] But while he noted the rumbling cadence of a preacher like Barber was unfamiliar or even somewhat uncomfortable for some, Bazán decided it was the substance that ultimately mattered most.

"The message was clear as a bell," he said.

What's more, Bazán pointed out that Barber's approach, combined with visuals of clergy, the elderly, and everyday North Carolinians being hauled away in handcuffs, was especially evocative in North Carolina.

"There's probably no better hook for local news than having a couple of ministers from Henderson arrested," he said. "From a news standpoint, it was genius."

(Bazán joked that local reporters couldn't avoid the demonstrations if they tried. Some even found themselves part of story: the religion reporter from the *Charlotte Observer* was inexplicably arrested while trying to report on one of the demonstrations.)[32]

Granted, the overlap of faith and activism isn't exactly unexpected in North Carolina, a state in which some 39 percent of residents regularly attend worship, and 80 percent of residents claim a religious affiliation.[33] It's a tradition that stretches back at least a generation: one of the earliest sit-ins of the civil rights movement was spearheaded by Rev. Douglas E. Moore, a Methodist minister, who lead a group of activists in 1957 into the whites-only section of the racially segregated Royal Ice Cream parlor in Durham (all were arrested).[34] Still, the Moral Monday movement's ability to interlock so many movements and leaders, including ones who claimed no faith affiliation whatsoever, surprised even veteran organizers like Bazán and Wilson-Hartgrove.

"It felt like a revival rooted in this prophetic black church experience, which didn't mean people were joining those churches— they were joining a movement," Wilson-Hartgrove said. "They were finding a way to exist in a public space with other people that represented their values, and a lot of people told us, 'You know, I'm an atheist and I'd never go in church, but I love coming out here and hearing this preaching!'"

At the heart of it all was the movement's *intersectional* nature. *Intersectionality*—the assertion that systems that oppress people based on race, sexuality, gender, class, and other attributes can overlap and intersect in ways that affect several groups at once—has become a despised term in many right-wing circles. Its correct usage is even debated among liberals, some of whom prefer only to invoke it in feminist contexts where it originated. But for many it is a concept that underlies many progressive movements, which often rely on broad, diverse coalitions to build power. Barber regularly notes the intersectional nature of his work in interviews, although he tends to use the word "fusion" instead. While reflecting on the Moral Monday movement during a 2017 speech, he laid out the power of his fusionist approach:

"[This movement exists so] preachers can 'fight for fifteen,' and workers can say 'black lives matter,' and a white woman can stand with her black sister for voting rights, and a black man can stand for a woman's access to health care, and LGBTQ folk can stand for religious liberty, and straight people can stand up for gay people and bisexual people and transgender people and queer people, and a Muslim imam can stand with an undocumented worker—that's why we march!"[35]

Barber was talking about solidarity, and evidence suggests that it was *precisely because* the North Carolina state legislature was impacting so many groups at once that the Moral Monday movement—using fusion methods framed as a way for citizens to express their own frustrations while also trumpeting those of others—took off. Barber detailed how he capitalizes off of this shared suffering in *The Third Reconstruction*, a half-memoir, half-organizing handbook that he cowrote with Wilson-Hartgrove in 2016. He explained that his strategy was not just to build a broad coalition "including moral and religious leaders of all faiths" but also to "intentionally diversify the movement with the goal of winning unlikely allies" within North Carolina.

"Fusion politics is about helping those who have suffered injustice and have been divided by extremism to see what we have in common," he wrote.[36]

Moral Monday participants told me these efforts often made that first wave of demonstrations feel like a family, and they pointed to how rallies targeted specific policy themes (health care, LGBTQ rights, labor issues, etc.) to focus on the voices of those who were negatively impacted by policies passed by conservative lawmakers.

"Testimonies from impacted people, then framed as a moral issue, became the moral fusion organizing model that Moral Mondays was built on," Wilson-Hartgrove said.

A MOVEMENT, NOT A MOMENT

Despite the chanting masses, the North Carolina legislature mostly ignored the pleas of Moral Monday protesters in 2013. But Barber assembled even larger crowds for a relaunch of the movement in 2014, kicking off a new wave of protests with a Moral March on Raleigh, which local NAACP leaders said assembled between eighty thousand and one hundred thousand people. It was not the first Moral March in Raleigh and attendance figures were disputed, with some claiming the crowd was closer to twenty thousand. But photos of the sprawling assembly garnered media attention all the same and jump-started another year of demonstrations in the Tar Heel State.[37]

Meanwhile, the movement began to spark brushfires of grassroots activism outside North Carolina. In January 2014, a coalition in Georgia announced a sister movement, Moral Monday Georgia, modeled after North Carolina's. The next day a group in South Carolina did the same, dubbing theirs Truthful Tuesdays.[38] Both spinoffs included visible participation from faith leaders as they pushed to protect voting rights and expand Medicaid—something many Republican governors had refused to do after the passage of the ACA. But activists tailored their work to the needs of each state: Truthful Tuesdays demonstrators often focused on longstanding frustrations over public education funding in South Carolina,[39] and Moral Monday Georgia activists occupied the office of then Georgia secretary of state Brian Kemp to demand he explain the disappearance of forty thousand voter registrations from the state's database.[40]

These satellite efforts attached themselves to existing events organized by state chapters of the NAACP and other groups, and kept themselves in the gravitational pull of the original North Carolina campaign by featuring speeches and sermons from Barber himself.[41] This proved to be a powerful model, and in August 2014 Barber announced a Moral Week of Action, which would launch a constellation of solidarity movements in Alabama, Arkansas, Florida, Indiana, Mississippi, New York, Ohio, Pennsylvania, Tennessee, and Wisconsin.[42] A nationwide progressive campaign against conservative state legislatures was blasting off, with Barber and other faith leaders in the cockpit with their hands on the controls.

As the phenomenon (and Barber's fame) swelled throughout 2014, however, the Goldsboro pastor was suddenly struck by a desire to step back and reassess where it all was going. He reached out to the Reverend Dr. Liz Theoharis, a Presbyterian minister, and asked about taking a sabbatical at Union Theological Seminary in New York City, where Theoharis ran the Kairos Center for Religions, Rights, and Social Justice. The two had met the previous November, when Barber spoke at the launch of the historically liberal school's Kairos Center, which focused on alleviating poverty. Theoharis, who graduated from Union, agreed to Barber's request, and the school raised enough money to host him for ninety days beginning in spring 2015.

"I believe [that] in the movement, there's a period where you should . . . step back, evaluate what's going on, retool, [and] deepen your understanding of the intersectionality of that movement to other things that are happening in the country and the world," Barber told *Politico* magazine at the time.[43]

During his time at Union, cloistered in a dorm room he kept intentionally spartan, Barber worked with Theoharis to hatch plans for projects even loftier than the ascendant Moral Monday movement. They eventually settled on two projects: a Moral Revival Tour of twenty states throughout 2016 to promote a "revolution of moral values" and a 2018 revival of the Poor People's Campaign, the last, unfinished project of civil rights giant Rev. Martin Luther King Jr.

The first goal was ambitious, but hardly impossible for activists of their experience. By structuring the effort as nonpartisan but otherwise blatantly political, they could work to reframe political debates about morality ahead of the 2016 election. Theoharis, speaking to me over the phone in 2019, explained that it paired well with the Kairos Center's existing efforts to combat poverty.

"This was work that we were already doing—and poor people across the country were already focused on—but we were trying to bring this explicit focus on a moral revival, on having faith leaders and people of faith at the very center of this work, battling around morality and theology," she said.[44]

Bringing back the Poor People's Campaign, however, was a much heavier lift. Rev. King and others launched the original campaign in 1968 to focus on the issue of economic inequality, something that the civil rights hero argued had an impact on all races but African Americans in particular. The campaign aimed to capture national attention with a march that would bring the "the tired, the poor, the huddled masses" to Washington, DC, but King was assassinated before he could bring that to fruition.[45]

Decades later, Theoharis knew that taking on the Poor People's Campaign—and King's legacy—was a daunting, generational task. Transforming the country's economic, social, and political structures to focus on the poor wasn't exactly something that could happen in one election cycle (or ten, or twenty). It was going to require long-term planning, with a focus on developing a network of like-minded spiritual leaders across the country.

To achieve this, Theoharis and Barber flew to cities weeks or months before scheduled Moral Revival Tour events to offer day-long "seminary without walls" trainings for local faith leaders. Together, they would address these groups through the vehicle of Repairers of the Breach, an organization that Barber founded in 2015. While Theoharis focused on theology, Barber presented the historical argument for a third reconstruction.

"A lot of that was seeding these ideas among faith leaders of the biblical, theological, and historical foundation for building moral movements," Theoharis told me, noting that she did similar work through the Kairos Center, independent of Barber. "So much of movement building is actually about moving minds, not just mobilizing bodies."

The result was the reawakening—spiritual and otherwise—of a long-dormant national progressive faith-based infrastructure, one with a strong history that predated Theoharis and Barber's efforts but which found renewed purpose and energy in the cause they championed.

But perhaps no other moment broadcast—literally—the power of a progressive faith message more widely than Barber's primetime address at the 2016 Democratic National Convention in Philadelphia. As millions turned on their televisions in expectation of seeing Democratic presidential nominee Hillary Clinton's address later that night, the North Carolina clergyman shuffled to the microphone and declared in his distinctive low and purposeful tone: "I come before you tonight as a preacher."[46] His shoulders hunched as he stared out at the crowd before continuing: "The son of a preacher. A preacher immersed in the movement at five years old . . . I come to talk about faith and morality."

Suddenly, members of the crowd rose to their feet, smiling and whooping with the energy of an altar call. The preacher's voice boomed over the next few minutes, easing into a practiced cadence as he skillfully guided entranced listeners to the heart of his talk. He insisted that America had a "bad heart" in need of a "shock," and he clenched his fists as he called on those present to be the "moral defibrillators of our time." As Barber conducted a call-and-response with his impromptu congregation, one attendee donned in red, white, and blue threw his hands into the air, closed his eyes, and swayed as if in prayer. With the crowd whipped into a frenzy, Barber concluded by roaring the lyrics to "Revive Us Again," one of his favorite hymns.

"Hallelujah, thine be the glory!" he bellowed before turning to exit the stage, leaving the crowd locked in an ecstatic state that a religious observer might describe as, well, revival.

The spectacle, combined with a healthy helping of other religious references at the DNC, triggered a flurry of articles expressing shock at the preponderance of spiritual displays in a modern progressive context. "Democrats shift to embrace the Religious Left," wrote the *New York Times*.[47] "Infused with the spirit of the black church, the Democrats became the party of optimism," observed Jamelle Bouie from *Slate*.[48] *Vox* didn't even try to hide its astonishment: "The Democratic convention's most surprising argument: Christianity is a liberal religion."[49]

And lest anyone think the party had co-opted Barber's cause, it's worth noting how the pastor got on that stage. Representatives from the Moral Monday movement and Repairers of the Breach traveled to the DNC and the Republican National Convention that year to try to present a list of moral demands to representatives of each party. According to Wilson-Hartgrove, the DNC received the demands and immediately invited Barber to Philadelphia to address the assembly. RNC officials took the exact opposite approach.

"They not only refused to receive them . . . they sent a security officer to say that that group would be arrested if they didn't leave," Wilson-Hartgrove said.

Indeed, 2016 proved to be a triumphant year for Barber and the Moral Monday movement. In August, the US Supreme Court deadlocked 4–4 on a lawsuit spearheaded by ninety-two-year-old Rosanell Eaton, a Moral Monday demonstrator who, at Barber's request, had agreed to become lead plaintiff in challenging the North Carolina voting law that helped spark the protest movement. The deadlock allowed a lower court ruling to stand, overturning many of the law's more restrictive provisions, which were deemed to be unconstitutional efforts to "target African Americans with almost surgical precision."[50]

And in November, after nearly three years of protests and arrests with relatively little response from state officials, North Carolina progressives finally scored a major electoral victory: Democratic gubernatorial candidate Roy Cooper eked out a win over Republican

Pat McCrory by ten thousand votes—a margin so thin it took weeks of recounts and legal challenges before the GOP incumbent finally conceded. It was a monumental achievement for progressives in the state, and several commentators credited the Moral Monday movement—particularly the voter mobilization efforts run by its numerous partner organizations—as the chief reason for the upset.[51]

Even that win, however, could not erase the shock of the night's other major electoral development: the election of Donald Trump. Along with the GOP maintaining firm control over the US House and Senate, Trump's rise seemed to contradict virtually everything the Moral Monday movement stood for. Worse, Trump had been catapulted to power with significant help from the Religious Right and white evangelicals, a group that appeared largely unconvinced by the intersectional liberation theology that permeated the Moral Monday movement.

Yet as other liberals wallowed in despair, Barber and his cohort were quick to reframe the development as another reminder that their work was far from over. The morning after the election, Wilson-Hartgrove received a phone call shortly after he woke at around 7:00am. It was Barber, saying he had spent his early hours poring over a passage from 1 Samuel, in which God tells the prophet, "They have not rejected you, but they have rejected me."

To Barber, the sentiment felt all too familiar.

"America is North Carolina now," he said.

AMASSING MORAL RESISTANCE

Just three weeks after Trump's inauguration, Barber found himself in Raleigh, standing before yet another crowd for yet another Moral March. Just as in 2014, the streets teemed with demonstrators waving signs of protest, and just as in 2014, supporters estimated eighty thousand people[52] (a figure that was, again, disputed).[53] But the subtext was different and so were the messages: instead of focusing on state-level concerns, many placards bore references to Trump and his policies, including #NoBanNoWall and Don't Make America Sick Again!

The shift in political winds wasn't lost on Barber, who cited scripture as he declared that the movement he helped birth in 2013 stood ready to tackle issues brought about by the Trump era.

"Four years later, we see that we have been preparing all along 'for such a time as this,'" he said during the rally, grinning as he referenced Esther 4:14. "The racist and greedy extremism that came to power in North Carolina four years ago now controls the White House and the Congress in DC."

The comparison was apt. In many ways, the Moral Monday movement had already provided a framework for what would become the nationwide Resistance movement in opposition to Trump, his administration, and its policies. Duke University professor Jedediah Purdy outright promoted the movement's achievements in North Carolina as "model for anti-Trump politics" in a February 2017 column for *The New Yorker*,[54] a position journalist Jelani Cobb would echo a year later in the same publication when he called Barber "the individual most capable of crafting a broad-based political counterpoint to the divisiveness of Trumpism."[55] Indeed, just as the 2012 election brought about an unexpectedly sharp power shift in North Carolina, so too did Trump's election leave political analysts the world over scrambling to make sense of it all. Just as the Moral Monday movement benefited from moral fusion organizing—sometimes called moral resistance—so too would Resistance demonstrations forge new alliances that only grew as the president and his administration targeted ever more marginalized groups. And just as those in North Carolina came to recognize the power of using moral language and repeated arrests when combating a political foe, so too would Resistance demonstrations lean heavily on direct confrontation and appeals to justice and morality.

As such, it's no surprise that Barber came to play such a prominent role in Resistance protests throughout 2017. When the GOP-led Congress threatened to repeal and replace the Affordable Care

Act that summer, Barber helped spearhead a spate of rallies, pray-ins, and protests on Capitol Hill, which included religious and secular groups alike.[56] The same strategies that benefited Moral Monday—dramatic arrests, multiple waves, and a direct appeal to a higher moral standard—garnered widespread news coverage for the demonstrations. These efforts, along with those of other grassroots activists, ultimately helped defeat the repeal effort.[57] (Barber and other religious groups reconstituted the method for other legislative fights, such as the battle over the Republican tax bill later in the year, with less success.)

Like in North Carolina, Barber orchestrated none of this by himself. By its very nature, fusion organizing relies on a broad network of groups, each of which offers its own resources to the cause. Throughout the Obamacare protests, for instance, Barber stood alongside other fixtures of the Religious Left, such as Rev. Jennifer Butler; Sister Simone Campbell; and Rev. Traci Blackmon, a prominent activist out of Ferguson, Missouri, who works with the Black Lives Matter movement.[58]

And while activism in the nation's capital garnered the most attention, it was augmented by localized faith-based protests that often wove together the elements of several movements. In December 2017, Republican senator Susan Collins of Maine was poised to vote for the GOP's controversial tax bill, which threatened to remove the ACA's individual mandate provision. In response, an interfaith group of Jewish, Buddhist, Unitarian Universalist, and Christian leaders—known as Moral Movement Maine—occupied her office while holding signs adorned with the Faith in Public Life logo until they were led away by police.[59] (Collins voted for the bill anyway,[60] although she insists she extracted some health care–related concessions from her Republican colleagues before doing so.)[61]

Nevertheless, Barber's fame and fiery rhetoric eventually made him the de facto head of America's new Religious Left. Articles about the resurgence of religious progressives in *The Washington Post* and *Reuters* cited him as a key leader of the movement.[62] He became a regular guest on MSNBC, particularly on Joy Ann Reid's show, *AM*

Joy,[63] where he was presented as speaking on behalf of religious progressives. And when *New York Times* readers picked up their Sunday edition on June 10, 2017, a photo of Barber stared back at them from within an above-the-fold story chronicling a potential "progressive religious revival."[64]

It should be noted that Barber, like many religious progressives, generally rejects the term *Religious Left*. Despite speaking from the DNC stage and repeatedly championing progressive causes, he decries the phrase as "too puny," arguing that "we are fighting for the moral center of our traditions"[65] and that liberals of faith have challenged Democrats in the past as well.[66] At times he insists he is an "evangelical," although he usually goes on to explain that he defines that word differently from many right-wing conservatives.

Still, Barber's fame gave him a national platform that few, if any, religious progressives since King have enjoyed, and it allowed him to needle out unusual responses from the Religious Right—an impressive achievement, given that conservative religious figures have largely ignored the Religious Left for decades. When Barber described a picture of Trump's evangelical advisory board praying over the president while remaining silent about the Obamacare repeal effort as "a form of theological malpractice bordering on heresy," it triggered an atypically intense round of theological sparring. Right-wing outlets such as *The Blaze*, *FOX News Insider*, and even *FOX and Friends* rushed to condemn his remarks, characterizing them as "hatred of President Trump."[67]

Barber dismissed the criticism, but was eager to, quite literally, debate right-wing evangelicals on issues surrounding the intersection of religion and politics. Prior to joining progressive evangelicals at the first Red Letter Revival in Lynchburg, Virginia, in 2018, to voice criticism of Jerry Falwell Jr., he signed a letter with Shane Claiborne, Wilson-Hartgrove, Theoharis, and others challenging the Liberty University president to a theological debate.[68] And during the faith-fueled outcry over the Trump administration's policy of separating immigrant families at the US-Mexico border, when Paula White pushed back on the claim that Jesus was a refugee, Bishop

Yvette Flunder of The Fellowship of Affirming Ministries joined Barber, Wilson-Hartgrove, and Theoharis in challenging her to a live television debate.[69]

White never responded, and it would be more than two years before a think tank attached to Liberty would tentatively accept Barber's challenge to debate (and without confirming whether Falwell would take part). But the media have at times taken it upon themselves to force a debate between Barber and Religious Right figures anyway. In November 2018, CNN's Christiane Amanpour brought Tony Perkins, head of the conservative Family Research Council (which the Southern Poverty Law Center classifies as a hate group, despite FRC's objections), on her show and asked him to respond to a clip of Barber asserting that the Bible calls on Christians to prioritize the poor and the immigrant. Perkins was visibly uncomfortable for several seconds before he regained his composure and mustered his answer, arguing that Christians should also respect the rule of law with regard to illegal immigration.[70]

Barber's status has allowed him to speak to several issues, constituencies, and systems of power at once, which has only benefited his relaunch of the Poor People's Campaign and boosted fusion organizing at the national level. It keeps him busy: he declined a lengthy sit-down interview for this book, as I was instead encouraged to catch up with him along the sidelines of his innumerable events. But his stardom is also why he and Theoharis were able to quickly assemble a slate of clergy to join him at a November 2017 Poor People's Campaign event in Birmingham, Alabama, to decry the candidacy and Christian nationalism of Roy Moore. It's why Barber's health care protests that same year included participation from prominent lawmakers and future presidential candidates such as New Jersey senator Cory Booker, who would later tell me he sees Barber as a powerful figure whose "charisma speaks, in an instructive way, toward my heart and my being" because he "believes that being poor is not a sin."[71] It's why California congressman and short-lived presidential candidate Eric Swalwell directly credited Barber's activism with helping Democrats take back the House of Representatives in 2018.[72]

And it's why I spotted South Bend, Indiana mayor and presidential candidate Pete Buttigieg standing silently in the crowd at a protest featuring Barber on a sunny summer Wednesday in 2019, when hundreds of faith leaders gathered to preach and protest outside the White House to condemn what they called the "evil" policies of the Trump administration. During the march to the White House—which, like that first Moral Monday protest, began with a service at a Presbyterian church—Barber, Theoharis, Blackmon, and others stood shoulder to shoulder and held a sign. It read: Moral Witness Wednesday.[73]

I tracked down Barber as he left the demonstration. We walked slowly, the White House at our backs, as he trudged toward a car waiting for him at the edge of Lafayette Square. He wore bright red vestments and still used a cane, this one wooden and chipped along the sides. I asked him about what had just transpired, noting that leaders from very different religious traditions had voiced concerns about a wide spectrum of issues including health care, gerrymandering, climate change, and the US Census.

The moment I started to say the word "fusion," he cut me off in excitement.

"This is moral fusion," he said. "We're not left. We're not right. We're not conservative or liberal. We're standing in the moral center . . . evangelicals were there . . . Pentecostals, Hindus all standing together. This is what moral fusion looks like."

Indeed, Barber is the first to admit that he is only as successful as the diverse coalitions he assembles, each of which is made up of issue-specific subgroups that existed long before he came calling. Fusion organizing requires subgroups to develop *first*, cultivating their own moral voice, agenda, strategic expertise, and leadership developed and expanded over the course of decades. Just like that first HKonJ coalition, these groups can represent a spectrum of concerns, be it immigration, climate change, or LGBTQ rights.

And when it comes to Religious Left organizing in the Trump era, one of Barber's frequent collaborators has become Traci Blackmon, who stood beside him that day in Washington holding the Moral Witness Wednesday sign. And while she, like Barber, can preach on many issues, she is perhaps best known for her work on a topic that not only has achieved new relevance under Trump, but also boasts arguably the most storied history of progressive faith-based organizing in US history: race.

★ ★ ★

CHAPTER FIVE

Keepers of the Story

T he pulpit Rev. Traci Blackmon approached that night wasn't anything out of the ordinary. It was attractive, but in a func-tional way: wooden, unassuming, accented with a green banner adorned with a gold cross. It wasn't all that different from the one that stands in front of the sanctuary at her home church in Florissant, Missouri. If anything, it was smaller. Her vestments were also fairly standard for a Protestant pastor: black shirt, white clerical collar, red stole.[1]

But if you looked closely, there were hints that *something* about that night was different. The image emblazoned on Blackmon's stole wasn't a rising dove or a Jesus fish—it was a raised fist.[2] The pews weren't occupied by a smattering of sleepy-eyed local churchgoers, but packed to the edges with a thousand or so ecstatic worshippers who hailed from different parts of the country and claimed different faiths, most already on their feet applauding or standing on tiptoe along the faded yellow sanctuary walls. And the tiny flashes of light that would soon flicker in the distance outside the windows weren't streetlights, but tiki torches held aloft by white supremacists.

It was August 11, 2017, in Charlottesville, Virginia, and Black-mon was there to talk about race.

"I must just say, this may be the first time that I have been in a standing-room-only church on a Friday," she joked, sparking peals of laughter from the crowd.

It was rare moment of levity in an otherwise grim context. The group of Charlottesville residents and clergy gathered at St. Paul's Memorial Church was but one subset of thousands that traveled to the sleepy Virginia city that weekend to muster counterdemonstrations against the so-called Unite the Right rally planned for the next day. Originally organized as an effort to oppose the removal of a Robert E. Lee statue in Lee Park at the heart of city, the right-wing event had ballooned into a rallying cry for a broad spectrum of racist groups that included neo-Confederates, white supremacists, and Nazi sympathizers.

Blackmon argued from the pulpit that evening that faith groups simply hadn't done enough to end the scourge of such racism and had "celebrated victory too soon." Her brow furrowed and her voice serious, the black UCC pastor of Florissant's Christ the King Church lamented the failures of the past.

"When violence and hatred are flourishing, it is necessary that love show up," she said. "When hatred is all around, when violence is the language of the day, when laws lack compassion and churches lose their way, then we who believe in freedom, we who believe in God . . . we must question: *Where have all the prophets gone?*"

She then recounted the biblical story of Goliath, comparing racists and their ilk to the camp of Philistines the giant emerged from to face David, the future king of Israel. "Until we close the camp, there will always be another Goliath," she said, noting that many preachers skip over the most gruesome part of the biblical tale: when the diminutive David defeated his colossal enemy with a stone and a sling, he didn't simply walk away triumphant.

"The text says that David doesn't just knock him down and kill him, but David takes his head off," she said, the crowd nodding solemnly in agreement. "The fact that David takes his head off is a message to the camp: what Goliath has wrought will no longer be tolerated."

Blackmon insisted that to defeat white supremacy in America—the same horrific ideology that has plagued the US since its founding—people of faith would need to do the same.

"Here I am at fifty-four years old, coming back because the Klan is still rising," she said, her voice trembling with passion as she pounded her hand on the pulpit.[3] "The Klan is still rising because we *never cut the head off!*"

After an outburst of applause, Blackmon clarified that she was advocating not for a physical altercation but a *spiritual* conflict—one in which faith-based activists would use love-focused methods of religious persuasion and nonviolent resistance. But just minutes after she concluded her sermon, volunteers anxiously informed her and other speakers of an ominous development just across the street: a column of torch-bearing white nationalists had crested the hill and marched down toward the University of Virginia's statue of Thomas Jefferson. The teeming mob, about three hundred strong with many in matching white polo shirts, was screaming racist and anti-Semitic slogans as they walked menacingly around a vastly outnumbered group of student counterprotesters who stood, arms linked, next to the statue.

The congregation in St. Paul's could hear the hateful chants and see torch flames flickering through the windows. Everyone feared the mass would approach the church next. Worse, police were nowhere to be seen, even as violent scuffles broke out between the racists and the students.

Goliath had arrived.

"They just surrounded the place," renowned academic and activist Cornel West told me.[4] "It took you back to the old days of the violence-ridden Jim Crow South, where you knew that you were being targeted, and that the use of violent power was arbitrary and could come your way. Most of us were pretty shaken, no doubt about it."

It's unclear whether the white supremacists descended on the spot specifically to counter the faith gathering or if any left the brawls near the statue to approach the church directly. Compared to the avalanche of reporters that blanketed the town the next day, press coverage during the torch rally was minimal. The only major media outlets in the area were *Sojourners*, which had a representative livestreaming the service to Facebook; a reporter from *The Guardian*, who was called away before the rally began; documentary crews from *National Geographic* and *VICE*, who were working on longer projects that wouldn't be released for days or months; and a lone *ThinkProgress* reporter—Joshua Eaton, an investigative journalist who also covered religion—who left the sanctuary to stand next to the student counterprotesters in the center of the torch rally.[5]

Inside the church, worship organizers were taking no chances. They locked down the building, held the doors shut, and instructed worshippers to stay inside. Unbeknownst to most attendees, the danger was already among them: a white supremacist had entered the church and was livestreaming the event to his followers.[6]

Meanwhile, the congregation tried to drown out the hateful bellowing with hymns of hope.

"We were locked in there for a couple of hours, just singing and praying," West recalled.[7]

At some point, organizers began escorting people out through the back doors to avoid attracting attention, but Blackmon was defiant. A black woman raised in Birmingham, Alabama—where she witnessed a Ku Klux Klan rally as a child—she wasn't about to slip out the back. She insisted she and West would leave through the front.

"When I opened the door, all I could see, as far as I could see, were flames," she said.[8] "People were chanting, 'You will not replace us! Jews will not replace us!' And I decided that, this one time, I might go out the back door."

★ ★ ★

To the casual observer, people of faith like Blackmon gathering to resist racism is almost expected. The vibrant activism and oratory of religious leaders in the 1960s-era civil rights movement is a story many Americans know well; the image of Jews, Christians, Muslims, and other faiths assembling to condemn white supremacy is one that has long been burned into the American psyche.

But that easy assumption belies the complex interaction between religion, race, and activism in recent years, particularly within liberal circles and the Religious Left. Progressive faith movements have risen to meet moral challenges throughout American history, but that doesn't mean the periods between are without controversy and missteps—or that the transitions into eras of activism don't require doing the hard work of reforging connections and reckoning with past mistakes.

And when it comes to race, American faith groups have much to reckon with.

FINDING FAITH IN FERGUSON

Racial justice activists have long told me the key to understanding the powerful but curious role that religion played in Charlottesville—and in today's larger progressive racial justice movement—lies in another frenetic moment in American history: the August 2014 protests in Ferguson, Missouri, that helped birth the Black Lives Matter movement, the largest racial justice campaign of our time.

It was a birth sparked by violent tragedy. On August 9, 2014, local police officer Darren Wilson shot and killed Michael Brown, an unarmed eighteen-year-old black man who had graduated from high school just eight days before. Grisly details of the incident—most notably that Wilson shot Brown at least six times within sight of the Canfield Green apartment complex—quickly became the subject of national debate and outrage. Within a day, there were reports of looting at Ferguson establishments, and elsewhere protesters were flooding the streets. Reporters flocked to the city to cover the fury, capturing dramatic images of frustrated demonstrators staring down police in riot gear. Activists began describing the events as the "Ferguson Uprising," a movement that turned the city into a catalyst for a national conversation about race, police brutality, the militarization of law enforcement, and the disproportionate killing of black men.

The light-speed escalation surprised many, including Blackmon, whose Christ the King Church sits about three miles from where Brown was killed. She remembers thinking that news of his shooting was undoubtedly tragic but not inherently different from the litany of local headlines detailing the deaths of black youths at the hands of police and others. Her pastoral profession made her painfully familiar with death: gun-related killings of young people had become so frequent that the area suffered from a shortage of funeral locations. Some churches refused to offer services for people who were not connected to their congregation. Their reasoning stemmed from safety concerns (in the case of shooting deaths, some worried that the church could be visited by the same violence) and from frustration with the sheer cost of hosting so many funerals.

But where others saw scarcity, Blackmon, who arrived at her church in 2009, saw a ministerial possibility. She opened the sanctuary at Christ the King to host funerals regardless of whether the deceased had any prior relationship with the congregation, offering the space to bereaved families free of charge. During one such funeral in 2013, a woman named Sierra came to pay respects to her best friend, a twenty-one-year-old woman killed in a drive-by shooting in Saint Louis when a bullet intended for her fiancé struck her as she cradled her nine-month-old child.[9] As Sierra left the church, she asked an usher for Blackmon's card.

A year later, Sierra and her two children left their home in the Canfield Green apartment complex for a family breakfast. When they returned, they walked past the bloody, uncovered body of Michael Brown, known to neighborhood kids as "Mike Mike." Horrified, Sierra rushed her distraught children home, found Blackmon's card, and dialed the number.

"She told me, 'You didn't know this, but since that funeral, you have been my pastor. And I'm asking my pastor to come to Ferguson,'" Blackmon recalled.[10] "I went to Ferguson because Sierra called me."

Before she left to visit the Ferguson police station that Sunday, Blackmon posted a message on her Facebook page asking fellow faith leaders how they planned to respond to the shooting. Many were hesitant. Some suggested they pray together as they awaited more information. But Blackmon, newly inspired, responded with a call to action, saying, "If all we're going to do is wait and pray, can we at least do it at the police station?" Clergy from multiple faiths suddenly reversed course, asking for more details before hastily organizing a prayer vigil at the station with a hundred or more faith leaders. Blackmon drafted a petition for participants to sign, demanding a thorough and transparent investigation into Brown's death, which she planned to deliver to city officials.

The tentativeness of clergy contrasted sharply with what Blackmon saw when she arrived at the police station a short time later. A crowd of perhaps five hundred demonstrators—primarily young people of color—stretched across the pavement in front of her. As a small group rushed over to ask about her plans, she realized that most were people who had taken to the streets the night before, hours after Brown's death. While Blackmon and clergy deliberated about how, or even *if*, to respond, these local activists had protested for hours before massing in front of the police station. And they never left.

As more clergy arrived, Blackmon hastily informed the demonstrators of her plans, and they agreed to participate. But their patience quickly ran thin: after nearly an hour of prayers, one young activist shouted, "That's enough praying—what are we going to do?" A group then peeled off from the vigil and began sitting in a nearby road, staging an impromptu protest to "sit down for Mike Brown." Blackmon and other clergy tried to stop them, voicing concerns that police would retaliate, but the activists refused. Realizing they were settling in for the long haul, Blackmon finally left the clergy, walked over, and asked the demonstrators if she could pray with them. They agreed, suddenly making Blackmon a participant in *their* protest, not the other way around.

It was likely an awkward moment—one that inverted the traditional paradigm of American racial justice organizing, particularly in black communities, where religious leaders such as Rev. Martin Luther King Jr. and Malcolm X have long been recognized as the chief authors of antiracist rhetoric and the poets of protest. But a new order emerged in Ferguson: the movement was orchestrated by a *coalition* of activists, often led by tech-savvy young people, and *assisted*—not necessarily *led*—by clergy.

One of those young activists was DeRay Mckesson, then a twenty-nine-year-old Minneapolis school administrator, who drove down to participate in the protests. He quickly emerged as one of the key online organizers of the Ferguson protests and the broader Black Lives Matter movement. He said that while religious leaders have historically been first responders to racial injustice, many clergy in Ferguson chastised the crowds who had taken to the streets.

"Pastors were actually some of the people telling us to go home and that this wasn't the way to make a difference," he told me.[11] "They were roundly ignored."

The ceaseless march of technological innovation also exposed generational divides, as many Ferguson activists skewed young. Whereas Civil Rights leaders of the 1960s often utilized ecclesiological structures to help organize and elevate their protests, activists in Ferguson leaned heavily on social media to orchestrate actions and share their message with the world. Following in the footsteps of virtual activists who spearheaded the Iranian Green movement, Arab Spring, and Occupy Wall Street, the origins of the Black Lives Matter movement date back to a hashtag that emerged after the acquittal of George Zimmerman, the Florida man who shot and killed seventeen-year-old Trayvon Martin—another black youth—in 2012.[12] Similarly, the death of Michael Brown triggered a flurry of posts tagged with #Ferguson and #MikeBrown, each reaching more people in seconds than a sermon could in days. According to CNN, between August 9 and August 25, 2014, the hashtag #Ferguson appeared on Twitter 1.9 million times without retweets, 11.6 million times with retweets.[13]

Mckesson, who claimed around eight hundred Twitter followers at the beginning of the protests and now boasts more than a million,[14] helped the fledgling Black Lives Matter movement make the most of new platforms.

"The internet changed our ability to build community without having to physically all be in one room," he said.[15] "I think the internet meant that we didn't need to convene at a church to figure out where we're going to go."

But the chasm of difference between church leaders and young activists yawned wider than tactics or technology; it involved religion as well. It is true that African Americans remain one of the country's most consistently God-fearing, churchgoing demographics, with 79 percent saying they identify as Christian, according to Pew Research's 2014 Religious Landscape Study.[16] That's higher than whites (70 percent) or Hispanics (77 percent), and black Americans attend weekly church services at higher rates. They are also disproportionately positioned within the black church tradition, as roughly half of all African Americans attend historically black Protestant churches. Without question, the black church remains a force to be reckoned with.

But while the rise of the religiously unaffiliated has not impacted African American Christians to the same degree that it has white Christians, there is still movement. Whereas only 12 percent of black Americans said they were religiously unaffiliated in 2007, according to Pew, 18 percent said so in 2014. That shift appears to be occurring primarily among young people, as roughly 29 percent of African Americans between the ages of eighteen and twenty-nine said they were unaffiliated, compared to only 7 percent of black adults sixty-five and older.

Blackmon witnessed this tension firsthand. She said many young people she encountered were not "pro-institutional religion" because they had been ostracized from the church for a variety of reasons ranging from sexuality to family dynamics to economics.

"These are the youth that the church rejected," she said.[17] "Whether it's because they were from single-parent homes and their parents had been ostracized or because they weren't married in conservative spaces where marriage was required if you were going to have a baby. Or whether these were the children of people who got caught up in the drug epidemic and had been shunned by the church, and therefore their children weren't raised in church. Whether it was the economic escalation of the black middle class—white flight is not the only flight. . . . Whether it's because these kids weren't going to go to college largely because they didn't have money to go. All of that played into it."

Blackmon's description upends the stereotype of religiously unaffiliated Americans as wealthy elites. Indeed, among African Americans who claim no religious affiliation, 57 percent make less than $30,000 a year, according to Pew,[18] compared to only 49 percent of black Americans who claim Christianity.[19] It's a distinct difference compared to whites, among whom only 31 percent of nones fall into that lower income bracket and roughly half earn $50,000 or more.[20]

And then there is the other major component that helps explain the complicated interactions between clergy and black youth in Ferguson: unlike unaffiliated whites, only 30 percent of whom are absolutely certain they believe in God, 63 percent of unaffiliated African Americans profess a belief in a higher power.

This group includes Mckesson, who noted that while he believes in God, he was one of many Ferguson activists for whom church "wasn't necessarily a safe place." He and others like him instinctively viewed clergy, even sympathetic ones, with skepticism.

The realization weighed heavily on Blackmon, who said it saddened her not only that youth were distant from faith communities but also that clergy like herself "had not missed them." As a result, she altered her activism to include elements aimed at healing longstanding wounds borne by those whom faith leaders had ignored. If she wanted Black Lives Matter protesters to trust her, she reasoned, she was going to have to do the difficult work of earning their trust.

In that spirit, the first time she led a march as part of the Ferguson demonstrations, she escorted it directly to the Canfield Green apartment complex. Once there, she didn't just criticize police—she called out the church.

"I did a public repentance, saying we weren't here, and we should have been here," she said.[21] "We had this relationship building to do in the middle of trauma."

There was also ample work to be done to rethink the dynamics of faith-based racial justice activism *within* faith-based activism itself, with a renewed emphasis on direct action and showing up at the front lines. Mckesson told of one tense encounter he witnessed between police and demonstrators outside a church parking lot, when furious protesters thought officers had killed a young man. As frustration mounted, Renita Lamkin, a white AME church pastor from nearby Saint Charles, walked between the two camps and lifted her voice in prayer.

"She just starts praying, and it was the first time that it had happened, so nobody really knew what to do," Mckesson said.[22] "The police got calm, the protesters got calm, and there was like, just, this moment.

"It was one of those moments where you're like, there must be a God somewhere," he added.

Blackmon explained that the clergy-as-mediator role served several overlapping functions that would be replicated in future protests. First and foremost, it allowed faith leaders to stand in solidarity with the demonstrators. ("We're not antipolice, but in that confrontation, there was an unequal balance of power, and we stand on the side of those who do not have the power," she said.) Their presence also tended to keep police from using force, but if violence did break out, clergy could use their status as community figures and moral exemplars to relate to the press what they saw.

"I titled us 'The keepers of the story,'" she said.[23] "Part of our role was to be present for everything that was happening in the street so that we could bear witness to the truth. That became very important: to have clergy who could say, 'No, that's not how this happened.'"

Sometimes clergy told their own stories, as religious vestments did not always guarantee safety. Four days after Brown was killed, Renita Lamkin was standing with protesters as they confronted a line of police. She later told reporters she was attempting to act as mediator, praying and chanting "Jesus, Jesus, Jesus." When officers warned the protesters to disperse, she shouted back, "They're leaving!"[24]

Suddenly, she felt a pop in her stomach and a pang of pain. She looked down to discover she had been struck by a rubber pellet that left a ghastly, bloody wound girded in dark bruises in her abdomen. Images of Lamkin's injury, juxtaposed with her smiling face, quickly became a fixture on social media.

The next day she was back in the streets, marching alongside her fellow protesters.[25]

"They say, 'You took a bullet for us.' I have no sense of taking a bullet for someone," she would later tell the St. Louis Post-Dispatch.[26] "My sense is that I'm in the struggle. I'm in it. We're in this together, and I was playing my role."

All of this upped the credibility of faith leaders in the movement, as did the actions of other religious groups and faith leaders who became de facto facilitators. Just as Mckesson was only one of thousands of demonstrators in the city, so too were Blackmon and Lamkin only two among many faith leaders. Despite the shift to using Twitter and Facebook as chief organizing tools, brick-and-mortar church buildings still served a purpose: congregations such as Greater St. Mark Family Church, headed by Rev. Tommie Pierson,[27] opened themselves up as "sanctuary churches" in which protesters could take refuge and organize.[28]

Rev. Starsky Wilson also opened his church, the UCC-affiliated Saint John's Church (The Beloved Community) in Saint Louis, a move that ultimately played a crucial role in the development of protest-focused liberation theology within the rapidly expanding Black Lives Matter movement.[29] In late August, the congregation played host to hundreds of Black Lives Matter activists who came to the city, allowing them to spend four days using its sanctuary for "teach-ins, healing stations, organizing actions, [and] reflecting."

While preaching a Sunday sermon entitled "The Politics of Jesus" to the activists and others gathered at the church, Wilson explained why the church had taken in the Black Lives Matter group, which was supposed to stay elsewhere before plans fell through.[30]

"We had to make a . . . decision: Would we be a space and a place that is welcoming to the work of God without God's name on it, or would we try to accommodate our own agenda for the sake of getting our name on it?" he said, sparking applause throughout the packed sanctuary. "God gave us an opportunity to do the politics of Jesus, and thanks be to God, somebody here answered the call. . . . We got a chance see the politics of Jesus played out in its radical, revolutionary, realistic form. Because the real deal is . . . Jesus's politics are both radical and revolutionary."

Wilson made the connection to the recent events explicit: "Jesus lived under Roman occupation and a militarized presence in his neighborhood. The Roman occupation in Jesus's neighborhood seems similar to the police state on the streets of Ferguson that we have seen in the last two weeks."

When hundreds of other activists returned a month later for Ferguson October, they used Saint John's basement to plan acts of resistance across the country.

"That's when you begin to see 'Shut down the streets in Chattanooga,' 'Shut down the streets in Atlanta,' 'Shut down the BART in Oakland,'" Wilson would later tell author Leah Gunning Francis.[31] "That was organized in a church basement where the BLM riders come back and then they begin to trade ideas."

As the movement in Ferguson matured and waves of activism continued to wash over the town, other faith groups joined, providing an impetus for religious leaders of all backgrounds to reengage with the topic of race. The St. Louis Metropolitan Clergy Coalition—an interfaith group that includes white and black clergy—convened a faith-based march in August that included an address by Blackmon.[32] It provided an opportunity to strengthen bonds between black faith leaders and white clergy, including the Rev. Michael Kinman of Christ Church Cathedral, an Episcopal church in Saint Louis, who helped organize the march. He would join others in taking a bolder stance on September 29, when a group of interfaith clergy knelt in prayer outside the Ferguson Police Department. Witnesses recall that Rev. Osagyefo Sekou—a dreadlocked activist, musician, and theologian who was born in Saint Louis—was the first to kneel, followed soon thereafter by Kinman and several others.[33]

But re-earning the trust of demonstrators estranged from the church would take time, and there was still more healing to do. The next month, an even larger group of interfaith leaders from across the country descended on the region in a show of spiritual force. It included Sekou and Lamkin and such prominent figures as Cornel West; Rev. Jim Wallis; Rev. Lisa Sharon Harper; and Rev. Michael McBride, of Faith in Action. Blackmon marked the auspicious occasion by hosting them that Sunday, October 12, in Saint Louis University's Chaifetz Arena, where several were slated to speak. A crowd of thousands awaited them as they arrived, eager to hear their thoughts on what was dubbed a "Weekend of Resistance."[34]

It foreshadowed future alliances within the movement, as several of those present would later march in the streets of Charlottesville. On the night of the right-wing torch rally three years later, West would note the powerful influence of Ferguson while introducing Blackmon, saying he had seen with his own eyes that Ferguson was "ground zero against the white supremacist treatment of our impressive young black brothers and sisters by too many of our police."

But that was still years away, and it wasn't long before fissures burst open between those on the stage and those on the floor of Chaifetz Arena. Activists in the audience began shouting at the stage about halfway through the program, and some turned their backs when NAACP president Cornell William Brooks began to speak. They demanded that the voices of those who had been in the street be heard alongside faith leaders from out of town, and several erupted into the chant "This is what democracy looks like!"

Blackmon, now well versed in such exchanges, acted quickly. She invited the young protesters to the stage, altering the program on the spot. She then turned to the faith leaders and, by way of explanation, declared, "This is what democracy looks like." The crowd responded with cheers.

Moved by the moment, West asked aloud the question on the minds of many: "How do we ensure that we love the younger generation enough to heal their wounds . . . so they can speak to us with dignity?"[35] He then made a promise that, in many ways, seemed to answer his own inquiry.

"I didn't come here to give a speech," he said.[36] "I came here to go to jail."

He made good on that promise, as did more than fifty people who were detained the next day—including Harper, McBride, Sekou, Wallis, and Lamkin. The group marched to the Ferguson police station arm-in-arm before presenting themselves to officers and asking them to "join them in repentance."[37] They were then led away in handcuffs alongside younger demonstrators, some of whom wore T-shirts that read "This ain't yo mama's civil rights movement."[38]

NEW ALLIANCES

The events of Ferguson proved to be a paradigm shift for faith-based organizing around race, particularly for African Americans. Georgia representative John Lewis described the protests as a "turning point" akin to the 1965 Selma March in Alabama,[39] an especially powerful proclamation given that Lewis was harshly beaten unconscious by police at that demonstration. But while both movements emerged from streets clouded with tear gas, the campaign that charged out of Ferguson was in many ways distinct from what marched off the Edmund Pettus bridge more than fifty years ago.

Instead of being primarily rooted in the black church, Black Lives Matter chapters cropped up around the country on their own. Activists helped stage die-ins to honor other black people felled by police officers, such as Freddie Gray in Baltimore, Maryland; Jonathan Ferrell in Charlotte, North Carolina; and Eric Garner in New York City. Meanwhile, the rise of white nationalist groups and racially motivated killings stretched the national conversation around race beyond policing policies and into broader discussions of systemic white supremacy.

Faith leaders also began to take seriously the spirituality of unaffiliated activists. While many demonstrators remained overtly secular, spiritual leaders recognized that activism and the communities it creates could be, for some, a form of faith.

"When you look at things like Black Lives Matter, you also look at other ways of exploring spirituality, other ways of creating a relationship between you and God that are not rooted in institutionalization," Blackmon said.[40]

Mckesson, who went on to become a successful podcaster, agreed. He guest-lectured a course at Yale Divinity School in 2015, where he led a band of theology students in a lengthy discussion of an essay entitled "In Defense of Looting" and facilitated theological debate on the declaration "Jesus was a protester."[41]

"I think that if I didn't understand a relationship with God before the protests, I certainly did in the midst and afterward," he said.[42] "I look back and think about so many moments when, if not for the covering of God, I wouldn't be here."

It should be noted that the Rev. Jesse Jackson and the Rev. Al Sharpton—both veterans of the civil rights movement—pilgrimaged to Ferguson in the early days of the protest, marching and speaking with protesters.[43] (Sharpton visited Michael Brown's grief-stricken family just days after the shooting and later spoke at Greater St. Mark.)[44] The two men were also in attendance when President Barack Obama gave his memorable June 2015 speech in a Charleston, South Carolina, sanctuary, where worshippers had gathered to mourn the deaths of nine Emanuel African Methodist Episcopal Church members killed by white supremacist Dylann Roof. Sharpton and Jackson sat alongside dozens of other ministers and politicians such as Republican leader John Boehner and Hillary Clinton—who had recently announced her campaign for president—and watched as Obama delivered what many would later describe as a sermon before launching into a rendition of "Amazing Grace."[45]

Even so, Ferguson helped usher in a new phase of activism that spawned a fresh pantheon of faith leaders who champion racial justice, at least in the eyes of many Black Lives Matter activists and their allies. Rev. angel Kyodo williams, a black, queer Zen Buddhist teacher, began challenging the mostly white American Buddhist community on its homogeneity, and she later joined Blackmon at protests around the country.[46] And in the aftermath of the Charleston shooting, artist and activist Bree Newsome recited scripture as she scaled the flagpole that flew a Confederate flag in front of the South Carolina statehouse, tearing down the banner and shouting, "You come against me with hatred, oppression, and violence. I come against you in the name of God—this flag comes down today!"[47] Less than a month later, on July 10, South Carolina officials took the flag down for good.

Voicing public support for Black Lives Matter soon became a cultural mainstay for progressive faith communities, with many houses of worship prominently displaying signs with the slogan outside their sanctuaries. The signs, in turn, made the churches a target: vandals were quick to deface Black Lives Matter signs at Unitarian Universalist congregations in Reno, Nevada, and Galloway Township, New Jersey, spray-painting them to read All Lives Matter[48] and White Lives Matter.[49] The same occurred in a number of congregations across the country, including churches in the Saint Louis area.[50]

For many predominantly white congregations the sign destruction was ultimately little more than a nuisance, as they often had relatively little to fear compared to the direct threats from white supremacists that black churches have faced for decades. But the signs were one of several expressions of solidarity that formed the foundation for renewed partnerships between African American church leaders and liberal white clergy, helping to push left-leaning denominations and individual churches to have serious conversations about race. After a rash of sign defacings in Saint Louis, for example, an interfaith coalition pooled its money to purchase a massive, electronic Black Lives Matter billboard on Missouri's Highway 44, making sure it was in place for the first anniversary of Michael Brown's death.[51]

These communal connections fueled the congregation-based organizing work of Faith in Action, which called on its massive activism network after Ferguson to embrace the idea of "prophetic resistance."[52] It even hosted a 2017 Prophetic Resistance Summit in Indiana, at which some faith leaders acknowledged that speaking out after Ferguson sometimes came with a cost. Pastors of color who oversee majority-white evangelical churches said they lost members after they broached issues of race. Some white clergy said they, too, had pews empty after denouncing white supremacy; a few were even pushed out of pulpits.[53]

But this kind of pushback, like the sign defacings, only cemented their resolve, and a new alliance of faith-based antiracism began to take shape. Michael-Ray Mathews, Faith in Action's director of clergy organizing, told me at the time that "race has to be at the center" of their faith-rooted work.[54] And it wasn't just about difficult conversations: race work, the leaders claimed, meant helping elect new local officials who would tackle issues of race. It also meant celebrating new leaders; not only did the summit include a panel discussion with Newsome and Sekou moderated by McBride, it also boasted Blackmon as its keynote speaker.

Indeed, Blackmon's star rose quickly in progressive faith circles after Ferguson. She was listed as one of Ebony magazine's Power 100 in 2015,[55] invited to Vatican City as part of a delegation to meet with Pope Francis's staff,[56] and elevated to a national position in the UCC—executive minister of Justice and Local Church Ministries. But even with her national role, which included participating in numerous protests alongside Rev. William Barber in Washington, DC, she remained convinced that localized activism was more effective than parachuting in as a jet-setting religious rock star. It's why she repeatedly turned down speaking invitations at numerous protests and demonstrations in the years after Ferguson, and why she initially turned down the invitation to preach in Charlottesville. (She agreed only when local activists assured her they didn't want her to lead, but just to offer a "word of encouragement.")

Sometimes, however, the movement came to her. When officials in Hillary Clinton's campaign were looking for a way to respond to the Charleston shooting, they didn't attempt to stage an event at a historic civil rights congregation. Instead, they reached out to Blackmon, largely due to her Ferguson activism—and, staffers said, the fact that Clinton wanted to attend a church led by a woman.

Blackmon initially resisted, noting that Emanuel in Charleston was an AME church, and referred the campaign to a nearby female-led

AME congregation. When that sanctuary proved too small, however, Blackmon relented and agreed to cohost the event at her church. But she accepted only with the same precondition she had demanded of Missouri lawmakers when they offered to visit her church during the Ferguson Uprising: Clinton couldn't just deliver a speech; she also needed to sit and listen to a panel of speakers from the community. Clinton readily agreed.

"The time is out for politicians to stop by and tell a bunch of lies and keep going," Blackmon said.[57] "So if you're going to come into the community, you should be coming to listen more than to talk."

DEFEATING GOLIATH

Although her job was to offer encouragement to others, Blackmon didn't feel especially encouraged that first night in Charlottesville. After witnessing the cabal of racists marching outside the church, Blackmon called Rev. William Barber, who was on tour as part of his campaign for moral revival, for advice. Barber said he was sending a security detail to protect her and that MSNBC's Joy Reid—after prompting from Barber—was preparing a film crew to cover the protests. Already, faith leaders were playing their role as keepers of the story.

Law enforcement did eventually arrive on the scene (far too late to stop several injury-ridden brawls), and the churchgoers were allowed to disperse. Blackmon used her phone to livestream the drive back to her hotel with Rev. Seth Wispelwey, a Charlottesville UCC pastor, in the driver's seat. As red-and-blue squad car lights lit the night, they could see white supremacists walking along the sidewalk near the car, chief Unite the Right organizer Jason Kessler among them.[58]

The tense moment was but a preview of the horrifying events that rocked the city the next day. Much has been written about the bloody clashes between white supremacist marchers and phalanxes of black-clad antifascist demonstrators, or Antifa, in the streets of Charlottesville on August 12. MSNBC and other cable news outlets broadcast images of shield- and baton-wielding racists who charged the lines of counterprotesters, sparking melees that left many maimed. As chaos consumed the town, protesters and reporters complained of an inadequate response by police as well as the unsettling presence of tight-lipped, gun-toting militia members who flanked Unite the Right protesters in the name of trying to "keep the peace."[59]

But while some counterprotesters responded in kind to violent assaults from white nationalists, many of those gathered to resist racism (including people of faith) were dedicated to nonviolence—a fact largely glossed over by the press.

According to Wispelwey, a white man who helped organize the counterprotests with the group Congregate CVille, many of the faith-based participants that day were from out of town for reasons that echoed the tensions Blackmon had seen in Ferguson. White and black pastors in the Charlottesville area had expressed discomfort with the direct-action style of counterprotest, arguing that it only provoked violence. But Wispelwey was unmoved, as were Don Gathers, cofounder of Charlottesville Black Lives Matter and a deacon at First Baptist Church Charlottesville, and Rev. Brittany Caine-Conley, a UCC minister and organizer who identifies as queer. Roughly a month before the demonstrations, they flew in Sekou to help prepare counterdemonstrators—faith-rooted and otherwise—with training simulations on how to respond to violence with nonviolence, disrupt hate speech, and obstruct law enforcement.[60]

As a result, many who showed up the day of the rally already had existing relationships with the faith-based organizers. Religious voices, in turn, tended to represent those who stood to be even further marginalized by the rise of hatred and white supremacy.

"Who you ended up mainly seeing on the front lines were queer rabbinical students and Muslim women and black civil rights leaders and lesbian clergy and stay-at-home parents," recalled Wispelwey.

Some well-known leaders of the Religious Left, such as Christian author Brian McLaren, also joined them the day of the Unite the Right rally, gathering with others down the street from the park for a religious counterdemonstration to denounce racism. The boldest among them marched directly into the fray: a group of faith leaders that included West, Sekou, and Lisa Sharon Harper walked to Emancipation Park and formed a line in front of militia members and white supremacists.

As West and the others knelt, prayed, and sang hymns for at least an hour, white nationalists responded by calling them "fake pastors"[61] and hurling homophobic slurs.[62] But many of the faith leaders had marched together before, making them a difficult group to break. And this time, they weren't alone: a group of Black Lives Matter protesters stood nearby and soon joined the clergy in chanting "Love has already won."[63] It was a small moment that stood as a testament to the relationship building that both groups—clergy and young activists—had done since Ferguson.

Shortly thereafter, a faction that included West, Sekou, Wispelwey, Caine-Conley, and Unitarian Universalist pastors in Black Lives Matter stoles made a difficult decision, one they said was inspired by nonviolent protests of the civil rights movement: they formed a line across an entrance to the park, locked arms, and dared the white supremacists to pass.

Witnesses said that some white nationalists did, in fact, break through the line, shoving the faith leaders aside with their shields to gain entrance to the park.[64] As the violence escalated, West grew increasingly concerned.

"I'm sitting there thinking, 'I'm always trying to keep alive the legacy of brother Martin Luther King, of sister Fannie Lou Hamer,'" he said.[65] "[But] it became clear to me that the space for prophetic witness was quickly shrinking."

Despite the planning, moments of friction arose between faith leaders and some counterprotesters. In the midst of slowly building mayhem, Antifa members mistook the clergy outside the park as white supremacist *supporters* when the racists blew past them, and it required several rapid-fire conversations before things were made right.

"I remember one guy was just like, 'Fuck you! What are you doing?! Fuck you!'—like, right in my face," Wispelwey recalled.

The situation shifted quickly once the alliances were clarified, however. Antifa members rushed to defend the clergy from an advancing line of white nationalists, giving the faith leaders just enough time to end their protest and flee the scene.

"They saved us, because we were going to get crushed like cockroaches, man," West said.[66] "Without the Antifa brothers and sisters we would have been goners, believe me."

Despite such frantic moments, there was ample evidence to suggest that the religious voices had won over some of the more secular antiracist activists. When faith leaders reorganized themselves later in the day, they once again locked arms and marched through the streets of Charlottesville. As they passed, members of Antifa, Black Lives Matter, Industrial Workers of the World, and others all stopped to offer them a standing ovation.[67]

The relationship became even stronger a short time later. As clergy recuperated near a safe house, a group of activists stumbled up, panting and out of breath. Between strained gasps and sobs, they explained that a white supremacist had plowed his car into counter-demonstrators nearby, leaving bodies strewn across the pavement. They needed their help.

Sekou, McLaren, Wispelwey, and others sprinted to the scene to offer what support they could, administering pastoral care and forming a protective human barrier around the wounded and dying. Beneath the busy hands of several paramedics lay Heather Heyer, a young activist who would tragically succumb to her injuries later that day. West was one of many who would describe Heyer as a martyr, and he told me that she had spoken to the clergy as they stood in front of the park.

But amidst such darkness, tiny glimmers of light and newfound community burned. As he observed the chaotic scene, Wispelwey, who is not Catholic, heard someone shout, "Father!" over his shoulder. He looked to see an Antifa member kneeling in the street—the same man who had been yelling in his face earlier that day. He was cradling a distraught victim of the attack.

"This woman needs help," he said, thrusting her into Wispel-wey's arms before disappearing into the crowd.

★   ★   ★

The experience of Charlottesville was a reminder that America's struggle with race is far larger than a divide between black and white. The white supremacists who marched in Virginia didn't just heap hatred upon black Americans; they also spewed vitriol at Jews, Muslims, LGBTQ people, and immigrants, among others. Blackmon bemoaned the role some Religious Right leaders played in backing controversial policies that she says embolden that hatred, and she pointed to the one issue that has galvanized almost universal faith-based pushback to the Trump administration: the treatment of immigrants, particularly the policy of separating families along the US-Mexico border.

But as Blackmon pointed out, anti-immigrant sentiment and other forms of hatred predate Trumpism. And like racism, they require a robust response from faith leaders if they are ever to be defeated.

"To get rid of Donald Trump does not change the sentiment that's happening in this nation now," she said.[68] "The whole thing must be uprooted, because you can get rid of Goliath and still have the Philistines, and another Goliath will emerge."

Luckily for Blackmon, a thriving, radical, faith-based immigrant-rights movement had spent decades trying to do just that and was already waiting for her.

CHAPTER SIX

★ ★ ★

Welcoming the Stranger

Southside Presbyterian Church in Tucson, Arizona, doesn't exactly exude power. It's not a soaring stone cathedral dappled with statues and flying buttresses, but a humble sanctuary built from cactus ribs, pine logs, and flagstones fashioned to resemble an ancient Native American structure. It's not a glitzy megachurch that packs its pews on Sundays with influential dignitaries, but a small congregation of fewer than 150 members. It's not even located in a powerful part of Tucson; it lies instead in one of the city's primarily low-income Latinx neighborhoods.[1]

But for people like Daniel Neyoy Ruiz and a growing network of progressive houses of worship across the country, Southside is a place of profound power. It is a place strong enough to spark a national movement and—along with the courage of immigrants like Neyoy Ruiz—stop the US government in its tracks.

Not that Neyoy Ruiz knew that in 2011, when he was pulled over by a police officer who claimed his tailpipe was emitting smoke. For some, this would be an annoyance, but Neyoy Ruiz, an undocumented Mexican immigrant, had likely lived in fear of just such an incident. According to reports, the arresting officer rejected his Mexican license and called US Border Patrol, who took Neyoy Ruiz to the Tucson sector headquarters and put him in what he later described as a crowded, frigid holding cell.[2] Three days later he was transferred to a separate detention center—one he told reporters was worse than the first—where he stayed for roughly a month, until his wife sold their car to pay his bond.[3] For the next three years, Neyoy Ruiz tried to get his deportation order dropped, reportedly shelling out nearly $20,000 in legal fees. But nothing worked, and by May 2014, the husband and father of a thirteen-year-old was approaching the date of his deportation.

In this hour of need, Neyoy Ruiz was directed to Southside pastor Rev. Alison Harrington, a clergywoman known for her progressive leanings and a spiritual demeanor perhaps best described as matter-of-factly firebrand. Soon thereafter, Harrington announced that her congregation would allow Neyoy Ruiz to move into a small, windowless room on church property until Immigration and Customs Enforcement (ICE) dropped his deportation order.

"In times such as these, we are called by our faith in Jesus Christ to act on behalf of those who suffer," Harrington, a former community organizer and the daughter of two preachers, wrote at the time.[4] "Throughout scriptures, people of faith are called to care for the orphan and the widow, but when it is a broken immigration system that is creating orphans and widows, we need to start intervening sooner."

It was a desperate, last-ditch play, and Harrington insisted her community was only acting out their faith in tandem with Neyoy Ruiz. But over time this small moment of defiance has snowballed into a nationwide interfaith network of progressive-leaning houses of worship, legal firms, and secular immigration advocates known as the New Sanctuary movement. Their work not only aided undocumented people during the Obama administration but also emerged as a key force within the broader progressive Resistance movement opposing Trump's immigration policies.

To understand the New Sanctuary movement is to understand how the Religious Left builds power through a mixture of moral arguments, liberation theology, and the art of protest.

★   ★   ★

Explaining the New Sanctuary movement requires a bit of history, much of which begins at Southside. Appearances notwithstanding, the tiny church has developed something of a tradition in starting movements. Its pastor emeritus is John Fife, a legendary figure in immigrant rights circles and one of the people widely credited with igniting the *original* Sanctuary movement in the 1980s. At the time, the southern border of the US was beset by a wave of Central American migrants, most of whom were fleeing horrific violence in their home countries—especially El Salvador and Guatemala. But the US government, which gave military training and aid to those nations, rejected more than 90 percent of Salvadoran asylum requests, insisting that they were simply "economic migrants."[5]

Fife, Southside, and five other congregations near the border were incensed by what they considered to be cruel negligence on the part of the federal government. The faith communities believed the migrants were refugees, full stop, and declared that they had a religious duty to offer the vulnerable some semblance of safe harbor. In direct defiance of federal law, volunteers began shuttling people across the border to offer them sanctuary in churches.[6] The movement captured national attention, spreading to as many as five hundred congregations at its peak and establishing what some would describe as an underground railroad that transported refugees to Canada.[7] Along the way, worship communities offered the beleaguered migrants legal aid, social services, transportation, resettlement assistance, and other forms of support.

Rev. Minerva G. Carcaño, now a bishop in the United Methodist Church, was active in the movement during the 1980s. She told me it was essentially a public, politicized version of what immigrants had been doing privately for each other for decades, if not centuries.

"Immigrant families themselves have provided sanctuary for other immigrants forever," she said, speaking with a preacher's cadence that wraps powerful concepts in an understated tone. "They may not have done all of the kind of public work, but they have been the core and the backbone of sanctuary in this country."[8]

Carcaño knows this because, as a child of immigrants, she lived it. For families like hers, private forms of sanctuary were simply a way of life.

"I lived in a family that, just out of Christian faith and out of a sense of community, would take in immigrants," she said. "When I was in high school, I began to learn that all those aunts and uncles that I assumed were just family members were actually people that my grandfather—sometimes my grandmother—would come across in life and find out they were people who had just come across the border from Mexico and didn't have a place to go. They would take them in and they would become family."[9]

Carcaño extended this same spirit to her own work with the Sanctuary movement. As a minister operating near the US-Mexico border, she worked with members of the Evangelical Lutheran Church in America (ELCA) to aid Salvadorans who left their country for the United States. When the ELCA told her of an eighteen-year-old undocumented Salvadoran woman and her infant child in need of housing, Carcaño took them in without hesitation. The mother and child stayed with Carcaño for two years, enough time for the minister to become the child's godmother, while the ELCA helped the pair gain residency status in the US. The family eventually moved to another home, but it wasn't long before Carcaño took in three other Central American women at the request of a local judge.

These radical forms of hospitality were second nature to many participants, but publicizing them was risky. In 1986, the FBI infiltrated Sanctuary movement groups and indicted sixteen activists, ultimately convicting nine—including Fife and Peggy Hutchison, another Methodist who worked with Carcaño—on felony charges that included smuggling and conspiracy.[10] But their sacrifice left a political legacy. The movement put pressure on the Reagan administration to address the refugee issue, and in 1990 the government settled a class-action lawsuit (*American Baptist Churches v. Thornburgh*) that a number of faith groups had brought against the Immigration and Naturalization Service (the precursor to today's Citizenship and Immigration Services, Customs and Border Protection, and ICE) on behalf of Guatemalans and Salvadorans. In the settlement, the government agreed to grant the immigrants new asylum hearings if they met certain criteria.[11]

Faith-based sanctuary activists were also credited with convincing municipal leaders in San Francisco, California, to pass a "City of Refuge" ordinance in 1989, which ended local cooperation with federal immigration enforcement and extended social services to all, irrespective of legal status.[12] San Francisco thus became the nation's first "sanctuary city," a designation that would make new headlines decades later when President Donald Trump blithely described it as a "ridiculous, crime infested & breeding concept" in a 2018 tweet.[13] (He went on to insist the Department of Justice could sue or even withhold funds from cities such as Chicago and New York City for declaring themselves sanctuary cities, igniting a legal battle.)[14]

More than thirty years after the original Sanctuary movement, Harrington saw her congregation's embrace of Neyoy Ruiz as a modern expression of this rich, spiritual activist tradition, just amended for a new context. Instead of refugees fleeing war zones, Harrington's moral challenge was the mass deportation of immigrants by the Obama administration, which removed more than 2.5 million people from 2009 to 2015 through immigration orders.[15] So intense was the forced expulsion of migrants under Obama that Latinx advocacy groups began referring to him as the "deporter-in-chief."[16]

With a new context came a new strategy. Southside's tactics differed from those of the original Sanctuary movement, which offered public assistance to refugees who were primarily hidden from public view. But local lawyer Margo Cowan—a key organizer of the original Sanctuary movement—urged Harrington and her church to pioneer a new kind of protest: to champion the narrative of the imperiled immigrant in order to *very publicly* hold Obama accountable to a pair of internal policy memos signed by ICE head John Morton. The first discouraged ICE agents from raiding "sensitive locations," such as hospitals, schools, and places of worship.[17] The second suggested that agents exercise "prosecutorial discretion," meaning they should prioritize violent criminals who are undocumented instead of those without a criminal record or who exhibit traits such as stateside family ties and a lengthy presence in the country.[18]

Openly pushing the Obama administration to stay true to its word was an experiment with limited precedent: in 2006, immigrant rights activist Elvira Arellano took sanctuary in a Chicago church, but left a year later to speak at congregations around the country and was arrested in Los Angeles and deported.[19] Cowan told me that she was initially ambivalent about using the decades-old strategy, because "as an organizer you really don't want to do the same thing twice." But she had proposed using sanctuary to prevent deportation—coupled with the threat of organizing events like a parade or a raucous church meeting to draw media attention—in at least two cases roughly eighteen months before suggesting it to Neyoy Ruiz. The government came back to the negotiation table before either of those immigrants took physical sanctuary, but they dug in on Neyoy Ruiz.

"Daniel's case was a situation where the government was wholly nonresponsive," Cowan said. "We wanted to call back upon the legend of sanctuary and open doors."[20]

Getting the attention of the public was key to opening those doors, and Neyoy Ruiz got it in spades. To handle the influx of interest, Harrington reached out to her friend Rev. Noel Anderson, a United Church of Christ minister who serves as the grassroots coordinator for immigrant rights at Church World Service, a national faith-based organization headquartered in Washington, DC. A California native who grew up in immigrant-heavy communities, Anderson is the kind of advocate who is just as likely to be seen walking into a meeting with government officials as he is to be dragged out of the same office in handcuffs chanting in protest.

Speaking with me in a dimly lit sports bar on the outskirts of DC in 2019, the young, slender, and perpetually earnest Anderson looked almost sentimental as he described how the Obama-era ICE memos helped stop as many as two hundred thousand deportations.[21] He said the mere existence of the memos sent a signal that "sort of showed the Obama administration was behind" immigrant rights activists—or was at least amenable to change.[22]

Despite Washington's best intentions, Anderson stressed, many undocumented people who met the criteria of the prosecutorial discretion memo still slipped through the cracks. Such was the case with Neyoy Ruiz, a father who reportedly paid his taxes, cared for his wife and son, had lived in the US for more than a decade, and lacked a criminal record. He was also a dedicated member of his community, having participated in an apartment watch program with the Tucson Police Department. As he told *The Daily Beast*: "I did everything I thought you needed to do."[23]

Thus, Southside and its allies were betting big that ICE, like the government in the 1980s, wouldn't risk the public relations disaster that would almost certainly follow if gun-toting federal agents stormed a church to apprehend Neyoy Ruiz. Instead, church leaders hoped the Obama administration would make good on its promises and drop the deportation case altogether.

It was a gamble. Internal policies are just that—policies, not law. Memo or not, ICE had the authority to deport Neyoy Ruiz at any time, and the federal government was well within its legal rights to raid a church sanctuary. In an extreme case, congregants could be held legally liable for aiding him, just like their forebears in the 1980s.

Meanwhile, Neyoy Ruiz continued to live in the church, by all accounts racked with anxiety. By day, he reportedly painted, played music, and occasionally talked with visitors from the community—those who weren't afraid to associate with him. By night, he slept on bunks with his family, his heart racing whenever he heard the wail of police sirens.[24]

But with Anderson lending a hand, Neyoy Ruiz and Southside had key allies: the media.

In addition to local newspapers printing op-eds and articles about sanctuary, NPR and other national outlets covered Neyoy Ruiz's plight, documenting the emergence of the New Sanctuary movement in Tucson.[25] As the days ticked by, others such as *The Daily Beast* followed suit,[26] and Harrington even made an appearance on an MSNBC show then hosted by Melissa Harris-Perry.[27]

It was a short segment, but one with an important audience. Harris-Perry is herself a religious progressive, a Unitarian Universalist who studied at the famously left-leaning Union Theological Seminary in New York. Her since-canceled show was then an influential voice among a vast audience of progressives, especially Hispanics and people of color.[28]

Harris-Perry is also a political science professor who studies the machinations of power, and she was visibly intrigued by the implications of Southside's protest. After admitting that her first reaction to the sanctuary tactic was puzzlement—"You can do that?"—she inquired about the strategy's potential.

"Is there a way to kind of capture your story, or your model, or the kind of ethical norms that you're presenting here, and actually influence policy as a result?" she asked.

"I hope so," Harrington replied.

Harris-Perry was also implicitly asking the same question that virtually every article on the protest had: Would the Obama administration really charge into a church and drag out a father while distraught pastors looked on?

The answer, it turned out, was no. ICE backed down roughly a month after Neyoy Ruiz moved into the sanctuary, issuing a one-year stay of deportation, which gave him time to obtain a work permit and apply to renew the stay.[29] When his attorney, after meeting with immigration officials, rushed back to the church to deliver the news, Neyoy Ruiz was overcome.

"When she told me, I just began to cry," he told the *Arizona Daily Star*.[30] "We were all crying there at the church."

It was a small but profound victory. Immigration activists had toiled for years fighting deportation orders through various legal channels, but Neyoy Ruiz and Southside had rediscovered an unorthodox method that drew attention to the issue and made a tangible, life-altering difference to the person at the center of it all. Immigrants and faith leaders stared down the United States government, and the feds blinked.

THE POETRY OF PROTEST

After word of Neyoy Ruiz's case got out, the New Sanctuary movement exploded.

Inspired by Southside, Shadow Rock United Church of Christ in nearby Phoenix, Arizona, offered sanctuary to undocumented immigrant Marco Tulio that same month, and his deportation order was dropped within twenty-four hours.[31] By September 2014, churches in Phoenix, Tucson, Chicago, and Portland, Oregon, were all actively housing immigrants on their property. At least twenty-four congregations across the country had declared a willingness to do the same, and some sixty additional communities had expressed support for the cause.[32] Organizations such as Faith in Action and Christian denominations such as the Presbyterian Church (USA) were joining Church World Service as either official partners of the movement or voices of solidarity on press calls. Rep. Raúl Grijalva, a Democrat from Arizona's Third District, called their activism "a cornerstone in pushing the decency of the American people to demand of its elected officials to do something."

Southside was just getting started. The congregation offered shelter to another immigrant just a few weeks after Neyoy Ruiz moved out. This time they opened their doors to Rosa Imelda Robles Loreto—a married, undocumented mother of two boys.

But sanctuary was not a guaranteed fix for all involved, nor was it a quick process. Robles Loreto ended up living in Southside's halls for fifteen months,[33] until her lawyer reached a confidential agreement with ICE that allowed her to live without fear of deportation.[34] Neyoy Ruiz had to reenter sanctuary in a different church a year after leaving Southside, because his stay of deportation had to be reexamined each year. (It was ultimately granted a second time.) And as the case of Elvira Arellano had made clear years before, if a person in sanctuary left their holy home for any reason—even to meet with immigration officials or accompanied by their children and religious leaders—they ran the risk of being detained and deported anyway.

Meanwhile, Harrington said, the burgeoning movement struggled with growing pains. She recalled that when she helped convene the first major gathering of those offering sanctuary in Phoenix in August 2015, the room was fraught with "healthy tension." Several participants had never attended a strategy meeting before, and the conference ended with many tasks unfinished. Attendees raised difficult issues, such as how to give a greater voice to the undocumented immigrants at the center the movement.

"A lot of times people living in sanctuary didn't feel like they were being empowered," Harrington said.[35]

Nevertheless, advocates saw the potential in what Southside had set in motion and continued to replicate the sanctuary strategy across the country. Against all odds, the tiny Tucson church had concocted the successful, scalable model of protest the Left had been seeking.

The secret to the scalability of the New Sanctuary movement lies in its appeal to the poetry of protest—the telling of a moral story through the medium of direct action. Think of it as a sonnet with interchangeable verses but always the same refrain: Organizers first orchestrate a demonstration to dramatize a larger moral quandary in a way that attracts media attention, usually through direct confrontation with authorities. The media attention, in turn, encourages the masses to sympathize with the protesters, draws more people to the cause, and—ideally—results in social or legislative change. It's an art form embraced by many throughout American history, but especially religious activists who preach moral arguments for a living. Hence its adoption by Martin Luther King Jr., who appealed to roughly the same logic when explaining the 1965 confrontation between Civil Rights marchers and Alabama state troopers on the Edmund Pettus Bridge.[36] He said the demonstration was meant to "dramatize the existence of injustice and to bring about the presence of justice by methods of nonviolence"[37] using methods that "must demand the attention of the press, for it is the press which interprets the issue to the community at large and thereby sets in motion the machinery for change."[38]

Several American social movements have seen media attention— and, as a result, popular support—mushroom after squaring off with police. An example: according to data maven Nate Silver, media outlets initially ignored the Occupy Wall Street movement, but the activists saw a spike in coverage after a video went viral that showed protesters being pepper sprayed by police and after officers arrested some seven hundred demonstrators on the Brooklyn Bridge.[39] The movement was unable to capitalize on that coverage in the long-term, but other progressive campaigns—such as the Moral Monday movement—clearly benefited from repeated, sustained arrests that were closely tied to a moral message.

The New Sanctuary movement took this approach and transposed it for their purposes, adding a beat or two to the existing prosody. It framed sanctuary as a *potential* conflict with authorities in a way that highlighted the larger concern of mass deportation and then used that potential to apply media pressure on authorities. Existing support for undocumented immigrants bolstered the approach: a 2014 poll by the Public Religion Research Institute found that all but one major religious group—white evangelical Protestants—voiced majority support for immigration reform legislation that included a pathway to citizenship for undocumented people.[40] Thus, the movement could encourage participation from a wide spectrum of groups that transcended religion, class, and geography, with multiple faith traditions interpreting the cause in their own terms.

Scripture was a starting point for many. Christians often cite Matthew 25: 31–40, in which Jesus says, "I was a stranger and you welcomed me."[41] Jews typically point to Exodus 23:9, which reads, "You shall not oppress a stranger, for you know the feelings of the stranger, having yourselves been strangers in the land of Egypt."[42] Other faith groups that have offered sanctuary also invoke sacred texts when explaining their support for the cause, be they Muslims ("We have indeed honored the Children of Adam," Qur'an 17:70),[43] Buddhists ("As long as a society protects the vulnerable among them, they can be expected to prosper and not decline," a paraphrase of words attributed to the Buddha in the Mahaparinirvana Sutta), or others.[44]

Not every New Sanctuary movement community would self-identify as progressive, since concern for immigrants tends to transcend religious traditions and party identification (at least until recent years, when the gaps have widened).[45] But most New Sanctu-ary movement participants leaned liberal and commonly interpreted scripture through the lens of liberation theology. Something of a lingua franca among Christian progressives in particular, liberation theology as a school of religious thought emerged in the 1950s and 1960s among Latin American Catholic theologians, the most famous of whom is Peru's Gustavo Gutiérrez. It has since proliferated to in-clude a number of faiths and subgroups; Jewish liberation theology, black liberation theology, Palestinian liberation theology, and queer theology all share a tie to Gutiérrez's work. Its various permutations are complex, multifaceted, and sometimes directly at odds with each other, but all are rooted in the same assertion: God is on the side of the oppressed.

This religious focus came up again and again when sanctuary participants spoke with me, and it's why sociologist Grace Yukich classifies the New Sanctuary movement as a "multitarget social movement." Its goal is to alter multiple institutions at once—both political *and* religious. Yukich stresses this point in her book *One Family Under God: Immigration Politics and Progressive Religion in America*, noting that even in its early stages "the New Sanctu-ary movement sought not only to challenge US immigration policy but also to change dominant representations of what it means to be religious today."[46] Thus, for faith-led New Sanctuary movement activists, their campaigns simultaneously pushed back on the narra-tive that religion is inherently conservative *and* helped pressure the Obama administration *and* responded to a deeply rooted faith claim. In theological terms, they contended that undocumented immigrants at risk of deportation and separation from their families were clearly the oppressed—meaning that aiding the immigrants' cause wasn't just the right thing to do, it was God's will.

The New Sanctuary movement also transcended class by *requir-ing* buy-in not just from groups that ICE targeted but also from those it didn't—namely, wealthy religious liberals. When cities formed sanctuary coalitions, they often followed the same pattern: many faith communities pledged to support the movement in a general sense, but houses of worship that tended to skew liberal, wealthy, and white were the ones that offered sanctuary. This wasn't because rich churches were intrinsically braver or bolder than their neighbors. It was a strategic choice: many poorer or immigrant-heavy churches already felt scrutinized by federal authorities or law enforcement; richer, whiter communities rarely suffered the same experience. Privilege was seen as a practical asset, should a church take in an undocumented immigrant, because it heightened the potential for media attention and made it even less likely that ICE would kick in their (often very expensive) door.

Harrington noted that while this approach had tactical benefits and its declarations of solidarity constituted a "very sweet bravado," it also had theological pitfalls.

"What was interesting is that it kind of became about us, about how *heroic* we were and about how *amazing* we were and how our grandchildren are going to be so *proud* of us," she said, speaking of the broader New Sanctuary movement. "It became about, 'We need someone in sanctuary to kind of prove that we're about it.' People who were thinking about going into sanctuary often felt very much as if they were kind of pawns in that. That's a bad look."[47]

Some sanctuary coalitions have worked to address this divide, and immigrants taking sanctuary have since organized amongst themselves. A few immigrants living in sanctuary even left the relative safety of their host congregations in 2018 to meet secretly in the basement of CityWell Church in North Carolina, where they compared experiences, cried together, and discussed ways to create support systems.[48]

One of the immigrants at that meeting was Hilda Ramirez, who described the experience as deeply cathartic.

"It felt good to share [my] story, to listen to the stories of others, and to talk about the sadness of being persecuted and followed by ICE," Ramirez told me, speaking through a translator. She was still living in a Presbyterian church in Texas nearly a year after the gathering and stressed the importance of solidarity: "We should all have the same voice, and we all have to fight because we are all immigrants."[49]

Indeed, righteous solidarity has long been the cultural glue binding the New Sanctuary movement. Although no one risks more than the undocumented immigrants themselves, many who joined the movement still faced potential consequences, which builds a sense of community. What's more, through trainings, workshops, rallies, and protests, religious groups were pushed to get to know other local communities with which they had never interacted, be they immigrants or other houses of worship in the sanctuary network. For many, it was their first sustained exchange with liberal religious groups outside their walls, much less with undocumented people, whom movement coordinators would refer to as "friends."

This solidarity extended beyond the spiritual, because the sanctuary community grounded its activism in a broader progressive legacy. Activists distributing movement tool kits to houses of worship drew parallels between the harboring of immigrants and the aid given by sympathetic Germans to Jews fleeing the Holocaust, or the assistance provided by Christian abolitionists to enslaved African Americans escaping to freedom.[50] And despite the obvious faith component, the New Sanctuary movement never consisted solely of religious groups in the first place: even at Southside, Harrington and others worked closely with local immigration attorneys, meeting frequently to seek guidance for Neyoy Ruiz's case and to discuss other undocumented immigrants who were potential candidates for sanctuary.[51]

As the movement grew, sanctuary networks expanded their focus beyond physical sanctuary. In New York, Sanctuary coalition members offered accompaniment services, which provided practical, emotional, and spiritual support for undocumented people enduring laborious immigration proceedings.[52] In Philadelphia, churches created a crisis hotline for people to call if they witnessed an ICE raid; when the call came in, a team of trained volunteers would rush to the site, film the arrests, hold a prayer vigil, and do their best to console any family members who were not detained.[53] During the waning years of the Obama administration, it was not uncommon to see groups marching at immigration-themed protests behind banners promoting their local sanctuary coalition.

The New Sanctuary movement represented a faith-led project that offered a tangible, pragmatic, and relatively accessible way to oppose the problem of mass deportation. It was a potentially hazardous solution, but the threat of retaliation from the government only *heightened* the profile of participants, earning them street cred among their progressive peers and accelerating the expansion of the movement.

But the real work was just beginning.

LAYING THE GROUNDWORK FOR #RESISTANCE

The New Sanctuary movement grew at a steady clip under the Obama administration, bolstered by robust support from national multifaith organizations such as Church World Service and Faith in Action. Their numbers ballooned whenever government officials led a sustained crackdown on immigrants, such as when ICE launched a series of raids targeting Central American asylum-seekers in early 2016.[54]

But the Obama-era spikes were nothing compared to the masses of impassioned faithful that flocked to the movement in response to the rise of Donald Trump.[55] His rhetoric ("They're rapists"[56] or "These aren't people. These are animals"[57]) and his policies (building a wall on the US-Mexico border, separating immigrant children from their parents) were widely seen as a direct threat to immigrants and, by extension, to the people of faith who spent years organizing to protect them.

Less than a month after Trump's inauguration, Southside's Alison Harrington stood before a gathering of faith leaders at her church and made it clear that Trump's ascension demanded an immediate response from the religious community.

"As people of faith and people of conscience, we pledge to resist the newly elected administration's policy proposals to target and deport millions of undocumented immigrants, and discriminate against marginalized communities," she said, echoing similar sentiments preached by progressive faith leaders across the country.[58]

And resist they did.

When Trump announced his ban on immigrants and refugees from several Muslim-majority countries, various sanctuary coalitions helped galvanize protesters to flood airports across the country,[59] where many held signs emblazoned with scripture.[60] When thousands rallied outside the Capitol in December 2017 to demand legislation reinstating DACA, sanctuary participants were there, too. And in 2018, when police arrested a cadre of protesters who were demonstrating outside an ICE building in Philadelphia to oppose the administration's policy of separating families detained at the southern border, members of the local sanctuary coalition were among them.[61]

These protests weren't the exclusive province of sanctuary groups. But the New Sanctuary movement successfully elevated progressive faith-based activists as a respected organizing force within the Left, as evidenced by a chant that became ubiquitous among religious and nonreligious progressives alike at Resistance demonstrations: "No ban, no wall, sanctuary for all!" The concept of sanctuary evolved rapidly in the face of Trump, retaining the core elements of the original faith-rooted moral protest while threading its way into more secular spaces. Taking a cue from sanctuary cities, students began pushing their colleges to become sanctuary campuses by refusing to cooperate with ICE, removing any reference to citizenship on applications, and providing legal support to students under threat of deportation.[62]

Yet the religious heart of the movement still beat. Whereas the New Sanctuary movement initially sought to reprimand a persuadable Obama, under Trump its actions were reimagined as prayerful defiance. During Faith in Action's 2017 Prophetic Resistance Summit in Indianapolis, a speaker asked more than 350 faith leaders if they had personally pressed lawmakers to make their home a sanctuary city. More than half raised their hands, some stretching to wave them in the air with excitement. By the end of 2018, the New Sanctuary movement had reached far beyond its humble beginnings at Southside Presbyterian. It had morphed into a slate of protest tactics, a potent mobilizing force, and a model for progressives of what resistance to Trump could look like.

The growth of the movement was partly due to the increased, urgent need among immigrants. Because of the prosecutorial discretion memo, 82 percent of those arrested by ICE during Obama's final months were immigrants *with* a criminal record. Donald Trump promised to target such "bad hombres" for deportation, but roughly two years into his tenure they account for only 63.5 percent of arrests. Those arrested under Trump *without* a criminal past, however, now represent a record-breaking 36.5 percent. And the percentages don't expose the raw numbers: as of March 2019, the Trump administration each month averaged 4,219 arrests of undocumented immigrants with no criminal record. By comparison, the Obama administration averaged only 1,352 such arrests each month in its final two years.[63]

Activists also revived the use of home sanctuary, in which immigrants at risk of deportation stay secretly in the houses of sympathetic individuals trained by sanctuary coalitions. It's a significantly more dangerous tactic than traditional sanctuary, since ICE does not consider homes to be sensitive locations. But activists—many of whom were faith-based—designed a remarkably furtive system: there was no comprehensive list of homes, hosts rarely knew each other, and organizations discouraged communication to make it harder to shut down a network should one person be arrested.[64]

"There's a lot of folk that have taken in people in their homes for sanctuary," Church World Service's Noel Anderson told me, noting that hosts are often connected to faith communities.[65] "Sometimes it's to buy some time to find a church to do a public sanctuary case. . . . [But] there is that sort of underground or private effort in the sanctuary movement."

Harrington argued that the use of this tactic was born out of necessity.

"Because there's zero tolerance [by immigration officials], my sense is you have more people living in sanctuary privately, not publicly, because they don't have strong cases—because nobody has a strong case underneath this administration," she said.

The cumulative result of all this organizing was the creation of a small, nonviolent army of faith-based activists spread across the country. The New Sanctuary movement claimed roughly 450 congregations before Trump's election, but by fall 2019 Anderson told me it had spread to more than twelve hundred congregations, with as many as forty networks and sanctuary coalitions in twenty-five states.[66]

As the movement grew, so too did the press attention, especially in the progressive media. *Mother Jones,*[67] *New Republic,*[68] and the *Huffington Post*[69] all published stories on sanctuary. In February 2017, MSNBC ran regular breaking news updates for an entire day about a family taking sanctuary in Colorado, with correspondents reporting live from inside the church.[70] And throughout 2018, *The Nation* penned a "Finding Sanctuary" series, which chronicled—in English and Spanish—one immigrant family's experience taking refuge in a New York City church.[71]

Legacy media caught wind of the phenomenon as well, bringing the cause to the masses. In addition to a 2018 CNN segment on home sanctuary,[72] which included an interview with a coordinating pastor, *The Washington Post*[73] and the *New York Times*[74] ran major stories on the subject. Dave Eggers, author of *The Circle* and *What Is the What*, penned a lengthy account in *The New Yorker* about a Pakistani immigrant family living in sanctuary. His subhead: "An immigrant family hides from Donald Trump in a Connecticut church."[75]

Once a one-off strategy by a tiny congregation, sanctuary had become the secret weapon of the Resistance.

BACKLASH TO THE BACKLASH

The New Sanctuary movement has become the central pole uplifting a much grander, faith-based, immigrant-justice tent that is neither new nor uniformly progressive. It had set up camp in the American consciousness before: an anomalous union of the Religious Left and the Religious Right, bolstered by the work of the Evangelical Immigration Table,[76] drove the push for immigration reform in 2013.

Their efforts failed, but Trump managed to give the faith-based immigration rights movement an unexpected shot in the arm in the way only The Donald can: by being openly, shockingly antagonistic toward religious support for immigrants.

One of the earliest instances came in February 2016, when Trump was riding high off his victory in the New Hampshire primary. So brazen was then candidate Trump's dismissal of religious activism on behalf of immigrants that he picked a fight with, of all people, the pope. In an interview with Fox Business Network, he called the pontiff a "political person" for praying with undocumented immigrants and immigration activists along the US-Mexico border and went on to imply that Mexico "got [Pope Francis] to do it" for financial reasons.[77]

His shot did not go unanswered. When Pope Francis was asked by a journalist a few days later about Trump's remarks and his immigration policies, he challenged the businessman's faith: "A person who thinks only about building walls, wherever they may be, and not building bridges, is not Christian."[78]

It was a theological clapback to end all theological clapbacks, although it did little to stymie Trump's ascension. If anything, the first two years of Trump's administration were *defined* by an adversarial posture toward faith groups that challenged his immigration policies.

This generated some gains for Trump and his allies but gravely miscalculated the growing influence of faith voices on debates over immigrant rights. The most dramatic example came in 2018, when the Trump administration implemented a zero tolerance policy that separated immigrant children from their families once they crossed the US-Mexico border to seek asylum. Faith-based pushback from immigration-focused groups such as Church World Service came swiftly,[79] followed by a letter condemning the policy that was signed by several prominent interfaith leaders, including Rabbi Rick Jacobs, president of the Union for Reform Judaism; the Rev. Dr. J. Herbert Nelson II, the stated clerk of Presbyterian Church (USA); and the Most Rev. Michael B. Curry, presiding bishop of the Episcopal Church. Not to be outdone, members of the US Conference of

Catholic Bishops suggested invoking "canonical penalties"—which range from a denial of sacraments to excommunication—for government officials who participate in zero tolerance.[80]

Even this blistering religious criticism paled in comparison to the firestorm that erupted after the Trump administration's next faith flub. Attorney General Jeff Sessions, seemingly rankled by the faith-fueled outrage, attempted to address his censure by "church friends" and justify the border policy by using scripture.

"I would cite you to the apostle Paul and his clear and wise command in Romans 13, to obey the laws of the government because God has ordained them for the purpose of order," he said, speaking during an event in Indiana.[81] "Orderly and lawful processes are good in themselves and protect the weak and lawful."

White House press secretary Sarah Huckabee Sanders backed up Sessions's comments that same day, saying, "I can say that it is very biblical to enforce the law. That is actually repeated a number of times throughout the Bible."[82]

American religious groups did not agree.

On the contrary, Sessions's attempt at theological debate quickly became one of the biggest embarrassments of Trump's young administration. Progressive activist groups and denominations alike rushed to condemn the argument, the undergirding policy, or both as immoral, with Quakers,[83] the Sikh Coalition,[84] and Methodist bishops[85] voicing outrage alongside Faith in Public Life,[86] leaders of the Poor People's Campaign (both William Barber and Liz Theoharis),[87] and a group of western Buddhists.[88] Conservative traditions also spoke out, with the Church of the Nazarene,[89] the Southern Baptist Convention,[90] and the Church of Jesus Christ of Latter-day Saints all publishing strongly worded refutations.[91] Even Trump's own religious allies, typically loath to criticize him or his administration, made their discomfort known: The Rev. Franklin Graham called the practice of family separation "disgraceful";[92] Johnnie Moore, the de facto spokesman for Trump's evangelical advisers, declared that Sessions "is no theologian";[93] and Rev. Samuel Rodriguez, who prayed at Trump's inauguration, signed on to an Evangelical Immigration Table letter decrying the policy as "horrible."[94]

It was, without question, the single most uniform theological denunciation of a policy I have ever encountered as a religion journalist.

The debacle rapidly eroded the Trump administration's claim to the moral high ground on immigration, but people of faith weren't done. More than six hundred Methodists signed a formal church complaint against Sessions (who is also Methodist), requesting that the UMC take formal action against him for implementing the policy. The denominational charges they levied were serious: child abuse, immorality, racial discrimination, and "dissemination of doctrines contrary to the standards of doctrine of the United Methodist Church."[95]

The charges were ultimately dismissed,[96] but the public relations chaos surrounding the family separation policy would haunt Sessions for the rest of his term as attorney general. So, too, would the outrage of faith groups: when Sessions attempted to deliver a speech on religious freedom in Boston in October 2018, he was interrupted by two progressive-leaning pastors.[97] Police forcibly removed the two from the banquet hall as they shouted Bible passages such as "I was a stranger, and you did not welcome me" and called on Sessions to repent. As police escorted them past the television cameras of national cable outlets, Sessions described their protest as an "attack."[98]

When Sessions resigned a little more than a week later, even *Saturday Night Live* acknowledged the role faith played in his ousting. In a satirical skit mocking the former Alabama senator's short tenure as attorney general, a forlorn Sessions (portrayed by comedian Kate McKinnon) sullenly packed up his belongings to leave his office for the last time. Naturally, the first object he grabbed was a Bible.

"My trusty Bible," said McKinnon/Sessions, holding the sacred text aloft. "I justified a lot of bad things with this book!"[99]

These and other moments added weight to the Religious Left's argument and emboldened faith-based advocates for more intense

immigration fights to come. When Trump focused national attention on immigration ahead of the 2018 midterm election by deriding caravans of Central American migrants then approaching the
southern border, several groups of faith leaders assembled their own
faith caravans to offer them aid. By December, hundreds of faith
leaders—including Liz Theoharis, Traci Blackmon, and Methodist
bishop Minerva Carcaño—led a procession to the vestigial end of the
US-Mexico border fence, which stretches along the beach near San
Diego and extends into the frothing ocean. Some clergy broke away
from the main group and directly confronted a line of armored, gun-
toting US Customs and Border Protection agents along the beach,
singing and praying in front of them for nearly two hours. A few
knelt and some stood in the surf before the guards, letting the waves
crash against them as they closed their eyes in prayerful ululation.

"Rise up my people, my condors, my eagles! No human being
will ever be illegal!" they sang.

In the end, more than thirty activists were detained. Video of the
event showed officials tugging some faith leaders headfirst onto the
beach and dragging them through the sand before wrenching their
arms behind their backs and binding their wrists.[100]

It was yet another example of the poetry of protest, and activists who were there told me that many of their number shared a
common thread: their worship communities were participants in the
New Sanctuary movement. Theoharis noted that just weeks before
the border protest, twenty-seven members of the CityWell Church
in Durham, North Carolina, had been arrested after they confronted
ICE officials who were detaining Samuel Oliver-Bruno, an undocumented Mexican immigrant. Oliver-Bruno had lived inside the
United Methodist Church for more than a year, but left briefly—
accompanied by congregants and their pastor—for a scheduled
meeting with immigration officials in nearby Morrisville. When ICE
agents detained him unexpectedly, congregants rushed to the parking
lot and surrounded the officials' van for two hours, refusing to move
until they, too, were arrested.[101]

Hundreds later gathered at the detention center in Raleigh to demand Oliver-Bruno's release, among them Jonathan Wilson-Hartgrove and William Barber. Barber laid out precisely why ICE's actions, fueled by the Trump administration's policies, served only to strengthen their cause.

"Evil always goes too far," he told the crowd.[102] "The pride cometh before the fall. And these dark moments now, where we see what's happening on the border, and we see what happens in Morrisville, may just be the birth pangs of our deliverance. . . . We may one day even have to say, 'Thank God that they touched Samuel [Oliver-Bruno].' . . . Because in that moment, evil and wrong went too far. And instead of shutting us down, their actions increased, intensified, and emboldened our activism."

Back in Tucson, the lawyer who helped birth the New Sanctuary movement now has misgivings about its use. Margo Cowan told me in 2019 that she no longer recommends public sanctuary, arguing that under the Trump administration it has "no positive results other than to put a bull's-eye" on most churches. She instead suggests private or home sanctuary, reasoning that it stands a better chance of directly benefiting an immigrant at risk of deportation. The point is to help, she says, noting that Neyoy Ruiz has since left the US after an amicable separation with his wife, returning to Mexico to be with his aging parents, who are both evangelical pastors. Cowan said that affording immigrants the right to make those kinds of simple life choices—ones US citizens too often take for granted—is at the core of her activism.

"That's the essence: people should be able to choose, and people should be able to move freely," she said.[103]

Over at Southside, Harrington and her tiny church never stopped advocating for the undocumented or, for that matter, decrying the Trump administration. Among other things, they organized a demonstration inside a local congresswoman's office—a playdate with children and their parents—to protest family separation.[104]

The endless stream of activism was exhausting, especially in an era of protest fatigue, as progressives scrambled to respond to a seemingly infinite barrage of crises under Trump.[105] But when I asked Harrington what motivated her, she offered a characteristically matter-of-fact answer that captured how giving up simply isn't an option.

"We're commanded to do this work," Harrington said.[106]

As long and difficult as the fight for immigrant rights may prove to be, many activists, immigrants, and scientists acknowledge a much larger, far more ominous phenomenon lurking in the background. It's one that experts say played a critical role in precipitating the Syrian refugee crisis that triggered Trump's travel ban, the migrant caravans that journeyed to the southern US border, and various mass migrations all over the planet: climate change.[107]

It's a daunting problem that secular-minded activists have spent years trying to humanize in order to capture national interest. But as progressive environmentalists recently learned, sparking the attention of the masses just required bottling the same lightning that galvanized the New Sanctuary movement—faith.

★ ★ ★

CHAPTER SEVEN

Creation Care

I once asked Native Hawaiian activist Joshua Lanakila Mangauil to explain the connection between his religious beliefs and his environmental advocacy. I think about his answer a lot.

"There is no separation from our spirituality and our environment—they are one and the same," he told me in 2016. I had reached him by phone at his home on the "Big Island" of Hawaii, where he runs the Hawaiian Cultural Center of Hamakua. I was interviewing him for what I thought would be a straightforward *ThinkProgress* piece on Indigenous spiritual movements, but Mangauil quickly reminded me that concepts of the divine are rarely uncomplicated: "Other religious groups have these debates over whether or not God exists—but I know my god exists. It's the mountain. I can *see* it."[1]

I could still hear his words repeating in my head three years later as I stared up at the Big Island mountain Mangauil called god: the towering peak of Mauna Kea. Sitting on the hood of a tiny rental car, I buttoned my travel-crumpled winter flannel and shielded my eyes as the first rays of dawn sunlight bounced off the black-and-green-streaked fields that wrapped around the base of the dormant volcano. There to cover the growing protest movement against the construction of the Thirty Meter Telescope (TMT) at the alp's summit, I watched hundreds of people emerge from rows of multicolored tents scattered across a crag of dried lava that more closely resembled a barren Martian landscape than a swath of Pacific paradise. The crowd blinked away sleep and slipped on heavy jackets to shield goose-pimpled skin from the morning chill, then meandered to a narrow access road that stretched up the mountainside.

I hopped off the car and followed from a distance, observing silently as they filled the small patch of asphalt directly in front of a tent occupied by *kupuna*, or Native Hawaiian elders. Suddenly, a man began shouting directions in the Hawaiian tongue, and a small symphony of horns crafted from wood and seashells droned four times. With each bellow, the crowd shifted to face a different direction.

Finally, after a complete revolution, they turned to face the mountain, its peaks just visible through a thin trail of tumbling rainclouds. Then they began to pray.

This was not how many Americans would envision an environmental protest. Technically, most in the camp wouldn't even use that term, preferring to describe themselves as *kia'i*, meaning "protectors," and their actions as a protection, not a demonstration. Yet their ceremony—performed multiple times a day—was an act of defiance all the same.

Earth-focused spiritual beliefs, like those of Native Hawaiians, predate the founding of the United States by several millennia. But they have achieved a new, politically influential relevance in recent years, especially among Indigenous communities. Through a series of dramatic protests rooted in claims that certain lands and waterways are sacred and worthy of protection, Indigenous protectors in Hawaii, North Dakota, and beyond have caught the eye of popes, politicians, and the progressive masses. The sheer magnetism of their spiritual activism has lit a fire underneath at least three burgeoning global movements at once: faith-rooted support for environmentalism, the push for Indigenous rights, and the campaign for climate justice.

I had caught murmurings of this Indigenous phenomenon for years while covering environmental protests. It was always passionate, but often piecemeal—sometimes proclaimed loudly from demonstration stages, more often relegated to the fringes. But as Indigenous activists grow more unified in their message, their influence over progressive politics is becoming more difficult to ignore. Others are now echoing their political vision, which mixes centuries-old denouncements of colonialism and empire with modern economic critiques of capitalism and its connection to climate change, all while extolling the power of prayer.

But to properly interpret the prayers of mountain protectors on a sunny, far-flung Pacific island—and decipher their significance within the broader environmentalist movement—one must first unpack what happened three years earlier along the banks of a cold North Dakota river.

★　★　★

For Chase Iron Eyes, one of the most memorable days of the Standing Rock protests began, fittingly, with water.

It was 2016, and he was just trying to enjoy a day with his kids. Family bonding was a coveted commodity for the Oglala Sioux lawyer and activist, especially since he also happened to be running for North Dakota's single congressional seat. Political campaigns typically don't lend themselves to lengthy personal outings, but he'd carved out the time anyway, which is why he found himself out on the water in a boat surrounded by his children when his phone rang.

On the line was a community member. He informed Iron Eyes that his spouse, Dr. Sara Jumping Eagle, had been arrested and led away in handcuffs by police at the construction site of the Dakota Access Pipeline (DAPL).

"My wife, she's not the type of person that could stand to see this trespass happen against us, this degradation," he told me. "We're all spirits, and a spirit is naturally inclined to seek a liberation."[2]

North Dakota would soon become a haven for such spirits. Jumping Eagle was one of more than four hundred people arrested that year in and around Cannon Ball, which sits within the Standing Rock Indian Reservation, where Iron Eyes grew up.[3] By the end of 2016, an estimated ten thousand others had descended on the region to sing, pray, and protest the DAPL, a project of Energy Transfer Partners, a Texas-based corporation.[4]

It was a seismic response to what was supposed to be a relatively uncontentious addition to America's ever-expanding energy infrastructure. The plan called for a more than thousand-mile run of pipe that would stretch across the Midwest before linking up with an existing pipeline to funnel crude oil from the Bakken Formation to refineries along the Gulf of Mexico.

But the proposed path of the DAPL burrowed beneath Lake Oahe, which sits less than a mile from the Standing Rock Sioux reservation. A potential spill, Standing Rock Sioux leaders argued, would threaten their water supply as well as lands that their people deemed sacred. Unsettled, tribal chairman Dave Archambault II and others pushed the Obama administration to pursue a requisite consultation process with the local Indigenous nation. It was a move with the potential to halt construction, but it quickly became clear that bureaucracy alone couldn't stop what some believed to be a prophesized "black snake."[5]

"When we were children, we always heard stories of the black snake that would come to destroy the world," said Lakota historian and elder LaDonna Brave Bull Allard, who lives at Standing Rock.[6] "When an oil spill happens, it destroys the environment; it destroys the earth; it destroys the animals, the insects, the plants, the medicines. It destroys the land. . . . And they said, 'Aha, that is what it is.'"

A spiritual threat, she reasoned, merited a spiritual response.

"When we first started talking about what was happening with the pipeline, we went into ceremony, we went into prayer," Allard recalled.

The ensuing battle over the pipeline's construction sparked a series of dramatic, sometimes harrowing showdowns between authorities and protesters, who preferred the term "water protectors." The #NoDAPL campaign, as it came to be called, would capture the hearts of hard-line progressives and the attention of national news outlets, serving as a boon for the environmental and Indigenous rights movements.

Yet few focused on the intense, pervasive religious undercurrent that fueled much of the support for those in Standing Rock. In fact, the demonstrations amounted to one of the most unabashedly *spiritual* progressive-leaning movements of the twenty-first century, drawing strength from a spiritual core that capitalizes on a broader religion-rooted campaign to protect the planet.

This movement didn't spring into action overnight, of course. The road map for confronting issues as large as climate change or challenging the immense power of the oil industry often features a tangled web of one-way streets and dead ends. This was especially true early on in the #NoDAPL fight, when Iron Eyes and others in Standing Rock faced days tinged with dread and defeatism.

"I remember going to those initial community meetings and not knowing what the hell we were going to do, how we were going to even stand up to 'big extraction,' 'big financial'—essentially the economic reality that rules the globe," he said.[7]

The pipeline threat reminded him of when European colonizers decimated Native American populations, invoking Christian theological ideas such as Manifest Destiny and its older cousin, the Doctrine of Discovery. Both beliefs anointed European colonialism and the American westward expansion with a spiritual justification for enacting systemic violence against Indigenous populations, whether by war, murder, or various forms of subjugation. Taking dominion over lands and the people that lived there, the logic went, wasn't just encouraged. It was a spiritual *mission*.

Iron Eyes drew a direct connection between the Dakota Access Pipeline and the Doctrine of Discovery, a concept first elucidated through a series of papal bulls issued by Pope Alexander VI in 1493. The doctrine has become an oft-referenced source of frustration among modern Indigenous activists like Iron Eyes, who described it as something the pope and his advisers "invented in order to justify legally, in their minds, the acquisition, enslavement, and genocide of people that were not like them." To him, the pipeline fight was simply "another coming of that." The difference this time was that the cold, hard verbiage of secular law and economics had replaced the language of spiritual conquest.

Conversely, protectors in North Dakota turned to their spiritual traditions to aid their fight against the pipeline. On April 1, 2016, they established a "spirit camp" in Allard's backyard, near the pipeline construction site, to serve as a staging area for protests and spiritual resistance. Later, they renamed it the Sacred Stone Camp, with leaders inaugurating it with pipe ceremonies, prayers, and blessings for the ground.[8]

Tribal chairman Archambault noted that while "prayer was present before any demonstrations," because it had undergirded Indigenous ways of life for eons, it also provided a common spiritual language for demonstrators who came into town to support the #NoDAPL campaign.

"It was a prayer camp: they'd bring their songs and bring their prayers, and they'd share," Archambault said.[9]

Tensions escalated in November, when construction crews began bulldozing a location that the water protectors reportedly identified as a sacred burial ground. Several demonstrators subsequently gathered in prayer before marching to the construction site with a small band of journalists in tow. After a few heated exchanges between protectors and construction staff, Indigenous activists broke through makeshift fences and confronted the workers, who called over private security officers. When the protectors pressed forward, security forces blasted their faces with pepper spray and released attack dogs into the crowd. Several participants were bitten, and cameras captured haunting images of snarling dogs, their snouts slathered with thick blood.[10]

Footage of the incident, which circulated on social media, thrust the Standing Rock demonstrations back into the national spotlight.[11] Camera crews from major news outlets rushed to North Dakota, where they found multiple thriving prayer camps dotted with tepees and prayer poles patrolled by Native Americans on horseback. The #NoDAPL fight had caught fire with Indigenous groups across the country, and the thousands of water protectors included members of more than three hundred federally recognized Native American tribes.[12]

"The spirit camp was busting at its seams," Archambault recalled.

AN INDIGENOUS CONSENSUS

The massive turnout at Standing Rock was something of a departure in the complicated history of twentieth-century Native American protest movements. Indigenous people are sometimes painted with a broad brush, lumped together in the minds of many Americans as a pantribal culture with a shared identity. The truth is dizzyingly more complicated: Native Americans, Native Alaskans, and Native Hawaiians all claim distinct histories and spiritual identities, as do various individual tribes and nations.

This hasn't stopped tribes on the continent from launching unified campaigns, of course, such as when Indigenous people banded together to form the American Indian Movement in 1968. Over the course of the next decade, Indigenous activists occupied Alcatraz Island in San Francisco Bay and the village of Wounded Knee in South Dakota, among other initiatives.[13] But infighting and factionalism eventually marred these powerful attempts at forging solidarity and political influence across cultural and tribal differences. The American Indian Movement has since split into at least two subgroups, and activists have struggled to find a unifying cause that would capture national attention for longer than a single news cycle. Add the logistical challenge of orchestrating campaigns across national boundaries—not to mention oceans—and it's easy to see why movement building in Indigenous communities remains a daunting task.

But in the years just prior to Standing Rock, something changed. In December 2012, four women in western Canada convened a teach-in to protest legislation that would erode approval and consultation processes required for construction near bodies of water in the country. Declaring that the change would disproportionately impact land sacred to First Nations people, the three First Nations women and their non-Indigenous ally called the protest Idle No More.

Discussion of the demonstration flooded social media, triggering waves of marches, peaceful protests, spiritual dance flash mobs, and solidarity demonstrations by Native American groups in the US.[14] The response set in motion a resurgence of Indigenous activism across North America and parts of the Pacific that was not only environmental in its scope but also often unapologetically religious (although some within the movement prefer the term *spiritual*). Indigenous activists joined other environmentalists in 2012 to demonstrate against the Keystone XL pipeline, with some creating a spirit camp at Cheyenne River Reservation in South Dakota near the construction route where activists prayed and taught classes in civil disobedience.[15] Archambault personally lobbied President Obama to halt the construction of the pipeline, and activists marched through Washington, DC, carrying signs that read "President Obama: Protect our Sacred Water."[16] Inspired, Native Hawaiians rallied the following year to halt the construction of the Thirty Meter Telescope on top of the volcano Mauna Kea, which they consider sacred. And in 2015, members of the Apache nation occupied land near a proposed copper mine at Oak Flat, Arizona—an area they describe as holy.[17]

Indigenous advocates repeatedly invoked Idle No More at these demonstrations, often posting the same slogans on social media or shouting the same chants at rallies. Activists from various tribes and traditions began crisscrossing the country—even from Hawaii—to show up in solidarity at each other's events, hoping to raise awareness of different causes.

Religion came up over and over again in my coverage of these demonstrations. When I called activists or visited protests, I usually didn't even ask participants about faith—they brought it up themselves, telling me that their religion and activism were one in the same. "Idle No More raised our consciousness," Caro "Guarding Red Tarantula Woman" Gonzales, a Standing Rock water protector of the Chemehuevi nation, told me during a 2016 *ThinkProgress* interview.[18] "When people are chaining themselves to bulldozers, that is prayer."

Spirituality lay at the core of their environmental activism, many told me, because while Indigenous spiritual traditions are diverse, they often share a common belief that the earth, in whole or in part, is sacred.

"While European philosophers were arguing over whether God

is separate from nature . . . our language doesn't even allow us to have that separation," Iron Eyes said.[19]

As explicit as many Indigenous faith claims are, advocates insist the US legal system fails to grant Indigenous people and their spiritual beliefs the same rights and privileges afforded to other religious groups. In the late 1980s, two Supreme Court cases—*Lyng v. Northwest Indian Cemetery Protective Association* and *Employment Division v. Smith*—drew national attention to this disparity. *Lyng* granted the US Forest Service the right to build a road through a region of California, despite a First Amendment claim by Yurok, Tolowa, and Karok tribes, who had considered the region sacred for more than two hundred years and who used it to gather materials for prayer ceremonies.[20] In *Smith*, the court upheld the state of Oregon's claim that it did not have to provide unemployment benefits to two Native Americans who were fired after they tested positive for traces of mescaline, a compound found in the illegal drug peyote, which they used as part of a religious ceremony.[21] *Smith* in particular incensed the general public, and Congress responded by passing the Religious Freedom Restoration Act of 1993 (RFRA) to overrule the decision and return the legal concept of religious liberty to a pre-*Smith* era.[22]

But Native Americans rarely win in legal courts—even when invoking the RFRA—and the #NoDAPL movement stood a far better chance of winning in the court of public opinion. Images of water protectors clashing with police and security guards garnered sympathy for their cause; it attracted the attention of the broader environmentalist movement and, more crucially, a resurgent interfaith campaign for ecological justice.

"I think the faith community is the strongest source of allies that we have," Iron Eyes told me.[23]

Iron Eyes was quick to cite the complicated nature of exchanges between Indigenous spiritual traditions and those adopted by colonizers—especially Christians. He felt that modern religious leaders needed to adapt so that they "no longer consider that [they] have a God-given right to dominate nature."

As it turned out, there was a wide array of religious leaders from non-Indigenous faiths that agreed with him, making the #NoDAPL campaign a unique opportunity to forge dialogue between different environmentally conscience spiritual movements. To wit, when I asked Iron Eyes for an example of someone who had already made this spiritual pivot, he pointed to the environmental writings of a man who now occupies the office that once crafted the Doctrine of Discovery: Pope Francis.

"Pope Francis is dope," Iron Eyes said.

ENCYCLICAL ENVIRONMENTALISM

When Cardinal Jorge Mario Bergoglio was elected pope on March 13, 2013, the reaction from the global Catholic community trended toward collective uncertainty. It wasn't that people had particularly strong feelings about the Argentine cleric, although many appeared elated about the first Latin American pope. It was that most of the world's more than one billion Catholics simply didn't know who he was and were uncertain as to what kind of agenda he would pursue.

All that changed six days later, when Bergoglio, now known as Pope Francis, delivered a homily at his inaugural mass in Saint Peter's Square. He spoke to a crowd of more than 150,000 people, which included 132 government delegations (a shades-wearing Vice President Joe Biden among them) and representatives from virtually all major global faiths.[24] Over the course of just a few minutes, he called on world leaders and his fellow Catholics to be "protectors" for God—specifically, protectors of the poor, the weak, and the planet.

"Please, I would like to ask all those who have positions of responsibility in economic, political, and social life, and all men and women of goodwill: let us be 'protectors' of creation, protectors of God's plan inscribed in nature, protectors of one another and of the environment," he declared.[25]

It was a sign of things to come for the pontiff, who went on to achieve enormous popularity for simultaneously voicing a concern for the poor *and* the planet. Within a year he was making headlines for holding scholarly summits on climate change at the Vatican and warning his fellow believers, "If we destroy Creation, Creation will destroy us!"[26]

His earth-focused theology struck a chord with Catholics and non-Catholics who already embraced the scientific consensus on climate change, including faithful in the United States. A 2014 PRRI survey conducted around the time of Francis's elevation found that Hispanic Catholics, not the religiously unaffiliated, were the group most distressed about climate change; 73 percent of Hispanics said they were "very" or "somewhat" concerned about climate change. The unaffiliated were next (60 percent), followed closely by Black Protestants (58 percent), non-Christian religions (54 percent), and Jews (53 percent).[27] For these and other religious groups, recognizing the looming threat of climate change while maintaining passionate religious beliefs wasn't strange or unusual. It was their spiritual everyday.

The very existence of these groups challenged lazy arguments that the debate over whether to "believe" climate research was somehow an extension of a wide rift between environmental science and religion. The reality was far more narrowly defined: a rift did exist, but it sliced between the scientific community and *white* Christian Americans. The same PRRI survey found that the groups *least* likely to say they were very or somewhat concerned about climate change were white mainline Protestants (43 percent), white Catholics (42 percent), and white evangelical Protestants (35 percent). Those same groups were also the least likely to hear clergy discussing the issue from their pulpits.[28]

Enter Pope Francis. The pontiff's unyielding rhetoric on climate change had massive political implications, representing an existential threat to white Catholic Republicans, who as a group had carved out a reputation as an intellectual force within conservative circles. Granted, Francis's theology was largely consistent with that of previous popes. Pope John Paul II declared "the *ecological crisis is a moral issue*" (emphasis his) as early as 1990,[29] and Pope Benedict XVI was called the first "green pope" for installing solar panels at the Vatican and speaking out about the dangers of greenhouse gas emissions.[30] But Francis's firebrand tone called into question the relevancy of a politicized conservative Catholicism that appeared far more concerned with contraception than carbon dioxide levels.

Francis's emergence produced awkward moments for public figures like Pennsylvania senator and then GOP presidential candidate Rick Santorum, who had centered his political identity on his conservative Catholicism. During a 2015 appearance on a Philadelphia radio show, when Santorum was asked about Francis's climate talk, he suggested the Catholic Church should stay out of the debate altogether. "The church has gotten it wrong a few times on science," Santorum said.[31] "We probably are better off leaving science to the scientists and focusing on what we're really good at, which is theology and morality."

Santorum was roundly mocked for his comments by progressive outlets such as the *Huffington Post*, inverting the modern conception that dogma-focused Roman Catholicism was the purview of the conservative wing of American politics.[32] The famously sweatered lawmaker's remarks proved even more ironic when Francis published an entire encyclical on the environment—*Laudato Si'*, or "Praise Be to You"—just two weeks later. Francis's encyclical took science seriously, earning acclaim from several climate scientists who said there was "little to disagree with" in its 180-plus pages.[33]

Still, the encyclical's scientific offerings were not its most impactful. What resonated most deeply with Catholics and other people of faith was the document's approach to a long-simmering theological debate among Christians and Jews regarding the nature of humanity's divine responsibility to the planet. For decades, theologians and Bible scholars have clashed over how to interpret Genesis 1:28, in which God instructs Adam and Eve to "fill the earth and subdue it" and "have dominion over the fish of the sea and over the birds of the air and over every living thing that moves upon the earth" (NRSV). The word *dominion* remains a point of contention, with exegetes falling into roughly two camps: religious environmentalists, who insisted that it points to a form of responsible environmental stewardship violated by the wanton use of fossil fuels, and their conservative opponents, who argued that dominion essentially gives humanity *carte blanche* to exploit the earth's resources.

Some conservatives further contend that even if climate change poses a threat, God's divine contract with humanity necessitates that the Almighty will eventually mend all.[34] When Rep. Tim Walberg of Michigan—who attended Moody Bible Institute and Wheaton College, both conservative Christian institutions—was asked by a constituent in 2017 about the looming threat of the planet's changing climate, Walberg invoked God: "As a Christian, I believe that there is a creator in God who is much bigger than us," said the Republican and former Baptist pastor.[35] "And I'm confident that, if there's a real problem, he can take care of it."

Laudato Si' first questioned such interpretations, then directly refuted them.[36] Francis put the might and authority of the Bishop of Rome behind the belief that God calls on humans to be stewards of the earth, and he planted his papal flag firmly in the environmentalist camp, saying:

"We are not God. The earth was here before us and it has been given to us. This allows us to respond to the charge that Judaeo-Christian thinking, on the basis of the Genesis account which grants man 'dominion' over the earth (cf. Gen 1:28), has encouraged the unbridled exploitation of nature by painting him as domineering and destructive by nature. This is not a correct interpretation of the Bible as understood by the Church. Although it is true that we Christians have at times incorrectly interpreted the Scriptures, nowadays we must forcefully reject the notion that our being created in God's image and given dominion over the earth justifies absolute domination over other creatures."

It was decisive rhetoric that helped legitimize the views of millions of Americans who argued that taking bold action to address climate change wasn't a position they held *in spite* of their faith but rather *precisely because of it.*

Catholics weren't the first religious leaders to use the pulpit to push for climate action in the United States, of course, where a web of faith-and-climate groups was already active. Interfaith Power and Light (IPL), founded in 1998 as a project of a few Episcopal churches in California, had grown steadily into a nationwide interfaith network that comprised forty state affiliates and twenty thousand congregations.[37] By the time Francis released his encyclical, IPL boasted decades of experience heading eco-justice campaigns; it had encouraged worship communities to go green by installing solar panels, fought against mountaintop removal in North Carolina,[38] and met with lawmakers at every level to lobby for legislation that would protect the environment.[39]

IPL's activism drew strength from a thick forest of theologies that shared a common concern for ecological caretaking. In Christian contexts, IPL and other groups espoused what is often called creation care theology, which pulls from concepts of stewardship and caring for God's creation and which often stresses the same scripture passages cited by Francis. Eco-conscious Jews sometimes cite the same verses, but they lean also on Jewish concepts such as *tikkun olam*, which in Hebrew means "Repair the world." Creation care appears also in Muslim climate activism: in 2008, the Islamic Environmental Group of Wisconsin partnered with a local IPL affiliate and encouraged local mosques to reduce their carbon footprint,[40] drawing inspiration from the Qur'an passage "He it is (God) Who appointed you vice-regents upon the earth."[41] Buddhists, Sikhs, and others draw on similar themes, albeit with different terms.

When *Laudato Si'* was published, IPL and other faith-rooted groups in the United States and across the globe pushed its message as far as it could go. IPL partnered with the Catholic Climate Covenant to produce an action kit that congregations could use to respond to the encyclical (for example, by lobbying Congress to apportion resources for the Green Climate Fund, a United Nations project that helps developing countries adapt to climate change).[42] Meanwhile, the Global Buddhist Climate Change Collective published a statement citing *Laudato Si'* and calling on world leaders to completely phase out fossil fuels. The statement was signed by the Dalai Lama,

Thích Nhất Hạnh, and such American leaders as Buddhist Association of the USA president Bhikkhu Bodhi.[43] (Both Bodhi and Rev. angel Kyodo williams had delivered talks at the White House earlier that year on climate change.)[44]

The general public may have been unaware of these groups, but hardcore climate activists had been partnering with them for years. Throughout the 2000s, the Sierra Club produced reports on religious eco-justice movements and promoted *The Green Bible*, which highlighted environmental passages in green and included commentary from progressive faith leaders such as Brian McLaren.[45] Shortly after Pope Francis delivered his encyclical, Bill McKibben, one of America's most renowned environmentalists (and a onetime United Methodist Sunday school teacher), penned an opinion piece for the *Boston Globe* titled "What Religion Can Teach Climate Scientists."[46] And Dr. Katharine Hayhoe, a premier climate scientist turned activist and one of *TIME* magazine's "100 Most Influential People" in 2014, lectures frequently on the intersection of religion and climate concerns from an evangelical Christian perspective.

Arguably the most prominent American religious environmentalist, however, is Al Gore, the former vice president, who reinvigorated the climate movement with his landmark film, *An Inconvenient Truth*. Gore, a divinity school dropout, led trainings for Christian, Muslim, Jewish, and Hindu climate activists eager to frame environmental issues in religious terms. "I trained two hundred Christian ministers and lay leaders here in Nashville in a version of the slide show that is filled with scriptural references," he told *Newsweek* in 2009.[47] "It's probably my favorite version, but I don't use it very often because it can come off as proselytizing."

In his 2015 encyclical, Pope Francis did not share Gore's reticence to fusing climate and spiritual matters, nor did he avoid matters of faith when he visited the United States later that year. During his first address on US soil, the pope spent most of his time talking about climate change while standing next to President Barack Obama on the White House lawn. The religious message was not lost on Obama, who celebrated the pontiff's "call to all world leaders to support the communities most vulnerable to changing climate,"[48] nor on White House press secretary Josh Earnest, who told reporters that Francis "was speaking with a passion and a conviction about the need to act on climate issues that was deeply rooted in his faith."[49]

By that point, support for *Laudato Si'* had become something of a litmus test for Democrats. After the encyclical was released, billionaire Democratic donor Tom Steyer praised both the papal letter and long-shot presidential candidate Martin O'Malley, arguing that the Maryland governor's climate policies were an example of American politicians "heeding [the pope's] call to action."[50] Other 2016 Democratic contenders senator Bernie Sanders and former secretary of state Hillary Clinton got the hint: both eventually lavished Francis with praise in different ways. Sanders embarked on a successful effort to meet the pontiff in Rome,[51] while Clinton took the less dramatic route of publishing an op-ed in the *National Catholic Reporter* titled "Heed Francis's Message: Be Good Stewards of the Earth."

"I'm grateful—as so many Americans are—for the pope's teachings," she wrote. "And as president, I hope to follow his example. I will make combating climate change a top priority of my administration."[52]

Meanwhile, Republicans suddenly found themselves on the defensive when discussing religion and continued to wrestle with how to react to the surge of spiritual environmentalism. Rep. Paul Gosar, an Arizona Republican and a self-described "proud Catholic," published a letter ahead of the pope's US visit expressing his intention to boycott the Holy Father's address before Congress. His reason? Francis's stance on climate change.

"Troubling is the fact that [the pope's] climate change talk has adopted all of the socialist talking points, wrapped false science and ideology into 'climate justice,' and is being presented to guilt people into leftist policies." he wrote.[53] "When the Pope chooses to act and talk like a leftist politician, then he can expect to be treated like one."

And just like that, the decades-old claim of spiritual dominion by the Religious Right in American politics began to slip away. Environmentalism and climate change had emerged as a religious issue—a *progressive* religious issue.

(SPIRITUAL) POWERS COMBINE

If Francis's *Laudato Si'* grafted institutional support to the tender sapling of religious environmentalism, then Standing Rock offered it a space to bloom into a full-on movement. It just needed some cultivating in the form of reconciliation.

In October 2016, Chief Arvol Looking Horse of the Lakota, Dakota, and Nakota nations called on faith leaders of all traditions to assemble at the camp. He cited fears that an influx of police and National Guard troops could pose a threat to younger demonstrators who were "standing in prayer."[54] Faith leaders, he argued, could help de-escalate the situation.

The invitation provided Christian clergy an opportunity to forge new alliances with Indigenous peoples and create a space in which to do the work of healing—or at least addressing—centuries-old wounds. A few days after the invitation video was posted, a group of more than five hundred interfaith clergy came to the camp to march, protest, and express solidarity with the water protectors and their cause. At one point, members of multiple faith traditions— including Episcopalians, Methodists, Lutherans, Presbyterians, and other Christian denominations—stood and read messages in support of those in Standing Rock or in repudiation of the Doctrine of Discovery. They then handed paper copies of the fifteenth-century document to elders in the Oceti Sakowin Camp—one of the largest of the protest camps—and asked if they would like to destroy it in a fire.[55]

"Burn it," one elder replied.[56]

As one of the documents was held aloft and set aflame, the crowd erupted in celebration.[57]

The moment culminated years of activism by Indigenous communities, which included many Christians in their ranks. Like other subgroups of the Religious Left, Native American Christians claim their own strain of liberation theology, penned by scholars like Lutheran pastor George "Tink" Tinker of the Osage nation. Other prominent voices include Mark Charles, a former minister and Navajo citizen, who wrote at length about the Doctrine of Discovery throughout the 2010s, penning pieces for such left-leaning religious publications as the blog *Red Letter Christians*.[58] By the time faith leaders marched into Standing Rock, at least six denominations and the World Council of Churches had repudiated the Doctrine of Discovery and issued reports acknowledging their complicity in the subjugation of Indigenous people.

The cause reached Pope Francis as well. In 2016, an Indigenous delegation traveled to Rome, where they met with Francis and his staff to implore the Holy Father to revoke the Doctrine of Discovery.[59] He did not, and Francis still has amends to make regarding his relationship with Indigenous populations in North America: he angered many in 2015 by canonizing Junípero Serra—a Roman Catholic Spanish priest who scholars such as Tinker say enslaved Native Americans.[60]

But the pope has also lifted up the concerns of Indigenous peoples throughout his papacy, so much so that Archambault sent the pope a video message in 2016,[61] thanking him for expressing a desire to "be a spokesperson for the deepest longings of Indigenous peoples . . . who are threatened in their identity and in their existence."[62] Archambault's message explained the situation in Standing Rock, where water protectors like Iron Eyes and others reportedly saw the pontiff as a spiritual ally. He asked the pope for his prayers, even as he repeated their request that he formally revoke the Doctrine of Discovery.[63]

Francis never responded directly to the message, but he did offer remarks on the issue of sacred lands a few months later. While greeting a group of Indigenous peoples at an international forum on agriculture development in early 2017, Francis spoke of the need to "reconcile the right to development . . . with the protection of the particular characteristics of Indigenous peoples and their territories." He explained this tension was "especially clear when planning economic activities which may interfere with Indigenous cultures and their ancestral relationship to the earth."[64]

The comments were widely seen as tacit support for Standing

Rock water protectors and their cause. Unfortunately for activists, Francis, who had publicly sparred with candidate Trump on immigration, had little if any sway over the president's administration, which had already taken steps to approve final permits for both the Dakota Access and Keystone XL pipelines.[65]

Low on conventional options, the #NoDAPL legal team finally made an unusual play in the form of a RFRA claim. In early 2017, the Standing Rock Sioux and Cheyenne River Sioux tribes jointly filed for a temporary restraining order to halt the construction of the Dakota Access Pipeline, arguing that the project violated the RFRA.[66]

"Our feeling about ritually pure water [is that it] should be considered to be exactly the same as a Jewish person's right to have kosher food or a Catholic person's right to take the sacrament," Nicole Ducheneaux, an attorney and member of the Cheyenne River Sioux, told the progressive magazine *In These Times*.[67] "Our hope is to jump in and say: Hey, if Hobby Lobby can expand the RFRA in the context of a major Western religion, you can understand how that expanded context also applies to a Native religion."

Yet even when invoking a law created largely *because* Native Americans often lose in the courts, the federal court ruled against the tribes on procedural grounds, adding another case to the long, frustrating history of Native American legal defeats.[68] There were more arrests in the demonstration's last days—including Iron Eyes, who lost his 2016 bid for Congress. On February 22, 2017, authorities finally expelled the water protectors from the main camp (most left voluntarily, with only a few arrested), and the first oil flowed through the finished pipeline later that summer.[69] A judge ordered an additional environmental review of the Dakota Access pipeline in June 2017, but the Trump administration rejected environmental concerns a little over a year later, arguing that the review didn't expose new issues.[70]

It was a crushing blow for the #NoDAPL efforts, which had also become known as the Water Is Life movement. But iterations of faith-fueled environmentalism began to spread, even as they faced compounding losses under the Trump administration.

For example, when the route for a planned natural gas pipeline, the Atlantic Sunrise, threatened to cross land owned by the Adorers of the Blood of Christ—a group of Catholic nuns in Pennsylvania— lawyers for the women religious argued that it violated their spiritual beliefs. They explained in court filings that the nuns had adopted a land ethic in 2005 that proclaimed a "long-held religious belief in the 'sacredness of all creation,'" and cited *Laudato Si'*.[71] Like the tribes in Standing Rock, the sisters argued the construction of the pipeline was a violation of the RFRA, and they erected a chapel along the pipeline's designated route. And, just as they did with the tribes, the courts ruled against the nuns. An appeals court ultimately sided with a lower court ruling that the RFRA wasn't applicable because the nuns had not made their religious objections known during the federal administrative process. The sisters appealed to the Supreme Court, but the justices declined to take up the case in 2019.[72]

Meanwhile, Al Gore apparently abandoned his fear of publicly fusing faith and environmentalism in 2019, when he began touring southern churches with Rev. William Barber as part of a Moral Call to Action on the Climate Crisis.[73] Around the same time, Barber gave his full-throated support for Native Americans in Arizona fighting to protect Oak Flat in a Medium post, and made reference to anti-pipeline demonstrations.

"We witnessed what happened after the Keystone XL Pipeline was allowed to drill [near the Lake Traverse Reservation] after all those promises were made about environmental protection, and we do not want to bear witness to that again," Barber wrote, linking to an article detailing reports of oil leaks along the Keystone XL pipeline route.[74]

It goes without saying that faith-rooted environmentalism is only one part of the broader eco-justice movement. Given the global scale of climate change, religious actors alone should hardly be expected to turn the tide (literally) on any number of environmental issues, climate change or otherwise. Yet the contributions of Indigenous spiritual fights to the environmental cause remain profound.

"A lot of people would say we're following the environmentalists," Archambault told me. "But the reality is Indigenous peoples around the world, no matter where you go, have a true understanding of what the environment is—they are the first environmentalists. What the environmentalists are talking about now is something that we have been saying for centuries."

And secular environmentalists, LaDonna Brave Bull Allard pointed out, sometimes have a difficult time parsing the spiritual approach of Indigenous protectors.

"We are still not on the same page with a lot of environmental groups, because they want to talk about the destruction of the environment, or being vegan, or something like that," she said. "They don't get to the core of what the earth is, what the water is, what the air is, what the wind is. There is a spirit in each one of these that we have to acknowledge, an entity greater than self."

And while faith-based repudiations of the Doctrine of Discovery are welcomed, they are sometimes seen as little more than a preliminary step.

"The Doctrine of Discovery is the basis for land titles. If you're going to repudiate the doctrine, you should give some land back," said Mark Charles, who, by 2019, was not only running for president and discussing the Doctrine of Discovery while on the stump,[75] but also publishing a book on the subject.[76]

Even so, the #NoDAPL fight showed the potential for Indigenous communities to unite around local fights in ways that can supercharge at least the Indigenous rights movement, if not broader faith-fueled environmental campaigns.

"Regardless of the outcome, it was probably the most significant and beautiful thing that happened in Indian country," Archambault said. "[It proved] we have the ability to come together and unite. The power of unity, the power of peace, and the power of prayer is present."

★　★　★

Three years after the #NoDAPL campaign hit its peak, I stood on the uneven lava field at Hawaii's Mauna Kea gazing up at a row of flags that flapped in the wind alongside the access road where demonstrators gathered to dance and pray. The string of standards included the banners of various Polynesian islands and symbols adopted by the protectors, such as upside-down Hawaiian flags.

I was focused on one ensign in particular: the flag of the Muckleshoot tribe, a Native American group that hailed from thousands of miles away in the Pacific Northwest. It reminded me of a similar "flag row" of Indigenous banners that waved near the camps at Standing Rock, where members of the Muckleshoot tribe had traveled to protest in 2016.[77] I stared at it while listening absentmindedly to Pua Case, one of the chief organizers at the protest camp, as she addressed the enraptured crowd in front of me. Then I heard her utter a familiar phrase.

"We are the rock standing," Case said. "We are the water protectors."

Such is the curious ripple effect of the Standing Rock water protectors, whose lasting legacy likely isn't what they did (or did not) achieve in North Dakota, but how their spiritual approach to ecojustice inspired an emerging generation of environmental activists and forged a new network of faith-rooted Indigenous protectors.

The rationale for opposing the TMT atop Mauna Kea, for instance, was partly environmental. A court-ordered environmental impact study concluded that previous construction projects on the summit had already had "substantial, significant, and adverse" impacts on the mountain, and protectors insisted that further building would affect nearby aquifers and local wildlife.[78] Marie Alohalani Brown, a religious studies professor at the University of Hawaii at Mānoa and a *kupuna* protector I met at the Mauna Kea camp in 2019, told me that for many Indigenous people—including practitioners of the island's traditional Polynesian spiritual traditions— environmental issues blend with another concern: the belief that the mountain is, quite literally, divine.

"Our shared connection . . . as Indigenous people is our visceral, genealogical connection to the land," she told me. "Especially Polynesians, but even some Native American or First Peoples consider the land and their elder relatives sacred. And the use of prayer, the use of nonviolence—that's a spiritual component, too."

This potent mixture of environmentalism and religion drove

activist Joshua Lanakila Mangauil and others to interrupt a ground-breaking ceremony for the TMT in 2014. It is also largely why they were able to halt construction the following year by gathering hundreds at the mountain to confront authorities, resulting in dozens of arrests.[79] A lengthy legal battle ensued that gave TMT opponents several short-term victories, but the Hawaii Supreme Court ultimately cleared the way for construction to begin in July 2019.

When construction vehicles were preparing to ascend the mountain that month, Native Hawaiians formed a human blockade across the road. Nearly forty blockaders were arrested—most of them *kupuna*, including Brown. Other protectors set out to build a more permanent obstruction along the road: a tent village, where they convened at least four ceremonies, or protocols, a day, each with religious elements such as prayer, song, and dance. Protectors slowly attracted political allies to their cause, including Sen. Elizabeth Warren[80] and spiritual author Marianne Williamson[81]; both Democratic presidential candidates tweeted out solidarity with those at the camp. Hawaii's own representative Tulsi Gabbard also visited the mountain in a show of support, setting up a stark contrast from the 2016 election cycle, when water protectors grew so frustrated with Hillary Clinton's silence on Standing Rock that they gathered outside her campaign headquarters to protest by drumming, singing, and erecting a tepee.[82] (Bernie Sanders came out against the DAPL after losing the 2016 Democratic nomination[83] and his supporters were fixtures at Standing Rock, often wearing Bernie 2016 shirts while helping out at the prayer camps.)[84] Celebrities such as Dwayne ("The Rock") Johnson and Jason (*Aquaman*) Momoa also visited Mauna Kea, and within a month the crowds had ballooned into the thousands.[85]

"In 2015, the biggest action day had just around eight hundred to nine hundred people come to the mountain," Mangauil said. "This round, when we were moving to occupy our position, we were all hoping and praying, 'Oh, I hope we'll get like five hundred people.' We're seeing numbers on the *mauna* in the thousands—three, four, even five thousand strong coming to the mountain, and almost every weekend."

Sitting with me underneath one of the Mauna Kea camp's many

tents to shield ourselves from the blaring sun, Brown said people flocked to the mountain for many reasons. Some were driven by environmental concerns, and others out of a desire to protect the rights of Indigenous people.

But her voice began to crack as she explained that for *kupuna* like herself, risking arrest to oppose the TMT wasn't simply an expression of practical concern. It was a spiritual necessity.

"This is what we do, we protect the sacred . . . and we will continue to do it until the last *aloha*," she said.

She paused for a brief moment, wiping away tears as they streamed beneath her spectacles and down her cheeks. Behind her, a crowd began to gather along the access road for a protocol. As the horns bellowed and people turned to face the mountain, Brown cut our interview short.

"I have to pray," she said.

Visitors who have come to pray with Brown included Native Americans and Native Alaskans from the mainland. While I was there *kupuna* ceremonially welcomed at least one man who identified as hailing from Alaska's Haida people.

Perhaps the most prestigious Native American visitor to the camp, however, was LaDonna Brave Bull Allard, who left shortly before I arrived. When I later asked her what she witnessed at Mauna Kea, she replied that it was like "Standing Rock but only better, stronger," explaining that the focus on Indigenous culture and spirituality was especially impressive.[86]

The Standing Rock connection was not lost on Native Hawaiian protectors, some of whom—such as Pua Case—had visited North Dakota during the demonstrations in 2016. The relationship even became a form of political leverage: Gabbard visited the mountain only after activists pointed out that she had traveled to show solidarity with Native Americans massing in North Dakota in 2016.

"Tulsi Gabbard, you went to Standing Rock, why are you not here on Mauna Kea standing with the people of Hawaii, where you reside?" one activist reportedly asked.[87]

Standing Rock continues to impact more prominent political circles as well. Among the hundreds of demonstrators who made the trek to the 2016 prayer camps in North Dakota was a twenty-something Puerto Rican woman working as a bartender in New York City. Frustrated by the 2016 election, she and her friends piled into an old Subaru and drove across the country to North Dakota. A Boston College graduate and avowed Catholic, she would later insist that she felt "called" to Standing Rock, saying it tugged at her "like a magnet" and describing the experience as "spiritually transformative." She would also credit the trip as inspiring her to return to New York City and begin a run for Congress.[88] That young woman was Alexandria Ocasio-Cortez, who not only won that congressional seat (emerging as a Democratic rising star) but also became the chief author of the Green New Deal, arguably the boldest environmental legislative proposal in US history. Tucked away in its pages was a none-too-subtle nod to her time in Standing Rock: the resolution listed as a chief goal "obtaining the free, prior, and informed consent of Indigenous peoples for all decisions that affect Indigenous peoples and their traditional territories, honoring all treaties and agreements with Indigenous peoples, and protecting and enforcing the sovereignty and land rights of Indigenous peoples."[89]

Republicans dismissed Ocasio-Cortez's Green New Deal and its warnings about the threat of climate change, with then-White House press secretary Sarah Huckabee Sanders saying, "I don't think that we are going to listen to her on much of anything, particularly not on matters that we are going to leave into the hands of a much, much higher authority."[90]

But the theological tables had already turned. Ocasio-Cortez fired back with a tweet that listed verses from Genesis and Leviticus to "serve and protect" God's creation.[91] As her source she cited an article from *Relevant*, an evangelical Christian magazine, which referenced many of the same scripture passages as Pope Francis' *Laudato Si'*.[92] She followed with another tweet that read, "You shouldn't need a Bible to tell you to protect our planet, but it does anyway."[93]

Like many activists, Ocasio-Cortez does not appear to see a conflict between her Christian faith and her experience with #NoDAPL movement. When met with a delegation led by Oglala Sioux Tribe President Julian Bear Runner in June 2019 to discuss the Green New Deal and the Keystone XL pipeline, she made her spiritual connection to Standing Rock clear.

"The spiritual power of protecting the water . . . I left that experience [at Standing Rock] willing to just give everything," she told the group, which included Iron Eyes. Leaning forward with intensity, she went on to say that she felt called to introduce a "paradigm shift" in society, adding: "It is first and foremost a spiritual battle, a spiritual transformation."[94]

Ocasio-Cortez would also lend a hand during the 2019 Mauna Kea protections. Alongside footage of *kupuna* being arrested, she tweeted out the message "From Puerto Rico to Hawaii, people are coming together to protect their dignity, rights, + sacred land w massive, peaceful, collective action."[95] She included a link to the Hawaii Community Bail Fund, which saw a windfall of hundreds of thousands of dollars in donations.

The bail fund was the work of the Democratic Socialists of Honolulu, and the video footage was shot by members of the group who had resided at the camp since its earliest days. The connection likely wasn't coincidental: For all the attention Ocasio-Cortez has drawn for her environmentalism, she is perhaps best known for her attachment to democratic socialism, which undergirds not only her politics (and her Green New Deal), but also that of a growing bloc of progressive voters. A deeply leftist economic theory, democratic socialism envisions a society with expansive welfare programs, social ownership of large swaths of the economy, and a vibrant democracy.

It's an idea sometimes cast as a construct of "godless liberals," but in truth it is tied to a rich history of faith-based activism. In fact, Native American activists I spoke with repeatedly invoked staunch criticisms of capitalism. And if you listen closely to a growing cadre of Religious Left leaders, Indigenous activists, and even Pope Francis himself, it's hard not to hear a growing chorus of support for a form of economic populism rooted in faith.

CHAPTER EIGHT

$\star$ $\star$ $\star$

Prophets over Profits

F or the roughly one thousand demonstrators who gathered in
New York City on September 17, 2011, the first day of the
Occupy Wall Street movement, the plan was simple. Scouts
had informed organizers that police barricades encircled large swaths
of Lower Manhattan in preparation for the protest, but that law enforcement had inexplicably left vacant Zuccotti Park, a patch of land
controlled in part by the investment banking giant Goldman Sachs.
The idea was to march down there, set up a camp, and usher in a
movement that would stand up for "the 99%"—a reference to the
staggering income gap between America's general population and its
wealthiest 1 percent of earners.

But as the anthem-chanting, sign-waving throngs of Occupy protesters rounded the corner of Zuccotti Park, they discovered another
group already there waiting for them. Along the march route stood
about a dozen young people draped in white albs, the traditional
vestments of many Christian traditions. They gripped makeshift
cardboard crosses or signs bearing slogans such as Blessed Are the
Poor. As the masses passed, the spiritual troop began singing "Ubi
caritas," a centuries-old Christian hymn whose first line translates as
"Where charity and love are, God is there."

Caught off guard, small gaggles of Occupy marchers paused to
listen.

"Their faces would just change and soften, and from that point on, we almost didn't have a chance to do anything else, because people were coming up to us and asking questions," Marisa Egerstrom, one of the group's organizers, told me at the time.[1] "In a group that had a lot of bandanas and black hoodies, we stood out."

Egerstrom and her friends had traveled from Boston to attend the event as self-declared Protest Chaplains. They were one of the first groups to offer what would become a more or less consistent religious presence at Occupy that year, giving voice to a spiritual critique of economic inequality that surprised some of their fellow progressives.

"People kept coming up to us and saying, 'You know, you are the first Christians I've seen at a protest . . . on our side," Egerstrom said. She added: "Advocating for the 99 percent is the same vision for the world that Christianity has, only rendered into secular language."

While the presence of faith voices may have shocked secular occupiers that day in New York—and rarely took center stage at famously egalitarian Occupy encampments—it was hardly the first time religious leaders have prayerfully condemned the capitalist economic system in the US. On the contrary, the Protest Chaplains of Occupy Wall Street were ensconced in a rich American tradition of faith-fueled economic criticism and concern for the poor, one long preached by civil rights leaders and proclaimed from the pulpits of society's most powerful faith groups—Protestants and Catholics—as well as smaller religious communities that rarely pierce national discourse. Theirs is the spiritual heritage that arguably sparked the broader American progressive movement in the first place, and which continues to animate many of today's lefty religious leaders and campaigns.

It's a legacy that stretches from Manhattan streets to Wisconsin church meeting rooms to Philadelphia group homes to the polished floors of the US Capitol, fueling the initiatives of major liberal activists and framing theological sparring sessions between Catholic nuns and former House Speaker Paul Ryan. In fact, in many modern Religious Left circles, voicing passionate critiques of the US economic system—or capitalism as a whole—isn't the exception. It's the norm. And as the broader progressive coalition warms to democratic socialism, an increasingly vocal subset of the Religious Left is proudly proclaiming what they say is an ancient faith in which the divine endorses the distribution of wealth.

ANTICAPITALISM: AN AMERICAN SPIRITUAL TRADITION

When asked to reflect on the Occupy movement, Gary Dorrien, a theologian and professor at Union Theological Seminary in New York City, kept coming back to the same two words: "fantastic" and "electrifying."

"We had forty-five Occupy chaplains just here at Union," he said. "We had an Occupy cell: they just sort of took over a big classroom."[2]

Most media outlets focused on the Occupy movement's secular components, but the wave of Occupy protests sparked a flurry of activity in progressive faith circles. In New York, a group of more than fifty clergy led a procession down to Zuccotti Park carrying a makeshift golden calf modeled on the New York Stock Exchange's famous bull statue. Participants declared, "Wall Street has become idolatrous." In Washington, DC, a local pastor oversaw a worship service at the request of Occupy K Street protesters. And at Occupy Boston's main encampment in Dewey Square, participants erected a Faith and Spirituality tent, which played host to Muslim prayers, yoga workshops, and a Yom Kippur service that drew more than 125 attendees.[3]

The movement also spawned a small corpus of religious reading material. Theologians and faith thinkers penned books such as *#Occupy the Bible: What Jesus Really Said (And Did) About Money and Power*, *Occupy Spirituality*, and *Occupy Religion: Theology of the Multitude*. Some religious protesters even produced their own protest prayer book designed to be easily sharable over the internet. They filled it with orisons from Buddhist monks, Catholic saints, and even Abraham Lincoln.

Their efforts were not always welcome. Dorrien acknowledged moments of tension between religious and secular occupiers who he

said were "hostile toward religion." The Occupy Boston tent city was
"very religion friendly," he said, but the same wasn't always true in
New York. Dorrien said Union faculty were sometimes called upon
to have "pastoral" conversations with seminarians who returned
from Zuccotti Park feeling berated and "beaten up" by their fellow
protesters.

Still, the preponderance of God talk during Occupy—well received or not—didn't surprise Dorrien. As a scholar who specializes
in the intersection of economics and faith, he spoke at several Occupy
encampments about the robust history of religious economic critique
in the US. Some of the earliest and most radical criticisms of America's capitalist economic system, he said, spun out of overtly religious
movements, particularly Christian ones, due to the outsized influence
of that faith on American politics. Paramount was the Social Gospel
movement, which dominated theological debates in the early twentieth century and featured Christian pastors who described the negative aspects of the Industrial Revolution as structural, or social, sin.

"The greatest figures of the Social Gospel are the ones that were
just outright socialists and said so: Walter Rauschenbusch, Harry
Ward, Reverdy C. Ransom, George Woodbey, and W. E. B. Du Bois,"
Dorrien said, rattling off the names of religious thinkers he links to
various iterations of the Social Gospel movement. "That goes way
back to the beginning of really talking about socialism per se [in the
United States]. It has Christian socialist roots in this country—roots
that are a big deal."

Indeed, America's spiritual brand of socialism is an often-forgotten
part of the broader movement's past. Technically, the term *socialism*
applies to a variety of views, although it traditionally refers to a belief
in collective—or social—ownership of the means of production and
support for workers managing themselves through unions and professional cooperatives. Not every devotee of the Social Gospel described
themselves as Christian socialists, although many signaled their affinity for socialist ideals by preaching spiritual critiques of capitalism. Chief among them was Walter Rauschenbusch, a white Baptist
minister who taught classes at the Rochester Theological Seminary

and authored the 1917 book *A Theology of the Social Gospel.* In it, he wrote that the ethics of capitalism are greedy, and "if we can trust the Bible, God is against capitalism, its methods, spirit, and results."[4]

Other Christians augmented Social Gospel thought, most notably those of the Catholic Worker movement, which Dorothy Day and Peter Maurin founded in 1933 to advocate for Christian pacifism and promote Catholic social teaching. The movement established farming communes and hospitality houses, which provided shelter and clothing to those in need, ultimately producing a "form of Catholic socialism," according to Dorrien. As such, Catholic Worker became a haven for left-leaning economic thinkers: Michael Harrington, author of the landmark 1962 study of American poverty, *The Other America*, joined the Catholic Worker movement in the 1950s before leaving to become a founding member of Democratic Socialists of America (he also eventually became an atheist).[5]

Members of other faiths embraced critiques of capitalism during this time as well. In 1897, a group of Jewish socialists founded *The Jewish Daily Forward*, a large-circulation Yiddish socialist newspaper based in New York City. It posited itself as a "defender of trade unionism and moderate, democratic socialism," and founder Abraham Cahan became a major voice in the Socialist Party of America.[6] Decades later, Malcolm X also criticized capitalism, comparing it to a blood-sucking vulture and predicting its eventual demise.[7]

Yet another religious thinker beloved by socialist-leaning faith leaders is Gustavo Gutiérrez, perhaps best known for his 1971 book, *A Theology of Liberation.* Gutiérrez, a Peruvian Catholic, helped popularize the idea of God's "preferential option for the poor"—a phrase that would later make its way into the mouths of popes. As discussed in previous chapters, he is widely credited with establishing the academic field that would become known as liberation theology, which would quickly branch out to other forms of Christianity and even other faiths.

Combined, these movements had a sizable impact on mainline Protestants, black church leaders, progressive Catholics, and labor activists of all faiths. Even Franklin Delano Roosevelt's New Deal implemented many of the policies and principles advocated by the Social Gospel movement. Its growing influence didn't always convert followers into socialists, but its work nonetheless shifted economic conversations among people of faith to such a degree that antisocialist movements formed in response, giving rise to the modern Religious Right.[8]

Carrying the banner of this corpus of economic theology, a succession of progressive religious leaders questioned elements of the US economic system throughout the twentieth century and pointed out how fiscal issues overlap with disparities in other areas—especially race. Rev. Martin Luther King Jr., for instance, called himself a "profound advocator of the social gospel."[9] In a 1952 letter to his future wife, Coretta Scott, King declared, "I am much more socialistic in my economic theory than capitalistic," although he added the caveat, "yet I am not so opposed to capitalism that I have failed to see its relative merits." Like Malcolm X and Cahan before him, King predicted the eventual demise of capitalism, saying it would take "quite a few more years."[10] King was even more leftist in a 1966 speech to the staff of the Southern Christian Leadership Conference, saying that, "there must be a better distribution of wealth, and that maybe America must move toward a democratic socialism" and "I think the earth is the Lord's, and since we didn't make these things by ourselves, we must share them with each other."[11]

Regardless of what political label one attributes to King's thinking, he clearly embraced the idea of an economic revival in the United States. He even suggested providing a "guaranteed annual minimum" income for all Americans decades before modern progressives reimagined the same concept as a universal basic income.[12] His most radical idea, however, was his plan to launch what he called the Poor People's Campaign, designed to pressure Congress into passing an Economic Bill of Rights by highlighting the plight of America's poor—irrespective of race—through a Poor People's March on Washington. The proposed demonstration would include mass civil disobedience and an occupation of the National Mall.[13]

King was assassinated in 1968 before he could bring his plan to fruition, but the idea did not die with him, and his followers mustered a version of the march that year. It failed to spark the national conversation King envisioned, but fifty years later, a different band of faith leaders would relaunch a tweaked—but no less passionate— version of the effort in the same state where Walter Rauschenbusch once preached.

CHANGING THE CHURCH

When Rev. Liz Theoharis told her Presbyterian Church (USA) ordination committee about her dream of eradicating poverty, she assumed it would play well. Jesus, after all, is well known for his concern for the poor.

They dismissed it entirely.

"[They] said to me, 'Well, you better not come back to us farther along in this process talking about ending poverty, because the Bible says the poor will be with you always,'" Theoharis told me.[14]

The offhand remark was a reference to Matthew 26:11, a Bible passage in which Jesus tells Judas, "For you always have the poor with you, but you will not always have me." It's a line sometimes cited by Republicans to push back against governmental efforts to eradicate poverty, but the members of Theoharis's committee were hardly archconservatives.[15] They were liberal mainline Christians from Theoharis's hometown of Milwaukee, Wisconsin. "Folks," as she put it, "that believed in feeding the poor and singing and praying for justice."

The exchange rattled Theoharis, who once broke into an abandoned Philadelphia church to provide homeless people with a place to sleep. She wasn't easily dissuaded from pursuing what she saw as her holy mission to fight for the poor, however. The child of activists, she remained dedicated to her call: she continued with her ordination process despite her committee's rebuke, attending Union Theological Seminary in New York City. Like most candidates for ministry in the PC(USA), she took four ordination exams, including a one-question essay test focused on theology. When she looked down at her test paper on exam day, a familiar question awaited her: "What should the church's response to poverty be?" Her fellow test takers, familiar with her interest in the topic, all turned to her expectantly.

Several weeks later, Theoharis received her test results. She had failed.

"I was in the ordination process basically struggling with the church at every stage about what their response to poverty should be," she said. "I saw that part of my call was to move the church."

Theoharis's experience is a reminder of just how complicated discussions of economics and poverty can be among people of faith, even in progressive religious communities. It's a topic rife with different opinions and approaches, and it still triggers disagreement among various factions of the Religious Left.

While studying at Union, Theoharis became consumed with Matthew 26:11, determined to unearth its true meaning. She crafted her doctoral dissertation (which she later developed into a book) around the question of how best to interpret the passage. Unlike her ordination committee, the seminary embraced her work and allowed her to set up a poverty initiative to equip faith leaders with the theological tools to address poverty.

But when it came to envisioning a faith-fueled movement to help the poor, Theoharis kept circling back to King's Poor People's Campaign. The movement proved so inspiring to her that in 2013 she rebooted the poverty initiative as the Kairos Center for Religions, Rights, and Social Justice, "with a very explicit focus on relaunching a Poor People's Campaign for today."

She knew just whom to invite as the keynote speaker for the kickoff: Rev. William Barber.

"[We] had very closely tracked this powerful [Moral Monday] movement of impacted folks and faith leaders, who were not just speaking and praying but putting themselves on the line and doing long-term nonviolent disobedience," she said.

After their initial meeting, Barber and Theoharis quickly became partners in their pursuit of social justice. It started small, with Barber emailing the Union exegete whenever he wanted help interpreting troublesome biblical passages.[16] Their spiritual synergy escalated quickly, and before long the two were openly planning to relaunch the Poor People's Campaign to coincide with its fiftieth anniversary. In December 2017, after months of preparation and training, they officially unveiled their new project: the Poor People's Campaign: A National Call for Moral Revival. It echoed King's ambition, aspiring for a series of protests to spread their message from Washington, DC, to smaller cities across the country.

It also updated King's vision, refining it for the modern era. Whereas the civil rights hero had focused his Poor People's Campaign on the three evils of racism, poverty, and militarism, Barber and Theoharis added "ecological devastation" and a "distorted moral narrative" to the list. It was part of an aggressively intersectional approach that used the power of protest to dramatize the links between poverty and issues such as racism, xenophobia, voting rights, Christian nationalism, the mistreatment of women, the cost of war, climate change, health care access, and income inequality, among others.

Barber and Theoharis worked to highlight these disparate concerns over the course of forty days during May and June 2018, when demonstrators affiliated by the Poor People's Campaign descended on some thirty state capitals and Washington, DC. Their tactics ranged from petitioning state legislators to stopping traffic,[17] and their protests resulted in roughly two thousand arrests in thirty-seven states.[18]

The new Poor People's Campaign also received cooperation from several major faith groups—including, to Theoharis's surprise, her own denomination. The PC(USA) declared "full participation in the campaign—from our grassroots to our highest levels of leadership" when the initiative launched in December.[19] And at the end of the forty days of action, the denomination invited Theoharis to address its General Assembly—a major meeting that convenes every two years. When Theoharis asked how many in the assembly audience had participated in Poor People's Campaign demonstrations, "dozens if not hundreds" raised their hands.

"It was pretty amazing," she said, "I was like, 'Wait, am I among Presbyterians?'"

RELIGIOUS SOCIALISM, REDUX

For all the talk of changing society in the Poor People's Campaign, its politics remain a strangely touchy subject.

The movement is unapologetically political in the broad sense and has accrued enough attention to catch the eye of prominent elected officials. Lawmakers hosted a hearing with the group on Capitol Hill in June 2018, offering poor and marginalized people organized by Barber and Theoharis a platform to speak about economic inequality, Indigenous rights, health care, union rights, voter suppression, and other issues. Participating lawmakers included the late Rep. Elijah Cummings and Sen. Dick Durbin as well as future presidential candidates Elizabeth Warren, Cory Booker, and Bernie Sanders—all of whom spoke at length to attendees.[20]

Still, Theoharis acknowledged that their campaign takes something of a catchall approach, which at times can appear unfocused. The strategy isn't laser-targeted on one policy proposal, but instead embraces a generational mission to change the national narrative on a slate of issues that impact the poor.

"We have to do this big work of going broad and deep," she said. "Because we know that . . . one program, one policy isn't gonna get us out of the situation we're in."

But as Barber and Theoharis have come to learn, a shared critique of America's economic and political systems does not a unified policy agenda make, nor does it create consensus for how best to bring about the change they seek. Some of the calls for reforming their movement came from inside the house: one of the earliest critiques of the Poor People's Campaign emerged from Union Theological Seminary itself, specifically from seminary students who identify as Christian socialists. It's a group experiencing something of a renaissance. While their numbers in the US remain small, Christian socialists I spoke with told me demand for their ideology is increasing, as evidenced by a slate of new Christian socialist podcasts created for what they say is a rapidly growing audience. "I think a lot of Christians are sympathetic to [socialism], in the sense that you've always heard a critique of capitalism," said Sarah Ngu, host of *Religious Socialism*, a podcast operated by the Democratic Socialists of America (DSA). "It's a pretty standard sermon to have a pastor preach about the ills of consumerism, or how people are overworked, too tired, burdened in debt, and how Jesus frees us . . . but [what] if you connect all the symptoms together and be like, 'Why are we in a rat race?'"[21]

This conglomerate of Christian socialists, which includes such organizations as Christians for Socialism (CFS) and the DSA's Religion and Socialism Commission, was initially jubilant about the Poor People's Campaign. But CFS members at Union grew concerned about the campaign's approach and rhetoric and were particularly frustrated by Barber's rejection of the term *Religious Left*—a moniker CFS members claim proudly in what they insist is its most accurate political meaning. But the North Carolina pastor often said that he preferred to characterize the Poor People's Campaign as representative of the "moral center."

"CFS people at Union were saying that [Barber's rhetoric] was kind of becoming a rhetorical trope that they feared was stopping people not just from being critical of capitalism, but also from signing on to a positive vision of socialism,"[22] said Dean Dettloff, co-founder of CFS.

Another activist group, the Philadelphia-based Friendly Fire Collective (FFC), echoed these concerns. FFC is a complex, multifaith religious community that was originally founded as a Quaker entity but which now transcends religious categories. Its members identify as "antifascist, anti-imperialist, and anticapitalist" and are bound together by "revolutionary leftism."[23] FFC member Hye Sung explained the collective's position to me this way: "God's love, when it's poured out, looks like tearing down the mighty and lifting up the oppressed."[24]

Hye Sung lamented what he said was Barber and Theoharis's aversion to speaking at length about the core evil at the heart of the US economic system.

"They don't talk about capitalism," he said.

Together, FFC and CFS published "A Christian Left, Not a Moral Center: An Intervention in the Poor People's Campaign"—a fifteen-hundred-word open letter listing their concerns. They never heard back, but Barber did find a roundabout way to address the issue while speaking at an August 2019 meeting of the Democratic National Committee.

"When we embrace moral language, we must ask: Does our policy care for the least of these? Does it lift up those who are most marginalized and dejected in our society? Does it establish justice? That is the moral question," Barber declared. "If someone calls it socialism, then we must compel them to acknowledge that the Bible must then promote socialism, because Jesus offered free health care to everyone, and he never charged a leper a co-pay."

It was not a direct endorsement of socialism per se, but it was perhaps telling that the crowd responded well to the line—and that DNC chairman Tom Perez, who was sitting behind Barber during the address, rose to his feet to join in the standing ovation. Equally telling was the outraged response from conservatives, such as FOX News host Laura Ingraham, who, in a televised conversation with Faith and Freedom Coalition chairman Ralph Reed, implied that Barber's interpretation was "dangerous." Reed, for his part, insisted that Jesus is not a "Birkenstock-wearing socialist" and that the Bible "talks about the importance of work." He also invoked *subsidiarity*—a concept embraced by many conservative Christians, but especially Catholics—to argue that scripture promotes small government.[25]

In the meantime, religious socialists appear interested in bolstering both their own influence and that of their fellow democratic socialists. When unabashed democratic socialist Bernie Sanders ran for president in 2016, Gary Dorrien, a charter member of DSA, stumped for him in front of religious audiences (something he said he did for Obama as well). Linda Sarsour, a veteran of Muslim American activism and a co-chair of the 2017 Women's March, also campaigned for Sanders at rallies[26] and tweeted that she was a "proud member of DSA."[27] Cornel West, a longtime DSA member and Union professor at the time, endorsed Sanders in 2015 and campaigned for him in places like South Carolina, where he told a crowd that the Vermont senator "represents so much of the best of the legacy of Martin Luther King Jr., and Rabbi Abraham Joshua Heschel, and Dorothy Day, and Mary McLeod Bethune." He then name-checked the "one percent" before describing Sanders's vision for a political revolution as "predicated on a moral and spiritual awakening."[28]

"The [DSA] religion and socialism caucus is strong," Dorrien told me. "It's vital."

CATHOLIC CLASH

Sister Simone Campbell has dismissed attempts to label her a socialist for years.[29] But as she sat across from me in her downtown Washington, DC, office, she admitted that the movements galvanized by democratic socialist firebrands such as Sanders and Alexandria Ocasio-Cortez were not easy to dismiss.

"As I understand it, these Wall Street Democrats, they're not worried—but they ought to be," she said, speaking to me in April 2019. "Because this level of inequality isn't sustainable."[30]

Still, when it comes to brass-tacks political strategy, Campbell, the charismatic head of Network, a Catholic social justice lobby, was less than impressed with the approach used by religious socialists—or, for that matter, the Poor People's Campaign. A politico by trade, Campbell is a lobbyist's lobbyist; it's just that she *happens* to be a Catholic nun of the Sisters of Social Service, and her constituency *happens* to be the poor. Naturally, her first concern is whether the Poor People's Campaign will be able to pass laws: Although she knows Barber well and endorsed Theoharis's book, Campbell said their campaign's lack of a targeted legislative strategy drove her "nuts" and potentially revives "every negative stereotype" of poor people.

"The reason why people are poor is because of the economic system we've got going on right now," she said. "Let's deal with the systemic analysis, and let's change the system."

She was similarly lukewarm about the Occupy movement, which

she described as more of a helpful "cry of anguish" than an effective legislative plan.

Economic policy is a sensitive topic for Campbell, who has spent so much of her life advocating for the poor in unusual ways that focus on policy. In spring 2011, several months before the birth of the Occupy movement, she began garnering attention for conducting a unique demonstration at speaking engagements. She calls it a "human bar graph," and it can be a bit of a workout. Campbell selects seven volunteers, telling five of them that each represents 20 percent of the American public, divided according to income bracket. She explains that she wants them to help her dramatize the percentage change in their income over the past thirty or so years, and that the number of steps she tells them to take across the room will symbolize those increases. Though she adjusts the math depending on her audiences or to reflect new economic data, the result is generally the same: the person representing the top 20 percent of income earners takes by far the most steps, because the percentage increase enjoyed by that income bracket has been the greatest. Meanwhile, the person representing the bottom 20 percent usually takes at least one step *backward*, if not two.

She then tells the two remaining volunteers that they represent Americans with the top 5 percent and 1 percent of income. The person representing the top 5 percent usually ends up walking across the entire room.

The person representing the top 1 percent has to take so many steps that they typically exit the room and walk all the way down the hall. Sometimes, that person finishes the demonstration outside the building.

As the head of Network, Campbell has presented this powerful demonstration of income inequality countless times. It's a part of her job, which requires her to make economic arguments on a regular basis in pursuit of her spiritual call to advocate for "economic and social transformation."[31] It's an atypical ministry, but she's uniquely gifted at it: under her leadership, Network has become well known on Capitol Hill and throughout Washington, and you can find their alumni at left-leaning economic think tanks like the Washington Center for Equitable Growth.

That kind of inside-the-Beltway clout would impress any lobbyist, but Campbell is more interested in whether it can influence lawmakers—especially those who share her Catholic faith. Of all the faith-based discussions of economics over the past decade, arguably the most far-reaching ones have occurred between Catholics, if for no other reason than they were who happened to hold positions of power in Washington. The most heated of such debates began in 2012, when Network launched Nuns on the Bus, a cross-country tour to criticize the budget proposal put forth by the GOP and then House Speaker Paul Ryan, a Catholic. The blitz of media coverage surrounding the bus tour elevated Campbell to the stage of that year's Democratic National Convention, where she derided Ryan's prized proposal on national television and instantly became his de facto theological sparring partner in the press.

Things got more complicated for Ryan in 2013, when Pope Francis became the head of the Catholic Church and soon after published *Evangelii Gaudium,* an apostolic exhortation in which he discussed the "preferential option for the poor." The document was widely seen as a scathing critique of capitalism, decrying what the pontiff called the "laws of competition" and the "idolatry of money." In a move that no doubt pained the free-market hearts of many Republicans, Francis declared that so-called trickle-down economics—a core element of Ronald Reagan's economic agenda and the cornerstone of GOP economic policies—"has never been confirmed by the facts."[32] Some conservatives, such as right-wing radio host Rush Limbaugh, retaliated, describing Francis's teachings as "pure Marxism." (Francis did not agree, saying that Marxist ideology was "wrong" but adding that he was "not offended" by the association because he knows some Marxists who are "good people.")[33] But things remained awkward for Ryan: when asked about Francis's argument, he dodged the question by suggesting that Francis, then in his mid-seventies, had simply never experienced capitalism at its best.

"The guy is from Argentina, they haven't had real capitalism in

Argentina," Ryan told the *Milwaukee Journal-Sentinel.* "They have crony capitalism in Argentina. They don't have a true free-enterprise system."[34]

The argument failed to impress nuns like Campbell, who continued to criticize Ryan's proposed cuts to social programs. Ryan eventually came face-to-face with the ire of Catholic nuns in 2017, when Sister Erica Jordan, a Dominican sister from the Speaker's home state of Wisconsin, confronted him during a CNN town hall. "It seems to me that most of the Republicans in Congress are not willing to stand with the poor and working class," she said, before asking: "How do you see yourself upholding the church's social teaching that . . . God is always on the side of the poor and dispossessed, as should we be?"[35]

Ryan responded by insisting that he shared Jordan's Christian concerns for the poor, but said, "Where we may disagree is in how to achieve that goal." He then argued that social programs are "discouraging and disincentivizing work," triggering a mixture of boos and tepid applause from the crowd.[36]

It was a response emblematic of a decades-long project initiated by conservative and libertarian-leaning Christian thinkers to craft a theology that attempts to merge biblical principles with the core tenets of free-market capitalism, with varying levels of success. There have been various attempts to fuse big business and the teachings of Jesus throughout American history, but the late University of Pennsylvania professor Michael B. Katz places the genesis of the most recent efforts during the rise of the Religious Right during the 1970s.[37] It was then that a group of primarily conservative Protestant pastors propped up the concept of the *undeserving poor*—that poverty can be an individual's *fault*—and lambasted government programs such as welfare because they "believed [the system] weakened families by encouraging out-of-wedlock births, sex outside of marriage, and the ability of men to escape the responsibilities of fatherhood."[38] Versions of these claims were bolstered by such groups as the American Enterprise Institute's Values and Capitalism Project and the Institute for Faith, Work, and Economics, both of which couple their support for free-market capitalism with a very specific understanding of the Christian faith. Their ideas permeated Catholic conservative circles too; Ryan, for example, has long insisted that his economic theories are within the realm of Catholic social teaching. Core to his argument is the idea that the Catholic concept of subsidiarity is "really federalism, meaning [that the] government closest to the people governs best . . . that's how we advance the common good by not having big government crowd out civic society . . . and take care of people who are down and out in our communities."[39]

Many of Ryan's fellow Catholics do not share this understanding of subsidiarity, and his view did little to advance his 2012 budget proposal, which failed in the Senate. It also did not aid his deeply unpopular 2017 effort to repeal and replace the Affordable Care Act, which failed to even garner a vote in the Senate.[40] Even Donald Trump called it "mean."[41]

Instead, the public tended to side with Campbell's views, which she articulates through a mixture of folksy wisdom and heady economic theory. She is especially fond of Richard G. Wilkinson and Kate Pickett's 2009 work, *The Spirit Level: Why More Equal Societies Almost Always Do Better,* which she cites as the inspiration for her "human bar graph." But the broader strokes of her thinking, she told me, emerge from her faith, which blends concern for the poor with racial justice issues and peacemaking.

When I asked her to explain this, Campbell walked to the corner of her office and pulled down a copy of Pope Francis's September 2015 address to Congress. Grinning despite herself, she read aloud a passage from the pontiff's speech: "A nation can be considered great when it defends liberty as Lincoln did, when it fosters a culture which enables people to 'dream' of full rights for all their brothers and sisters, as Martin Luther King sought to do; when it strives for justice and the cause of the oppressed, as Dorothy Day did by her tireless work, the fruit of a faith which becomes dialogue and sows peace in the contemplative style of Thomas Merton."

"I got tears in my eyes at the end, because it was like the summary of my life," Campbell said after she finished, adding with barely concealed nostalgia that she watched the pope's speech from the Senate gallery the day he delivered it.

It helps that Campbell isn't fighting by herself. In addition to Barber, Theoharis, and others, several other DC-based faith groups have also worked for years to rebuke the idea of the undeserving poor and to defend government safety nets such as Medicaid, SNAP (food stamps), and the Earned Income Tax Credit. One of the most effective of these groups is the Circle of Protection, a coalition of faith-based organizations that sent a stern letter to President Trump shortly before he took office in 2017. Its member organizations are by no means exclusively progressive, theologically or otherwise. In addition to traditionally left-leaning groups such as Sojourners, Bread for the World, the National African American Clergy Network, and the National Council of Churches, its participating organizations include the US Conference of Catholic Bishops and the National Association of Evangelicals.[42]

During Trump's first year, Circle of Protection joined with Campbell and others to express misgivings about the passage of the Republican-sponsored Tax Cuts and Jobs Act, arguing it could encourage Congress to target social safety net programs. But the bill passed and was signed into law in December 2017, with many seeing it as Ryan's greatest success as Speaker. He even produced a six-part documentary celebrating the passage.[43] Four months after his legislative coup, Ryan announced he would retire from public office after the 2018 midterm elections.

Campbell wasn't quite through prodding Ryan yet, though. When she launched the 2018 Nuns on the Bus tour—which concluded by driving past Trump's Mar-a-Lago resort in Palm Beach, Florida—she updated her human bar graph to depict the effects of the Republican tax-cut bill. After finishing the traditional exercise, she had volunteers pace off steps to signify every hundred dollars of income they would get back in a refund. The volunteer representing the bottom 20 percent of earners took a half step forward. The volunteer representing the top 1 percent took 1,930.

"They just kept walking around the room counting," she said. "They never finished."

Even operating under an administration as bullish as Trump's, Campbell is unlikely to give up her role as Capitol Hill's resident economic gadfly. She told me she still plans to push for specific legislative proposals, such as raising the federal minimum wage to fifteen dollars an hour.

And unlike the stunned looks that greeted the Protest Chaplains of 2011, these days God talk is almost an expected part of economic political discourse—one that Republicans ignore at their peril.

"I miss Paul Ryan," Campbell told me shortly before I left her office, her face settling into an almost wistful smile. "He was so much fun to poke at."

* * *

The spiritual heirs to the Social Gospel tradition of Walter Rauschenbusch, George W. Woodbey, Dorothy Day, and others are many, occupying a multitude of perspectives that often overlap but rarely align. Some are also literal heirs: Rauschenbusch's great-grandson Paul Raushenbush is a Baptist minister and a former editor of the *Huffington Post's* religious section. In 2011, he championed his progenitor's work while discussing the Occupy Wall Street movement with radio host Krista Tippett.

"What I'm really actually thrilled about right now is this kind of, in a sense, reuniting of the social and the private religious fervor and, in some ways, working together to really see some of the common issues that we all want to face, such as hunger," he said, speaking of young evangelicals taking an interest in the poor.[44]

But unlike his ancestor, Paul Raushenbush—a gay minister—is perhaps better known as a voice in a different, more modern social movement that has had just as much if not *more* of an impact on the Religious Left: the faith-grounded side of the LGBTQ rights movement.[45]

CHAPTER NINE

The Hard Work of Transformation

B ishop Gene Robinson could just make out the music as he shuffled through one of the shadowy back passageways of Washington National Cathedral, his clerical vestments billowing behind him. The tune was slightly atypical for an Episcopalian service, and the choir, too, was slightly atypical, at least by the standards of a cathedral that regularly hosts funerals for presidents and senators. The song was "Beautiful City" from the musical *Godspell*, performed by the Gay Men's Chorus of Washington, DC.

The rendition made perfect sense to the seventy-one-year-old Robinson, the first openly gay bishop of the Episcopal Church. As he paused in a tiny, hidden room that October 2018 morning, he hoped it would have meant something to his companion as well. In his hands Robinson cupped a vessel containing the ashes of Matthew Shepard, an openly gay University of Wyoming student who had been brutally beaten, tortured, and left to die by assailants in 1998. The twenty-one-year-old succumbed to his injuries six days after the attack. Widely remembered as a symbol of the harm done by antigay violence, Shepard is sometimes described as a martyr to the cause of LGBTQ rights. What many people *didn't* remember was that Shepard was also a devoted churchgoer. An Episcopalian, to be exact.

Robinson remembered. He thought about this fact as he listened to the practiced crooning of the altos echo through the cathedral. As the final notes began to fade, he took a breath and joined his fellow clergy at the back of the church. Still holding Shepard's ashes, he processed down the wide, center aisle of the cavernous sanctuary. He stared straight ahead, his eyes fixed on the altar, as a lone flute played a soaring version of the hymn "Morning Has Broken." Some two thousand pairs of eyes stared back at him as he passed, many already glistening with tears.

The bishop later explained to me that by interring the young man's remains at the cathedral, he saw the day as an occasion to celebrate Shepard and an opportunity to unite, if only for a moment, two groups that have long clashed in US history: institutional Christianity and the LGBTQ community. For centuries, Christian theology has been used to hurt and oppress LGBTQ people in innumerable cruel ways, and Robinson knew all too well that for many people in the pews that day, even showing up at a church was, as he put it, an "act of courage."

"For those two hours, I felt like those two communities of my life came together," Bishop Robinson told me. "For that brief moment, they understood each other and loved each other in a way that is still not common."[1]

As with many funerals, an unknowable number of stories wove their way into that moment. One begins decades earlier, when Robinson and others started working tirelessly to clear a space for LGBTQ people in faith communities that once rejected them, particularly among mainline Christians. It's a complicated, multifaceted form of LGBTQ advocacy that often isn't directed *outward* at the larger society. Instead, queer faith activists often argue that to change the way other religious Americans see them, they must first operate *within* religious communities—that is, doing the hard work of what Robinson often calls "transformation."

It's a form of spiritual work that is ultimately deeply political, with theological debates over LGBTQ ordination and same-sex marriage—particularly among mainline Christians such as Robinson—that have a direct impact on secular political fights for LGBTQ equality. And it continues to be a crucial, if unsung, aid to progressive campaigns that stretch from raucous activist conferences and dusty courtrooms to glitzy presidential campaigns.

BLAZING A PATH

Shepard's service at the cathedral grew out of a relationship that began on a cold November day in 2003, when Robinson was preparing to be consecrated as the Episcopal Church's bishop of New Hampshire. He was busily readying himself for the ceremony, fussing over the details of the day, when someone walked in and handed him a note from Judy Shepard, Matthew's mother.

It read: "I know Matthew will be smiling down upon you."

Robinson, deeply moved, held the note for a moment before tucking it into his pocket.

Then he went back to strapping on his bulletproof vest.

It was one of many security precautions the Kentucky-born cleric took as he prepared to venture to the University of New Hampshire for the service. Robinson's partner also wore a bulletproof vest, although it wasn't clear what good it would do against the chillingly detailed attacks described in the reams of death threats they received prior to the ceremony. The clergyman was so unsettled that he insisted his son-in-law and four-month-old grandchild sit in a skybox at the far end of the university hockey arena used for the ceremony. "If a bomb went off, they would be the least likely to be hurt by it," Robinson told me in 2019, recalling the security preparations of that day as if they were now little more than practical, uninteresting details.

He was terrified back in 2003, of course, but drew strength from his supporters. Despite the fearmongering—and the mass of anti-gay protesters that had gathered nearby to decry the first openly gay bishop—nearly four thousand people crammed into the arena to observe the service, many rising to their feet to applaud as officials placed a golden miter atop Robinson's head. It was an auspicious occasion; accounts of his ecclesiological ascendancy graced the front page of newspapers such as the *New York Times*, highlighting his trailblazing achievement and its potentially divisive impact on the denomination he served.[2]

Division proved to be a running theme during the consecration. When the bishop overseeing the service asked the crowd if anyone had reason why they shouldn't proceed, three people—a priest and two members of the American Anglican Council—stood up and spoke against Robinson. One of the Anglicans called the consecration an "unbiblical mistake which will not only rupture the Anglican Communion, it will break God's heart." When they finished, the trio filed out of the hall to attend an "alternative" service at a nearby evangelical church.[3]

For all the fuss the event caused, Robinson is the first to acknowledge that he is hardly the only LGBTQ person to face such criticism, and by no means is he the only gay man to claim a Christian identity proudly and in public. He wasn't even the first openly gay priest in the Episcopal Church: that mantle belongs to Rev. Ellen Marie Barrett, a lesbian ordained in 1977.[4] The club expanded in 1989, when Bishop John S. Spong ordained Rev. J. Robert Williams, an openly gay man who authored one of the earliest works of pro-LGBTQ mainline Christian theology before he died of AIDS in 1992.[5]

Yet even those milestones came years after the 1968 founding of the Metropolitan Community Church, an entire Christian denomination dedicated to welcoming LGBTQ people. Never mind that the United Church of Christ (UCC) ordained its first LGBTQ minister in 1972.[6] *Or* that gay and lesbian synagogues began to appear in the 1970s in the aftermath of the 1969 Stonewall rebellion in New York City.[7] *Or* that Indigenous LGBTQ people in the 1990s, in their pursuit of full acceptance among their fellow Native Americans, increasingly embraced the term *two-spirited*[8] to describe themselves—a phrase that refers to much older Indigenous concepts that never mapped perfectly onto western sexual categories in the first place.

Or that one of the great unsung heroes of the civil rights movement is Bayard Rustin, a gay Quaker and confidant of Martin Luther King Jr., who helped organize the Southern Christian Leadership Conference and once delivered a speech in which he declared "the new 'n*****s' are gays."[9]

When Robinson took the stage in New Hampshire, the path for faith-based LGBTQ equality advocates was still perilous, but its lanes were wide and well trodden. In many ways, his ascension was only possible because of that work.

"One of the things I don't like about my community is how ignorant our younger members are about our history," Robinson said. "It's heartbreaking to me."

If there is one faith community whose LGBTQ activism is well documented, though, it's mainline Christians. Depending on whom you ask, the reasons for the disproportionate attention paid to their work vary, although most agree it has a lot to do with privilege, race, and power. Their debates also coincided with national conversations about homosexuality, and mainliners faced a steeper climb on LGBTQ rights compared to many other religious groups. In some ways, they still do: As of 2017, same-sex marriage enjoys massive support among majorities of Unitarians (97 percent), Buddhists (80 percent), Jews (77 percent), and Hindus (75 percent), and similar percentages back nondiscrimination policies to protect LGBTQ people. By contrast, only 65 percent of white mainline Protestants and 34 percent of white evangelical Protestants support the same rights.[10]

Robinson's election also attracted attention because white Christian leaders wield significant power in American politics and culture. This includes conservative Christian voices, whose passionate opposition to Robinson's consecration drove home just how difficult his task as bishop would be. For decades, if not centuries, religion—and, in the United States, particularly Christianity—had been one of the key forces used to disempower LGBTQ people, identities, and relationships. Now Robinson had become a *leader* in a major Christian denomination, putting him in the crucial (albeit uncomfortable) position of translating for two communities at once.

"I've pretty much spent my whole life helping the church understand the LGBTQ movement and the LGBTQ movement understand the church," Robinson told me. "Those are two very different tasks."

Thankfully for Robinson, he wasn't the only one tackling such a project. A constellation of denomination-level LGBTQ rights groups joined him in the early 2000s, focusing their campaigns within their own mostly white, liberal-leaning mainline branches of Christianity; Presbyterians, Methodists, Lutherans, and others mustered robust efforts to push their traditions to embrace LGBTQ people. Their work seemed cutting edge at the time, but many of these organizations were at least old enough to rent a car. Since 1974, five years after the Stonewall riots, ReconcilingWorks: Lutherans for Full Participation has operated in various capacities.[11] That same year, More Light Presbyterians, an organization focused on the Presbyterian Church (USA), was hatched after Rev. David Sindt stood up at the denomination's General Assembly with a sign that read "Is anyone else out there gay?"[12] And Reconciling Ministries Network, which works with United Methodist churches, developed out of a 1982 meeting in which advocates proposed seeking out congregations that could do the work of reconciliation between the UMC and gays and lesbians—both inside and outside the church.[13]

The shared mainline Protestant Christian context ultimately gave rise to a subcommunity of religious LGBTQ activists.

"There's a kind of wisdom that says a progressive Methodist and a progressive Presbyterian have more in common than [with] people in their own denomination," said Alex McNeill, a transgender man and the current head of More Light.

Advocacy groups also drew upon a shared pool of religious thinking that is today known as "queer theology," subversively reclaiming the term queer from decades of use as an anti-LGBTQ slur. Emerging out of the 1990s philosophical approach known as queer theory, the thinking added a crucial religious dimension that built on the work of liberation theologians such as Gustavo Gutiérrez and more secular-oriented scholars, such as Michel Foucault and Judith Butler. Books such as *Queer Theology: Rethinking the Western Body* and *The Queer Bible Commentary* helped popularize a number of LGBTQ-friendly theological and biblical interpretations, which ranged from the practical (the scriptures typically cited to condemn same-sex relationships weren't talking about the modern conception of homosexuality) to the radical (gender categories applied to God are human-constructed and thus fundamentally inadequate for comprehending the divine). Scholars quibble over the precise dimensions of queer theology versus the similarly named gay theology, but they generally define the former as primarily Christian writing that is penned by LGBTQ people, rooted in the idea of uplifting oppressed LGBTQ people, and seen as a challenge to many of society's core assumptions about gender and sexuality.[14] One finds these same principles in queer theological works in other traditions, such as Judaism.[15]

Iterations of queer theology cropped up in various intrachurch LGBTQ advocacy efforts, but the prevailing theology, geography, history, leadership, and polity (a fancy word for church governance) of their respective denominations impacted each group differently. While the participants could share general tactics and approaches, each denomination grappled with unique challenges that weren't always applicable to their colleagues. Presbyterians, for instance, do not have bishops and were thus less likely to create a moment with the same media-grabbing pageantry as Robinson's consecration. Episcopal polity is also more hierarchical than that of the United Church of Christ—which while overwhelmingly liberal still allows for a diversity of opinion. To this day, the UCC plays host to congregations who actively support *and* oppose same-sex marriage.

Regardless, these groups learned what they could from each other, and by the time of Robinson's consecration many had already launched efforts to support same-sex marriage and the ordination of gay and lesbian people. (In 2001, Presbyterians voted against an overture that would have banned clergy from blessing same-sex unions.)[16] Their campaigns also received a boost in November 2003, when the Massachusetts Supreme Judicial Court ruled in favor of same-sex marriages. In her decision, Chief Justice Margaret H. Marshall pointed out that while religious objections to same-sex marriage exist, "many [also] hold equally strong religious, moral, and ethical convictions that same-sex couples are entitled to be married, and that homosexual persons should be treated no differently than their heterosexual neighbors."[17] Marshall—who was raised Anglican/Episcopalian in South Africa[18]—also noted that many of the same-sex couple plaintiffs in the case were "active in church," as several belonged to Unitarian Universalist or UCC congregations. Both denominations already claimed worship communities that affirmed LGBTQ relationships and allowed clergy to officiate same-sex unions.[19]

Suddenly, the goal of dismantling an anti-LGBTQ culture, both inside and outside religion, was a far more achievable reality. And more important for faith-based champions of the cause, the lines between religious work and secular political work were starting to blur.

As the first decade of the century edged into the 2010s, the efforts of activists began to pay off. In 2009, the Evangelical Lutheran Church in America (ELCA) voted not only to allow gay and lesbian clergy but also to remove a stipulation that they remain celibate.[20] Two years later, the PC(USA) did roughly the same.[21] Episcopalians had essentially allowed for various forms of same-sex weddings to be performed for years, but they codified the practice through two resolutions in 2015 that, among other things, approved gender-neutral and same-sex marriage ceremonies. (The denomination would extend same-sex marriage rites to all couples in 2018.)[22]

Things were more complicated for United Methodists who supported LGBTQ inclusion, as they would remain ensnared in a lengthy debate over same-sex marriage and LGBTQ ordination for many years. Unable to win many institutional victories, Methodist activists adopted a method of sustained dissent, with pastors such as Rev. Frank Schaefer defrocked (and later reinstated) for officiating same-sex weddings in defiance of church rules.[23] Even powerful churches joined the minirebellion: by 2008, Foundry United Methodist Church in Washington, DC—a congregation long frequented by Bill and Hillary Clinton—was offering up its pastor to officiate same-gender services. By 2011, it was hosting concerts with the Gay Men's Chorus of Washington and hiring a full-time coordinator of LGBT advocacy.[24]

Within a decade of Robinson first raising his bishop's crook, Christian LGBTQ advocacy wasn't a fringe movement to be dismissed. It was a force that would test the spirit of those in the pews and push the limits of people in power.

SACRED MEETS SECULAR

As religion-focused activists made strides in mainline communities, secular LGBTQ advocacy groups took notice and increasingly turned to faith voices—especially mainline Protestant leaders—for help in efforts to legalize same-sex marriage.

Alex McNeill traced the formalization of this partnership to October 2010, when the National Gay and Lesbian Task Force (since renamed the National LGBTQ Task Force) tapped him and others to help lead the Believe Out Loud Power Summit in Orlando, Florida. The event gathered three hundred pro-LGBT Christians and allies, drawn primarily from mainline Christian pro-LGBTQ organizations such as More Light, Reconciling Ministries Network, Reconciling-Works, and others.[25] Secular groups such as the Gay & Lesbian Alliance Against Defamation (GLAAD) offered training sessions on leadership development and how to interact with media.[26]

McNeill described the conference as a pivotal moment for the mainline Christian LGBTQ rights movement. He led one training that focused on how to push advocates "out of the pews and into the streets," and he explained that the overarching message of the gathering inspired faith-based groups to explore the question "How do we take this movement work we're doing within our denominations and move it into some secular work?"

The scions of this union were, politically speaking, a powerful bunch. In 2012, four states put initiatives involving same-sex marriage on the ballot. In the Northwest, when a coalition of groups that included the Gay and Lesbian Task Force, Human Rights Campaign, and the American Civil Liberties Union launched the Washington United for Marriage coalition in 2011, they brought on Rev. Debra Peevey as a faith director. Peevey, who spoke at the Believe Out Loud conference and worked on the Presbyterian LGBTQ ordination campaign, coordinated with local congregations and distributed thousands of green buttons that read "Another Person of Faith Approves R. 74"—a reference to the ballot measure that would legalize same-sex marriage in the state.[27]

Similar campaigns in Maine, Maryland, and Minnesota brought on faith directors, hired religion-related staff, and developed faith strategies of remarkable sophistication. Maryland organizers worked with black churches, Maine and Washington state campaigns focused on lay Catholics, and Minnesota leaders targeted the state's large Lutheran population.[28] Some ran advertisements with clergy openly endorsing marriage equality,[29] including one ad in Maine that featured a collared Methodist pastor—this despite the fact that his denomination did not condone it.[30]

When the votes were finally counted, LGBTQ advocates won victories in all four states.

"The reason those four states were successful in 2012 is because they had deep faith teams working within a multifaith and multicultural religious experience," said McNeill, who worked on the Maryland campaign.

The ideological separations between faith-based LGBTQ advocacy and secular activism narrowed even in legal battles. In 2011, UCC minister Rev. Jasmine Beach-Ferrara founded the Campaign for Southern Equality (CSE), a pro-LGBTQ rights organization that operated out of the basement of a UCC church in Asheville, North Carolina. A year later, the state voted to approve Amendment One, a ballot referendum with considerable support from conservative Christian groups that was designed to be an ironclad prohibition against same-sex marriage. Amendment One was unique in how it interacted with existing North Carolina law: ministers *already* faced arrest or a fine for solemnizing *any* union without a valid marriage license, and Amendment One made it illegal for same-sex couples to obtain a license. It was an ethical conundrum for progressive clergy who saw it as their religious duty to marry same-sex couples: either set your faith aside and abide by the law or act on your religious principles and end up in handcuffs.

Beach-Ferrara and the CSE saw the potential for a legal challenge on First Amendment (religious freedom) grounds and set about finding plaintiffs. She didn't have to look far: her denomination, the UCC, signed on to the case in 2013 as a collective entity. It was quickly followed by a slate of clergy from the same tradition as well as faith leaders from Reconstructionist Judaism, the ELCA, and others. The case, which would eventually become known as *General Synod of the UCC v. Reisinger*, was filed in April 2014 and paired its religious freedom challenge with a host of Fourteenth Amendment claims on behalf of North Carolina same-sex couples, who argued that Amendment One denied them constitutionally mandated due process and equal protection under the law.

There was a small but notable rash of media coverage around the proceedings. Reporters focused on how the case unsettled popular beliefs that religion and same-sex marriage were somehow incompatible. MSNBC's *The Last Word with Lawrence O'Donnell* ran an interview with three of the plaintiffs—Diane Ansley and Cathy McGaughey, a lesbian couple, and Rev. Joe Hoffman, head pastor of First Congregational UCC, which houses CSE—answering questions in the church.[31]

"In my tradition and in my congregation, I have been empowered and authorized to marry any couple that's mutual, loving, and wants to get married," Hoffman said during the segment, his voice rolling around a thick southern drawl. "This law prevents me from doing that for same-sex couples."

The lawsuit even won something resembling tepid support from Albert Mohler, a prominent conservative Christian and head of the Southern Baptist Theological Seminary. Speaking on his radio show, he said that the UCC's cause highlights an issue that "might be of genuine concern" to conservative Christians, although he stopped short of arguing that Amendment One should be overturned.[32]

Six months later, the US Supreme Court declined to review a case involving a different same-sex marriage ban in Virginia, which a federal district court had declared unconstitutional on Fourteenth Amendment grounds. The Supreme Court's inaction allowed the lower court's ruling to stand and set in motion a domino effect for other cases filed in the Fourth Circuit Court of Appeals—including the case brought by CSE.

It was US District Judge Max Cogburn who finally issued a ruling on *General Synod of the UCC v. Reisinger* in October 2014, declaring Amendment One unconstitutional on Fourteenth Amendment grounds, per the new precedent. He did not rule on the religious freedom argument, but Judge Cogburn noted in his decision that any action that "threatens clergy or other officiants who solemnize the union of same-sex couples with civil or criminal penalties" would also be unlawful under the Fourteenth Amendment.[33]

Shortly after the ruling, I visited Beach-Ferrara on a *ThinkProgress* reporting trip. From her office, she and I walked across the street to attend one of the first same-sex weddings at the Asheville Register of Deeds building. Beach-Ferrara stood smiling in the back of the room as pastor Hoffman officiated the ceremony for the same couple he appeared with on MSNBC months earlier, the steeple of his church clearly visible in the window behind him.

"Now, by the authority given me by the First Congregation of the United Church of Christ," he said to the giddy crowd packed into the diminutive government office, "and the power given me now by the state of North Carolina . . ."

Hoffman had to pause, as he was suddenly drowned out by a wave of cheering and several shouts of "Amen!"

After a moment, he delivered the final line: ". . . I now pronounce you married—wife and wife."[34]

Two years later, Beach-Ferrara ran for Buncombe County commissioner, pushing a message that focused on a "politics of empathy." She defeated two primary opponents and won the general election in 2016 unopposed, thus becoming the first openly gay commissioner in the county's history.

When a reporter asked her about CSE on the night of her primary victory, she maintained that her religious advocacy and her political message were the same. "We will always be empathic toward those who oppose our rights, toward those who condemn us," she said. "For me that comes from a place of faith, ultimately."[35]

(QUEER) THEOLOGY MEETS POLICY

The wave of religious LGBTQ activism didn't just alter denominations and LGBTQ advocacy groups. It also helped carve out a theological space for people of faith to affirm LGBTQ relationships and identities in public.

Sometimes this shift meant incorporating LGBTQ religious voices into the liturgy of American civil religion, such as when Bishop Gene Robinson was selected to deliver a major prayer at Barack Obama's inaugural festivities in 2009.[36] Many saw the invite as a response to the outcries from liberals after Obama invited evangelical pastor Rick Warren to pray at his inauguration, but Robinson's relationship with Obama—in public and in private—both predated and outlasted that moment. During Obama's 2008 campaign, the bishop had advised the candidate on LGBTQ issues and later was asked to deliver an impromptu prayer at the 2014 Easter Prayer Breakfast.[37]

The influence of faith-rooted LGBTQ advocacy could also be seen in a string of high-profile Democratic endorsements of same-sex marriage in the 2010s. When Hillary Clinton, a Methodist, endorsed same-sex marriage in March 2013, she did so while invoking religion, saying that her personal views on the topic had been shaped by "the guiding principles of my faith."[38] So, too, did Missouri senator Claire McCaskill, a Catholic, when she voiced support for marriage equality on Tumblr a week later. She headed her post with a reference to Corinthians 13: "And now abide faith, hope, love, these three; but the greatest of these is love."[39]

But undoubtedly the most dramatic religion-infused endorsement of same-sex marriage came from Barack Obama. When he famously explained his support for the cause during a May 2012 interview with ABC's Robin Roberts, he named his faith as a factor that shaped his "evolution" on the issue.

"[Michelle Obama] and I are both practicing Christians, and obviously this position may be considered to put us at odds with the views of others," he said. "But when we think about our faith, the thing at root that we think about is, not only Christ sacrificing himself on our behalf, but it's also the Golden Rule—you know, treat others the way you would want to be treated. And I think that's what we try to impart to our kids, and that's what motivates me as president."[40]

It's unclear whether Obama's spiritual argument was the product of a rhetorical strategy on the part of White House staff, which by multiple accounts scrambled to prepare Obama's endorsement after Vice President Joe Biden expressed support for same-sex marriage on *Meet the Press* a few days earlier. Michael Wear, Obama's 2012 faith outreach director and former White House staffer, noted in his book *Reclaiming Hope* that appealing to the Golden Rule was a message the pro-LGBTQ group Freedom to Marry had previously tested.[41] Joshua DuBois, head of the White House's faith-based office at the time, declined to comment on the record about whether he advised the president on the remarks. Neither Bishop Robinson nor Democratic National Committee faith outreach director Rev. Derrick Harkins recalled telling the president to use any religious elements in the endorsement, and Harkins had to be reminded that Obama had mentioned his faith at all.

But the debate over whether or not the president—a politician whose every speech is meticulously crafted by teams of people—was coached by staff or used poll-tested language obscures the far more important political and cultural development at play. The mere fact that groups had even *bothered* to study faith-oriented language supportive of LGBTQ issues was already a victory for religious LGBTQ advocates, much less that those ideas would be eventually repeated by the president of the United States.

And while Harkins didn't recall Obama's God talk, he vividly remembered preparing to handle the *impact* of the president's support for marriage equality. He began making phone calls to primarily black pastors in the wake of the announcement, "with nanosecond precision," hoping to preempt potential Republican efforts to use Obama's endorsement as a way to win over African American voters who opposed same-sex marriage.[42]

Harkins insists his calls proved any such effort would have been futile. Pastors he spoke with were amenable to the argument that legalizing same-sex marriage, while perhaps not something they would endorse *theologically*, was nonetheless about "justice and access." The board of the NAACP formally voted to endorse same-sex marriage ten days later, a crucial turning point for an organization with long-standing ties to the black church.

"Growing up as a black Baptist in Cleveland, Ohio, I can tell you that in just about every church you could imagine, in back of the sanctuary or down in the fellowship hall, there was usually an NAACP membership sign," Harkins said. "Those two institutions have been inextricably linked."

Not everyone was convinced by Obama's logic, of course. One member of the NAACP board—Rev. Keith Ratliff Sr.—resigned in protest.[43] But by year's end, NAACP leaders were running radio ads in support of the campaign to legalize same-sex marriage in Maryland, framing it as a civil rights issue.[44]

UNFINISHED BUSINESS

Despite the movement's various successes, religious opposition is still a significant hurdle for many who champion LGBTQ rights, inside the church and out.

Sometimes issues are more complicated than a simple yes-or-no answer. For example, evidence suggests that when the issue is framed as a legal rather than a theological matter, African American communities are highly supportive of LGBTQ rights campaigns. When a 2017 survey polled support for so-called religious refusals, or whether a business owner should have the right to refuse products or services to gay or lesbian people if doing so would violate their religious beliefs, black Protestants were one of the religious groups least likely to agree, with 65 percent voicing opposition (only Jews, Buddhists, and Unitarian Universalists were more opposed).[45]

However, LGBTQ advocates I spoke with argued that anti-LGBTQ theology—even if paired with legal support for equal rights regardless of sexual or gender identity—is still harmful. Hence the continued work of groups such as The Fellowship of Affirming Ministries, which pushes for more inclusive spaces in African American Protestant communities, where support for same-sex marriage still lags behind several other Christian groups. The fellowship's work often skews political: Derrick Harkins noted that the group was represented on a panel during an event at the 2012 Democratic National Convention.

In other instances, internal religious debates can be exacerbated for political purposes. Conservative (and liberal) pundits will sometimes deride Islam as somehow uniquely anti-LGBTQ, for instance, but a 2017 poll reported that a slim majority (51 percent) of American Muslims support same-sex marriage (significantly more than white evangelicals).[46]

This discrepancy became apparent in the aftermath of the tragic shooting in Orlando, Florida, in 2016, when a man claiming to be a member of ISIS murdered forty-nine people inside Pulse, a gay nightclub. Donald Trump and other Republicans were quick to characterize the attack as a direct result of "radical Islam" being "antiwoman, antigay,"[47] but multiple news outlets highlighted the voices of groups such as the Muslim Alliance for Sexual and Gender Diversity and a group of LGBTQ Muslims that gathers to pray regularly in New York City.[48]

Perhaps one of the most widely covered religious debates over LGBTQ identities rages among American Catholics, who since at least 2012 have, as a group, consistently voiced majority support for marriage equality, despite a church hierarchy that virulently does not.[49] Even with Pope Francis making headlines in 2013 for responding to a question about gay priests with the quip "Who am I to judge?,"[50] church teaching on the subject—which describes homosexual tendencies as "objectively disordered"—has yet to change. In fact, Francis has repeatedly affirmed the Church's position over the course of his papacy.[51]

The result has been a series of public kerfuffles among Catholics over even the simplest of expressions of support for LGBTQ people and identities, regardless of whether Catholic leaders sanction either side's view. For example, when author, Jesuit priest, and consultant to the Vatican Secretariat for Communications James Martin published his 2017 book *Building a Bridge: How the Catholic Church and the LGBT Community Can Enter Into a Relationship of Respect, Compassion, and Sensitivity*,[52] he was initially inundated with admiration, some of it coming from the top. The book garnered endorsements from leaders in the Society of Jesus (Martin's order of priests), his fellow Jesuits, cardinals, archbishops, and bishops. Martin told me that even Pope Francis has communicated "through intermediaries" that he supports the priest's work on the subject, and the two met privately at the Vatican in 2019 to discuss ministry to LGBTQ people.[53]

Martin attributed such institutional support to the fact that the book argues mostly for a change in tone regarding the Church's treatment of LGBTQ people, not in Church teaching itself. But his conversations with everyday Catholics reminded him that anti-LGBTQ sentiment still runs deep in the Church—even when gay parishioners remain chaste, an approach that LGBTQ activists widely condemn. He recounted a story to me of parents who told him that fellow parishioners stopped speaking to their teenage children when the worshippers discovered the children claimed LGBTQ identities.

"These are kids, and they're doing nothing against Church teaching," he told me, his voice rising with frustration. "They're not in any sexual relationship. They're certainly not married. And people are still treating them like dirt."

Martin also faced backlash himself from what he referred to as "alt-right Catholics." The head of the conservative Catholic website Church Militant chastised Martin after his book was published, calling him a "homosexualist" and a "heretic." Martin was subsequently disinvited from several speaking opportunities, reportedly due to a rash of phone calls from people railing against his book.[54]

Yet even Martin's ordeal pales in comparison to the firestorm of hostility faced by LGBTQ advocates who operate among white evangelical Protestants. They're working with a tough crowd: Strong majorities of white evangelicals, along with members of the Church of Jesus Christ of Latter-day Saints, still oppose same-sex marriage and most, according to the Public Religion Research Institute, also support religious refusals.[55]

Nevertheless, emerging leaders like Matthew Vines, a young author and LGBTQ activist, remain dedicated to the task of changing evangelical hearts and minds. Vines grew up in Kansas, where he attended the same Presbyterian church as Christian conservative and Trump secretary of state Mike Pompeo. But when Vines came to terms with his sexuality as an undergraduate at Harvard, he struggled to articulate his identity within the theological construction of his evangelical faith. Frustrated by a lack of online resources for people like himself, he set about crafting an hour-long theological talk to help his fellow LGBTQ evangelicals and their allies probe the topic through the lens of scripture. Eventually, in March 2012,[56] he uploaded his talk to YouTube. A million views, several glowing media profiles, and a few years of work later, Vines now has a book—*God and the Gay Christian: The Biblical Case in Support of Same-Sex Relationships*[57]—and an organization, the Reformation Project, to his name. Both are dedicated to creating a more inclusive space for LGBTQ people within evangelicalism.

Naturally, Vines's efforts evoked blistering theological criticisms from prominent evangelical figures like Tim Keller[58] and led to meetings between Vines and Southern Baptist pastors, Focus on the Family employees, and Albert Mohler.[59] According to Vines, the theological criticism isn't evidence of defeat. It's a signal that his arguments are being taken seriously.

"That was a sign to me," he said.

Vines hasn't exactly reversed decades of theological teaching within evangelical circles. But he has become a leading voice for those wishing to claim proudly an LGBTQ identity in evangelical spaces. And that, in turn, has established the mere *possibility* of such a position in the minds of many young evangelicals, which itself only creates more opportunities for activism.

To wit, Vines and others paved the way for Church Clarity, an online database project created in 2017 with the goal of systematically assessing the LGBTQ stance of churches across the country. Sarah Ngu, who identifies as a queer Christian and attends Reformation Project conferences, cofounded Church Clarity after realizing that some evangelical churches avoid advertising their stance on LGBTQ issues in the hopes of attracting young, often liberal-leaning churchgoers. The database has since expanded its investigative lens to include determining whether churches allow women to serve in leadership roles, and the project now boasts as many as fifty volunteers who scour church websites daily.

"What we're doing is not necessarily about LGBTQ issues and women in leadership," Ngu said. "I think what we're fundamentally doing is trying to shift power from institutions to individuals."

The push to clarify LGBTQ stances has become a flashpoint in progressive Christian circles, led in part by the advocacy of Eliel Cruz, a bisexual Seventh-day Adventist and creator of #FaithfullyLGBT—a hashtag, photo series, and organization promoting the stories of LGBTQ people of faith. Cruz has challenged the progressive credentials of liberal-leaning evangelicals who do not openly affirm LGBTQ identities, and made waves by criticizing Shane Claiborne for not being more openly pro-LGBTQ ahead of the 2018 Red Letter Revival. (The gathering eventually included an LGBTQ workshop headlined by Brandan Robertson, another bisexual evangelical activist.)[60]

Cruz has encountered what he described as a hesitancy among progressive faith groups to engage in new LGBTQ advocacy fights, even among mainline Christian institutions that openly affirm LGBTQ relationships and identities. Their reticence left Cruz exasperated: After a series of heated phone calls and a mountain of unreturned emails from one group, he grew so frustrated that he eventually halted some of his advocacy.

"I'm tired and I've stopped a lot of my work," Cruz said, noting that he has begun talks to restart some of his efforts after a year's sabbatical. "It has definitely had a toll on my own faith."

LGBTQ faith leaders are also not shielded from criticism from within their ranks. A few weeks after my interview with Vines, the entire staff of the Reformation Project unexpectedly quit en masse, citing frustrations with their founder, who they said had rescinded a consensus-based leadership structure and transformed their workplace "from an atmosphere of collaboration and openness to one of fear, intimidation, and confusion." The staff also accused the board of silencing them and keeping them from "having any say in the trajectory of the organization."[61]

In a lengthy blog post, Vines disputed their characterization of events, arguing that efforts to create a less hierarchical leadership structure never changed his leadership role.

"The LGBTQ Christian community has already weathered too much suffering from schisms in our support networks, and the Board and I are deeply saddened that any developments at [The Reformation Project] have added to that suffering rather than helped to alleviate it," he wrote.[62]

Despite the challenges, frustrations, and missteps that come from faith-rooted LGBTQ advocacy, the collective effect of the wide-ranging work continues to have an impact on society, culture, and politics. A few weeks after Pete Buttigieg, the openly gay mayor of South Bend, Indiana, announced his candidacy for president in January 2019, he triggered an explosion of media attention for talking openly about his faith. Buttigieg, an Episcopalian married to another man, garnered applause at a CNN town hall for questioning the authenticity of Vice President Mike Pence's Christianity in light of his support for the "porn-star presidency" of Donald Trump.

It proved to be a deft political strategy—one that showcased the waxing influence of religious rhetoric that affirms LGBTQ people.

"Just this one individual speaking about his faith has really shifted how people think about this false dichotomy between religion and

LGBTQ people in just a few months," Cruz said of Buttigieg. "We should have been doing this a long time ago, and we should have been doing it a lot more. We should have multiple people who look way different than Pete speaking about their queerness and their faith in profound and important ways."

Vines told me that since Buttigieg announced his candidacy, he has seen a spike in sales of *God and the Gay Christian*. And when *The Washington Post* asked Buttigieg to name some of his spiritual influences, he cited James Martin by name.[63] Two months earlier, Buttigieg and Martin had received awards from the Gay and Lesbian Alumni of Notre Dame and Saint Mary's and had exchanged "quick emails," according to Martin.[64]

Another past winner of that award is Gene Robinson, who perked up when I mentioned Buttigieg. With excitement, he described how impressed he was that a LGBTQ candidate could muster a serious campaign for the highest office in the land. The bishop said he would "never claim" that Buttigieg's comfort in discussing his faith was the result of the bishop's own advocacy, but Robinson didn't hide his enthusiasm for aiding the mayor's fledgling campaign, if only to help him get on the debate stage.

"I just donated the other day," Robinson said, smiling.

★　★　★

The fight over LGBTQ ordination and same-sex marriage helped establish a core subset of organizations and theologies that continue to guide queer Christian activists, even as progressive faith-based advocates pivot to conversations about other segments of the LGBTQ coalition.

The campaign for transgender equality, for instance, has included instances of liberal institutions engaging with the theological while defending transgender rights—seen by many advocates as the latest beachhead in the fight for equality. While working as a senior fellow at the Center for American Progress (he was brought onboard in 2010), Robinson initiated a project in 2015 to produce a theological document he called "Transgender Welcome"—a first for the secular think tank. To consult on the project, he called in Alex McNeill; Cameron Partridge, a transgender man and Episcopal priest from Boston; and Justin Tanis, adjunct professor at Berkeley's Pacific School of Religion.[65]

The resulting document developed from existing works of transgender-affirming theology, such as Tanis's own *Trans-Gendered: Theology, Ministry, and Communities of Faith*, which McNeill described as the field's "OG book." LGBTQ affirming faith expressions had also impacted another member of the advisory committee: Sarah McBride, a transgender woman on CAP's LGBT team, who would go on to speak at the Democratic National Convention in 2016 and run for office in her home state of Delaware in 2019. According to McBride, part of the impetus for drafting the document was to replicate the influence that religious groups wielded in the fight for same-sex marriage.

"I knew from my own advocacy just how powerful voices of faith—and particularly faith leaders—are in our political conversations, particularly around LGBTQ equality," she told me.[66] "I had seen so many faith leaders and people of faith talk about their own faith and advocate for marriage equality."

McBride, an ordained Presbyterian elder, also knows the far more personal role that progressive religious leaders can play in the lives of LGBTQ people. When she came out to her parents as transgender, they turned to the pastors of their local Presbyterian church in Delaware for guidance. McBride said the clergy responded "affirmingly and supportively," a response that proved critical for McBride's family as it moved forward.

LGBTQ-affirming faith would continue to touch her life years later in 2014, when McBride married Andrew Cray, a transgender man and fellow CAP staffer, shortly after he was diagnosed with incurable cancer. Robinson officiated their wedding, and when Cray passed away a few months later, the bishop was among those in the hospital room, holding hands with family members and a group of LGBTQ advocates who had traveled to be by Cray's side in his final hours.

McBride said the entire experience, while agonizing and tragic, was also "probably the most faith-affirming experience I've ever had." Indeed, Robinson witnessed a similar response among bereaved CAP employees when he oversaw a memorial service for Cray a short time later.

"It was a remarkable opportunity to take on a chaplain's role at a thoroughly secular institution," he recalled. "Do you know that those twenty- and thirty-somethings—even before Andy's funeral—almost demanded that I wear my collar? . . . I think they wanted to believe that one could believe in God, in whatever form, and be relevant in the world, do good things, and take risks for justice. They wanted to believe that somebody could put those two things together."

Advocates are quick to note that goodwill established by leaders such as Robinson, McNeil, Beach-Ferrara, Ngu, Cruz, Vines, and McBride does not erase the fact that faith is still often used as a weapon against queer people. Some religious groups still quietly support things like gay conversion therapy, and many leaders still invoke faith when calling for policies that grant religious Americans the right to discriminate against LGBTQ community members.

But while the fight for equality rages on, in the pews and in the streets, Robinson remains convinced that progress is possible in both secular and religious arenas. He said as much while officiating Matthew Shepard's memorial service, which took place only a few days before the midterm elections in 2018. After tearfully recounting Shepard's life; sharing anecdotes about Matthew's parents, Judy and Dennis; and telling the biblical story of the prodigal son, Robinson made a direct appeal to parishioners on behalf of the transgender community.

"Violence takes many forms, and right now the transgender community is the target," he said. "There are forces about who would erase them from America. Deny them the right they have to define themselves. And they need us to stand with them. That's the kind of transformation today makes possible."

He then added: "I want you to remember, and Dennis would want me to say: 'And then go vote.'"

The cathedral burst into applause, the loudest that day. Robinson repeated the call a few minutes later as he closed his sermon, his voice echoing off the towering stone walls of the Washington National Cathedral.

"Remember. And vote. And get to work," he said. He then turned to look over his shoulder at the vessel holding Shepard's ashes, his voice scratchy, his eyes welled to the brim. "Oh yeah, and Matt: Welcome home."

After the ovation that followed died down, the service turned back to music. It was a song written with Shepard in mind, a booming choral piece pulled from a hundred-minute oratorio titled *Considering Matthew Shepard*. Called "All of Us," the song and its closing lyrics, belted throughout the sanctuary by Grammy Award–winning group Conspirare with backup from the Gay Men's Chorus, sounded a whole lot like queer theology.

> *What could be the song?*
> *Where do we begin?*
> *Only in the Love, Love that lifts us up.*
> *All of Us.*
> *All.*

But to continue the fight for inclusivity, faith leaders like Robinson would need to sing songs of protest that reached far beyond the halls of the National Cathedral and reverberated outside Christianity itself. As Robinson would stress to me several times in our conversation, the only way for progressive people of faith in the US to create lasting political change in today's world is to team up with as many other faiths groups as possible—sometimes out of solidarity and sometimes simply to survive.

CHAPTER TEN

★ ★ ★

Troubled Waters

L inda Sarsour, an internationally known progressive Muslim activist and one of the co-chairs of the historic 2017 Women's March, was chatting on the phone with a friend when she heard the doorbell ring. Peering out the window of her home in Brooklyn, she spotted two white men standing just outside. Unsettled, she began to describe the scene to her friend.

"Don't open your door," her friend pleaded.

The men weren't especially intimidating, visually speaking. Their attire was somewhere on the spectrum between Brooklyn hipster and average white guy: flannel shirts, vests, jeans, and sneakers. Rather it was their sudden appearance—unannounced and oddly timed—that gave Sarsour pause. As a onetime advocate for Muslim immigrant families in the city in the aftermath of the September 11 attacks—not to mention a Muslim herself—she was well acquainted with the array of deceptive methods sometimes used by law enforcement when raiding homes. Keeping her door shut didn't seem like a terrible idea.

She eventually relented, however, reasoning that if the men really were interested in arresting or mistreating her, they were unlikely to do so in broad daylight, much less in front of the burly construction crew toiling away just down the street. When she finally opened the door, her fears weren't exactly assuaged: the men immediately identified themselves as officials with the New York field office of the FBI.

Her mind reeled, cycling through nightmare scenarios in which one of her many anti-Islam opponents concocted a story to frame her. As she inwardly panicked, the long-dormant know-your-rights training that she spent years teaching others suddenly roared to life. She demanded to see the officials' badges, inspected their business cards, and told them she was uncomfortable speaking to them without a lawyer.

It was only then that they announced they were not there to investigate her or anyone she knew.

"It was the biggest sigh of relief that I think I've ever made in my whole entire life," Sarsour later told me, her words clipped by the staccato of her thick Brooklyn accent.[1]

The men then proceeded to explain that they were visiting her as part of an investigation into sixteen packages containing pipe bombs that had been mailed across the United States earlier that month. The recipients included CNN's headquarters along with the homes or offices of people perceived to be critics of President Trump, such as former president Barack Obama, former vice president Joe Biden, former secretary of state Hillary Clinton, liberal billionaires George Soros and Tom Steyer, and Senators Cory Booker and Kamala Harris, among others. No one was hurt or killed, but the incidents made international headlines in October 2018. Police ultimately raided properties connected to the primary suspect in the case: a Florida resident who lived in a van blanketed in pro-Trump stickers.

According to Sarsour, the officials at her door said the raids unearthed a list of what they believed were other potential mail bomb targets. Her name appeared on the list alongside three addresses: her former office at the Arab American Association of New York, her home, and her mother's residence.

For most Americans, being named on a bomber's hit list would be enough anxiety for a lifetime. But while she was shocked, Sarsour—no stranger to death threats—found the news eerily comforting.

"I was more relieved to know that I was the target of a potential bombing [and not] under investigation by the Federal Bureau of Investigation," she told me. "That's the psychological warfare that I deal with every day as a Muslim."

The FBI declined to comment when I asked them about the alleged visit, but Sarsour's experience is not all that uncommon among American Muslims. *Islamophobia,* as anti-Muslim sentiment is often labeled, spiked in the aftermath of the September 11 attacks and has never really let up since. Recent years have only seen the problem worsen, with mosques and Islamic centers across the country enduring armed protests, vandalism, desecration, and even arson. Everyday instances of Islamophobia, such as Muslim children bullied at school or Muslim men and women harassed in public simply for what they believe, only compound the collective trauma.[2]

Worse, Islamophobia is increasingly politicized, usually by conservative political pundits and politicians. Early attempts to bolster electoral victories using anti-Islam rhetoric were largely unsuccessful, but all that changed when Trump successfully recast politicized Islamophobia into a tool for victory at the ballot box in 2016—namely, by proposing to temporarily ban all Muslims from entering the country.[3]

However, if the rash of hate crimes and incidents surrounding Trump's election proved anything, it's that this new wave of bigotry isn't narrowly targeted at Muslims. Sarsour told me she was at her house the day of the FBI visit because she was taking a break to process two other horrific incidents of hate, neither of which singled out her religious community. The first had taken place the week before, when a gunman—after failing to gain entry into a mostly black church—walked into a Kentucky supermarket, shot two black patrons, and spared a white man on his way out, saying, "Whites don't kill whites."[4] The second occurred three days later, when another gunman stormed the Tree of Life synagogue in Pittsburgh, Pennsylvania, and unleashed a torrent of gunfire that left eleven worshippers dead. That suspect was known for posting anti-Semitic *and* anti-Muslim *and* anti-refugee content on social media, effectively boiling down a trifecta of hate into his own evil stew: shortly before the shooting, he published comments on the internet that railed against the Hebrew Immigrant Aid Society, a Jewish group that helps resettle refugees—including Syrian refugees.

"I'm not directly impacted by any of those incidents, or at least I

thought I wasn't," recalled Sarsour, a mother of three. "I was very triggered and really traumatized. I was crying for days. Especially after the
Tree of Life shooting. That whole weekend I didn't leave the house."

Sarsour's mixture of first- and secondhand trauma echoes similar accounts described to me by several Religious Left leaders, many
of whom are regularly harassed and threatened as a byproduct of
their advocacy. But if the goal of bigots and hate groups who target
American religious minorities is to terrify their victims into obscurity,
their efforts have failed spectacularly. In an ironic twist, evidence
suggests Sarsour and others have refashioned their pain into a form
of power—namely, interfaith or multifaith coalitions based on solidarity and common experience.

In fact, interfaith alliances are now not only one of the Religious
Left's greatest strengths, but also rapidly becoming a rich resource
for secular progressives as well.

STRENGTH IN DIVERSITY

If you were to ask a Religious Left activist to name a historical par-
allel to modern-day interfaith social justice organizing, odds are they
would eventually name the civil rights movement. They have a strong
case; the push for the equal treatment of black citizens not only benefited from robust ecumenical alliances but also sparked fledgling
interfaith movements. Rev. Martin Luther King Jr., has been lauded
as an interfaith visionary for marching with Rabbi Abraham Joshua
Heschel, gleaning his nonviolent protest philosophy from Mahatma
Gandhi (a Hindu), and opposing the war in Vietnam after striking up
a friendship with Buddhist monk Thích Nhất Hạnh (the two eventually issued a joint statement on the conflict).[5]

But organizing across faiths can be dicey, and even King had his
missteps when attempting to coalesce an interfaith coalition. His
efforts to collaborate with emerging Muslims leaders such as Malcolm X were tenuous at best, and King was criticized in 1961 by a
Jewish leader for referring to the US in a speech as a "Democratic
and Christian nation." King did course-correct, however, writing a

letter saying he was misinterpreted and explaining, "It is my sincere conviction that no religion has a monopoly on truth and that God revealed Himself in all of the religions of mankind." Five years later, he penned a different public letter condemning a black civil rights activist for spewing an anti-Semitic Hitler reference during a protest, arguing that black people should be "intolerant of intolerance" and welcome the support of "Hebrew prophets."[6]

It was because of this mixture of humility and empathy that interfaith collaborations between Heschel, King, and others largely succeeded, even as they proved to be difficult learning experiences for all involved. Over time, a pattern developed: They grounded themselves in a form of religious pluralism that celebrated religious differences but prioritized common principles; and they trumpeted a shared sense of solidarity among minority groups that was equal parts spiritual altruism and a belief that what affects one group can impact all, an expression of King's concept of "a single garment of destiny."

These traits would underpin many American interfaith efforts for years to come, threading their way into the fabric of faith-based community organizing campaigns in major cities throughout the 1980s and 1990s. They were especially prevalent among community organizing groups such as the Direct Action and Research Training Center, the Gamaliel Network, Industrial Areas Foundation, and Faith in Action (then called PICO), which unified diverse religious communities to pressure local lawmakers into addressing regional urban concerns.

"We shifted in the early-to-mid-'80s from organizing neighborhood groups—like on housing issues—to beginning to organize through faith institutions," Gordon Whitman, senior adviser to Faith in Action, told me. "Most large cities in the United States over the course of the '90s developed, to some degree, a faith-based organizing group."

Their legacy persists. When I asked Sarsour about interfaith organizing, she spoke glowingly of how work with other religious groups influenced her as an activist. She was talking to me over the phone at the time, apologizing repeatedly as she rushed back to her hotel after a speaking engagement. Our call was constantly interrupted by short conversations with drivers and awkward silences during elevator rides. But even in her hurry, her voice was notably warm as she described a New York City interfaith campaign that successfully pushed local officials to recognize Islamic holidays for Muslim students. The tagline of the campaign, she said, was "recognition, inclusion, and respect," and many of her fellow participants weren't Muslim.

"I was really moved by it, because I was like, 'You don't get nothing out of this,'" she said, leaning into her Brooklyn accent. "I always say to people, 'That's what solidarity looks like, and that's what faith-rooted action looks like.'"

There are those who dismiss interfaith activism as ineffective, insignificant, or even inauthentic. Such was the position of Bernard Haykel, a Princeton University professor of Near Eastern Studies, when he derided those who argued in 2015 that the murderous Islamic State does not represent Islamic ideals. He argued people who decried the terrorist group as un-Islamic were either ignorant or followers of an "interfaith-Christian-nonsense tradition." (Haykel later attempted to clarify to me that he was specifically referring to the "Christian tradition of interfaith dialogue," although I remain flummoxed as to what exactly that clarifies, given that it was often prominent, scholarly *Muslims* who lambasted the Islamic State's claims to represent their tradition.[7]) The clear implication was that religious groups who forge interfaith alliances often obscure each other's differences— even, some may say, their flaws—in favor of eradicating conflict.

But activists say this critique fundamentally misunderstands how interfaith organizing actually works, particularly in recent years, when it has sought to address a spike in literal attacks on religious minorities. According to FBI statistics, the raw number of hate crimes increased substantially around 2014, particularly in two subcategories: incidents targeting people because of their race/ethnicity/ancestry and those singling out people because of their religion.[8] There is some evidence to suggest that the uptick is partly due to an increase in people informing law enforcement about hate crimes, but nearly half still go unreported.[9] And tracking *hate crimes*—a specific legal definition that can vary by state—is indicative only of the worst *hate incidents*, or hateful actions that may not rise to the level of a crime. Hate incidents also appear to have spiked in various ways, particularly around the 2016 election: in the three months after Trump's victory, *ThinkProgress* tracked 261 hate incidents, more than 41 percent of which had some connection or reference to Trump's campaign, rhetoric, policies, or victory.[10] Most were anti-Jewish, followed by anti-Black, anti-LGBTQ, and anti-Muslim.

The Southern Poverty Law Center (SPLC), which used a different methodology and verification approach than *ThinkProgress*, tracked more than three hundred hate incidents in the first week following Trump's election alone—the same amount it usually encounters in a six-month span. According to the SPLC, incidents were mostly anti-Black, followed by ones that were classified as anti-immigrant and anti-Muslim. One category was simply labeled "Swastika."[11]

This data is even more jarring when one considers that Sikhs, Hindus, Muslims, Jews, and other religious minorities make up only a tiny fraction of the American religious landscape. According to the most recent Pew research data, Jews represent slightly less than 2 percent of the US population, Muslims less than 1 percent, and all non-Christian faiths together just 6 percent.[12] Yet the surge of hateful acts that spiked before and after Trump's election disproportionately targeted these groups and religious populations that align with them (or simply appear to). Local news outlets were awash with harrowing reports of Muslims stabbed outside houses of worship,[13] Sikh men accosted and followed,[14] black churches spray-painted with hateful slogans,[15] Jewish seminaries[16] and openly LGBTQ churches defaced with swastikas,[17] and even largely white progressive faith churches damaged by bricks thrown through their windows.[18]

Yet in the midst of such wanton violence, a curious thing occurred. The negative experiences of these faith communities became a common bond that anchored a new, ever-expanding web of local interfaith organizing.

Take the example of the Episcopal Church of Our Savior, a congregation in Silver Spring, Maryland, just outside of Washington, DC. Less than a week after the 2016 election, vandals defaced a sign outside the church that advertised a Spanish-speaking worship service, scrawling Trump Nation Whites Only across it in angry black letters.[19] As if that weren't enough, the vandals also wrote Trump Nation on the wall surrounding a columbarium on the other side of the church. According to Our Savior's then-pastor Rev. Robert Harvey, it was an unambiguous attack on a congregation that was 85 percent immigrants and skewed heavily nonwhite. Distraught, he set about installing new security cameras throughout church grounds.[20]

But just a few hours after the desecration was discovered, the church was overwhelmed by an outpouring of support from the local community. Hundreds packed the pews the next Sunday in a show of solidarity, and the church promptly erected a new sign out front donated by a band of concerned neighbors: "Silver Spring loves and welcomes immigrants!"[21]

A few weeks later, Harvey and his congregation received a box in the mail filled to the brim with more than 550 cards, each bearing the message "There is strength in the diversity of our community. We stand with you against hatred and prejudice." The cards, signed by children, featured hand-drawn pictures written in crayon and carried an inscription on the back: "Your neighbors at the Muslim Community Center Weekend School."[22]

The experience moved the members of Our Savior, especially since congregational leaders had never contacted the Muslim community center in the past. But in the chaos that was the early days of the Trump era, they quickly found a way to pay it forward. The nearby Jewish Community Center of Greater Washington was one of the first victims of a rash of bomb threats that targeted Jewish organizations across the country in 2017. Church of Our Savior responded by instructing their Sunday school students to send letters encouraging the center to stand firm in the face of animosity.

"A good deed was done to us, so we wanted to pass it on to somebody else," Harvey told me at the time.

The Jewish community center was eventually able to complete the circle of solidarity. When threatening letters began arriving at several mosques and Islamic centers in the area—including the

Muslim Community Center—the JCC reached out to the Muslim Center with words of comfort.

The common experience of trauma created a spontaneous new interfaith community, and as any organizer knows, community is the foundation of power building. Although leaders at the three institutions had rarely, if ever, interacted in the past, they all reported a renewed interest in attending interfaith gatherings. The JCC hosted an interfaith Community Solidarity Rally in March 2017 and a Multifaith Film Festival later that same month. Church of Our Savior began hosting interfaith discussions for people interested in joining the New Sanctuary movement. And as of March 2019, the Muslim Community Center is still hosting interfaith gatherings at its facilities.[23]

Versions of this story happened over and over again across the country in the years immediately prior to and following Trump's election, especially among Jewish and Muslim groups. During the height of anti-Muslim sentiment in 2016, Dr. Mohamed Elsanousi, then the director of Community Outreach and Interfaith Relations for the Islamic Society of North America, collaborated with Rev. Richard Killmer, founder of the National Religious Campaign Against Torture, to create the Shoulder to Shoulder campaign. The group dedicated itself to forging interfaith coalitions to combat anti-Muslim hatred, and it successfully organized the heads of Jewish, Muslim, and Christian organizations and denominations to join a press conference at the National Press Club to condemn Islamophobia and vow to continue to do so in the future.[24]

Others broadened this work. Within a week of the 2016 election, the American Jewish Committee and the Islamic Society of North America teamed up to form the Muslim-Jewish Advisory Council, a thirty-one-person group that aspired to "develop a coordinated strategy to address anti-Muslim bigotry and anti-Semitism in the US" and "protect and expand the rights of religious minorities."[25] A broad array of leaders whose expertise touched on business, religion, law, and politics came together to form the board, including former senator Joe Lieberman, the Connecticut lawmaker who became the first Jew to receive a major party's nomination in 2000; Eboo Patel, the founder of Interfaith Youth Core, who served on President Obama's Inaugural Advisory Council; Rabbi Julie Schonfeld, the executive vice president of the Rabbinical Assembly, who served on President Obama's Advisory Council on Faith-based and Neighborhood Partnerships; and Rabia Chaudry, a prominent attorney and Muslim made famous by NPR's wildly successful *Serial* podcast for advocacy efforts on behalf of Adnan Masud Syed.

Meanwhile, worship communities continued to offer tangible support for each other, with campaigns that were national and even international in scope. In the days following the Tree of Life synagogue shooting, Muslim groups helped raise more than $230,000 dollars for the victims' families in just four days. After blowing past their initial goal of $25,000 in only six hours, the group eventually gifted $155,000 for families of victims and more than $84,000 for "projects that will help foster Muslim/Jewish collaboration, dialogue, and solidarity."[26] When a white supremacist murdered scores of Muslims at mosques in Christchurch, New Zealand, the following year, the Tree of Life congregation and other Pittsburgh-based Jewish groups raised more then $310,000 to support the Muslim community on the other side of the globe.[27]

The end result was the slow, piecemeal construction of networks that—while often minuscule on their own—integrated themselves into a larger, progressive-leaning effort that could flex political power when needed.

When the Trump administration began discussing the idea to create a database of Muslims,[28] Shoulder to Shoulder convened a press conference in Washington, DC, in which Muslim, Christian, Jewish, and Buddhist leaders condemned the idea, and some—such as Rabbi Jack Moline of Interfaith Alliance—pledged to register as Muslim in solidarity.[29] Anti-Defamation League head Jonathan Greenblatt[30] and former secretary of state Madeleine Albright soon issued similar pledges, both citing their faith as they did so.[31] While some criticized such pledges as ultimately toothless,[32] the sentiment nonetheless set the stage for Sen. Cory Booker to introduce legislation that would outlaw such a registry. When Booker, known for his ability to navigate interfaith spaces,[33] posted a Facebook video explaining his bill, which was designed to protect Muslims, a Tanakh and a Bible sat propped up on the desk behind him.[34]

Interfaith coalitions excelled as organizations that could quickly voice collective outrage. When the Trump administration implemented the first iteration of its travel ban in January 2017, thousands of demonstrators rushed to protest at airports. Among them were leaders of various interfaith coalitions, including Imam Omar Suleiman, cofounder of the Dallas-based group Faith Forward. Suleiman—whom CNN later named one of country's most influential Muslims[35]—stood with fellow faith leaders as he helped negotiate with airport personnel and relay updates to the crowd about detained travelers.[36]

"Let me say to you that Donald Trump will never make me hate you," he told a crowd at a candlelight vigil the next day. Flanked by other religious leaders from Faith Forward, he added: "And I hope that no politician will ever make you hate me."[37]

Sometimes even the smallest interfaith groups found ways to make their voices heard. Throngs of protesters also flooded Dulles International Airport just outside Washington, DC, in reaction to the ban, attracting national attention and participation from lawmakers—including Booker. The mass of well-wishers at Dulles exploded in revelry every time a group of immigrants exited the international terminal, chanting "Welcome home!" and waving signs that featured scripture references.[38]

Among the crowd, a small, diverse band of demonstrators huddled together clutching a large sign. The banner's glossy sheen made it look like a professionally designed rejection of anti-immigrant hate—and it was, just not for *that* protest. It was Church of Our Savior's new sign, bearing a message that would get a lot of use under Trump: "Silver Spring loves and welcomes immigrants!"[39]

GOD(S) OF THE GRASSTOPS

For many Religious Left leaders, the epicenter of the country's political interfaith movement is a literal place.

To get there, you have to walk down West 120th street in Manhattan, past Columbia University heading toward the Hudson River.

Don't be distracted by the neo-Gothic structures near the water, which feature soaring towers that look like someone removed a magical envelopment surrounding an American satellite campus of Hogwarts—that's Union Theological Seminary and Riverside Church. The place you're looking for is *inside* the brutalist square, nineteen-story limestone building across the street, deep within the bowels of the Interchurch Center—or as some call it, "the God box."

It's not flashy, but the building is something of a monument to older liberal mainline Protestant institutions shifting away from their historical emphasis on ecumenism—that is, connecting different Christian groups—and toward an embrace of modern interfaith work. Dedicated in 1960, its proximity to Riverside and Union Theological Seminary, both historic progressive Christian institutions, isn't an accident. It once housed the national offices of mainline denominations such as the Presbyterian Church (USA) and the Evangelical Lutheran Church in America, as well as the National Council of Churches.

Those groups have since relocated, although the building retains a Bible room and a chapel, and some Christian groups such as Church World Service remain. But many of the center's current tenants are more closely tied to the progressive interfaith tradition, such as Interfaith Community, the Interfaith Center of New York, the Interfaith Center on Corporate Responsibility, and the National Council of Jewish Women, among others.

The real standout is on the eighteenth floor, however, where you will find the eleven-thousand-square-foot offices—complete with a four-thousand-square-foot "design space" used for interfaith gatherings—of Auburn Seminary. It is from there that staff work toward their stated mission to "trouble the waters, heal the world," which in practice usually means molding the Religious Left in both visible and invisible ways.

Both parts of Auburn Seminary's name are misnomers, although it comes by them honestly. It was once a traditional Presbyterian seminary, founded in its namesake upstate New York town more than two hundred years ago with the goal of training ministers, and now proudly touts a social justice–minded history befitting a liberal main-line Christian institution. Auburn served as a stop along the Under-ground Railroad; helped originate the Auburn Affirmation, which signaled a shift away from fundamentalism in Presbyterian circles; and admitted women for instruction (in 1917) long before the de-nomination began ordaining female pastors (in 1956). It eventually relocated to the campus of Union Theological Seminary in New York City, another historically progressive religious institution.

Hints of its Presbyterian legacy remain to this day, as Auburn retains a "covenant agreement" with the PC(USA) and is still run by an ordained PC(USA) minister, Rev. Katharine R. Henderson, a Union graduate.[40]

But the goals and scope of Auburn have changed over time, es-pecially in the past two decades. Unlike most seminaries, the school no longer convenes traditional classes in dedicated, brick-and-mortar classrooms, nor does it grant theological degrees in the formal sense. Instead, it has reimagined itself as a clearinghouse for conferences, media trainings, and fellowship gatherings for faith leaders and ac-tivists across the religious spectrum—especially high-profile leaders of the Religious Left.

This transition was largely shepherded by Henderson, a short-haired, bespectacled woman who was elevated from vice president to president of Auburn in 2009. She speaks with the rehearsed inflec-tion of a mainline preacher, stretching out her sentences and deliv-ering them in an almost aggressively inoffensive tone that sometimes makes it hard to detect traces of her upbringing as a preacher's kid in Louisville, Kentucky. She does have at least one tell, though: her accent peeks out when she refers to *multifaith* (mole-*tie*) work, a term she prefers to *interfaith* because she feels the latter is dated and "insufficient."[41]

Drawing on a personality that projects a mixture of pragmatism, intellectualism, and progressivism, she inherited an institution that largely functioned as three separate research-and-training centers. Where others saw disorganization, Henderson saw the potential for something new.

"We began asking the 'So, what?' question of multifaith or interfaith work," she told me. "It's not for Kumbaya purposes or even to learn about each other's traditions. It's 'How do we do the work of justice together?' Trying to create an institution that works on this edge of justice."

The emphasis on justice inspired Auburn projects such as the online service Groundswell, the brainchild of filmmaker, lawyer, activist, and Sikh leader Valarie Kaur. She told me the idea for the site struck her as a student at Yale Law School, when she worked with local faith leaders to challenge what she described as a corrupt police department in Connecticut.[42] She went on to launch Groundswell in 2011 as "a multifaith network that connects, mobilizes, and amplifies the moral center around urgent social causes," and organized its first campaign to coordinate events of "hope and healing" on the tenth anniversary of the September 11 attacks.[43]

"I saw up close on the ground how powerful it was to build those kinds of coalitions where you have faith leaders partnering with advocates, and then mobilizing community support behind them," she said. "The vision behind Groundswell was to be able to connect pockets where that kind of activism was happening with different pockets all throughout the country."

Eight years later, the platform has evolved to drive interest toward faith-related campaigns using online petitions, fashioning itself as the scrappy progressive religious equivalent to the liberal mobilization site MoveOn.org. Scrolling through its many pages reveals sections dedicated to progressive issues such as LGBT equality ("Faith Leaders to President Trump: Don't Use Religion to Discriminate"), immigration ("Cancel the Deportation of Vicky Chavez!"), gun violence ("Ban Assault Weapons in Oregon"), and reproductive rights ("People of Faith Stand with Planned Parenthood"). Click through on any of these petitions and you'll find authors that include influential interfaith and Religious Left organizations such as Shoulder to Shoulder, Faith in Action, Interfaith Power and Light, various local sanctuary coalitions, and the Poor People's Campaign.[44]

Meanwhile, Auburn Media, a shop that trains faith leaders and activists who Henderson describes as "focused on justice issues," has been equally impactful. Under the leadership of filmmaker Macky Alston, the group has taught more than six thousand religious leaders how to interact with and speak to the media, a helpful skill for clergy and others who rarely if ever face a reporter.

These efforts are designed to model a flavor of interfaith activism that is geared toward building power, an approach that is distinct from the "Kumbaya" efforts Henderson cautioned against. Kaur, who has since left Groundswell but remains affiliated with Auburn, argued that in today's world, interfaith organizing should be rooted in action, not just discussion.

"I see people of multiple faiths coming together around shared moral imperatives and organizing together—and grieving together—with an eye towards social justice goals," she said. "What is most urgent right now is organizing across differences and around shared moral values for change that is supported by dialogue, but not replaced by it."

Henderson agreed, noting that she rarely hears dismissive opprobrium about interfaith work in the wake of rising hatred directed at religious minorities after the election of Trump.[45] Instead, Auburn was one of several progressive faith institutions that reported a windfall of funding after the 2016 election (Sojourners and Faith in Public Life were others).

"I think people realize the dangers in this current moment and the ways in which regressive forces—including conservative forms of Christianity—try to break apart adherents of other traditions," Henderson said. "I think people are realizing more and more the need for people to come together across lines of religious difference."

Of all of Auburn's projects, arguably its greatest contribution to the Religious Left has been the faith leader cohorts that it facilitates across the country. Chief among them is the Auburn Senior Fellows, which the seminary launched in 2015 as "inspired by the multifaith work of civil rights successes in Selma and other key moments in history in which people from many faiths found common ground."

The fellows now number more than twenty-five, and the list reads like an invitation to a Religious Left all-star banquet. Among its ranks are Kaur, Rev. William Barber, Rev. Traci Blackmon, Rabbi Sharon Brous, Bishop Gene Robinson, Bishop Minerva Carcaño, Fr. James Martin, Rev. Jennifer Butler, Brian McLaren, Sister Simone Campbell, Imam Dawud Walid, and Linda Sarsour. The group meets throughout the year at gatherings where Auburn officials facilitate discussion and dialogue between these titans of progressive faith movements.

It's a tweaked example of what is often called *grasstops* organizing, a strategy whereby prominent leaders from various faith traditions network so as to increase their collective power and present a united front. The method is common among conservative evangelicals, who often lean heavily on powerful pastors to wield political influence. But it has seen less play among liberal religious groups, which prefer to operate at the grassroots level.

Auburn is looking to change that, beginning with the fellows. Participants say the meetings have proven helpful and that they stay in contact via email, sharing notes about their often difficult experiences advocating for a progressive religious vision.

"I believe wholeheartedly that Islam, in and of itself, is a progressive faith," Sarsour told me, noting that she regularly speaks at mosques that express more conservative views on LGBTQ rights and reproductive rights—issues on which she holds a decidedly progressive stance. Others may see this as a contradiction, but she sees paving a different theological path for fellow believers to be a key part of her activism, even if it confuses secular progressives.

"I say to people all the time: It's not my job to preach to the choir," she said. "What's the point of me talking to people who are already in agreement with what I'm saying and what I believe? It just doesn't make sense for me as an organizer."

Other Auburn senior fellows echoed the dedication of Sarsour, who refers to Auburn as "my seminary." For community leaders who often speak in the plural, their descriptions are atypically personal and intimate: several said Auburn offers them a sense of community that, for the heads of disparate, faith-based social justice organizations, can be difficult to find.

"We're all out there in pretty public but often pretty solitary ways," said Rabbi Jill Jacobs, head of the Jewish social justice group T'ruah Rabbis. "So it's important to have that network and that community of people who can support each other and who can talk about difficult issues."

Sometimes those difficult issues include intense personal experiences. Their meetings give them space to vent frustration with their own communities or to ask advice for how to handle seemingly infinite waves of hate.

"When Linda Sarsour is getting untold death threats and so on, you know, I've been through that," Robinson said, recalling the promised violence that threatened to disrupt his consecration as bishop. "Somebody in the group has probably been through this thing that you're struggling with. Having already built a trust relationship with that person, you can just pick up the phone and call them."

Other times, senior fellows say the conversations allow leaders from different corners of the progressive faith universe to hold download sessions about each other's movements. Robinson recalled how Rev. angel Kyodo williams, a black Buddhist minister who is also in the cohort, helped improve his ability to engage with racial issues. Similarly, when Jacobs spoke to me in spring 2019, she noted that she learned about the United Methodists' acrimonious row over same-sex marriage from another fellow.

"I finally said to somebody, 'Can you just explain this to me?'" Jacobs said. "And [a fellow] just explained a lot more about the internal dynamics. That's important, because it actually helps me understand what some people I know are dealing with that I hadn't really understood before."

It's not always sunshine and rainbow coalition building, however. Disagreements can sometimes spiral into what Sister Simone Campbell referred to as "prickly, painful exchanges." The rifts can be so intense that they sometimes make her question the long-term efficacy of the group; Auburn fellows, she said, are only collectively useful when their relationships transcend ideological or theological differences.

"I don't know if there's a strong enough commitment to the group to engage it [in activist spaces]," Campbell said.

Several fellows mentioned discussions of Israel and the occupied Palestinian territories as especially charged, with Jewish, Muslim, and Christian leaders in particular debating deeply held views on Zionism, the occupation, and the Boycott, Divestment, and Sanctions (BDS) movement. Some fellows represent movements where advocating for Palestinians or Israelis—sometimes at the same time, sometimes separately—is a core value, and it's not a subject that is always easy to avoid. Even Henderson, as head of Auburn, weighed in on the topic in the past: when the PC(USA) voted to divest from companies that are involved in the occupation, she spoke out against the action in the press[46] and added her name to a list of Presbyterians who penned open letters[47] and took out a full-page advertisement in the *New York Times* opposing the decision. (PC USA) officials insisted that the vote didn't constitute support for the BDS movement.[48])

Yet discussions of Israel and Palestine among Auburn fellows were arguably ahead of the curve, pre-dating what some see as occasionally conflicting claims of Islamophobia and anti-Semitism that have rocked the larger US progressive movement. Here again, the Religious Left and the larger left are not easily extricable: Sarsour and other Women's March leaders were criticized for failing to list Jewish women in the group's Unity Principles ahead of the first demonstration, in 2017, and were later accused of internal anti-Semitism ahead of the 2019 march.[49] Sarsour was specifically blasted for supporting BDS and for allegedly enlisting a security detail connected to Louis Farrakhan's Nation of Islam, although Sarsour derided the Farrakhan allegations as a "smear" and a "litmus test."

"I have never breathed the same air" as the often overtly anti-Semitic minister, she told me.[50]

Yet it is in these moments of conflict that the power of the Auburn fellows is made clear. After months of controversy surrounding the Women's March, *The Forward* reported in December 2018 that three Jewish organizations were advising the Women's March regarding anti-Semitism: the National Council of Jewish Women, Jews for Racial and Economic Justice, and Bend the Arc: Jewish Action.[51]

Bend the Arc is run by Stosh Cotler, whom Sarsour already knew well because Cotler, too, is an Auburn senior fellow. When Sarsour published an extensive letter in November 2018 to address the Farrakhan allegations, she used an image taken during an interfaith vigil outside the White House organized a month before by Bend the Arc in the aftermath of the Pittsburgh synagogue shooting.[52] The picture showed Sarsour addressing the crowd, with Cotler standing close behind her.[53]

The Women's March eventually added three Jewish women to its steering committee along with Rev. Liz Theoharis, who cofounded the Poor People's Campaign with Barber.[54] For his part, Barber reasserted his support for the Women's March in a tweet and noted that they had stood with the Poor People's Campaign.[55]

Sarsour, born of Palestinian immigrant parents, said this kind of I've-got-your-backmanship is common among Auburn fellows and showcases the Religious Left's sometimes undetectable influence within the broader progressive left. She pointed to when the fellows debated the idea of anti-Zionism, a position she claims. Sarsour insisted she mostly observed the conversation, but said it exhibited a greater potential for nuance than the secular progressive spaces where she often spends her time.

"I think what the Religious Left brings to the table is the way in which we can have dialogue that is different from the larger progressive movement," she said. "There's a lot more empathetic, theological, ideological, deeper conversations that the Religious Left can have that you can't have in the larger left, particularly in the secular left. . . . Like in the secular left, you'll notice people tearing each other to shreds about something they disagree on, but they really haven't actually heard each other. . . . I think in the Religious Left there is more opportunity for that nuance to happen."

She added: "I became a much better active listener organizing in faith-rooted spaces."

Bishop Robinson said intimate relationships forged at Auburn also inevitably led fellows to "show[ing] up at each other's things."

When Valarie Kaur led an event at the Pentagon as part of an effort to allow Sikhs to wear turbans in the US military, Robinson accompanied her, and she referenced him in her sermon.[56] When Sarsour needed religious leaders to speak at the main stage at the 2017 Women's March, she pulled directly from her Auburn cohort, booking Rabbi Sharon Brous and Sister Simone Campbell[57] to deliver short addresses to the record crowd.[58] And when Campbell hosted protests on Capitol Hill to defeat the Republican attempt to repeal and replace the Affordable Care Act, she contacted William Barber and other fellows through Auburn channels to encourage them to attend.

Barber was already headed to a meeting with the American Black Baptist caucus at the time. But after receiving the nun's message, which he described as a "school of prophets call," he canceled his plans and headed to DC. He referenced the Auburn connection while addressing a gaggle of activists gathered in front of the US Capitol.

"When a modern-day prophetess calls . . . whatever is needed, you drop [what you are doing]," Barber told the crowd, referring to Campbell.[59]

Interfaith collaboration expands the potential influence of each Auburn fellow's community and movement, allowing leaders to draw attention from several groups at once. By way of example, Sarsour pointed to the controversy that erupted over comments made by Minnesota Democratic representative Ilhan Omar in early 2019. The newly elected congresswoman was accused of invoking anti-Semitic tropes after she suggested on Twitter that money drives political support for Israel in the United States. Omar issued an apology, but other lawmakers began working on legislation rumored to condemn anti-Semitism, a move many saw as a none-too-subtle reference to Omar's comments.

Sarsour, ever the organizer, immediately swooped into action. Concerned that the backlash was quickly (and ironically) morphing into a form of Islamophobia, she drafted a sign-on letter. Within twenty-six hours, the letter boasted signatures from more than six hundred progressive leaders expressing support for Omar and urging

Congress to pass a resolution condemning anti-Semitism *as well as* Islamophobia, anti-Black racism, xenophobia, and other forms of hate.

"In today's political climate," the letter read, "anti-Semitism and Islamophobia are frighteningly prevalent."

Signatories included Auburn fellows Brian McLaren, Rev. Traci Blackmon, and Rev. Lisa Sharon Harper, although notably not Cotler or many other Jewish members of the Auburn cohort. The list also included other prominent clergy such as Rev. Michael McBride of Faith in Action, Rabbi Alissa Wise of Jewish Voice for Peace, and Rev. Kaji Dousa of New York's Sanctuary Coalition, who serves as a spiritual adviser to leaders of the Women's March. It also featured leaders from major secular progressive organizations, such as the Working Families Party and Indivisible.[60]

When Sarsour marched into House Speaker Nancy Pelosi's office to present the signatures, she did so with an interfaith entourage that included leaders from the Council on American-Islamic Relations and Jewish Voice for Peace. Congress did, in fact, vote and pass the resolution the next day, but not before House leaders changed the final text. The resolution no longer focused narrowly on anti-Semitism, but instead issued explicit condemnations of white supremacist hatred against "Jews, Muslims, Hindus, Sikhs, the LGBTQ community, immigrants, and others."[61]

"It was the first time ever in the history of our country where our Congress stood up and condemned Islamophobia," Sarsour said. "It really showed that the Democratic leadership, whether they like us or not, whether they agree with us or not, knew that they were not going to be able to pass a resolution that looked like a response to Ilhan and ignore the real threats to all of our communities—Jewish, Muslims, and others—which is white nationalism and white supremacy."

Solidarity is no guarantee of success, of course, nor does it grant members immunity from criticism. Despite the expressions of support, Sarsour and two other Women's March board members stepped down in September 2019, roughly six months after I spoke with her.[62]

And the power of interfaith work does not always stand on its own. Sometimes it can even be fleeting: representatives from Church of Our Savior told me the congregation's renewed interest in interfaith alliances lasted only a few months after the sign defacing incident, losing its vigor after Rev. Robert Harvey departed to lead another church. The majority-immigrant congregation has since turned its focus inward, searching for other means of protecting its beleaguered community in the Trump era.

Even at the grasstops level, there are concerns that current approaches to interfaith organizing fall short. Simran Jeet Singh, a Sikh author, activist, and professor at Union seminary who regularly attends interfaith events, told me that even though other progressive institutions outside of Auburn—including the Democratic Party—have begun to embrace diverse faith voices, their approaches can often be "both Eurocentric and Christocentric."[63] He and Kaur both expressed frustration at being the only Sikh in the room at meetings, an uncomfortable feeling compounded by what they said was a tendency to emphasize clergy—which Sikhs don't have.

"I think it's problematic to have a single voice from a community serve as that tokenized representation," said Singh, who won an award from Auburn in 2016 for being a scholar-activist. "It ends up being a flattening, homogenizing, and actually misrepresentative at a time when we're trying to be representative. It's a real problem, and I think the solution there has to be that we bring in more voices, not less."

But the work continues. And in the years ahead, one of the greatest challenges facing the interfaith movement may be convincing the progressive political establishment to take their various constituencies seriously—not as tokenized nods to diversity but as powerful voting blocs to be courted. It's a struggle that has increased relevance looking toward the 2020 election and beyond, especially given the growing distance between Democratic operatives who see faith outreach as a tool to reach conservative voters and those who envision it as a new way to shore up support among variegated religious elements of the Democratic base.

CHAPTER ELEVEN

The New God Gap

On the second day of the 2012 Democratic National Convention, party officials realized they had a God problem.

They weren't in trouble so much with God as with Republicans. Someone, somewhere, noticed that the Democrats had removed the only explicit use of the word *God* from their party platform, excising the phrase "God-given" that appeared in the draft from 2008. Conservatives pounced: Mitt Romney told FOX News that the change was evidence that the Democratic Party was "veering further and further away into an extreme wing that Americans don't recognize."[1] His vice presidential nominee, Paul Ryan, called the omission peculiar and "not in keeping with our founding documents, our founding vision."[2] The outrage was enough to make one believe the DNC—convened that September in Charlotte, North Carolina—was rife with antireligious sentiment, evoking images of secret backroom meetings dedicated to re-creating America in secularism's image.

Such a conclusion would be difficult to draw, however, if you *attended* the convention, where you would have to somehow disregard that each day began with prayer sessions and devotionals led by Hindus, Buddhists, Christians, Jews, Sikhs, and Muslims. Never mind the plethora of faith-related panels and forums scattered throughout the schedule, including events dedicated to "loving our neighbor," "caring for the poor and those in need," and "being our brother's and sister's keeper." Ignore that a cadre of liberal activists at the convention who happened to belong to the Church of Jesus Christ of Latter-day Saints quietly launched a new group for Mormon Democrats.[3] Pay no attention to the DNC staffer paid to help orchestrate religious activities.

"We had more faith-related programming in Charlotte than at any previous Democratic convention," said then director of faith outreach Rev. Derrick Harkins.[4] A former pastor at a heavily African American congregation, Harkins added that he believed the omission of God from the platform was unintentional. "We could even point quantitatively to how many of the speakers on the platform spoke about their own faith."

Faith and God were, in fact, mentioned numerous times on the convention stage throughout the event. AME Bishop Vashti Murphy McKenzie opened one session with a prayer and implored the crowd to squeeze the hand of their neighbor and say amen—*twice*.[5] Julián Castro—then mayor of San Antonio, Texas—called upon the Almighty in the event's keynote address, invoking his grandmother's faith-fueled benediction in Spanish and English ("*Que Dios los bendiga*," or "May God bless you").[6]

But the most memorable God talk at the convention proved to be a blockbuster speech by a white-coated Sister Simone Campbell, who capitalized on her fame with the Nuns on the Bus tour to chastise Paul Ryan's budget proposal.[7] Her address was unusual for many reasons, but especially because Campbell—who vigorously criticized Romney and Ryan during her speech—did not officially endorse Barack Obama. Campbell had insisted on a nonendorsement when convention organizers first approached her, primarily because she was (and is) a religious activist, not an elected official or DNC employee. She assumed that the party would push back, but organizers readily agreed, seemingly unconcerned with her preconditions.[8]

The crowd didn't care either. Applause repeatedly interrupted the beaming Campbell during her speech, and she eventually received a deafening standing ovation.

The outrage over the omission of the word *God*—a term that applies only to some monotheistic religious traditions and ignores the various polytheistic faiths claimed by many Americans—missed this entirely, primarily because it misunderstood how party leaders had come to engage with religion. Even if Democrats had omitted the *word* (they added it back after Obama personally intervened), party officials had already dedicated an *entire section* of the 2012 platform to faith.[9] The document spilled more ink on the subject than on middle-class tax cuts, voting rights, or the freedom to marry, and it described faith as not only "a central part of the American story" but also "a driving force of progress and justice throughout our history"—in other words, as an important source of liberal *activism*.

Indeed, the controversy highlights a different kind of God gap—not between Democrats and faith, but between competing visions for *how* progressives should engage with faith. Despite Obama's band of accomplished outreach experts, his second term—while hardly divorced from faith—saw a rupture crack open between grassroots Religious Left activists and Washington insiders. Fracturing also occurred within Washington's once tight-knit progressive faith community, with leaders disagreeing over what proper faith outreach should look like for liberals, or even which religious populations to court.

The result was an uneven mix of successes and half starts for progressive political faith engagement that rippled into the 2016 election season and—with the possible exception of outreach to Mormons in Utah—helped Donald Trump clinch the presidency. The lessons from that era spell out just how much the religious landscape has changed since Obama first ran for president and offer more than a few hard-earned lessons for 2020 Democratic presidential hopefuls.

THE OBAMA ERA

Most campaign workers who cut their teeth in Barack Obama's 2008 Religious Affairs team landed jobs in the administration. They were good jobs, too, not the "spoils of war" assistant-to-the-assistant métiers typically handed off to lower-tier staffers.

The lion's share stuck with faith. Rev. E. Terri LaVelle and Mark Linton ran the religion-related operations at the US Department of Veterans Affairs and the Department of Housing and Urban Development, respectively. Others went to work directly with the president at the White House's faith affairs office, which was headed by Joshua DuBois. Despite having worked outside the campaign, Mara Vanderslice Kelly became close with DuBois and was eventually anointed as his number two. Over the course of her time in the administration, Kelly would serve in the faith office of the Department of Health and Human Services and as senior policy adviser to the White House operation. Michael Wear, a former intern, was brought on board to work with DuBois.

Other alumni blazed a different path: Max Temkin, who is listed as an intern on the Religious Affairs campaign team, went on to create the popular party game Cards Against Humanity.

For some, success came with a tinge of bitterness. Washington's progressive faith community had atomized during the 2008 election, with some working for Obama and others working for Clinton. When the dust settled, bad blood remained.

"The movement got split a little bit," Kelly said. "That was hard. . . . There were some really hard feelings from all that stuff." She recalled deep divisions that lasted years, adding "people didn't trust each other."[10]

Obama's God squad plowed forward all the same, making manifest a vision he first articulated during a July 2008 campaign speech in Zanesville, Ohio. In the speech, which many viewed as a play for conservative votes, Obama proposed expanding the White House Office of Faith-based and Community Initiatives, created under George W. Bush, though Obama later renamed it the Office of Faith-based and Neighborhood Partnerships. He pledged $500 million a year in federal funds to religious groups and programs that aid the poor and disadvantaged.[11]

Some liberals expressed concerns about the implications of out-religioning the Bush administration. But Obama made good on his promise to embrace faith groups, which he hoped would enhance interactions between his administration and the communities it served.

According to DuBois, the expansion came with a heavy dose of bureaucracy building. Church-state boundaries that were "assumed" under the Bush administration, he said, were made concrete under Obama, and the White House faith office embarked on a rigorous process to clarify what it could and could not do.

"We strengthened the legal and constitutional underpinnings of this office," he said. "We ran a rule-making process. We pulled together an advisory council of faith leaders and community leaders for the first time that informed and produced hard regulations and rules that brought greater clarity to the inherent legal issues."[12]

The advisory council included some conservative and evangelical voices, including National Association of Evangelicals head Leith Anderson and Richard E. Stearns, president of World Vision US. But many who filled out the board over the course of Obama's two terms were well-known figures in progressive-leaning faith circles, including Rev. Traci Blackmon; Rev. Jennifer Butler; Rev. Jim Wallis; pastor Michael McBride; progressive Christian author Rachel Held Evans; Rabbi David Saperstein, director of the Religious Action Center of Reform Judaism; Harry Knox, head of the Human Rights Campaign's Religion and Faith Program and later CEO of the Religious Coalition for Reproductive Choice; and Rami Nashashibi, director of the Inner-City Muslim Action Network.[13]

But while Obama's religion experts rapidly expanded his administration's clout with progressive religious groups, his reelection faith outreach apparatus got considerably less attention. The biggest shift was in leadership: it was Wear, not DuBois, who ended up leaving the administration to run faith outreach for Obama's campaign in 2012, while DuBois stayed behind at the White House.

Wear faced different challenges from his predecessor. For starters, he was only twenty-three when he got the job, older than many bright-eyed Obama field organizers but still young enough—despite his years of service—to raise concerns that he did not have enough experience for a national position. As author and journalist Amy Sullivan told *The Washington Post*, "Republicans would put somebody senior with years and years of experience and a big Rolodex in that position . . . I guess that tells you something about how Democrats still view faith outreach and its importance."[14]

What's more, reelection campaigns usually differ greatly from a candidate's initial outing and often generate less enthusiasm. This was especially true for Obama's 2012 bid, which was less about "hope and change" and more about "hold the line." It didn't help that a series of religion-related conflicts erupted between Obama and religious conservatives. The administration continued to battle multiple lawsuits lobbed at the Affordable Care Act by religious conservatives who opposed its contraception mandate, and Obama's 2012 announcement in support of same-sex marriage brought backlash from some.

All of this weighed on Wear, who demurred when asked about direct comparisons between himself and DuBois. (He noted only that "the president wasn't inviting me over for drinks—I was not an 'inside circle' kind of guy.") Instead, he told me that the scope of faith operations in 2012 often hinged on whether state directors viewed them as advantageous, and many did not. The campaign also lacked the impressive slate of faith-specific outreach directors that it had in 2008. Wear's team was reduced to himself and two interns, a downsizing offset partly by the fact that elements of campaign faith outreach (especially to Catholics) were added to the portfolio of Obama's senior advisor, Broderick Johnson. In addition, the reelection campaign benefited from the work of the DNC's Derrick Harkins, whose faith outreach position did not exist in 2008, when Wear said the party relied more on consultants.

Despite all these obstacles, Wear was able to bootstrap a faith outreach operation that outshined anything assembled by Al Gore or John Kerry in 2000 and 2004, respectively. The campaign website once again had a page dedicated to people of faith, and it included an Obama video message to religious voters, penned by Wear in collaboration with David Axelrod, one of the president's closest advisers. Faith lit also returned, this time with a direct-mail piece sent to Catholics in Ohio and Iowa that featured Sister Simone Campbell alongside a message about Catholic values and economic fairness.

Still, Wear grew frustrated with what he saw as the campaign's apparent disregard for the sensibilities of theological conservatives. In *Reclaiming Hope*, Wear recounted an instance when a faith leader expressed his dismay that the campaign had sent out a mass email with the word *damn* in the subject line. When Wear complained to a fellow staffer about what he thought was a "crass decision," the staffer explained that emails with profanity got better open rates.

"Data-driven politics is incompatible with aspirational politics," Wear wrote. He likened the tactics to those used by such groups as the National Rifle Association, arguing that the strategy is "willing to sacrifice a broader coalition for a few bucks, a dozen hours of free airtime, and an angrier base."[15]

Obama won in 2012 anyway, profanity-laced emails and all, routing GOP opponent Mitt Romney by a slightly smaller margin than the Democrat's 2008 victory. But Wear's discontent continued to simmer, stoked by a run-in with the more progressive wing of the Democratic Party around the time of Obama's second inauguration.

The inaugural committee initially selected Louie Giglio, the evangelical pastor of Passion City Church in Atlanta, Georgia, to deliver a prayer at the formal ceremonies. But reporters at *ThinkProgress* unearthed an old sermon in which Giglio condemned homosexuality and argued that it is possible for gay people to change through "the healing power of Jesus."[16] The news sparked outrage among many liberals, and Giglio withdrew the next day. Writing of the incident, Wear commented, "Liberals were the sharks who smelled blood in the water."[17]

The consternation of Wear, a proud evangelical Christian, hastened a debate over how religious outreach should work within a progressive context. For Wear and others, reaching out to religious moderates and conservatives—people like Giglio—was crucial.

But for secular liberals and other religious progressives, removing Giglio was a triumph *because* there were alternatives such as Rev. Luis León, whom the White House chose to deliver the prayer instead. León, an Episcopal priest, served at St. John's Church, across the street from the White House. Sometimes called the "president's church," St. John's had openly gay, noncelibate priests and expressed a willingness to bless same-sex partnerships and ordain transgender clerics.[18] It was evidence that progressives no longer had to play it safe around religious conservatives when it came to issues such as LGBTQ rights, and it hinted at the emergence of a new breed of doggedly progressive religious activists who would change the future of how Democrats engaged with faith.

Faith outreach was no longer just about courting African American churchgoers or reaching across theological and political aisles to tempt conservative Christians to vote blue. It could now curry favor with newly activated parts of the Democratic Party's shifting progressive base, including non-Christians and those sometimes classified as the *hard* Left.

Meanwhile, members of the Obama-era progressive Grassmere group continued to go their separate ways. DuBois left the White House in 2013,[19] eventually wrangling Wear to help him lead Values Partnership, a consulting firm working "at the intersection of race, politics, entertainment, faith, and culture." That same year, Harkins left the DNC to work at Enroll America, a group run by 2008 Obama campaign staffers tasked with helping people sign up for health care under the Affordable Care Act. (Harkins would eventually end up at Union Theological Seminary in New York.) Kelly waited until 2014 to leave the faith office at Health and Human Services to jump ship for United Way.

The team that replaced them was more expressive of Obama's aggressively right-brained approach to governance. Melissa Rogers, a lawyer and legal scholar who in 2008 published a paper on a vision for the White House faith office, took over for DuBois in 2013, thus becoming one of the few academics in history to implement her own ideas about better governance.

"In certain sectors of the legal field, there's skepticism about this kind of work," Rogers told me, referring to partnerships between the government and religious organizations to serve people in need. "So what I've tried to say is, 'This work can be done in a way that's consistent with the Constitution.'"[20]

But as the new guard of lawyers and academics made their moves, the campaign and party infrastructure for faith-conscience advocates began to atrophy. The DNC did not replace Harkins for the 2016 campaign after he left his post, and while the party did religion-related work around Pope Francis's 2015 visit to the US, much of it was done as volunteer work by John McCarthy, a young, Catholic twenty-something largely unknown to the faith-and-politics power players that surrounded Obama.

They would know him soon enough.

DO ALL THE GOOD YOU CAN

Criticizing Hillary Clinton's 2016 campaign is something of a new-found pastime among Washington Democrats. Most failed attempts to win the White House endure postmortem scrutiny, but the razor-thin margins of Clinton's loss to Trump—combined with the sheer shock that it happened at all—turned how-Clinton-could-have-won theories into a cottage industry. From podcasts to op-eds to cable news segments, armchair analysts and seasoned political operatives alike repeatedly trumpeted the same theory: the former secretary of state could have turned it all around if she and her team had done just *one thing* differently.

The critics may all be right in their own way. But for faith outreach veterans, that one thing is Clinton's targeting of religious voters—or presumed lack thereof. Almost every operative I spoke with for this book had harsh words for the 2016 campaign (many of them unsolicited), but few were as critical as Wear, who didn't hesitate to blast the campaign publicly.

"What kind of data-mined campaign looks at a country that identifies itself as 70 percent Christian and says, 'We're going to run the first post-Christian campaign?'" Wear asked during a 2018 panel at Georgetown University, before answering his own question. "A losing one, that's the kind."[21]

E. J. Dionne—who Wear cited as having heard the "post-Christian" remark from a Clinton campaign official—later clarified to me that Wear had misunderstood him. He said he may have asked campaign staff about the line, but he never personally heard anyone say it. Prominent writers repeated the quote anyway, advancing the general perception that the Clinton campaign functionally abandoned faith outreach in 2016.[22]

The reality of Clinton's faith operation is a bit more complicated, and, as with many Clinton campaign postmortems, not all of the ire aimed at her failed presidential bid is fair. Organizers *did* wait until June 2016 to hire a formal faith outreach director, but Obama's reelection campaign brought on Wear in a similar capacity only a month earlier by comparison—in May 2012. Clinton's efforts *were* smaller than Obama's 2008 operation, but not significantly smaller than his reelection faith efforts, and Clinton had more institutional faith support than anything Kerry had in 2004. The Clinton campaign *mostly* stuck to more traditional forms of faith outreach, but it did explore the option of bringing in someone from the outside; the campaign even took meetings with staunch progressives such as Religious Left advocate Guthrie Graves-Fitzsimmons.[23]

(Full disclosure: I know a bit about Clinton's job search because—in a bewildering and unexpected turn of events for any journalist—the Clinton campaign also contacted *me* to discuss taking the position. It never resulted in any sort of job offer, however, and my none-too-subtle attempt to steer those conversations into an on-the-record interview with Clinton for *ThinkProgress* proved laughably unsuccessful.)

The man Clinton ultimately hired for the position was John McCarthy, who was a spritely twenty-four-year-old at the time. But he was far from a neophyte in the small world of liberal religion-and-politics operatives. In addition to his work around the pope's 2015 visit, McCarthy had assisted with Catholic outreach for Obama's

2012 campaign. He was volunteering for the Clinton campaign when they elevated him to a full-time position, helping facilitate conference calls with faith leaders. (He noted that John Podesta's role as chairman of Clinton's campaign "brought in a lot of institutional Catholic voices.")

McCarthy's work differed from that of his predecessors in significant ways, however. He wasn't exclusively focused on religious voters. Instead, he split his time between faith outreach and various forms of heritage outreach, which covered everything from broad-based groups (Irish Americans for Hillary) to smaller, more targeted populations (Macedonians for Hillary). He produced two internal briefing books a day—one for faith outreach, another for his other programs. It was a regular reminder that he was essentially working two full-time campaign jobs at once.

Despite the workload, McCarthy argued his strength derived from his existing ties within the Democratic Party. "I think a lot of the folks who've done faith outreach in the past came at it from an outsider angle—coming in to advise the campaign," McCarthy said. "I was a Democratic operative who happened to also do faith."[24]

He added: "I was an operative more than I was from the faith world—in that I wasn't a pastor or theologian—so I could make the argument that this was electorally beneficial to the party more than I think some of my predecessors were able to."

There were also people tasked with reaching religious voters while working under other programs. McCarthy said campaign staffers who worked in outreach to African Americans—"AfAm" for short—and Hispanic/Latinx populations incorporated faith into their work, as did those who targeted the Arab American vote.

Even so, outsiders expressed disappointment with the Clinton campaign's engagement with faith, primarily because they saw the former secretary of state as a natural fit for a dedicated, aggressive push for religious voters. A proud member of the United Methodist Church (UMC) who has spoken several times at UMC events, Clinton often invokes Methodist thinkers and sayings in her public addresses—just as she did during her 2016 Super Tuesday victory speech. "Like many of you, I find strength and purpose in the values I learned from my family and my faith," she said, sparking cheers. "They gave me simple words to live by, an old Methodist saying. 'Do all the good you can, for all the people you can, for as long as you can.'"[25]

The fact that Clinton described the line as an "old Methodist saying" rather than repeat the common misconception that it was penned by Methodism founder John Wesley, hints at her deft grasp of matters divine. She was also effusive about her faith during a campaign town hall when a woman stood up and voiced frustration with how she had to defend herself to friends who saw progressivism and Christianity as inherently incongruous. When the woman asked Clinton how the candidate grappled with the issue, Clinton launched into a lengthy, nuanced articulation of faith that, when fully transcribed, runs to about six hundred words.

"I am a person of faith. I am a Christian. I am a Methodist," Clinton said. "My study of the Bible . . . has led me to believe the most important commandment is to love the Lord with all your might and to love your neighbor as yourself, and that is what I think we are commanded by Christ to do. And there is so much more in the Bible about taking care of the poor, visiting the prisoners, taking in the stranger, creating opportunities for others to be lifted up . . . I think there are many different ways of exercising your faith."[26]

Clinton said similar things when she spoke in 2016 at the conferences of majority-black denominations, such as the National Baptist Convention[27] and the African Methodist Episcopal general conference.[28] Both visits earned her media attention, as had her 2015 visit to Rev. Traci Blackmon's church near Ferguson, Missouri (broadcast live on C-SPAN) in the aftermath of the Charleston church shooting.[29]

Still, glad-handing with religious leaders isn't the same as targeted ads and on-the-ground faith outreach, which were rarer occurrences in 2016. McCarthy said his operation worked similarly to Wear's for Obama in 2012 in that both had to shape their programs largely around the whims of the state directors. And like Wear,

McCarthy discovered that many were less than keen on religious campaigning—except, he said, for Utah.

THE MORMON EXCEPTION (THAT PROVED THE RULE)

The room—a drab, dull-colored rectangular office space—was packed to capacity. The mass of chattering bodies were pressed together so tightly that simply lifting my camera above my head to take a photo felt as if I was committing multiple personal space violations. The air crackled with electricity, a kind of anticipatory, I-can't-believe-this-is-happening energy usually reserved for a secret show in Brooklyn or a backstage encounter with a celebrity.

But the person who bounded onto the makeshift stage at the front of the room wasn't an indie musician or a famous actress. It was a staffer for the 2016 Hillary Clinton campaign, announcing the opening of a new office just outside of Salt Lake City.

In response, the crowd—most of whom wore blue stickers with slogans like "I'm With Her" and "Utah Together"—went berserk.[30]

August is a bit late for a campaign office opening, but the context was unusual. As election day drew nearer, campaign leaders (and more than a few voters) became convinced that Clinton would not only win but also have a rare opportunity to expand the electoral map for Democrats by seizing states long held by Republicans. Nowhere were their goals more ambitious than in Utah, where political analysts were surprised to discover simmering discontent about Donald Trump among members of the Church of Jesus Christ of Latter-day Saints. Looking back, the Salt Lake City office opening, which I chronicled for *ThinkProgress,* was a glimpse at Clinton's ad hoc approach to faith outreach as well as the complex, symbiotic relationship between grassroots progressive faith movements—yes, even Mormons—and presidential campaigns.

Members of the LDS Church, often called Mormons, represent around 47 percent of Utah's population as of 2018,[31] and statistically are the most reliably Republican major religious group in the country.[32] Yet Utah was one of the few states in which Trump fared particularly poorly during the primary season: Ted Cruz clinched the Utah caucus with 69 percent of the vote; Trump placed a distant third with an underwhelming 14 percent.

Trump's rhetoric failed to capture the imagination of the Beehive State—which he would describe as a "tremendous problem" midway through the campaign[33]—for several of reasons.[34] Trump's infamously brash demeanor and remarks about sexual assault, for instance, didn't mix with the traditionally genteel culture embraced by many Latter-day Saints. But the disconnect ran deeper and older: the businessman's December 2015 proposal to ban Muslims from entering the country triggered a rare public response by the leadership of the LDS Church, a religion that was *itself* almost banned from the US in 1879 by then secretary of state William M. Evarts.[35]

"The Church of Jesus Christ of Latter-day Saints is neutral in regard to party politics and election campaigns," the response to Trump read in part. "However, it is not neutral in relation to religious freedom."[36]

A newly emboldened population of LDS progressives in the state added to the Mormon frustration with Trump. Members of the so-called Latter-day Left are a statistical minority among their religious peers, but they have been around for decades, claiming prominent Democrats such as Sen. Harry Reid among their number. The group didn't find its organizational footing until 2012, when it launched Mormon Democrats (later rebranded LDS Dems) during that year's Democratic National Convention. Reid was one of several Mormon Democrats who spoke at the inaugural gathering, which took place in a Holiday Inn conference room. Crystal Young-Otterstrom, then chairwoman of the group, described the event to NPR as "like a missionary effort."[37]

By 2016, Young-Otterstrom and LDS Dems had developed their own website and a impressive social media presence, and they saw the faith-fueled backlash to Trump in Utah as an opportunity—one that didn't even require a victory to be successful. Former CIA officer and LDS member Evan McMullin, an independent presidential candidate, was accruing significant support in the state as a protest against Trump. All Clinton had to do was split the vote enough to cost Trump the state and its six electoral votes.

It was the first time a Democrat had made a major play in Utah in decades, and it was coupled with a surprising investment in Utah religious voters by Clinton's team.[38] In addition to a campaign presence, Clinton published an op-ed in the *Deseret News* (which is owned by the LDS church), in which she mentioned the near ban on Mormon immigration in 1879. She also gushed about heroes of the faith such as Sister Rosemary M. Wixom, a prominent modern female leader in the tradition, and Joseph Smith, founder of the religion.

"Generations of LDS leaders, from Joseph Smith and Brigham Young to Gordon Hinckley and Thomas Monson, have noted the infinite blessings we have received from the Constitution of the United States," Clinton wrote. "The next president will swear an oath to preserve, protect, and defend that document for successive generations. And if you give me the honor to serve as your president, I will fight every day to carry out that sacred responsibility."

The effort was capped off with a bona fide campaign video, "We Are Mormons for Hillary," released roughly a month before Election Day. The ad featured a bipartisan group of Mormons—including both former GOP state representatives and a Democratic candidate for Utah state senate—reading a passage from Clinton's autobiography, *It Takes a Village*. They provided the voice-over for slow-motion footage of children frolicking across a picturesque Utahan landscape, laughing and rolling in the grass as the Wasatch Mountains towered in the distance.

"We are Mormons for Hillary," the video concludes. "Join your friends and family and vote on November 8."

Annette Harris, an LDS member who was working as a policy fellow in the Utah for Clinton campaign at the time, said the ad was the result of prodding from the campaign's state director, who "really advocated for more help in Utah." Harris found the Clinton campaign's interest in Utah's religious voters "really validating," because it meant that "finally someone was seeing that this is important and worth investing in."[39]

But Eric Biggart, the current LDS Dems chair, noted the outreach was geared not necessarily toward Mormon Democrats but rather toward "moderate Republicans and Never Trumpers" to "convert some moderates to realize that our gospel views line up with [Democratic] party views a lot closer than they line up with Republican Party views."

It was a gutsy ploy to snare a constituency long written off by Democrats as hopelessly conservative, but Election Day results revealed the extent of Mormon distrust of Trump. According to the Utah Colleges Exit Poll, Trump won less than 45 percent of Mormon voters, or roughly half of what Romney secured in 2012 and 30 points below what John McCain garnered in 2008.[40] Trump's share of the overall state vote was roughly the same: he won 45.5 percent of the popular vote in Utah, far worse than McCain, who won 62.3 percent in 2008, and miles behind Romney, who garnered a staggering 72.8 percent in 2012.[41] McMullin made an impressive showing for an independent, picking up 21.5 percent of the vote behind Clinton's 27.5 percent.[42]

Trump actually performed better in Utah than most preelection polls in the state predicted, just as he did elsewhere. But there was a significant disparity between Utah and the rest of the country, where Trump won 61 percent of the overall Mormon vote.[43]

For Crystal Young-Otterstrom, the results spoke for themselves.

"The final numbers really did justify that investment," she said. "We came in much higher than a Democratic presidential candidate usually does in Utah. Our efforts really did pay off."

And yet for all that work, Clinton failed to secure Utah's electoral votes, raising questions as to whether faith outreach resources could have been better spent targeting the Democratic base elsewhere. Turnout among black voters in 2016, for instance, was the lowest since at least 2004.[44] Granted, religious messaging can't erase voter ID laws, which in states like Wisconsin are shown to disproportionately disenfranchise people of color. Still, religious outreach may have urged more progressives to the polls—be they black, white, Hispanic, or otherwise.

But according to McCarthy, the urgency for faith outreach simply doesn't resonate with many Democratic operatives.

"The culture of this is still just off," he told me, shaking his head in frustration. "If you ask a lot of the political operative folks that I work with, they would say, 'That's just not part of our coalition anymore.'"

Worse, the tiny tribe of liberal faith operatives was rocked by scandal. In 2018, it was revealed that Burns Strider—a longtime faith adviser to the Clintons and a regular at Grassmere gatherings—had been accused of sexual harassment on the campaign in 2008, but Hillary Clinton declined to fire him.[45] Burns went on to run an independent super PAC that supported her 2016 candidacy, where he also allegedly harassed multiple women.[46]

And even if an entirely new group of people take over faith outreach, McCarthy stressed, the Democrats will still be forced into an awkward choice between divergent opinions about which votes they should target.

"Are we going to be the party of just Catholic Midwestern voters in Ohio and Pennsylvania, or are we going to be just Union Seminary? I think those are two very different things—we can be both."

Indeed, solving the new God gap may require less either-or and more both-and. Election night 2016 was a bleak moment for many Democrats, but there was a notable highlight on an otherwise catastrophic night, a glimmer of hope amidst the darkness. In North Carolina, a state Hillary Clinton lost by nearly four points, a Democrat narrowly unseated the incumbent Republican governor. Pundits credited the electoral shift to Moral Mondays as lead by Rev. William Barber—a grassroots faith activist, not a Washington insider—who assembled a coalition with the goal of putting a Democrat in office in the Tar Heel State. Barber, the head of the longstanding protest, had even delivered a fiery address at the 2016 Democratic National Convention.[47]

As discussed in previous chapters, the 2016 convention surprised many political writers for its unusually religious flair, and Clinton's team had been in regular contact with Barber.[48] The pastor even stopped by the campaign's New York City headquarters one day in September to "fire people up." It was a mostly impromptu rah-rah session (technically *not* an endorsement, as Barber, like Campbell in 2012, never endorsed any candidate); Barber happened to be in town that day for an event at Union Seminary to condemn Trump's rhetoric. But McCarthy wasn't surprised by the visit, since "at that point I was talking to [Barber] pretty regularly."

In the Trump era, the best indicator of the progressive faith community's power likely won't be found at a political convention, or even by looking at the size of a candidate's faith outreach team. It likely won't be found in Washington at all, but rather at the far-flung rallies and spiritual gatherings headlined by Barber and others, ones that assemble disparate and unusual religious groups—some of which are only just now beginning to wade into political waters.

CHAPTER TWELVE

★ ★ ★

The Future of Faith

W hen I pulled my comically oversized rental truck into the field-turned-parking-lot set aside for the 2019 Wild Goose Festival, the first thing I noticed was the mud. The second thing I noticed was the politics.

I'm sometimes asked if the Religious Left is really a *thing*, but people who ask me that have clearly never been to Wild Goose, an annual event held at a picturesque Appalachian campground that stretches alongside the rushing French Broad River in Hot Springs, North Carolina. Every year, for three or four days, thousands of liberal Christians make the trek to this patch of the Blue Ridge Mountains for what organizers describe as the "largest progressive gathering footprint in North America."[1] The result is a spectacle that is one part Burning Man, one part Netroots Nation, and two parts old-school tent revival.

Or as some like to call it, Jesus Coachella.

Officially, I was there to cover the event for *Religion News Service*.[2] But if I'm being honest, I had an ulterior motive. I'd always wanted to visit Wild Goose, primarily to figure out why so many progressive faith activists—particularly liberal white mainline Christians and evangelicals—mentioned it as one of the most important spiritual gatherings of the year. The answer became obvious in seconds: Just walking along the dirt road to the main stage is like watching the patches stitched across a liberal Christian activist's backpack spring to life. There were brightly colored booths for progressive faith groups such as Sojourners, The Resistance Prays, Network, and the Creation Care Alliance. Musicians of various stripes belted out left-leaning spirituals from a hodgepodge of stages as fans—some branded with religiously themed tattoos, some sporting dreadlocks, more than a few with both—swayed back and forth, singing along.

People passed me adorned in shirts and hats bearing slogans such as Black Lives Matter; Make America Native Again; Feminist; Who Would Jesus Execute?; and I Met God—They're Queer, Y'all. As an expression of respect for the LGBTQ community, many wore buttons delineating their preferred pronouns—*he*, *she*, *they*, *them*, etc. One man milled about the crowd in a sandwich board that read Free White Ally Coaching.

As I approached a crowd in front of the main stage, I heard the booming voice of Rev. William Barber.

"I've seen the spirit," Barber declared, flanked by a rainbow flag and a makeshift cage-like structure designed to remind attendees that children were being detained along the US-Mexico border. "I've been in Kentucky, in rural Appalachia, up in Harlan County. They told me you can't go to Harlan County to organize because that's so-and-so's [Trump's] country. I said, 'Well, I heard the earth is the Lord's and the fullness thereof, and all them that dwell therein.'"

The preacher went on to list groups he had organized with and protested alongside as part of leading the Poor People's Campaign, closing the section of his speech with an anecdote from a teachers' march in North Carolina.

"I asked one of the teachers, 'Why are you here?' She said, 'Because the Holy Ghost said I had to be here.' I said, 'Oh, my God.'"

The crowd erupted in response, some whooping and shouting "Hallelujah!" When Barber slowly exited the stage several minutes later, droves of attendees mobbed him, clamoring for selfies. Some said they were praying for him; others asked him to pray on their behalf. At one point, Barber laid hands on a seminarian to pray for the young man's pursuit of ordination.

I watched as the line of supporters slowly winnowed over the course of several minutes. It took a while for the flurry of hugs and handshakes to dissipate, but when Barber finally had a moment alone, I leaned in to ask if he saw his activism as creating its own spiritual community, one that spans multiple faiths. He rejected the premise of my question as a "false dichotomy," insisting that the spirit—presumably, the holy variety—isn't beholden to such petty distinctions.

"You know, the spirit is like wind: You don't see the wind, you see the effects of wind," he said. Beads of sweat dripped from his brow as he spoke, plopping across the front of a black preacher's shirt ill designed for the summer heat. He reached out a hand to lean against the car that had pulled around to whisk him away, nodding to an assistant who hustled to keep him hydrated. Partly filtered by the trees, the mountains towered behind him. "When we see people willing to put their bodies on the line for immigrants, we see the wind. When we see people coming together across these lines in deep spiritual ways, you see wind. We even see people who don't necessarily believe, but they are pulled to this justice and this love. When you see people saying, 'We're not going to stand down in this moment,' I see something much deeper than just the political conversation, and much deeper than a left versus right, conservative versus liberal context."

I chewed on Barber's answer as I wandered around Wild Goose interviewing attendees. I was eager to learn as much as I could about why their faith compelled them to spend hundreds of dollars on a ticket to a place where tree-slung slack lines and hammocks (approximately a dozen) significantly outnumber cell phone towers (approximately zero). As they answered my questions over craft beer and samosas from nearby food trucks, a basic truism emerged: for modern religious progressives, there is little, if any, distinction between the spiritual and the political, and activism is often seen as a religious edict.

This is the opposite of new. As earlier chapters in this book have detailed, generations of faith-fueled liberals have preached similar beliefs throughout US history. But the oft-obscured subtext of the modern Religious Left is that it emerged from *religious communities,* many of which were already in states of transition or reevaluation.

When the political winds in the Trump era shifted in a direction that faithful liberals found abhorrent, flocks of (often white) faithful leveraged theological liberalism as a means to become hubs of activism, typically guided by other (often nonwhite) faith traditions that have enthusiastically engaged in advocacy for decades.

With all the marching and protesting, it can be easy to forget that left-leaning religious groups are far more than activist organizations that conveniently help Democrats. They are a living, breathing community of religious Americans who are passionate about their faith and who attend a temple or a mosque or a house church as often as secular liberals walk into a Whole Foods (although more than a few religious progressives buy their avocados there, too). And as the modern Religious Left continues to take shape, enjoying moments of influence in debates both denominational and presidential, preexisting religious communities with politicized spirituality are impacting the future of politics and, increasingly, the nature of American faith itself.

To understand what the Religious Left wants, you have to understand how—and why—they worship. That means you need to look at some of the major faith groups that are helping it to organize and craft a unifying theology: namely, the emergent church, longstanding coalitions of largely nonwhite faith groups, and a new crop of progressive religious communities led primarily by women.

FROM EMERGENT CHURCH TO EMERGING POWER

Wild Goose wasn't always hyperpoliticized, at least not explicitly so. The conference is the culmination of what is often called the *emergent, emergence,* or *emerging church* movement, an enigmatic and often purposely ineffable phenomenon that picked up steam in the years just after 2000 and, at least in early iterations, was not overtly political in its outlook.

The origins of the emergent church are tough to trace and a matter of dispute, but the leaders most frequently associated with the movement are primarily white evangelical authors and pastors, including Rob Bell, Doug Pagitt, and Brian McLaren. Defining what they helped create is tricky, in part because the participants disagreed among themselves about its precise dimensions and even who was in the club. Some insisted on referring to emergence as a conversation instead of a movement. Others, such as evangelical megapastor (and eventually *disgraced* megapastor) Mark Driscoll, were initially seen as part of the emergent in-crowd only to distance themselves later as the liberal undertow became apparent.

Still, there were shared—or at least overlapping—tendencies. Leaders in the movement often shepherded communities that emphasized new styles of preaching and worship or revamped ancient styles for new occasions (celebrating the Eucharist in a bar), signaled a willingness to question traditional theological beliefs and dogmas (flirting with versions of universalism), and voiced an inherent skepticism of institutions and traditional voices (forming new ministry networks instead of relying on old ones).

The attention paid to *evangelical* emergents, however, obscured a related movement that bubbled up among mainline Christians. Unlike the evangelical iteration, the loudest voices among mainline emergent churches included people of color, like former PC(USA) moderator Bruce Reyes-Chow and women such as Lutheran pastor Rev. Nadia Bolz-Weber, Episcopal priest and author Rev. Stephanie Spellers, academic Phyllis Tickle, and religious history scholar Diana Butler Bass. They, too, challenged dogmas and hierarchy—complete with conversational sermons that insisted on open dialogue with the congregation. But they also brought with them a robust academic approach that was often unabashedly liberal: in a departure from their evangelical Christian brethren, these mainline emergents were far more likely to openly embrace LGBTQ identities, with several leading faith communities with heavy LGBTQ contingents.

Mainline emergents were also generally more likely to engage in direct political activism. Several Protest Chaplains who appeared at the inaugural Occupy Wall Street demonstrations, for example, attended Spellers's church—an Episcopal congregation in Boston known as the Crossing. (Full disclosure: as a graduate student in divinity school, I attended and interned at this church.)

The commonalities outweighed the differences, however. Evangelical and mainline emergents both engaged heavily with postmodern thought, inculcating the practice of deconstructing ideas and systems of power into their theology. This emphasis on deconstruction triggered a wealth of religious debate but had the unintentional effect of hamstringing efforts to organize an expanding emerging community. A movement inherently skeptical of labels and institutions was *also* skeptical of efforts to build yet another institution with a label, and several attempts to establish defined emergent church databases and networks were eventually abandoned.

Database or no, a complex, organic emergent church community existed all the same. It was made up of diverse communities that often discovered they had more in common with *each other* than with congregations in their respective denominations. It was this impetus that inspired members from both evangelical and mainline branches—McLaren, Pagitt, Tickle, and Bolz-Weber—to organize and speak at the inaugural Wild Goose in 2011. Partly modeled on the Greenbelt Festival, a similar celebration in the United Kingdom, it was meant to focus on church-specific questions.

At the time, McLaren voiced his frustration with critics who derided the festival as liberal.[3] But his critics had a point: McLaren had long been more political (and arguably more liberal) than other evangelicals in the emergent church movement, sometimes identifying as an activist and participating in protests. In addition to serving on the board of Sojourners, he openly (but as a private citizen) endorsed Barack Obama during the 2008 election on the website of the Matthew 25 Network—the independent group founded by Mara Vanderslice Kelly to bolster faith-rooted support of Obama's campaign.[4]

Even so, political labels worried McLaren, an earthy bald man with a Yoda-esque smile that effortlessly evokes a sense of concentrated spiritual wisdom. An avid nature lover, he spoke to me from his home near the Florida Everglades which, while not *exactly* Dagobah, is close enough.

"Because I grew up evangelical/fundamentalist, the word *liberal* is the worst word," he said.[5] "Liberal is synonymous with evil."

He frets over pragmatic concerns as well. Stories abound of prominent evangelical authors who faced direct consequences for being deemed too liberal. When Eugene Peterson—a Presbyterian minister and theologian popular among evangelicals—told evangelical writer Jonathan Merritt in a 2017 interview that he would perform a same-sex marriage,[6] LifeWay Christian Resources threatened to pull Peterson's books from its store shelves, including his popular Bible translation, *The Message: The Bible in Contemporary Language*.[7] Within twenty-four hours, Peterson reversed course, saying, "On further reflection and prayer, I would like to retract that."

For evangelical emergent church authors, simply *gesturing* toward a more liberal theology had consequences. Albert Mohler, president of the Southern Baptist Theological Seminary and a titan of evangelical thought, decried Rob Bell's 2011 book *Love Wins* as universalist (the idea that everyone goes to heaven) and further chided the emerging church movement as "pushing Protestant liberalism—just about a century late."[8] McLaren rushed to Bell's defense,[9] and Bell rejected Mohler's assertion. (He contended that he merely set out a range of exploratory options for the afterlife, one of which just so *happens* to closely resemble a version of universalism.)[10] But the conservative evangelical dismissal of the emergent church movement persisted and ultimately caught up to McLaren.

"In my earliest books, I was trying to open the door for people who are conservative to think a little more broadly on issues," he said.[11] "Of course, my fear was that I was going to be outed or labeled as liberal because as soon as I am labeled in that way, nobody's going to read my books. I just knew how that was going to go—and that's exactly how it went."

Hand-wringing notwithstanding, McLaren ended up embracing his liberal persona. In 2012, he officiated a "commitment ceremony with traditional Christian elements" at the same-sex wedding of his son, whose nuptials were covered by the *New York Times*. Despite blowback, he retained a robust audience among progressive Catholics and liberal mainliners.[12] Pagitt, Bell, and others followed suit to varying degrees.

By the time of the 2019 Wild Goose Festival, the merger of starry-eyed emergent church theological liberalism and vintage mainline Protestant progressivism was complete. Festival attendees flocked to a panel entitled "What ever happened to the emerging church?," cramming into a tiny dirt floor tent to listen to a conversation between Mike Clawson (a scholar and onetime "emerging church planter"), Diana Butler Bass, and Brian McLaren. The three agreed that while the emerging church movement no longer appeared cohesive, the most obvious echoes of the conversation could still be found in mainline churches.

"Institutionally, the mainline actually heard this," said Bass, a former evangelical turned Episcopalian.

Indeed, if Wild Goose is seen as a product of the emergent church, several mainline denominations have bought its wares wholesale. The Episcopal Church, the Evangelical Lutheran Church in America, and the United Church of Christ were all listed as official partners of Wild Goose in 2019, and all three sported booths at the festival. A smattering of mainline seminaries also erected tables, which they covered with glossy brochures advertising their ministries. Elements of other denominations, including the Young Adult Volunteer program of the PC(USA) and the United Methodist Church's Global Mission Fellows, also partnered for the event. The emergent church's penchant for cheeky, alternative forms of worship was on display as well. One group convened a Communion service in which the traditional bread and wine were replaced by doughnuts and bourbon. People raved about it for days.

But what the emergent panelists *didn't* discuss was just how political many leaders of the movement have become in recent years. Bass, for her part, has embraced a firebrand political voice under the Trump administration, mixing her religious acumen with strident critiques of the president and his policies on Twitter and in opinion pieces for CNN. When Trump's campaign manager referred to the president as a "savior" provided by God, Bass quote-tweeted the official and replied, "I'm so old that I remember when Christians believed that Jesus Christ—and not Donald Trump—was their savior."[13]

McLaren did make an offhand reference during the panel to a

moment when he realized the sociological dimensions of his theology. He recounted a story of meeting an African theologian and confessing what he thought was a profound revelation: "Postmodern is postcolonial." The theologian's response: "You finally got it!"

McLaren declined to detail precisely how that realization pushed him toward more political work, but he didn't really have to. If participants wanted to hear how he connected the spiritual with the political, they had only to wait a few hours to hear him moderate a panel entitled "Faith in the Age of Tyranny." It was organized by Faith in Public Life (FPL), the same group that helped mobilize and organize religious groups to pass the Affordable Care Act.

The first panel question: What to make of the Religious Left?

"What I always say is I am progressive because of my faith, not despite my faith," said panelist Jennifer Butler, head of FPL and whose husband, Glenn Zuber, leads an emergent church community in Washington, DC. Although she expressed ambivalence about the Religious Left title, she recalled how her organization received a wave of positive responses after an NPR article described FPL as emblematic of the term. The organization's in-boxes overflowed with elated emails from people gushing over the association, telling Butler it was something they had been looking for all their lives.

Moved, Butler responded with a spurt of evangelism.

"One of the joys of my life was connecting [with] people who contacted us after that piece," she said, raising her voice slightly above the sound of the French Broad River rushing behind her. "I spent a day reaching out to people and helping them find a congregation in their area that they could worship in."

McLaren would later explain to me that his own interest in the Religious Left (although he, too, isn't sure about the term) is mirrored in his ever-more-political activism. In addition to assisting Obama's 2008 campaign—during which he traveled to states like Iowa giving speeches—he worked with Doug Pagitt ahead of the 2018 midterms on a Vote Common Good initiative, which targeted liberal religious voters through a bus tour and a series of rallies in roughly thirty battleground congressional districts across the country.[14] It was after speaking in

October 2018 at one such rally in Iowa—which included a mixture of speeches and hymns—that McLaren encountered J. D. Scholten, a former minor-league baseball player and then congressional candidate running against Republican representative Steve King in Iowa's Fourth District.[15] McLaren said that Scholten, a Catholic, approached him after the session and expressed shock at how the pastor had outlined progressive support for abortion rights in a religious context.

"[Scholten] came up and said that in every single town hall he did, one of the first questions asked was 'How can you be a Democrat and a baby killer?'" McLaren said. "And he said something like, 'Boy, you talked about that so directly . . . I learned more tonight about how to address these issues than I've learned in all of my campaigns so far.'"

It was too late to help Scholten, who made a strong showing at the polls but still lost to King by a little more than 3 points (47 percent to 50.4 percent, an 8-point swing in favor of Democrats compared to 2016). But the experience inspired McLaren to help more candidates talk about faith. Ahead of the 2020 election, he has expanded his involvement with Vote Common Good's work, and partnered with Pagitt to help candidates craft religious messaging. McLaren had just finished meeting in Washington, DC, with three Democratic candidates for public office when I spoke to him in July 2019.

"We need to help Democratic candidates in general to learn to speak about their own faith," said McLaren, who declined to name his three trainees. "Even if they're not religious, we need to help them learn how to understand religious voters."

The political footprint of the emerging church movement can be found in other circles as well. William Barber's communications director, Stephen Roach Knight, was once an active participant in emerging church circles, and Rev. Stephanie Spellers is the canon to the presiding bishop of the Episcopal Church for evangelism and reconciliation, a position that works closely with Presiding Bishop Michael Curry. (Curry achieved international fame for preaching at the wedding of Meghan Markle and Prince Harry, but a week later he was marching through the streets of DC, arm-in-arm with Jim Wallis, protesting the Trump administration.[16])

There is also the undeniable influence of older, left-leaning evangelicals who have mixed religion and politics for decades, such as Jim Wallis and Tony Campolo—the latter of whom Barber referred to as "the man who changed my life" when Barber spotted him at Wild Goose. Although they are rarely thought of as radicals, as they were in the 1970s, Wallis and Campolo retain a dedicated audience of progressive Catholics and mainliners that overlaps deeply with emerging church leaders. They have struggled to embrace LGBTQ rights with the same fervency as mainliners, but their publications—especially *Sojourners* and *Red Letter Christians*—remain sought-after reading material among many at Wild Goose.

This old guard has present-day disciples. Author and activist Shane Claiborne, having distanced himself from both the emerging church and more overtly LGBTQ-affirming positions, is nonetheless a constant at progressive Christian events and at Barber's protests—when he's not organizing his own, that is. He was an early leader of the New Monastic movement, which overlapped with emerging church circles and which revolved around several intentional residential communities among the urban poor, led by people who had studied with Campolo.[17] He also partnered with Barber confidant Rev. Jonathan Wilson-Hartgrove and author Enuma Okoro to pen the 2010 book *Common Prayer: A Liturgy for Ordinary Radicals.* The daily prayer book—which, naturally, is also available in app form—emphasizes social justice and is widely used in progressive Christian circles.

Even with this groundswell of political theology among white mainliners and progressive evangelicals, however, their organizing efforts ultimately pale in comparison to the mobilization apparatus of nonwhite and non-Christian faiths. Many liberal white Christians are several decades late to the game, but they are eager to learn.

TRAINING PROPHETS OF RESISTANCE

Judged purely by optics, the Prophetic Resistance Summit in October 2017 is the aesthetic opposite of Wild Goose.

Instead of thousands amassed in a remote, boggy campground in the Blue Ridge Mountains, some 350 faith leaders—carefully assembled by Faith in Action (then called PICO National Network)—convened in a J. W. Marriott hotel in downtown Indianapolis, Indiana. Instead of focusing primarily on Christianity, the gathering was an aggressively interfaith affair, featuring attendees and speakers who identified with Islam, Buddhism, and Native American spirituality in addition to Christianity. And instead of hosting a predominantly white crowd, the ballroom that housed the Prophetic Resistance Summit was filled with people of color.

And there were exactly zero slack lines.

Black Christian leaders in particular were core facilitators at the Prophetic Resistance Summit, which took place just two months after the violence-ridden march of white supremacists in Charlottesville, Virginia. Organizers specified that a chief goal of the gathering was to confront "white supremacy and structural racism," and Rev. Traci Blackmon was one of many speakers who focused their remarks on the central theme of race.[18] Invoking the biblical story of Moses, she argued that combating injustice with acts of resistance is not just a holy calling, but also something God prepares faith leaders to do—just as God prepared Moses. "For forty years, Moses had been demoted from the palace to the pasture," she said. "And for forty years he kept showing up, not knowing what was going to happen. See, God was preparing Moses not just for the moment in the desert, but for what was going to come after—for liberation."

Blackmon then brought the subject back to the present, insisting that when leaders in the audience participate in demonstrations, the divine accompanies their every step.

"God is there in those places where things seem to be going up in flames today," she said, her voice rising. "God is still at the border! God is in the midst of the DREAMers! God is among the state-sanctioned poor! God is inside the human warehouses where we cage 2.2 million of our citizens in what we call a prison industrial complex! God is with our LGBTQ family! . . . And whether you call us

Black Lives Matter, or the movement for Black lives, or protesters, or Black identity extremists, the fact is God is with us!"

As I roamed the halls to report on the summit for *ThinkProgress*, I quickly noticed the depth of experience among attendees when it came to mixing faith and politics. Most told me that they had been reared in congregations that have framed faith as a pathway to civic participation for generations, and they themselves had participated in faith-fueled activism for as long as they could remember. Rather than view progressive religious expressions as subversive, conference participants—including then Women's March co-chair Linda Sarsour and Charlottesville veteran Rev. Osagyefo Sekou—saw them as a baseline. So fervent was this belief that summit organizers insisted their gathering was "not a conference, but a strategy session" to prepare "prophetic spiritual leaders" to organize their own faith communities for campaigns ahead of the 2018 and 2020 elections.[19]

It all reflected a mindset that showed a far more tactical approach to electoral politics than what I found at Wild Goose. One presentation in Indiana, led by a staffer from Faith in Action's 501(c)4 wing, detailed strategies for how faith leaders could impact local elections. As the staffer spoke, participants could be seen peering down at the official conference pamphlet, which listed the religious affiliation of every member of Congress. After describing how Faith in Action helped elect a new county prosecutor in Florida, the staffer asked the crowd who that elected official was accountable to.

"To the people!" the crowd shouted.

"That's right, to the people—to the faith community," the staffer replied.

Yet Wild Goose and the Prophetic Resistance Summit remain spiritually linked, as both are expressions of the overarching theology that permeates the modern Religious Left. They just currently serve different roles: whereas Wild Goose evoked a politicized spiritual community ready to *participate* in campaigns/protests, the Indianapolis summit gave *leaders* of those same campaigns/protests an opportunity to fine-tune their theology and tactics.

The summit also included a smattering of progressive white evangelicals, although they adopted a posture that focused less on preaching and more on listening. It's a disposition I would find again when covering a separate gathering in Virginia a few months later: the 2018 Red Letter Revival, an evangelical-led religious protest-slash-revival aimed at Liberty University. It was there that left-leaning white evangelicals spoke openly about their desire to learn from nonwhite faith leaders regarding all things activism—especially the black church.

I was told this explicitly by Jonathan Martin, a white evangelical author, who was forcibly removed from the Liberty campus after criticizing the school's president, Jerry Falwell Jr.

"People like me, from some of the spaces we come from, we're grappling with these issues for the first time—like, 'Oh, what's the relationship of faith to politics supposed to be?'" Martin said as we sat in my car, hiding from the rain. My CRV isn't small, but I still had to move the seat back to make room for his towering build. "The black church just has those resources in ways a lot of our traditions don't. So I know what I'm trying to do here is a lot of listening and learning from my brothers and sisters in that tradition, because the resources are there. We don't have to just make this up as we go."

Rev. Lisa Sharon Harper, a black evangelical who spoke at the Red Letter Revival and who stared down white supremacists in Charlottesville, later explained that while white clergy learning activism from people of color isn't exactly unprecedented, demographic changes are likely to make it a more common occurrence in the future.

"I think it's really important that the Christian faith is browning as much as the nation is browning," she told me via video chat in 2019.[20] "Because as the Christian faith browns, I think we'll be much more likely to find allies within the Christian faith for that radical redistribution of power in our society."

The shift is big. According to Pew data, the traditional indicators of faith are increasingly dominated by people of color, particularly African Americans and Hispanic Americans. When asked in 2014 about the importance of religion in their lives, black and Latinx people were far more likely to describe faith as "very important" (75 percent and 59 percent, respectively) than white people (49 percent). The same is true for worship attendance: black and Latinx people (47 percent and 39 percent, respectively) are more likely than white people (34 percent) to attend worship at least once a week.[21]

Back at the Prophetic Resistance Summit, Michael-Ray Mathews, the director of clergy organizing for Faith in Action, told me that the emergence (or, depending on your perspective, resurgence) of a race-conscious, action-oriented form of faith reflects what he described as a "theology of resistance." A minister who effortlessly intertwines sermon-like imagery into normal conversation, he said that although *resistance* has become a catchword for liberal demonstrators in the aftermath of Trump's election, Faith in Action and its thousands of affiliated congregations first began employing the term after the 2014 Ferguson protests. "Many of us saw the dragon of white supremacy and empire [in Ferguson] in ways we had never seen before, and we realized we needed to draw on something much deeper to be able to face that dragon," Mathews said.[22] "It begged this question: Are we chaplains to the empire or prophets to the resistance?"

If the summit was any indication, being a prophet to the resistance—or as Mathews also puts it, prophets *of* the resistance[23]—involves drawing upon a web of activist-minded congregations usually led by people of color. Halfway through the three-day summit, attendees visited Friendship Missionary Baptist Church, a majority-black congregation in the city's West Side neighborhood. They were there to witness a youth action by the church, which is a member of the local Faith in Action coalition, IndyCAN (since renamed Faith in Indiana). The mass of interfaith leaders—some in yarmulkes, more than a few in collars, still others in tribal garb—filed into a broad sanctuary, where they sang, worshipped, and watched a band of young leaders press a local police chief to help with a campaign to end gun violence in the city.

Later in the service, Bishop Dwayne Royster, a black United Church of Christ pastor and Faith in Action's national political director, bounded up to the pulpit. Adorned in a vintage dark suit and what looked like a hip pair of thin rimless glasses, he delivered a passionate talk that spelled out precisely what kind of theology he hoped the group would embody.

"We're not the 'nice' faith people!" he bawled over shouts of affirmation from the crowd, many of whom nodded along or leaped to their feet in support. "We're not just going to show up to a vigil and be glad [a politician] invited us! We have some demands. We are prophets of the people and we have something to say!"

The crowd roared in response, raising their hands in jubilant prayer as Royster stared out at them. Below him sat a hand-painted banner, its defiant message wrapped around the aging wooden pulpit: Moral Vision, Political Muscle.

FAITH = REBELLION

Rabbi Sharon Brous addressed the crowd at the Prophetic Resistance Summit with a steady, confident voice that was just audible above the crowd's boisterous shouts. The opening keynote speaker for the gathering, she drew on her experience at IKAR—the Jewish community she leads in Los Angeles, California—to outline three different kinds of faith that she said frustrate younger generations: religious extremism, or the "exploitation of sacred texts to justify hatred and violence in God's name"; religious routineism, a "dead" faith she described as "rote, soulless, empty religiosity"; and religious escapism, a "pacifier," "diversion," or "thoughts-and-prayers religion."

Brous then posited a fourth option, one rooted in an appreciation for activism.

"My Jewish tradition is centered around obedience to God and observance of *mitzvot*, commandments, and yet the central charge of our tradition is to stand in defiance of unjust power structures," she said.[24] "Our heroes are those who stood up for the vulnerable, who risked everything, challenging both God and man to fight for what is just and right."

She later added: "Faith is a rebellion against [the] world. The goal is not to be quieted, to feel good, to get comfortable and settled while the palace burns. It is to be awake and to fight—with love—for the courage we need, for the family we yearn for, for the beloved community we're called to be, for the world we want our children to inherit."

The religious community Brous leads, IKAR, makes this connection between faith and activism obvious on its website, plastering the phrase "We are activists," alongside a litany of descriptors on its landing page. Brous also made it clear in her talk that she takes this justice-focused approach to faith seriously, recounting how she was recently arrested in Washington, DC, for participating in a protest opposing the Republican Party's 2017 efforts to repeal the Affordable Care Act.

Granted, action-focused theology is familiar to many American Jews. Like the black church, Jewish communities have long been a mainstay of progressive faith organizing. Among the extensive list of faith-led liberal Jewish activists you'll find Rabbi Abraham Joshua Heschel, who famously marched with Martin Luther King Jr., and Marshall Ganz, a civil rights organizer credited with helping craft Obama's 2008 field operation (and who now, with a rabbi, coteaches a Harvard course on moral leadership). The modern heirs to this tradition include DC-based organizations such as Bend the Arc: Jewish Action and the Religious Action Center of Reform Judaism (known as "the RAC"), both of which are cornerstones of contemporary progressive protests. In a country where 64 percent of Jews lean toward or identify as members of the Democratic Party according to Pew, faith-fueled progressivism is practically assumed in many Jewish communities.[25]

Yet even in a deeply progressive religious context, Brous represents a small but significant shift toward a different form of spiritual progressivism. IKAR is not your average Jewish synagogue: it is not tied to any one Jewish denomination. Its founding can be traced to a 2004 email that Brous and her friend (a civil rights lawyer) sent out inviting friends and others to a "conversation" aimed at those who might "bail on religion." (It included the promise of scotch as a peace offering.) It ultimately became one of seven Jewish communities that banded together in 2016 to form the Jewish Emergent Network, a loose conglomeration of what are often described as "nontraditional"

Jewish communities. Their number includes experimental bands of believers like San Francisco's the Kitchen as well as more prominent, established synagogues such as Sixth&I in Washington, DC.

If the use of *emergent* in the network's title sounds familiar, you're not the only one who thinks so. Self-declared emergent Jewish leaders and Christian emerging/emergent church leaders have been in conversation for more than a decade, regularly discussing the overlap between their respective missions. One such meeting of the theological minds took place in Simi Valley, California, in 2006, organized by a group that went by the peculiarly futuristic name Synagogue 3000. The *Jewish Journal* covered the event and noted the commonality between both flavors of emergent faith. "Both 'emergent' Jews and Christians share a progressive outlook, a philosophy of welcoming and hospitality, a commitment to community and social justice," wrote the *Journal*. "Both are using creativity to build engaging, spiritual communities."[26]

Brous, who offered a prayer at an interfaith service commemorating Barack Obama's second inauguration, celebrated the connection between the community she heads and similar progressive, activist-minded religious communities in other faiths during a TED Talk she gave at TEDWomen 2016 in San Francisco. "There is a shared religious ethos that is now emerging in the form of revitalized religion in this country," she told the TED audience, referencing women's mosques and Catholic groups like Nuns on the Bus. "And while the theologies and practices vary very much between these independent communities, what we can see are some common, consistent threads between them."

In addition to an action-forward ethos, members of the Jewish Emergent Network share another thing in common: women lead many of the communities, another trend that extends beyond Judaism. As Christian scholar Diana Butler Bass explained to me in an interview, the gradual rise of women in religious leadership within mainline Christian denominations, which began in the 1950s, has led to an uptick in women's voices in Christian discourse and, by extension, in political discourse. "They used to say you couldn't imagine a church surviving without women as members," said Bass, who once "got in trouble" with her colleagues when she was teaching at an evangelical college for hosting roundtables on women's ordination. "But now I can't imagine, say, the Presbyterian Church (USA) without women in leadership. . . . And the reality is, once women become religious leaders, they bring women's issues to the fore. And women's issues have often—not always, but often—been the idea of creating a society that is more just, more compassionate."

It's a difficult point to rebut, especially considering how many of today's progressive faith leaders are women—including many of the voices profiled in this book. Whether it's leading Faith in Public Life (Rev. Jennifer Butler) or fighting white supremacy in its various forms (Rev. Traci Blackmon); whether it's organizing the Women's March (Linda Sarsour) or helping craft a new vision for the interfaith movement (Valarie Kaur); whether it's helping pass marriage equality laws in southern states (Jasmine Beach-Ferrara) or taking part in discussions of Israel-Palestine (Rabbi Jill Jacobs); whether it's leading the immigrant rights struggle (Bishop Minerva Carcaño) or helping get the Affordable Care Act across the finish line (scores of Catholic nuns)—women lead a staggering number of modern Religious Left movements.

Meanwhile, some women are already creating their own more liberal religious expressions. In Chicago, Muslims can now gather at Masjid al-Rabia, a "woman-centered" mosque that does not separate men and women during prayers, replaces Friday sermons (*khutba*) with discussion circles, and features leadership that is openly LGBTQ.[27] Although still a fledgling community, the mosque embraces advocacy as central to its identity, particularly its outreach to more than six hundred prisoners who are both LGBTQ and Muslim.

The liberalizing trend has also impacted a subset of aging, historic congregations in major cities across the country. The emphasis on action—particularly forms that focus on justice rather than charity—has changed not only how they worship but also how they use their worship spaces.

Take Judson Memorial Church, a Protestant congregation near

Greenwich Village in New York City, headed by Rev. Donna Schaper. When you visit the church's website, the first tab doesn't announce worship times or give sermon transcriptions. It links to a Justice page that proudly details the community's dedication to LGBTQ rights, reproductive justice, and taking action on climate change. Judson also hosts the offices of the New Sanctuary Coalition and regularly rents out its spaces to activists. When Alexandria Ocasio-Cortez, then thought to be a long shot to win a congressional seat, cut an advertisement for her campaign, it included images of her silhouetted against stained glass windows. Those were Judson's windows, as the church was hosting a convention of the New York City Democratic Socialists.[28]

Religion scholar Simran Jeet Singh told me these kinds of bold, public-facing activist stances by houses of worship have the potential to attract a generation of younger, more justice-focused Americans.

"Showing publicly the power of religion to produce and sustain justice makes religion more compelling," he said. "[Young people] have sincere empathy and sincere commitment to justice. They really feel like they want to be doing good in this world. A lot of people are having trouble finding a system of ideas—coherent ideas—that gives them a home, roots, and a place where they can look for guidance. . . . And I think as we see more of a spotlight on the Religious Left, it will make religion more compelling for them."[29]

There are numerous other women-led communities in other cities (for one, Central Presbyterian Church in Atlanta, Georgia, is currently led by two women), although not all liberal religious leaders belong to traditions that embrace female religious leadership. But Bass argues that the secular and religious streams of the women's movement empty into the same harbor, lifting all feminist boats, and she suggests that the prominent role of women in the Religious Left helped the movement transcend the patriarchal constraints of individual denominations.

Similarly, as an ever more diverse band of faith leaders occupy positions of prominence—be they LGBTQ, immigrants, or non-

Christians—so too will the religious institutions they lead reflect a broader, more progressive slate of political concerns.

"Whenever you create those alternative spaces, it always has political consequences," Bass said.

KINGDOM COMING

The tilt toward justice-focused theology streamlined activist cooperation across denominations, faith groups, and advocacy organizations. It's partly why the Poor People's Campaign lists entire denominations such as the Presbyterian Church (USA), the Episcopal Church, the Christian Church (Disciples of Christ), the Progressive National Baptist Convention, the Union of Reform Judaism, the Unitarian Universalist Association, and the United Church of Christ among its formal partners. Arms of other denominations are also affiliated with the movement (the United Methodist Church's General Board of Church and Society and the Friends Committee on National Legislation), as are umbrella organizations (the Islamic Society of North America) and even individual worship communities (Rabbi Sharon Brous's IKAR).[30]

I mulled over these and other communities as I stood near the stage at the 2019 Wild Goose Festival, which attendees told me had a more political vibe than usual. They meant this in the most literal way possible: the speaker who followed William Barber was none other than Marianne Williamson, a long shot for the 2020 Democratic presidential nomination (organizers told me they had invited other candidates, but only Williamson showed up).

Williamson is Jewish but earned her fortune by writing a series of books that invoke a spirituality she describes as universal. We spoke briefly about faith before she took the stage to speak, taking refuge from the sun in a golf cart as Wild Goose attendees mulled past, seemingly unaware of our presence.

"I was told—and what I was told has proven to be correct—that this is a place of many like-minded people," she said.[31] "The intersection of religion and spirituality and social justice is my tribe. It's the space I inhabit."

Millions of potential voters would say the same. Only some of them would gravitate toward Williamson's particular brand of spirituality and policy. Others recoil from it and prefer other candidates. Still others find spiritual and political fulfillment far from Wild Goose, be it at the Prophetic Resistance Summit, immersed in a Red Letter Revival, or simply when communing with their worship community. But all would willingly call the ever-widening umbrella of progressive faith home.

And after years of uneven collaboration, these groups are finally working in lockstep to make their voices heard in politics. As I left Wild Goose, I spotted Brian McLaren and a few others huddled under an abandoned festival tent. I would later learn that McLaren and Pagitt's Vote Common Good project entered into a partnership with Faith in Action—complete with a formal memorandum of understanding—to impact the 2020 elections, from local races all the way to national contests. Sitting near McLaren was Rev. Bryan Berghoef, an emergent-influenced pastor who runs a *Pub Theology Live* podcast. The group spoke to him with hushed intensity, leaning over and gesturing excitedly as I passed.

A little more than a week later, Berghoef announced (from a bar) that he was running for Congress, hoping to unseat Republican representative Bill Huizenga in Michigan's Second, the same district that Secretary of Education Betsy DeVos calls home. When asked by a local reporter to explain his political message, Berghoef didn't hesitate to invoke religion. "My faith compels me to take action when I see my neighbors hurting, when the marginalized are ignored and mistreated, and when God's creation is under siege."[32]

Berghoef is in good company. All signs point to a resurgent Religious Left that, complicated and fragile though it may be, is gearing up to transform American politics—primarily because it has *already* transformed whole swaths of American faith.

Yes, the Religious Left is definitely still a *thing*. And it's not going anywhere.

Epilogue

On a blazing early morning in August 2019, a friend dropped me off in downtown Charleston, South Carolina. She put the car in park while I awkwardly fished my camera case out from the back seat. The zippers on my battered black canvas bag wobbled and clinked at odd angles as I pulled it across my chest, their once ovular shapes twisted and warped from years of overuse.

The camera I slid inside the case wasn't much better off. I was using it once again for journalism that day, but my pre-reporting preparation left a lot to be desired. I had lost a backup memory card a year prior at some Religious Left demonstration that I couldn't remember—in my defense, there were *a lot* of them at the time—and was forced to rely on a single memory card that I kept forgetting to replace. I dimly recalled a time when I was sure I would never fill it, but those days were long gone. I had spent the drive over from my friend's house absentmindedly cycling through the digital library of images to free up disk space, deleting what I could bring myself to erase from protests past.

We're a long way from that tent city in Boston, I thought, inspecting the camera's finicky latch. I'd jury-rigged it back into place more than once over the years, and it had yet to earn back my trust.

Eventually, I extricated myself and the case from the car and gave my friend a quick wave goodbye. I pivoted on my heels as she pulled away, sauntering down the narrow sidewalk and quietly cursing myself for wearing a blazer in the heat of the Carolina Lowcountry. I walked slowly, partly because that's the expected pace in my home state and partly because I was only a few steps from my destination: the sacred sanctuary of Emanuel AME Church, the site of the horrific 2015 shooting that left nine African American churchgoers dead at the hands of a white supremacist.

I had pitched my editors earlier that week on flying down to cover a major speech at the church by Democratic presidential candidate and New Jersey senator Cory Booker. It probably seemed like an odd request: the official press release said Booker's remarks would focus on racism and gun violence, a chance to offer a presidential-style speech in the aftermath of two mass shootings that had rocked the country the week before, one of which was tied to white nationalism. A cynical politico might have concluded that the choice of Emanuel Church was more about pageantry—condemning one racist shooting from the site of another—than faith.

But I knew Cory Booker and, for that matter, South Carolina politics. So I had a hunch religion would come up. Sure enough, when Booker took the stage a few minutes later, he opened with a reference to his own faith. "We're here this morning in the wake of yet another act of hatred in America," the senator began, his broad frame illuminated by the towering stained glass windows that lined the two-story sanctuary.[1] "But I come here today because of love. The kind of love I learned about in church growing up."

Booker condemned racism and gun violence, but repeatedly referenced religion as he did so. He invoked Galatians 6:7 from the New Testament ("Do not be deceived, God is not mocked; for whatever a man sows, this he will also reap"). to argue that acts of hatred come from hateful rhetoric "sowed" by others—particularly Donald Trump. He spoke of the faith that guided the Emanuel community out of their grief in the aftermath of the shooting and how religion, in its best moments, has threaded itself into the tapestry of the American experiment in ways that made society slightly more just, slightly more fair.

"We are here today because of our ancestors' sacrifices," he said. "They did what was difficult. Because they had faith. In God, in each other, and in a bolder, broader, and more inclusive patriotism. For patriotism is love of country, but you cannot love your country unless you love your fellow countrymen and women—all of them."

It was one of the more deeply religious political speeches I'd heard that year. And yet it was by no means the *only* one. On the contrary, the early stages of the 2020 Democratic primary season turned out to be an unabashedly religious affair, with candidates speaking openly and repeatedly about religion. Former US secretary of housing and urban development Julián Castro announced his candidacy across the street from the church in which he was baptized, and he frequently referenced his Catholicism on the trail.[2] Sen. Kamala Harris also invoked the divine during her announcement speech, loudly proclaiming a religious argument that sounded a lot like liberation theology. "Let's remember: when abolitionists spoke out and civil rights workers marched, their oppressors said they were dividing the races and violating the word of God," Harris said.[3] "But Frederick Douglass said it best and Harriet Tubman and Dr. King knew—to love the religion of Jesus is to hate the religion of the slave master."

So, too, was it with Pete Buttigieg, the mayor of South Bend, Indiana, whose rise from relative unknown to household name was arguably a direct result of his willingness to discuss matters of faith, whether by criticizing conservative iterations or discussing his own. After questioning the faith of Vice President Mike Pence live on CNN—"Is it that [Pence] stopped believing in scripture when he started believing in Donald Trump? I don't know"[4]—Buttigieg decried the causes of climate change as "a kind of sin"[5] and repeatedly called for a revival of the Religious Left during prominent appearances on shows like MSNBC's *Morning Joe*.[6]

Buttigieg would later walk back his comments slightly by acknowledging that the Religious Left had been operating "without much attention" for some time, but even that slight pivot signaled the encroaching influence of religious progressives on a Democratic field that didn't shy away from God talk.[7] Sen. Elizabeth Warren often cited Matthew 25, and Sen. Kirsten Gillibrand brought the spiritual fire by declaring Trump to be "contrary to the gospel."[8] In addition, longtime spiritual author Marianne Williamson constantly alluded to spiritual ideas—some mainstream, others decidedly not—and called for a "blooming" of the Religious Left.[9]

Booker and Buttigieg not only cited scripture during the early televised debates but also threw institutional weight behind their rhetoric; by the end of August, each was preparing to hire a national faith outreach director. The Democratic National Committee was way ahead of them: Rev. Derrick Harkins returned to the helm, hosting listening sessions with diverse groups of faith leaders and telling me that faith "will be a priority going into 2020, but even more importantly, beyond 2020."[10]

But two events that took place in June stand as perhaps the most concrete evidence of the Religious Left's rising power, and both were led by Rev. William Barber and Rev. Liz Theoharis as part of the Poor People's Campaign. The first was a protest outside the White House to decry the Trump administration. By all appearances, it was an archetypal Religious Left demonstration, featuring attendees and speakers from several progressive faith movements, including Rev. Traci Blackmon, Shane Claiborne, Rev. Jacqui Lewis, and Wendsler Nosie of the San Carlos Apache tribe. But there was also another unexpected participant: Pete Buttigieg, who stood silently in the crowd—never speaking—throughout the protest. It offered a striking contrast to how similar instances are handled among the Religious Right, as the photo that emerged from the rally wasn't of Buttigieg holding court with an enraptured crowd but of him literally sitting at Barber's feet.[11]

The influence of progressive faith activists became even clearer a few days later when the Poor People's Campaign convened a candidates' forum in Washington to pepper presidential hopefuls with questions about poverty, climate change, health care, and other issues. Nine candidates showed up, including then frontrunners Joe Biden, Bernie Sanders, Kamala Harris, and Elizabeth Warren. (Julián Castro was slated to attend but was unable to make it.) By comparison,

Netroots Nation, a massive progressive gathering that has met annually for years, managed to secure only four candidates for its forum.[12]

Sometimes the impact of Religious Left activism on the campaign cycle was explicit. When Biden claimed at the forum that "almost half the people in the United States [are] living in poverty"—a bungled version of the Poor People's Campaign claim that 43.5 percent of Americans are "poor" or "low income"—the *Washington Post* published an official fact-check of Biden's remark. (He got three Pinocchios, but the authors blamed Biden, not Barber.)[13]

At other times, the influence was subtler. When I checked back in with Network in December 2019, staffers told me Sister Simone Campbell was in active conversation with several 2020 Democratic presidential candidates. Buttigieg met with her to discuss faith and economics, for instance, and Warren's team had expressed interest in putting her on a potential faith advisory group. The nun had also forged an especially close relationship with Biden's campaign, and was in "semi-regular contact" with his campaign manager Greg Schultz.

There were moments where the role of the Religious Left was more pastoral than political, such as when Buttigieg visited the Washington National Cathedral in October 2019. He wasn't there to campaign, but to make a pilgrimage to the cathedral's Chapel of St. Joseph of Arimathea—the spot nearest to where Matthew Shepard's ashes are interred. He was escorted there by—who else?—Bishop Gene Robinson.[14]

Meanwhile, candidates attended several forums hosted by faith or faith-related groups that have received less attention in the past. Two separate forums hosted by Muslim groups garnered pledges to attend (virtually or otherwise) from Warren, Sanders, and Castro.[15] A conversation with young black church leaders, organized by the Black Church PAC and moderated by Faith in Action's Michael McBride, boasted attendance by Booker, Castro, Buttigieg, Warren, and Sanders. And a Native American forum—which included mention of Indigenous sacred land claims—attracted Sanders, Warren, Castro, Williamson, and Amy Klobuchar, as well as independent candidate

Mark Charles, a member of the Navajo nation and a former pastor.[16] More than one was asked about the Doctrine of Discovery.[17]

By the time Democratic candidates attended Iowa's annual Steak Fry, it was no longer a question of *whether* progressive faith expressions would play a role in the 2020 election cycle. It was only a question of *how*.

But Religious Left activists have not let their newfound clout slow their spiritual activism or their pursuit of a more progressive America. Advocates frustrated by the Trump administration and other systems of power organized protests to defend immigrants, support LGBTQ people, champion equal pay, condemn racism and religious bigotry, and demand action on climate change. Arrests were frequent, as were tense confrontations with authorities: a group of Jewish demonstrators protesting outside an immigrant detention center in Rhode Island made headlines in August 2019 when a law enforcement official appeared to try and run them over with his truck.[18]

There have also been murmurings of progressive faith movements that haven't yet risen to the same level of intensity or influence as others profiled in this book, but which stand poised to make wide-ranging impacts in the near future.

Robust and longstanding efforts continue to articulate a religious message in support of abortion rights, for instance. There is ample history of religious support for abortion rights, albeit much of it ignored by members of both parties; religious leaders were actually among the first to speak out in favor of abortion rights in the 1960s, aiding women who needed abortions performed safely in New York City, for example.[19] While the movement continues unabated to this day, the organizational heirs to this legacy still struggle to gain traction outside of progressive spaces—religious or otherwise—and have yet to manifest as a broad-based counterbalance to the influence of antiabortion religious activists, whose fervor refuses to wane.

But as the abortion debate continues to escalate, its liberal allies continue to come forth. When Alabama passed its deeply restrictive abortion ban in the summer of 2019, Rev. William Barber and the Poor People's Campaign headlined a rally in the state, at which the pastor held hands with Planned Parenthood advocates and denounced the law as "immoral hypocrisy."[20]

Some movements have extended beyond the progressive faith community entirely, particularly the #MeToo or #ChurchToo movements. Although #MeToo emerged from a historically progressive sense of women's empowerment and protection of the vulnerable, some of the movement's most recent high-profile impacts have occurred within conservative faith communities. At Willow Creek Community Church in Chicago, pastor Bill Hybels was accused of "sexually inappropriate words and actions" (he eventually resigned),[21] while within churches of the Southern Baptist Convention, a *Houston Chronicle* investigation uncovered records detailing sexual misconduct by hundreds of clergy, lay leaders, and volunteers.[22]

Progressive faith communities have grappled with their own #MeToo incidents, although some have included added levels of nuance and complexity. In July 2019, the *New York Times* published that Rev. Amy Butler was leaving New York City's historically liberal Riverside Church, reportedly due to alleged incidents of harassment from male parishioners she endured while serving there.[23] The next day, the *New York Post* and *Slate* revealed that Butler had *also* been accused of harassment, which allegedly also contributed to her departure. Some parishioners later challenged the allegations against Butler and petitioned to have her reinstated.[24]

There are also progressive faith movements that are fighting for net neutrality,[25] animal rights,[26] reparations for African Americans,[27] and likely other issues that will have emerged between the time I submit this manuscript and the day you read this book.

And then there are the movements that are just now hitting their stride, such as the religious groups who have spent decades advocating for various pieces of gun control legislation. Their efforts—which arguably peaked in 2013, at least at the federal level[28]—were unable to force Congress to pass meaningful gun control, but the networks they forged aided students from Parkland, Florida, in 2018, when they rallied thousands in Washington, DC, to push gun violence issues back into the public consciousness.[29] Faith groups have continued to contribute in other ways as well: interfaith coalitions such as Faiths United to Prevent Gun Violence have called for specific legislation such as background checks to prevent more gun deaths,[30] and the Presbyterian Church (USA) has even ordained its own minister of gun violence prevention.[31]

But perhaps the most dramatic example of this submovement involves Shane Claiborne, who, when not organizing Red Letter Revivals, helps orchestrate a campaign that takes firearms and reshapes them into garden tools—a living expression of the biblical exhortation to beat "swords into plowshares." Claiborne's group had an anvil and an open flame set up for just such a purpose when I saw him at the Wild Goose Festival in 2019.

"We've had two guns donated since we've been here," he whispered to me excitedly.

It was at Claiborne's tent that Rev. Sharon Risher—a pastor whose mother, Ethel Lee Lance, was among the nine members killed inside Mother Emanuel AME Church in Charleston—personally hammered a glowing, molten fragment of a firearm with all her might.

"I hit this, Mama," she shouted as she pummeled the remains of the gun, her voice cracking. "I hit this for you!" The crowd around her remained silent, the quiet pierced only by the strength of her voice and the dull clang of metal on metal.[32]

As I sat in the pews of Emanuel AME Church that August morning in Charleston, I wondered what Risher would think as Booker finished his soaring, heartfelt speech. The applause that erupted after he finished was immediately followed by a spontaneous meet and greet, with people darting through the pews to pose for selfies and grab a few fleeting seconds of conversation with the candidate. Around the edges of the room, a familiar coda resounded as I and other journalists—television, magazine, daily newspaper—pulled onlookers aside for quick reaction interviews.

But even after securing a few quotes, I couldn't bring myself to leave the sanctuary. I reclined in one of the pews cordoned off for press, carefully put away my camera, and watched the curious intersection of religion and politics play out in front of me. It was a moment of no less political or theological significance than similar gatherings of the Religious Right, and yet when Americans think of places where faith and politics mix, few would list Mother Emanuel. This, despite it being a place that helped change state policies, take down Confederate flags from government grounds, and host aspiring *and* sitting presidents—all after enduring unspeakable tragedy.

Then again, perhaps that is *why* so many people underestimate the Religious Left. Much of its power comes from religious communities who, for so long, have been presumed to have none. But as I looked out at that church that day, it was clear that their power remains.

I caught a glimpse of this power shortly before I departed the church. As Booker left and the crowd thinned out, I looked over my shoulder and noticed a small group of men standing near the back pews, speaking softly to each other. I walked over and asked if any of them had listened to the speech. Only one said yes, a man named Melvin Graham. Sheepish at first, he explained that not only was he a member of the church but also that he'd lost his sister, Cynthia Graham Hurd, in the 2015 shooting.

I asked him if he appreciated Booker's references to faith. He offered an enthusiastic yes, insisting that he found spiritual resonance in the senator's activism-minded approach to religion. Then his voice began to waver as a kaleidoscope of colors washed over his face, tiny fractal-shaped glimmers of the nearby stained glass window.

"We don't want 'thoughts and prayers' anymore—we want action," he said, his eyes welling with tears. "God is good. God is great. God can do all things. But God gave you the power to do some things on your own. Use that power He's given you. Use that authority He's given you to make things better. Don't hold it back for yourself. Take those talents He's given you—don't bury them in the sand. Use them for good, for justice. Power is not yours to hold on to exclusively. Power is there for you to help people, to uplift people."

He paused for the briefest moment, steadying himself. Then he added a fiery addendum, his voice thick with the indignant pain that comes with loss: "And unless the politicians decide to do what is morally right and not what is politically expedient for themselves, this will continue."

His words clung to my chest. I asked a few more questions and then concluded my interview, thanking him for his time. I tried to keep it together, I really did. I fiddled with my camera aimlessly as I exited the dark church back into the blinding sun. My attempt at steely resolve was a force of habit; journalists are often expected to keep their emotions in check while working, because the best reporters are ostensibly those who remain visibly unmoved by the tragedies we discover and witness.

I reflected on just how stupid that expectation is as I sat on a park bench and broke down in tears.

I also reflected on the profound power of progressive faith on those who claim it, inspiring action and activism—sometimes boisterous, sometimes quiet—on any number of issues. He reminded me that faith is one of the few things that can, at its best, exist outside the often bleak narratives we journalists paint for the world, inspiring millions to hold fast to hopeful truths in the face of a society that bitterly insists that all is lost.

I followed up with Graham a few months later. He told me that, like many faith-rooted advocates, he doesn't necessarily align his gun violence prevention activism with one ideology or party (although he was leaning toward supporting former vice president Joe Biden in the Democratic primary). "It doesn't matter if it's Republican or Democrat, just do the right thing," he said. But his work—which requires him to repeatedly relive his own experience of tragic loss—is inspired by his family and his faith, things on which he refuses to compromise.[33]

And that's precisely why the modern Religious Left, broadly defined, is likely to impact politics for years to come. It draws from a seemingly bottomless well of resilience that is paradoxically adaptable *and* immutable. It is undeterred by those who mock it, and even if the cameras vanish from the rallies, or the flood of activists slows to a trickle, or the politicians stop listening to them altogether, religious communities dedicated to progressive causes will endure. For they have the audacity to believe in a faith that gives them no other choice but to cry out.

As I have chronicled throughout this book, this menagerie of communities, activists, and everyday believers will not always agree with each other, nor will they avoid mistakes. But if you know where to look, you will still find them in the streets, along the picket lines, or even in the halls of power.

And sometimes all you have to do is turn around to spot people like Melvin Graham standing in the backs of churches, synagogues, prayer circles, and temples across the country, living out their faith the only way they know how: by doggedly insisting, to anyone who will listen, on a better world.

Just as prophets always have.

Acknowledgments

My father used to have an expression: "Nothin's easy." He said it whenever he was frustrated, but it was forever welded to an unspoken addendum: do it anyway, preferably with help.

That phrase became my mantra throughout the writing of this book, which turned out to be a significantly larger undertaking than I could have ever imagined. To describe it as a labor of love would require a very creative definition of love, especially since I chose to write it during a time in my life that was, as one friend put it, "either perfect or preposterously unsuited for book writing." It turned out to be a bit of both, and if I'm being honest, the book you are holding only exists because there are a lot of truly amazing people in this world that inexplicably decided to help me.

I am indebted to my fearless agent (I know, I can't believe they let me have one of those either) Roger Freet, as well as my eternally patient (and surprisingly gracious) editor Miles Doyle at HarperOne, both of whom managed to shepherd an untested author through the tumultuous process of writing his first book.

What's more, this project would have been a lost cause were it not for a constellation of brilliant minds and beta readers that helped me edit, fact check, and hunt down key details. I am particularly grateful to Rev. Cara Rockhill, who not only pushed me to write this book in the first place but also read *profoundly* awful first drafts of almost every chapter. I also was humbled by the expertise and thoughtful feedback of Emily Atkin, Joshua Eaton, Erin Edwards, Zack Ford, Liza Ryan Gill, Meghan Goldenstein, Aysha Kahn, Esther Yu Hsi Lee, Emily Miller, Jeff Spross, and Lauren Williams. Oh, and I owe a thank you to Alejandro Dávila, who helped me reimagine structure when he *really* should have been finishing his own book.

I am tremendously thankful to those who provided me *spaces* to write. A special shout-out to Talyah Alpern of H Street's Shopkeepers coffee shop/store/event space, who tolerated my weekend visits despite random theological conversations and incessant requests for tea. And I am beholden to David and Dana Cozad, who graciously allowed me to hole up in their gorgeously simple stream-side cabin for weeks in Montreat, North Carolina (forever my spiritual home), where I was only attacked by a snake once.

I am forever grateful to various mentors who led me to this topic and to writing in general. Rev. Dr. Jeri Perkins, who saw a future for me when I couldn't. Rev. Stephanie Spellers, a prophet in her own right who taught me how to pray. Dan McKanan, who endured my asinine questions when I took his course on the Religious Left in divinity school. Kevin Eckstrom, who let an untrained graduate student write stories and changed my life. Igor Volsky and Judd Legum, who decided that maybe reporting on the Religious Left full-time was a pretty good idea after all. And all the good folks at *Religion News Service*, who still put up with me.

Lastly, I would never have been able to do any of this were it not for my incredible family: a sister (Lathem) who never stopped encouraging me my entire life; a brother-in-law (Jason) always willing to endure my rambling thoughts; nieces (Dargan and Mance) who provide an eternal fountain of joy; an awe-inspiringly loving mother who taught me to write (and rightly insisted throughout this process that I "add more story"); and a doting father who never stopped rooting for me, including as I wrote the proposal for this book next to his hospital bed in his final months of life.

You were right, Dad: nothin's easy. But we do it anyway, and we do it together.

That's what makes it worth doing.

Notes

INTRODUCTION

1 Harmeet Kamboj, "The Media's 'Religious Left' is Erasing Marginalized Communities of Faith," *Sojourners*, February 6, 2019, https://sojo.net/articles/media-s-religious-left-erasing-marginalized-communities-faith.

ONE Faith in Public Life

1 John Podesta (founder of the Center for American Progress), phone interview by the author, April 1, 2019.
2 "The Employment Situation: June 2003," US Bureau of Labor Statistics, June 2003, https://www.bls.gov/news.release/archives/empsit_07032003.pdf.
3 "Faith, Politics & Progressives: A Conversation with John Podesta," moderated by Michael Cromartie, Pew Research Center, April 26, 2005, https://www.pewforum.org/2005/04/26/faith-politics-and-progressives-a-conversation-with-john-podesta/.
4 David Paul Kuhn, "Kerry's Communion Controversy," CBSNews.com, April 6, 2004, https://www.cbsnews.com/news/kerrys-communion-controversy/.
5 Barbara Bradley Hagerty, "Profile: Silent Evangelical Support of Bush's Proposed War Against Iraq," *NPR Morning Edition*, February 26, 2003, https://www.npr.org/programs/morning/transcripts/2003/feb/030226.hagerty.html.
6 Laura Blumenfeld, "Soros's Deep Pockets vs. Bush," *Washington Post*, November 11, 2003, https://www.washingtonpost.com/archive/politics/2003/11/11/soross-deep-pockets-vs-bush/c7c8f9a0-d902-4298-ac8e-9132ad499238/.
7 Podesta, "Faith, Politics & Progressives."
8 Podesta, phone interview.
9 "Current Work," Res Publica, accessed via Web Archive. https://web.archive.org/web/20041206190705/http://therespublica.org/CurrentWork.htm.
10 Tom Perriello (former congressman), Skype interview by the author, May 20, 2019.

11 Joe Feuerherd, "Res Publica: A Public Works Project," *National Catholic Reporter,* December 29, 2004, http://www.ncrnews.org/washington/wnb122 904.htm.

12 Podesta, phone interview.

13 Res Publica, "The Future of the Progressive Faith Movement," December 7, 2004.

14 Jennifer Butler (head of Faith in Public Life), interview by the author, February 15, 2019.

15 Mara Vanderslice Kelly (former progressive faith operative), interview by the author, May 31, 2019.

16 David Gibson, "Catholic Voter Guide Differs from Two Catholic Candidates," *Religion News Service,* March 1, 2012, https://www.ncronline.org /news/politics/catholic-voter-guide-differs-two-catholic-candidates. See also: "Pro-Obama Catholic rewarded with government job at HHS," Catholic News Service, June 4, 2009, https://www.catholicnewsagency.com/news /proobama_catholic_rewarded_with_government_job_at_hhs.

17 Gordon Whitman (senior adviser, PICO/Faith in Action), phone interview by the author, March 28, 2019.

18 Andrea James, "Religious Liberals Say Health Care Is a Life-and-Death Moral Issue," *RNS Daily Digest* (blog), *Religion News Service,* January 26, 2005, https://religionnews.com/2005/01/26/rns-daily-digest762/.

19 Ricardo Alonso-Zaldivar, "Liberal group proposing plan for health coverage for all," Associated Press, February 22, 2018, https://apnews.com/dea22d 80e24d44baa055249c9144b36d/Liberal-group-proposing-plan-for-health -coverage-for-all.

20 Podesta, "Faith, Politics & Progressives."

21 Podesta, phone interview.

22 "About," the website of the *Catholic Health Association of the United States,* https://www.chausa.org/about/about.

23 Sister Carol Keehan (CEO, Catholic Health Association), phone interview by the author, April 25, 2019.

24 Ezra Klein, "A Lack of Audacity," *The American Prospect,* May 30, 2007, https://prospect.org/article/lack-audacity-0.

25 "Is Obama All Style and Little Substance?," Associated Press, March 27, 2007, http://www.nbcnews.com/id/17811278/ns/politics-decision_08/t/obama-all -style-little-substance/.

26 Keehan, phone interview.

27 Keehan, phone interview.

28 Butler, interview.

29 Eric Kleefeld, "Town Hall Attendee Tells Specter: 'One Day, God's Gonna Stand Before You,'" *Talking Points Memo,* August 11, 2009, https://talking pointsmemo.com/dc/town-hall-attendee-tells-specter-one-day-god-s-gonna -stand-before-you.

30 Stephanie Condon, "Faith Groups to Help Obama on Health Care," CBS News,

August 10, 2009, https://www.cbsnews.com/news/faith-groups-to-help-obama-on-health-care/.

31 "People of Faith for Health Reform," Faithful America video, accessed on You-Tube, August 9, 2009, https://www.youtube.com/watch?v=OaBq0QeM3-8.

32 Paul Raushenbush, "The Health Care Call with Faith Leaders and President Obama," *Progressive Revival* (blog), *Beliefnet,* https://www.beliefnet.com /columnists/progressiverevival/2009/08/the-health-care-call-with-fait.html.

33 Whitman, phone interview.

34 Jessica Rettig, "10 Things You Didn't Know About Ben Nelson," *US News & World Report,* March 29, 2010, https://www.usnews.com/news/articles/2010 /03/29/10-things-you-didnt-know-about-ben-nelson. See also: "Nebraska Right to Life OKs Dave Heineman, abandons Ben Nelson," *Lincoln Journal Star,* April 14, 2010, https://journalstar.com/news/local/govt-and-politics /nebraska-right-to-life-oks-dave-heineman-abandons-ben-nelson/article _d12751ba-4804-11df-a831-001cc4c002e0.html.

35 "On Capitol Hill, Religious Leaders Take Stand for Working Families," Episcopal News Service, October 20, 2009, https://www.episcopalchurch.org /library/article/capitol-hill-religious-leaders-take-stand-working-families.

36 Kevin Whitelaw, "Next Step: Getting A Health Bill To Obama's Desk," NPR, December 24, 2009, https://www.npr.org/templates/story/story.php?storyId =121838784&ps=cprs.

37 Thomas C. Fox, "Two Dozen Nebraska Religious Leaders Support New Health Care Abortion Language," *National Catholic Reporter,* December 18, 2009. https://www.ncronline.org/blogs/ncr-today/two-dozen-nebraska-religious -leaders-support-new-health-care-abortion-language.

38 David M. Herszenhorn and Carl Hulse, "Democrats Clinch Deal for Deciding Vote on Health Bill," *New York Times,* December 19, 2009, https://www .nytimes.com/2009/12/20/health/policy/20health.html.

39 Steve Jordon, "What Was the 'Cornhusker Kickback,' the Deal that Led to Nelson's Crucial ACA Vote?," *Omaha World-Herald,* July 20, 2017, https://www .omaha.com/livewellnebraska/obamacare/what-was-the-cornhusker-kickback -the-deal-that-led-to/article_a2eb3a1d-df14-513b-a141-c8695f6c258e.html.

40 Democratic National Committee, "Doing Right," copy of the advertisement provided to author.

41 Sister Carol Keehan, "The Time Is Now for Health Reform," *Catholic Health World,* March 15, 2010 (distributed on March 13), https://web.archive.org /web/20100316234927/http://www.chausa.org/The_time_is_now_for_health _reform.aspx.

42 Keehan, phone interview.

43 Sister Simone Campbell (executive director, Network), interview by the author, April 18, 2019.

44 Daniel Burke, "Catholic Bishops, Hospitals Split on Health Care," *Religion News Service,* March 17, 2010, https://religionnews.com/2010/03/17/the -president-of-the-us-bishops-conference-broke-with-catholic-hospital-adm/.

45   Dennis Coday, "Thousands of Catholic Sisters Support Health Care Reform,"
     National Catholic Reporter, March 17, 2010, https://www.ncronline.org/blogs
     /ncr-today/thousands-catholic-sisters-support-health-care-reform.

46   "Catholics Share Bishops' Concerns about Religious Liberty," Pew Research
     Center, August 1, 2012, https://www.pewforum.org/2012/08/01/2012-catholic
     -voters-religious-liberty-issue/.

47   Graham Moomaw, "Responding to criticism of abortion vote in Congress,
     Perriello says Northam backed 'most anti-choice president' ever," *Richmond
     Times-Dispatch,* April 21, 2017, https://www.richmond.com/news/virginia/
     responding-to-criticism-of-abortion-vote-in-congress-perriello-says/article
     _61fcaadf-7899-5275-9c06-cf7d0841d2cd.html.

48   Tom Perriello, Facebook post, January 6, 2017, https://www.facebook.com
     /TomPerriello/posts/10155393796305400.

49   Michael Sean Winters, "Cong. Kildee Defends Decision to Support Health Care
     Bill," *National Catholic Reporter,* March 18, 2010, https://www.ncronline
     .org/blogs/ncr-today/cong-kildee-defends-decision-support-health-care-bill.

50   "US Bishops, Dissenting Catholics Face Off in Health Care Debate," Catholic
     News Agency, March 20, 2010, https://www.catholicnewsagency.com/news
     /u.s._bishops_dissenting_catholics_face_off_in_in_health_care_debate.

51   Campbell, interview.

52   "Obama Thanks CHA for Backing Health Care Reform," *America,* June 21,
     2010, https://www.americamagazine.org/issue/741/signs/obama-thanks-cha
     -backing-health-care-reform.

53   "The President Speaks on Health Care Reform at the Catholic Health Associ-
     ation Conference," White House video, accessed on YouTube, June 9, 2015,
     https://www.youtube.com/watch?v=UNG6xNT1ObU.

54   "Catholic Bishops: CHA Wounded Church Unity with Health Care Endorse-
     ment," *Catholic News Agency,* May 23, 2010, https://www.catholicnews
     agency.com/news/catholic-bishops-cha-wounded-church-unity-with-health
     -care-endorsement.

55   Daniel Burke, "Bishop Nixes Nuns' Recruitment Drive over Health Care Spat,"
     Religion News Service, April 20, 2010, https://religionnews.com/2010/04/20
     /a-62-year-old-new-jersey-nun-is-on-a-nationwide-quest/.

56   Laurie Goodstein, "Vatican Reprimands a Group of US Nuns and Plans
     Changes," *New York Times,* April 18, 2012, https://www.nytimes.com/2012
     /04/19/us/vatican-reprimands-us-nuns-group.html.

57   Campbell, interview.

58   Jack Jenkins, "This Catholic Nun Pushed Obamacare Through Congress.
     Now She's Fighting to Save It," *ThinkProgress,* June 30, 2017, https://think
     progress.org/simone-campbell-health-care-663083582f55/.

59   Podesta's connection to the Catholic groups became a topic of debate among
     conservative Catholics in 2016 after his private emails were hacked and
     published by WikiLeaks. A few 2012-era emails published as a result of the
     hack drew attention for their discussion of Catholics United and CACG

as possible catalysts for a "Catholic Spring," although Podesta claimed the groups "lack the leadership" to muster such a challenge to church hierarchy. And despite outrage at Podesta's affiliation with the groups, his ties weren't exactly a secret: he told *Washington Post* that CAP helped guide their work as early as 2006. See: Caryle Murphy and Alan Cooperman, "Religious Liberals Gain New Visibility A Different List of Moral Issues," *Washington Post,* May 20, 2006, https://www.washingtonpost.com/archive/politics/2006/05/20 /religious-liberals-gain-new-visibility-span-classbankheada-different-list -of-moral-issuesspan/e86fa1c7-b704-496d-83a8-517c56dea08a/.

60 Adelle M. Banks, "Religious groups play key role in Obamacare insurance sign-up," *Religion News Service,* March 20, 2014, https://religionnews.com /2014/03/20/religious-groups-play-key-role-obamacare-insurance-sign/.

61 Adam Liptak, "Supreme Court Rejects Contraceptives Mandate for Some Corporations," *New York Times,* June 30, 2014, https://www.nytimes.com /2014/07/01/us/hobby-lobby-case-supreme-court-contraception.html.

62 Ian Millhiser, "Religious Groups Line Up to Support Affordable Care Act," *ThinkProgress,* February 21, 2012, https://thinkprogress.org/religious-groups -line-up-to-support-affordable-care-act-cd8b2ece986d/.

63 Jack Jenkins, "Religious leaders arrested in act of civil disobedience against Senate's 'immoral' health care bill," *ThinkProgress,* July 13, 2017, https://think progress.org/faith-leaders-protest-health-care-676c674ac077/.

64 Jack Jenkins, "Faith groups hold day-long vigil against 'sinful' GOP health care bill," *ThinkProgress,* June 29, 2017, https://thinkprogress.org/faith-vigil -gop-health-bill-b80448b43f5c/.

65 Jack Jenkins, "Faith groups launch major push to stop GOP health care repeal," *ThinkProgress,* July 27, 2017, https://thinkprogress.org/faith-groups -push-obamacare-e200406c21ad/.

66 Jane Adams (policy analyst, Bread for the World), Twitter direct message to author, May 7, 2019.

TWO The Personal Is Political—and Spiritual

1   Joshua DuBois, phone interview by the author, May 10, 2019.

2   "Religion Communicators Council's 2015 Convention," Newseum video, accessed on YouTube, June 5, 2015, https://www.youtube.com/watch?v=qm V_1wjNeRA.

3   Cathleen Falsani, "Barack Obama and The God Factor Interview," *Sojourners,* February 21, 2012, https://sojo.net/articles/transcript-barack-obama-and -god-factor-interview.

4   Barack Obama, *The Audacity of Hope* (New York: Crown Publishers, 2006), 203–204.

5   Falsani, "The God Factor Interview."

6   Colin McNulty and Jennifer White, "Obama 1: The Man in the Background," WBEZ Chicago Public Radio, February 8, 2018, https://www.wbez.org/shows

/making-obama/obama-1-the-man-in-the-background/52566713-83d4-4875
-8bb1-eba55937228e.

7   Peg Knoepfle, *After Alinsky: Community Organizing in Illinois* (Springfield,
    IL: Illinois Issues, July 1, 1990), 36–40.

8   Barack Obama, "President Obama's Farewell Address," Obama White House
    Archives, January 10, 2017, https://obamawhitehouse.archives.gov/farewell.
    See also: Falsani, "The God Factor Interview."

9   Knoepfle, *After Alinsky*, 36–40.

10 "The YouTube Interview with President Obama," conducted by Destin San-
    dlin, Ingrid Nilsen, and Adande Thorne, YouTube, January 16, 2016, https://
    www.youtube.com/watch?v=Tjl8ka3F6QU.

11 Daniel Burke, "Saguaro seminar stays with Obama," *Religion News Service*,
    June 11, 2009, https://religionnews.com/2009/06/11/bowling-alone-seminar
    -stays-with-obama3/.

12 Jim Wallis, interview by the author, May 15, 2019.

13 E. J. Dionne, phone interview by the author, June 20, 2019.

14 "Jim Wallis on President Obama's Understanding of Faith and Public Life,"
    Berkley Center, YouTube, May 10, 2013, https://www.youtube.com/watch?
    v=0QyT_naqKOA.

15 Jim Wallis, in person interview.

16 The Web Editors, "Obama's 2006 Sojourners/Call to Renewal Address on
    Faith and Politics," *Sojourners*, February 21, 2012, https://sojo.net/articles
    /transcript-obamas-2006-sojournerscall-renewal-address-faith-and-politics.

17 E. J. Dionne Jr., "Obama's Eloquent Faith," *Washington Post*, June 30, 2006,
    http://www.washingtonpost.com/wp-dyn/content/article/2006/06/29/AR
    2006062901778.html.

18 E. J. Dionne Jr., *Souled Out: Reclaiming Faith and Politics after the Religious
    Right* (Princeton: Princeton Univ. Press, October 12, 2009).

19 DuBois, phone interview.

20 Obama, *Audacity of Hope*, 195–226.

21 "Barack Obama's Presidential Announcement," BarackObamadotcom, You-
    Tube, December 10, 2017, https://www.youtube.com/watch?v=gdJ7Ad15WCA.

22 DuBois, phone interview.

23 Mara Vanderslice Kelly, phone interview by the author, May 31, 2019.

24 Susan Q. Stranahan, "Beyond the Wafer Watch," *Columbia Journalism Re-
    view*, May 23, 2004, https://archives.cjr.org/politics/beyond_the_wafer_watch
    .php.

25 Matea Gold, "Ex-Clinton Spokesman McCurry Joins Kerry," *Los Angeles
    Times*, September 15, 2004, https://www.latimes.com/archives/la-xpm-2004
    -sep-15-na-mccurry15-story.html.

26 Jodi Wilgoren, "Kerry Invokes the Bible in Appeal for Black Votes," *New York
    Times*, September 10, 2004, https://www.nytimes.com/2004/09/10/politics
    /campaign/kerry-invokes-the-bible-in-appeal-for-black-votes.html.

27 2004 CNN Exit polls, available at http://edition.cnn.com/ELECTION/2004 //pages/results/states/MI/P/00/epolls.0.html.

28 David D. Kirkpatrick, "Consultant Helps Democrats Embrace Faith, and Some in Party Are Not Pleased," *New York Times*, December 26, 2006, https://www.nytimes.com/2006/12/26/us/politics/26faith.html.

29 Michael Wear, phone interview by the author, May 17, 2019.

30 "Families," Matthew25Network video, accessed on YouTube, August 14, 2008, https://www.youtube.com/watch?v=6eUkc9GCMEQ.

31 "Obama: Faith 'Plays Every Role' In My Life," CBS/AP, October 8, 2007, https://www.cbsnews.com/news/obama-faith-plays-every-role-in-my-life/.

32 "Religion Communicators Council," Newseum video.

33 Barack Obama, "A Politics of Conscience," *United Church of Christ*, June 22, 2007, https://www.ucc.org/a-politics-of-conscience.

34 Lisa Miller, "Faith: Barack Obama's Mobile Ministry," *Newsweek*, May 31, 2008, https://www.newsweek.com/faith-barack-obamas-mobile-ministry-89551.

35 Bob Allen, "Obama Campaign Introduces Faith-Based Merchandise," *Ethics Daily*, September 18, 2008, https://ethicsdaily.com/obama-campaign-introduces-faith-based-merchandise-cms-13203/.

36 Eve Fairbanks, "Huckabee Doesn't Want Anybody to See Him at Church?," *New Republic*, December 29, 2007, https://newrepublic.com/article/38828 /huckabee-doesnt-want-anybody-see-him-church.

37 Buttons available at Obama '08 campaign store, accessed on September 25, 2008, via the Web Archive, https://web.archive.org/web/20080925192536/http://store.barackobama.com/Buttons_s/200.htm.

38 Peter Hamby, "Obama addresses evangelical megachurch," *Political Ticker* (blog), CNN, October 7, 2007, http://politicalticker.blogs.cnn.com/2007/10 /07/obama-addresses-evangelical-megachurch/.

39 Jodi Kantor, "Obama's Christian Campaign," *The Caucus* (blog), *New York Times*, January 25, 2008, https://thecaucus.blogs.nytimes.com/2008/01/25 /obama-and-faith-on-the-stump/.

40 "American Values Report, Volume 3," Barack Obama campaign newsletter, copy procured by author, 2008.

41 James Guess, "Obama's General Synod speech prompts IRS to investigate UCC's tax-exempt status," *United Church of Christ*, February 25, 2008, https://www.ucc.org/obama-speech-in-2007-prompts-1.

42 Amanda Adams, "IRS Drops Investigations of United Church of Christ and First Southern Baptist," *Center for Effective Government*, May 28, 2008, https://www.foreffectivegov.org/node/3698.

43 Kantor, "Obama's Christian Campaign."

44 Andrea Elliot, "Muslim Voters Detect a Snub from Obama," *New York Times*, June 24, 2008, https://www.nytimes.com/2008/06/24/us/politics/24muslim .html.

45 Alexander Marquardt, "Obama's Muslim affairs coordinator resigns," CNN,

August 6, 2008, http://politicalticker.blogs.cnn.com/2008/08/06/obamas-muslim-affairs-coordinator-resigns/.

46 Susan Schmidt, "Obama's Staff Slips Up With Muslim Outreach," *Wall Street Journal*, October 10, 2008, https://www.wsj.com/articles/SB122360316634321799?mod=rsswn.

47 "Hassan Shibly, Chief Executive Director for CAIR Florida, visited the White House," CAIR-FL, March 14, 2016, https://www.cairflorida.org/index.php/tag-cair-fl-in-the-news/269-hassan-shibly-chief-executive-director-for-cair-florida-visited-the-white.

48 "CAIR-Chicago Trains US Customs & Border Patrol Officers," CAIR Chicago, October 18, 2019, https://www.cairchicago.org/blog/2019/10/cair-chicago-trains-us-customs-amp-border-patrol-officers?fbclid=IwAR2T8ydIPy6wYzAOJ4pnjkxvsae_08Is0YVccI9Ogka0qRSst9MNRHAB0xU.

49 Barack Obama, "A More Perfect Union" (full speech), BarackObama.com video, accessed on YouTube, March 18, 2008, https://www.youtube.com/watch?v=zrp-v2tHaDo.

50 Katharine Q. Seelye and Jeff Zeleny, "On the Defensive, Obama Calls His Words Ill-Chosen," *New York Times*, April 13, 2008, https://www.nytimes.com/2008/04/13/us/politics/13campaign.html.

51 "Remarks of Senator Barack Obama: AP Annual Luncheon," BarackObama.com, archived from April 13, 2008, https://web.archive.org/web/20080426094150/ https://barackobama.com/2008/04/14/remarks_of_senator_barack_obam_57.php.

52 Adelle Banks and Daniel Burke, "Obama hashes out his stance with liberal, conservative church leaders," *State Journal-Register*, June 22, 2008, https://www.sj-r.com/article/20080622/NEWS/306229984.

53 Jake Tapper, "Purpose Driven Candidates: Obama, McCain Seek Rick Warren's Blessing," ABC News, August 15, 2008, https://abcnews.go.com/GMA/Politics/story?id=5586670&page=1.

54 "Faith and the Faithful in the Democratic Party," Global Georgetown video, accessed on YouTube, June 28, 2018, https://www.youtube.com/watch?v=i8ajxgqsrBI.

55 "Obama Reaches Out to Religious Voters," AP/CBS News, October 16, 2007, https://www.cbsnews.com/news/obama-reaches-out-to-religious-voters-16-10-2007/.

56 Laurie Goodstein, "Obama Made Gains Among Younger Evangelical Voters, Data Show," *New York Times*, November 6, 2008, https://www.nytimes.com/2008/11/07/us/politics/07religion.html.

57 James Guth, "Religion in the 2008 Election," *The American Elections of 2008* (Lanham, MD: Rowman & Littlefield, 2009).

58 Mike McCurry, "How My Party Found God," *The Daily Beast*, December 15, 2008, https://www.thedailybeast.com/how-my-party-found-god.

59 "Obama's 2006 Sojourners/Call to Renewal Address on Faith and Politics," *Sojourners*.

THREE When God Chooses a Leader

1 *Religion News Service*, Twitter, January 18, 2016, 8:06 a.m., https://twitter .com/RNS/status/689116742614958080.

2 Russell Moore, Twitter, January 18, 2016, 8:33 a.m., https://twitter.com /drmoore/status/689123499173122048.

3 Russell Moore, Twitter, January 18, 2016, 8:47 a.m., https://twitter.com /drmoore/status/689126932353519616.

4 Russell Moore, Twitter, January 18, 2016, 8:51 a.m., https://twitter.com /drmoore/status/689128085359300609.

5 Russell Moore, Twitter, January 18, 2016, 8:36 a.m., https://twitter.com /drmoore/status/689124286209085440.

6 Russell Moore, Twitter, January 18, 2016, 8:24 a.m., https://twitter.com /drmoore/status/689121147166822405.

7 Russell Moore, "Have Evangelicals Who Support Trump Lost Their Values?," *New York Times*, September 17, 2015, www.nytimes.com/2015/09/17 /opinion/have-evangelicals-who-support-trump-lost-their-values.html?smid =tw-share.

8 Russell Moore, Twitter, October 8, 2016, 11:39 a.m., https://twitter.com/ drmoore/status/784825668257316873.

9 Russell Moore (president, Ethics and Religious Liberty Commission, Southern Baptist Convention), phone interview by the author, March 13, 2019.

10 Kevin Kruse, *One Nation under God: How Corporate America Invented Christian America.* (New York: Basic Books, 2016).

11 Trump has a surprisingly direct link to Spiritual Mobilization. In 1947, the head of the movement, Rev. James W. Fifield, sought out an increasingly popular author and pastor, Norman Vincent Peale, to take his place. Peale, head of Marble Collegiate Church in New York City, popularized a theology that fused self-love and self-help, particularly his 1952 book *The Power of Positive Thinking*, which is often cited as a catalyst for the modern prosperity gospel movement. Peale turned Fifield down because, according to Kruse, he could likely make more money at his church and on his book tours. But his theological and political legacy has endured all the same: Trump grew up attending Peale's church, and Peale remains one of the few historical religious figures he can mention by name.

"The great Norman Vincent Peale was my pastor," Trump told an audience in Iowa during the 2016 campaign. "*The Power of Positive Thinking*— everybody's heard of Norman Vincent Peale. He was so great. He would give a sermon (and) you never wanted to leave. . . . I'm telling you, I still remember his sermons. It was unbelievable . . . When you left the church you were disappointed that it was over."

12 Kate Bowler, *Blessed: A History of the American Prosperity Gospel* (New York: Oxford Univ. Press, 2018).

13 David Van Biema and Jeff Chu, "Does God Want You to Be Rich?," *TIME,*

September 10 2006, http://content.time.com/time/printout/0,8816,15334 48,00.html.

14　Albert Mohler, "The Black Church and the Prosperity Gospel," Albert Mohler.com, October 1, 2010, https://albertmohler.com/2010/10/01/the -black-church-and-the-prosperity-gospel/.

15　Associated Press, "Falwell Shuns 'Prosperity Theology,'" *Free Lance–Star* (Fredericksburg, VA), June 6, 1987.

16　Russell Moore, "How the Prosperity Gospel Hurts Racial Reconciliation," *Desiring God*, April 25, 2015, https://www.desiringgod.org/articles/how -the-prosperity-gospel-hurts-racial-reconciliation.

17　Katie Glueck, "Donald Trump's God Whisperer," *Politico*, July 11, 2016, https://www.politico.com/story/2016/07/donald-trump-pastor-paula-white -225315.

18　"SiriusXM Town Hall with Joel & Victoria Osteen," SiriusXM video, November 7, 2014, accessed on YouTube, https://www.youtube.com/watch?v= vCLwEfnt2vE.

19　Russell Moore, Twitter, June 21, 2016, 12:26 p.m., https://twitter.com/dr moore/status/745337004007686144.

20　"RWW News: Paula White Says Opposition to President Trump Is Opposition to God," Right Wing Watch, August 21, 2017, accessed on YouTube, November 12, 2018, https://www.youtube.com/watch?v=STcgXcxOhNc.

21　Jack Jenkins, "Trump faith adviser regrets saying the president was anointed by God, insists he isn't racist," *ThinkProgress*, September 9, 2017, https:// thinkprogress.org/trump-faith-adviser-regrets-remarks-af48c1bd8e93/.

22　Steve Inskeep, "Religion, Politics a Potent Mix for Jerry Falwell," NPR, June 30, 2006, https://www.npr.org/templates/story/story.php?storyId=5522064. See also: "Transcript: Is America a Christian Nation?," FOX News, July 9, 2004, https://www.foxnews.com/story/transcript-is-america-a-christian-nation.

23　Joan Biskupic, "Roy Moore: The judge who fought the law," CNN, September 27, 2017, https://www.cnn.com/2017/09/27/politics/roy-moore-judicial -fight/index.html.

24　For an excellent treatment of this phenomenon, see Michelle Goldberg's *Kingdom Coming: The Rise of Christian Nationalism* (New York: W. W. Norton & Company, 2007).

25　Jack Jenkins, "Why Christian Nationalists Love Trump," *ThinkProgress*, August 7, 2017, https://thinkprogress.org/trumps-christian-nationalism-c6fe20 6e40cc/.

26　Donald Trump, Twitter, May 9, 2016, 3:05 a.m., https://twitter.com/realDonald Trump/status/729613336191586304.

27　Russell Moore, Instagram, May 9, 2016, https://www.instagram.com/p/BFL 0R2WTMdM/.

28　Gregory A. Smith and Jessica Martínez, "How the Faithful Voted: A Preliminary 2016 Analysis," Pew Research Center, November 9, 2016, accessed

November 30, 2018, http://www.pewresearch.org/fact-tank/2016/11/09/how
-the-faithful-voted-a-preliminary-2016-analysis/.

29   Moore, phone interview.

30   Donald Trump, "The Inaugural Address," WhiteHouse.gov, January 20, 2017,
https://www.whitehouse.gov/briefings-statements/the-inaugural-address/.

31   Donald Trump, "Remarks by President Trump at National Prayer Breakfast,"
WhiteHouse.gov, February 2, 2017, https://www.whitehouse.gov/briefings-state
ments/remarks-president-trump-national-prayer-breakfast/.

32   Donald Trump, "Read President Trump's Liberty University Commencement
Speech," *Time*, May 13, 2017, http://time.com/4778240/donald-trump-liberty
-university-speech-transcript/.

33   Donald Trump, "Remarks by President Trump to the People of Poland," White
House.gov, July 6, 2017, https://www.whitehouse.gov/briefings-statements
/remarks-president-trump-people-poland/.

34   Donald Trump, Twitter, July 4, 2017, 6:38 a.m., https://twitter.com/realDonald
Trump/status/882186896285282304.

35   Andrew L. Whitehead, Samuel Perry, and Joseph Baker, "Make America Christian Again: Christian Nationalism and Voting for Donald Trump in the 2016
Presidential Election," *Sociology of Religion* 79, no. 2 (January 2018), https://
www.researchgate.net/publication/321807766_Make_America_Christian
_Again_Christian_Nationalism_and_Voting_for_Donald_Trump_in_the
_2016_Presidential_Election.

36   Jack Jenkins, "How Trump's presidency reveals the true nature of Christian
nationalism," *ThinkProgress*, September 13, 2017, https://thinkprogress.org
/christian-nationalism-religion-research-b8f9cdc16239/.

37   Samuel Perry, Andrew L. Whitehead, and Joshua T. Davis, "God's Country in
Black and Blue: How Christian Nationalism Shapes Americans' Views about
Police (Mis)treatment of Blacks," *Sociology of Race and Ethnicity*, July 4,
2018, https://osf.io/preprints/socarxiv/gj5zr/.

38   Greg Smith (associate director of research, Pew Research Center), phone interview by the author, November 20, 2018.

39   Jack Jenkins, "Steve Bannon's radical faith," *ThinkProgress*, April 14, 2017,
https://thinkprogress.org/radical-faith-steve-bannon-politics-4d347f068648/.

40   J. Lester Feder, "This Is How Steve Bannon Sees the Entire World," *BuzzFeed*,
November 15, 2016, https://www.buzzfeednews.com/article/lesterfeder/this
-is-how-steve-bannon-sees-the-entire-world.

41   Emily McFarlan Miller, "Liberty University board member resigns over
Trump endorsement," *Religion News Service*, May 5, 2016, https://religion
news.com/2016/05/05/mark-demoes-liberty-board-trump-evangelicals/.

42   Daniel Burke, "7 types of evangelicals—and how they'll affect the presidential race," CNN, January 25, 2016, https://www.cnn.com/2016/01/22/politics
/seven-types-of-evangelicals-and-the-primaries/index.html.

43   Chris Moody, "The survival of a Southern Baptist who dared to oppose

Trump," CNN, July 2017, http://www.cnn.com/interactive/2017/politics/state
/russell-moore-donald-trump-southern-baptists/.

44 Sarah Pulliam Bailey, "Dozens of evangelical leaders meet to discuss how Trump era has unleashed 'grotesque caricature' of their faith," *Washington Post*, April 16, 2018, https://www.washingtonpost.com/news/acts-of-faith /wp/2018/04/12/when-you-google-evangelicals-you-get-trump-high-profile -evangelicals-will-meet-privately-to-discuss-their-future/?noredirect=on &utm_term=.a8810bb5aa55.

45 Samuel Smith, "Evangelical Leaders' Wheaton College Meeting Was Not Anti-Trump, Organizer Clarifies," *Christian Post,* April 18, 2018, https:// www.christianpost.com/news/evangelical-leaders-wheaton-college-meeting -was-not-anti-trump-organizer-clarifies-223070//.

46 Katelyn Beaty, "At a private meeting in Illinois, a group of evangelicals tried to save their movement from Trumpism," *The New Yorker,* April 26, 2018, https:// www.newyorker.com/news/on-religion/at-a-private-meeting-in-illinois-a -group-of-evangelicals-tried-to-save-their-movement-from-trumpism.

47 Emily McFarlan Miller, "Evangelical leaders discuss future of their movement in Trump era," *Religion News Service,* April 17, 2018, https://religionnews .com/2018/04/17/evangelical-leaders-discuss-future-of-their-movement-in -trump-era/.

48 Beaty, "At a private meeting in Illinois."

49 Katelyn Beaty, phone interview by the author, November 30, 2018.

50 Daniel Cox and Robert P. Jones, "America's Changing Religious Identity," Public Religion Research Insititute, September 6, 2017, https://www.prri.org /research/american-religious-landscape-christian-religiously-unaffiliated/.

51 "When Americans Say They Believe in God, What Do They Mean?," *Pew Research Center*, April 25, 2018, http://www.pewforum.org/2018/04/25/when -americans-say-they-believe-in-god-what-do-they-mean/.

52 See "Pew Research Center's Religious Landscape Study: Views about abortion" at http://www.pewforum.org/religious-landscape-study/views-about-abortion/ and "Pew Research Center's Religious Landscape Study: Views about same-sex marriage" at http://www.pewforum.org/religious-landscape-study/views -about-same-sex-marriage/.

53 Amelia Thomson-DeVeaux and Daniel Cox, "The Christian Right Is Helping Drive Liberals Away from Religion," *FiveThirtyEight*, September 18, 2019, https://fivethirtyeight.com/features/the-christian-right-is-helping-drive-liberals -away-from-religion/.

54 Daniel Cox and Robert P. Jones, "America's Changing Religious Identity."

55 Greg Smith, "RNA 2018 Sponsored panel from Pew Research Center: Religion and Politics" (lecture, annual conference of the Religion News Association, Columbus, OH, September 19, 2018). https://www.facebook.com/Religion NewsAssociation/videos/vl.296287831101295/235662297113806/?type=1.

56 Jack Jenkins, "Cory Booker Could Be a Candidate for the 'Religious Left,'"

Religion News Service, October 24, 2018, https://religionnews.com/2018/10/24/cory-booker-fashions-himself-as-a-candidate-for-the-religious-left/.

57 Carol Kuruvilla, "Christian Pastors in Alabama Seek to Build Momentum in Opposing Roy Moore," *HuffPost,* November 20, 2017, https://www.huffingtonpost.com/entry/christian-pastors-in-alabama-seek-to-build-momentum-in-opposing-roy-moore_us_5a131a42e4b0aa32975cc552.

58 Yonat Shimron, "In Alabama Senate Race, African-American Christians May Hold the Key," *Religion News Service,* December 7, 2017, https://religionnews.com/2017/12/07/in-alabama-senate-race-african-american-christians-may-hold-the-key/.

59 Morning Consult, "Morning Consult National Tracking Poll #180221 February 28-March 02, 2018," https://morningconsult.com/wp-content/uploads/2018/03/180221_crosstabs_POL_ENDORSE_v1_DK-1.pdf.

60 Erickson deleted the tweet along with many others, but it can be found at the Internet Archive's WayBack Machine, https://web.archive.org/web/20170612071305/https:/twitter.com/EWErickson/status/786591688890290176.

61 Ben Howe, "Jerry Falwell Jr. Is a Disgrace to Liberty University and Should Resign," *RedState* (blog), October 13, 2016, https://www.redstate.com/aglanon/2016/10/13/jerry-falwell-jr.-disgrace-liberty-university-resign.

62 "Liberty United Against Trump," petition, 2016, accessible at https://docs.google.com/forms/d/e/1FAIpQLScdLe5fbVw0d12MtiYcJCf-hLDjpr7AdiYTIkMBttqdLuTQbg/viewform.

63 Ben Collins, "Student: Jerry Falwell Jr. Axed Anti-Trump Story from Liberty University's School Newspaper," *The Daily Beast,* October 18, 2016, https://www.thedailybeast.com/student-jerry-falwell-jr-axed-anti-trump-story-from-liberty-universitys-school-newspaper.

64 Jerry Falwell Jr., Twitter, August 16, 2017 at 8:42 a.m., https://twitter.com/JerryFalwellJr/status/897845928337559552.

65 "Jerry Falwell Jr. on President Trump: He 'doesn't say what's politically correct,'" ABC News, August 20, 2017, https://abcnews.go.com/ThisWeek/video/liberty-university-president-jerry-falwell-jr-49319982.

66 Beaty, phone interview.

67 Jonathan Martin, Twitter, October 27, 2017 at 11:14 a.m., https://twitter.com/theboyonthebike/status/923976122391506944.

68 Jack Jenkins, "Liberty University police detain anti-Trump evangelical pastor who planned protest at school," *ThinkProgress,* November 1, 2017, https://thinkprogress.org/liberty-university-police-detain-evangelical-pastorl-9d63dfe35acb/.

69 Jack Jenkins, "At 'Red Letter Revival,' leaders give voice to evangelicals on the margins," *Religion News Service,* April 9, 2018, https://religionnews.com/2018/04/09/at-red-letter-revival-leaders-give-voice-to-evangelicals-on-the-margins/.

70 Jenkins, "At 'Red Letter Revival.'"

71 Elizabeth Podrebarac Sciupac and Gregory Smith, "How religious groups voted in the midterm elections," *Pew Fact Tank* (blog), November 7, 2018, http://www.pewresearch.org/fact-tank/2018/11/07/how-religious-groups-voted-in-the-midterm-elections/.

72 Smith, phone interview.

FOUR Revolutionary Love

1 Yonat Shimron, "Pastor and activist William J. Barber II wins MacArthur 'genius' grant," *Religion News Service*, October 2, 2018, https://religionnews.com/2018/10/04/pastor-and-activist-william-j-barber-ii-wins-macarthur-genius-grant/.

2 David Menconi and Camila Molina, "NC's Rev. William Barber wins a MacArthur 'Genius Grant' and its $625K prize," *News & Observer*, October 4, 2018, https://www.newsobserver.com/news/local/article219483790.html.

3 Tommy Tomlinson, "Reverend Resistance," *Esquire*, April 26, 2017, https://www.esquire.com/news-politics/a54573/reverend-william-barber-progressive-christianity/.

4 "North Carolina Disciples Pastor Chosen for National NAACP Board," Christian Church (Disciples of Christ), March 11, 2009, https://disciples.org/people/north-carolina-disciples-pastor-chosen-for-national-naacp-board/.

5 Cleve R. Wootson Jr., "Rev. William Barber builds a moral movement," *Washington Post*, June 29, 2017, https://www.washingtonpost.com/news/acts-of-faith/wp/2017/06/29/woe-unto-those-who-legislate-evil-rev-william-barber-builds-a-moral-movement/.

6 William Barber and Jonathan Wilson-Hartgrove, *The Third Reconstruction: How A Moral Movement Is Overcoming the Politics of Division and Fear* (Boston: Beacon Press, 2016), 44.

7 Barber and Wilson-Hartgrove, *The Third Reconstruction*, 50–66.

8 James L. Hunt, "Fusion of Republicans and Populists," NCPedia, 2006, https://www.ncpedia.org/fusion-republicans-and-populists.

9 Kim Severson, "G.O.P.'s Full Control in Long-Moderate North Carolina May Leave Lasting Stamp," *New York Times*, December 11, 2012, https://www.nytimes.com/2012/12/12/us/politics/gop-to-take-control-in-long-moderate-north-carolina.html.

10 Robbie Brown, "North Carolina Approves Steep Benefit Cuts for Jobless in Bid to Reduce Debt," *New York Times*, February 13, 2013, https://www.nytimes.com/2013/02/14/us/north-carolina-approves-benefit-cuts-for-unemployed.html.

11 Will Wrigley, "North Carolina Voter ID Opponents React to Bill's Passage, Vow to Continue to Fight," *HuffPost*, April 25, 2013, https://www.huffingtonpost.com/2013/04/25/north-carolina-voter-id_n_3156191.html.

12 John Frank, "Legislation would repeal N.C. tax credit for low- and moderate-income taxpayers," *News & Observer*, February 14, 2013, https://www.newsobserver.com/news/weather/article10344959.html.

13 "NCGA-17 Promo," NC Forward Together Moral Movement Channel video, accessed on YouTube, May 2, 2013, https://www.youtube.com/watch?v=s3 gRvwPYZ4A.

14 "Civil Disobedience Leads to Arrests at NC General Assembly," NC Forward Together Moral Movement Channel video, May 3, 2013, accessed on You-Tube, January 5, 2019, https://www.youtube.com/watch?v=GyIgUz4hgn4.

15 John Frank, "17 arrested outside N.C. Senate-NAACP leader, Duke scholars, detained in protest against GOP policies," *News & Observer*, April 30, 2013.

16 "'Moral Monday' crowd rallies for women's rights; 101 arrested," *WRAL. com*, July 14, 2013, https://www.wral.com/-moral-monday-crowd-rallies-for -women-s-rights-/12661852/.

17 "84 more arrested on 'Moral Monday' as protesters decry 'outsiders' label," *The Times News*, June 18, 2013, https://www.thetimesnews.com/20130618 /84-more-arrested-on-moral-monday-as-protesters-decry-outsiders-label/30 6189900.

18 David Forbes, "'We fight': Moral Monday brings thousands to downtown Asheville to protest legislature," *Mountain Xpress*, August 5, 2013, https:// mountainx.com/news/community-news/moral_monday_brings_thousands_to _downtown_asheville_to_protest_legislature/.

19 Abby Ohlheiser, "The Religious, Progressive 'Moral Mondays' in North Caro-lina," *The Atlantic*, July 15, 2013, https://www.theatlantic.com/national/archive /2013/07/North-carolina-moral-monday-protests/313301/.

20 Mary C. Curtis, "North Carolina protesters look forward and reach back to faith," *The Washington Post*, June 12, 2013, https://www.washingtonpost .com/blogs/she-the-people/wp/2013/06/12/north-carolina-protesters-look -forward-and-reach-back-to-faith/?utm_term=.546b37eb1a72.

21 Kim Severson, "Protests in North Carolina Challenge Conservative Shift in State Politics," *New York Times*, June 11, 2013, https://www.nytimes.com/2013 /06/12/us/weekly-protests-in-north-carolina-challenge-conservative-shift -in-state-politics.html.

22 David Weigel, "'It Was Awesome Getting Arrested,'" *Slate*, July 23, 2013, https:// slate.com/news-and-politics/2013/07/inside-the-moral-mondays-protests -the-rev-william-barber-and-his-campaign-to-fight-north-carolinas-gop.html.

23 Scott Keyes, "The Biggest Liberal Protest of 2013 in 35 Photos & Video," *ThinkProgress*, June 28, 2013, https://thinkprogress.org/the-biggest-liberal -protest-of-2013-in-35-photos-video-ef93ca1c1e3c/.

24 "Moral Monday, July 15," *WRAL.com*, July 15, 2013, https://www.wral.com /news/state/nccapitol/image_gallery/12665743/.

25 Keyes, "The Biggest Liberal Protest."

26 Jonathan Wilson-Hartgrove (director, School for Conversion), phone inter-view by the author, January 26, 2019.

27 Barber and Wilson-Hartgrove, *The Third Reconstruction*, 35–39.

28 Jonathan Merritt, "How American Christians can break free from 'slave-holder religion,'" *Religion News Service*, May 2, 2018, https://religionnews

.com/2018/05/02/how-american-christians-can-break-free-from-slaveholder
-religion/.

29 Barber and Wilson-Hartgrove, *The Third Reconstruction*, 38.

30 "Scholars, Seniors, Clergy & Students Arrested at NC General Assembly,"
North Carolina NAACP video, May 9, 2013, accessed on YouTube, January
3, 2019, https://www.youtube.com/watch?v=h4EpVIyev-U.

31 Jim Bazán (activist), phone interview by the author, February 4, 2019.

32 Andrew Beaujon, "Charlotte Observer reporter arrested while covering protest," *Poynter*, June 11, 2013, https://www.poynter.org/reporting-editing/2013
/charlotte-observer-reporter-arrested-while-covering-protest/.

33 "American Values Atlas," Public Religion Research Institute, accessed January 5, 2019, http://ava.prri.org/#religious/2017/States/religion/m/US-NC and
"Religious Landscape Survey," Pew Research Center, accessed January 5, 2019,
http://www.pewforum.org/religious-landscape-study/state/north-carolina/.

34 Bart Barnes, "Douglas Moore, provocative presence in civil rights and D.C.
politics, dies at 91," *The Washington Post,* September 4, 2019, https://www
.washingtonpost.com/local/obituaries/douglas-moore-provocative-presence
-in-civil-rights-and-dc-politics-dies-at-91/2019/09/04/4fe6a1ee-ca92-11e9
-a4f3-c081a126de70_story.html.

35 "Moral March on Raleigh, 2017," Fusion Films/Facebook Live video, Facebook, February 13, 2017, https://www.facebook.com/RevDrBarber/videos/12
04610509658820/.

36 Barber and Wilson-Hartgrove, *The Third Reconstruction,* 129.

37 Thomasi McDonald, "Turnout of the Moral March on Raleigh varies, depending on who you ask," *The Charlotte Observer*, February 14, 2014, https://
www.charlotteobserver.com/news/local/article9097277.html.

38 Adam Beam, "State House: Progressive groups plan 'Truthful Tuesday' protest
at SC State House," *The State*, January 6, 2014, https://www.thestate.com/news/
politics-government/politics-columns-blogs/the-buzz/article13833467.html.

39 Allison Kilkenny, "Hundreds Turn Out for Georgia's Moral Monday," *The
Nation*, January 15, 2014, https://www.thenation.com/article/hundreds-turn
-out-georgias-moral-monday/.

40 Alice Miranda Ollstein, "Georgians Occupy Secretary of State's Office to Protest Voter Suppression: 'Let Us Vote,'" *ThinkProgress*, October 28, 2014, https://
thinkprogress.org/georgians-occupy-secretary-of-states-office-to-protest
-voter-suppression-let-us-vote-2d9bd8afcbc6/.

41 Kilkenny, "Hundreds Turn Out."

42 Cathy Lynn Grossman, "'Moral Monday' expands to a week of social justice
action across US," *Religion News Service*, August 19, 2014, https://religion
news.com/2014/08/19/moral-monday-voting-rights-naacp/.

43 Errin Whack, "The Moral Voice of the South," *Politico*, July 30, 2015,
https://www.politico.com/magazine/story/2015/07/rev-william-barber-moral
-mondays-civil-rights-120832.

44   Liz Theoharis (codirector, Poor People's Campaign), phone interview by the author, January 25, 2019.

45   Martin Luther King Jr., "Remaining Awake Through a Great Revolution," The Martin Luther King Jr. Research and Education Institute at Stanford, March 31, 1968, https://kinginstitute.stanford.edu/king-papers/documents /remaining-awake-through-great-revolution.

46   "Rev. William Barber: Full Remarks at Democratic National Convention," C-SPAN video, July 28, 2016, accessed on YouTube, https://www.youtube .com/watch?v=aw3PUghqlAA.

47   Samuel G. Freedman, "Democrats Shift to Embrace the Religious Left," *New York Times*, August 27, 2016, https://www.nytimes.com/2016/08/28/us/for -hillary-clinton-and-democrats-a-public-shift-toward-god-talk.html.

48   Jamelle Bouie, "Bright Shining as the Sun," *Slate*, July 29, 2016, https://slate. com/news-and-politics/2016/07/how-the-black-church-transformed-the- democrats-into-the-party-of-optimism.html.

49   Emily Todd VanDerWerff, "The Democratic Convention's Most Surprising Argument: Christianity Is a Liberal Religion," *Vox*, July 29, 2016, https://www .vox.com/2016/7/29/12320252/democrats-christian-religion-dnc-convention.

50   Adam Liptak, "Supreme Court Blocks North Carolina from Restoring Strict Voting Law," *New York Times*, August 31, 2016, https://www.nytimes.com /2016/09/01/us/politics/north-carolina-supreme-court-voting-rights-act.html.

51   Vann R. Newkirk II, "North Carolina's New Rainbow Coalition," *The Atlantic*, November 30, 2016, https://www.theatlantic.com/politics/archive/2016 /11/identity-politics-north-carolina-governor/509153/.

52   Paul Blest, "Over 80,000 People Joined the Biggest-Ever Moral March in North Carolina," *The Nation*, February 13, 2017, https://www.thenation.com /article/over-80000-people-joined-the-biggest-ever-moral-march-in-north -carolina/.

53   Will Doran, "Claims of 80,000 protesters at Raleigh 'Moral March' appear to be inflated," *PolitiFact*, February 13, 2017, https://www.politifact.com/ north-carolina/article/2017/feb/13/claims-80000-protesters-raleigh-moral -march-appear/.

54   Jedediah Purdy, "North Carolina's long moral march and its lessons for the Trump resistance," *The New Yorker*, February 17, 2017, https://www.new yorker.com/news/news-desk/north-carolinas-long-moral-march-and-its-lessons -for-the-trump-resistance.

55   Jelani Cobb, "William Barber takes on poverty and race in the age of Trump,' *The New Yorker*, May 7, 2018, https://www.newyorker.com/magazine/2018/05/14/ william-barber-takes-on-poverty-and-race-in-the-age-of-trump.

56   Jack Jenkins, "Religious leaders arrested in act of civil disobedience against Senate's 'immoral' health care bill," *ThinkProgress*, July 13, 2017, https://think progress.org/faith-leaders-protest-health-care-676c674ac077/.

57   "Senate Healthcare bill and the moral call to defend healthcare," *MSNBC*

.com, July 29, 2017, https://www.msnbc.com/am-joy/watch/senate-healthcare -bill-and-the-moral-call-to-defend-healthcare-1016566339795.

58 Jack Jenkins, "This Catholic nun pushed Obamacare through Congress. Now she's fighting to save it," *ThinkProgress*, June 30, 2017, https://thinkprogress .org/simone-campbell-health-care-663083582f55/.

59 Jake Bleiberg, "Faith leaders arrested for trespassing after hours-long sit-in at Sen. Collins' Portland office," *Bangor Daily News*, December 7, 2017, https:// bangordailynews.com/2017/12/07/news/portland/faith-leaders-stage-sit-in at-sen-collins-portland-office/.

60 Naomi Jagoda, "Collins pens op-ed explaining tax bill vote," *The Hill*, December 27, 2017, https://thehill.com/policy/finance/366586-collins-pens-op -ed-explaining-tax-bill-vote.

61 Joe Lawlor, "Sen. Collins now says tax reform vote wasn't contingent on support for her bills to boost Affordable Care Act," *Portland Press Herald*, March 22, 2018, https://www.pressherald.com/2018/03/22/democrats-slam-sen-collins -over-aca-stabilization-comments-votes/.

62 Scott Malone, "'Religious left' emerging as US political force in Trump era," *Reuters*, March 27, 2017, https://www.reuters.com/article/us-usa-trump-religion /religious-left-emerging-as-u-s-political-force-in-trump-era-idUSKBN16Y114 and Julie Zauzmer, "People are looking for a 'Religious Left.' This little-known network of clergy has been organizing it," *The Washington Post*, April 26, 2017, https://www.washingtonpost.com/news/acts-of-faith/wp/2017/04/26/people -are-looking-for-a-religious-left-this-little-known-network-of-clergy-has-been -organizing-it/.

63 *AM Joy* w/Joy Reid, Twitter, July 29, 2017, 10:54 a.m., https://twitter.com/am joyshow/status/891310902091186176.

64 Laurie Goodstein, "Religious Liberals Sat Out of Politics for 40 Years. Now They Want in the Game," *New York Times*, June 10, 2017, https://www .nytimes.com/2017/06/10/us/politics/politics-religion-liberal-william-barber .html.

65 William Barber, Twitter, January 24, 2019, 6:15 p.m., https://twitter.com/Rev DrBarber/status/1088576034608480256.

66 William Barber, Twitter, January 24, 2019, 6:17 p.m., https://twitter.com/Rev DrBarber/status/1088576448527519744.

67 Jack Jenkins, "The Religious Left is getting under right-wing media's skin," *ThinkProgress*, July 19, 2017, https://thinkprogress.org/conservative-media -sure-seems-nervous-about-the-religious-left-4d40e4445976/.

68 "An Open Letter to Liberty University to 'Engage in Peaceful Debate,'" *Red Letter Christians*, November 3, 2017, https://www.redletterchristians.org/an -open-letter-to-liberty-university-to-engage-in-peaceful-debate/.

69 "We Challenge Trump's Evangelical Defenders to Live TV Debate About Faith & Public Policy," petition, Groundswell, accessed February 1, 2019, https:// action.groundswell-mvmt.org/petitions/we-challenge-fellow-evangelical -leaders-to-live-tv-debate-about-faith-public-policy.

70 Christiane Amanpour, "What does the Bible teach about immigration?," Facebook video, November 5, 2018, https://www.facebook.com/camanpour /videos/1988672174763637/.

71 Jack Jenkins, "Full interview with Cory Booker: 'I'm calling for a revival of grace in this country," *Religion News Service*, October 24, 2018, https:// religionnews.com/2018/10/24/cory-booker-im-calling-for-a-revival-of-grace -in-this-country/.

72 Jack Jenkins, "Joe Biden and other candidates speak to diverse faith leaders, activists," *Religion News Service*, June 17, 2019, https://religionnews .com/2019/06/17/joe-biden-and-other-candidates-speak-to-diverse-faith- leaders-activists/.

73 Jack Jenkins, "Boisterous faith leaders and a silent Pete Buttigieg rally against Trump at White House," *Religion News Service*, June 12, 2019, https://religion news.com/2019/06/12/boisterous-faith-leaders-and-a-silent-pete-buttigieg -rally-against-trump-at-white-house/.

FIVE Keepers of the Story

1   "Charlottesville Mass Prayer Service," *Sojourners* video, accessed on Facebook, August 11, 2017, https://www.facebook.com/SojournersMagazine /videos/10154913829892794/.

2   "Charlottesville Prayer Service," *Sojourners* video.

3   "Charlottesville Prayer Service," *Sojourners* video.

4   Cornel West (activist, professor, Harvard Divinity School), phone interview by the author, February 16, 2019.

5   Joshua Eaton, "Violence Erupts at Klan-like Rally Through the University of Virginia Campus," *ThinkProgress*, August 12, 2017, https://thinkprogress.org /hundreds-of-white-nationalists-march-through-virginia-campus-with-flaming -torches-sparking-violence-84ebbc552bbe/.

6   Sines v. Kessler (3:17-cv-00072). (2017) https://www.courtlistener.com/recap /gov.uscourts.vawd.109120.1.0.pdf.

7   West, phone interview.

8   Traci Blackmon (pastor), phone interview by the author, March 12, 2019.

9   Jack Jenkins, "This Missouri pastor is working to 'reclaim the language of faith,'" *ThinkProgress*, November 13, 2017, https://thinkprogress.org/rev-traci -blackmon-c81f140e144f/.

10 Blackmon, phone interview.

11 DeRay Mckesson (activist), phone interview by author, March 5, 2019.

12 Jessica Guynn, "Meet the woman who coined #BlackLivesMatter," *USA Today*, March 4, 2015, https://www.usatoday.com/story/tech/2015/03/04 /alicia-garza-black-lives-matter/24341593/.

13 Emanuella Grinberg, "What #Ferguson stands for besides Michael Brown and Darren Wilson," CNN.com, November 19, 2014, http://www.cnn.com /2014/11/19/us/ferguson-social-media-injustice/index.html.

14 "Transformational Leadership: DeRay McKesson," Yale Divinity School video, October 11, 2016, accessed on YouTube, https://www.youtube.com /watch?v=WlFIuVA5GXs.

15 Mckesson, phone interview.

16 David Masci, "5 facts about the religious lives of African Americans," *FactTank* (blog), Pew Research Center, February 7, 2018, http://www.pewresearch.org /fact-tank/2018/02/07/5-facts-about-the-religious-lives-of-african-americans/.

17 Blackmon, phone interview.

18 "Nothing in particulars who identify as black," Pew Religious Landscape Survey, https://www.pewforum.org/religious-landscape-study/racial-and-ethnic -composition/black/religious-family/nothing-in-particular/.

19 "Christians who identify as black," Pew Religious Landscape Survey, https:// www.pewforum.org/religious-landscape-study/racial-and-ethnic-composition /black/christians/christian/.

20 "Nothing in particulars who identify as white," Pew Religious Landscape Survey, https://www.pewforum.org/religious-landscape-study/racial-and-ethnic -composition/white/religious-family/nothing-in-particular/.

21 Blackmon, phone interview.

22 Mckesson, phone interview.

23 Blackmon, phone interview.

24 Lilly Fowler, "Pastor paves her own way to Ferguson's frontlines," *St. Louis Post-Dispatch*, November 3, 2014, https://www.stltoday.com/lifestyles/faith -and-values/pastor-paves-her-own-way-to-ferguson-s-frontlines/article_464 e9965-2cf4-50b5-b0dc-4813756259d2.html.

25 Dr Kathleen Bachynski, Twitter, August 14, 2014, 8:23 p.m., https://twitter .com/bachyns/status/500075320435691522.

26 Fowler, "Pastor paves her way."

27 Lilly Fowler, "Churches to serve as safe spaces after Ferguson grand jury an- nouncement," November 21, 2014, https://religionnews.com/2014/11/21 /churches-serve-safe-spaces-ferguson-grand-jury-announcement/.

28 David Montgomery, "Greater St. Mark Family Church among those offering 'safe place' in Ferguson," *Washington Post*, November 23, 2014, https://www .washingtonpost.com/politics/greater-st-mark-family-church-among-those -offering-safe-place-in-ferguson/2014/11/23/59a6fa78-734c-11e4-9c9f-a 37e29e80cd5_story.html.. See also Mckesson, interview.

29 DeRay Mckesson, *On the Other Side of Freedom* (New York: Penguin Publish- ing Group, Kindle Edition), 113.

30 "Politics of Jesus, sermon by Rev. Starsky Wilson," Roots of Justice video, September 8, 2014, accessed on YouTube, https://www.youtube.com/watch ?time_continue=1&v=suI1FmwMDs8.

31 Leah Gunning Francis, *Ferguson and Faith: Sparking Leadership and Awaken- ing Community* (Saint Louis: Chalice Press, Kindle Edition).

32 Jack Jenkins, "Ferguson Faith Leaders Take to the Streets, March with

Protestors," *ThinkProgress*, August 15, 2014, https://thinkprogress.org/fer guson-faith-leaders-take-to-the-streets-march-with-protestors-b78567134445/.

33 Francis, *Ferguson and Faith*.

34 Tim Lloyd, "Young Demonstrators Demand to Be Heard; Monday Begins with Early-Morning Games and Silent March," St. Louis Public Radio/NPR, October 13, 2014, https://news.stlpublicradio.org/post/young-demonstrators -demand-be-heard-monday-begins-early-morning-games-and-silent-march.

35 "Interfaith gathering calling for end to police violence brings hundreds to arena," *St. Louis Post-Dispatch*, October 12, 2014, https://www.stltoday.com /lifestyles/faith-and-values/interfaith-gathering-calling-for-end-to-police -violence-brings-hundreds/article_fa174bab-4e69-5351-9c71-ceafce1d60b8.html.

36 Howard Koplowitz, "Ferguson October: Cornel West Came to St. Louis 'To Go to Jail,'" October 13, 2014, https://www.ibtimes.com/ferguson-october -cornel-west-came-st-louis-go-jail-1703698.

37 Lisa Sharon Harper, "Why I got arrested in Ferguson," CNN.com, October 15, 2014. See also http://religion.blogs.cnn.com/2014/10/15/why-i-got-arrested -in-ferguson/; https://sojo.net/articles/arrested-ferguson-act-repentance; https:// www.theguardian.com/us-news/2014/oct/13/cornel-west-arrest-clergy-ferguson -protest; https://www.wbur.org/news/2014/10/14/osagyefo-sekou-ferguson -arrest.

38 Heather Wilson, "This Ain't Yo Mama's Civil Rights Movement," HW Cre- ative photo at https://www.dustandlightphoto.com/index/G0000A7Hjy4yW Gvs/I0000HhtYcZEY3yI.

39 Tina Nguyen, "Rep. John Lewis Calls for 'Massive, Non-Violent Protests' Na- tionwide if Wilson Isn't Indicted," *Mediate*, November 18, 2014, https://www. mediaite.com/online/rep-john-lewis-calls-for-massive-non-violent-protests -nationwide-if-wilson-isnt-indicted/.

40 Blackmon, phone interview.

41 Vicky Osterweil, "In Defense of Looting," *New Inquiry*, August 21, 2014, https://thenewinquiry.com/in-defense-of-looting/.

42 Mckesson, phone interview.

43 "Jesse Jackson joins protests as hundreds turn out in Ferguson," AP/CBS News, August 16, 2014, https://www.cbsnews.com/news/jesse-jackson-leads-peace ful-protests-in-ferguson-missouri/.

44 Jenkins, "Ferguson Faith Leaders."

45 Ed Pilkington, "Obama gives searing speech on race in eulogy for Charles- ton pastor," *The Guardian*, June 26, 2015, https://www.theguardian.com/us- news/2015/jun/26/obama-charleston-eulogy-pinckney-amazing-grace.

46 Jack Jenkins, "The black queer Buddhist teacher who is smashing stereo- types and leading an awakening on the left," *ThinkProgress*, August 28, 2017, https://thinkprogress.org/angel-kyodo-williams-0357aa186187/.

47 Ari Phillips, "Sick of Waiting, Woman Takes Down South Carolina Confed- erate Flag Herself," *ThinkProgress*, June 27, 2015, https://thinkprogress.org

/sick-of-waiting-woman-takes-down-south-carolina-confederate-flag-herself
-67a404c50acb/.

48 Donna Weaver, "'Black Lives Matter' sign defaced at Galloway church,"
September 3, 2015, https://www.pressofatlanticcity.com/news/black-lives-
matter-sign-defaced-at-galloway-church/article_01e0a042–51c1–11e5-bf68
–6f462d82c281.html.

49 Seth Richardson, "'Black Lives Matter' sign defaced at Reno church," August
27, 2015, https://www.rgj.com/story/news/crime/2015/08/28/black-lives-matter
-sign-defaced-reno-church/71282886/.

50 Elaine McArdle, "Black Lives Matter banners at Unitarian Universalist churches
have been defaced and stolen—sometimes repeatedly," August 24, 2015,
https://www.uuworld.org/articles/blm-banners-defaced.

51 McArdle, "Black Lives Matter banners."

52 Jack Jenkins, "'We're not the "nice" faith people!': Faith leaders are battling
white supremacy, Trump," *ThinkProgress*, October 31, 2017, https://think
progress.org/prophets-resistance-undermine-trump-8cfdda05ab1a/.

53 Jenkins, "'We're not the "nice" faith people!'"

54 Jenkins, "'We're not the "nice" faith people!'"

55 "Ebony Power 100: Honoring the Heroes of the Black Community," *Ebony*,
2015, http://www.ebony.com/power100-2015/.

56 D. J. Wilson. "The Rev. Traci Blackmon on Ferguson, Hillary Clinton, and the
Pope," *St. Louis* magazine, January 14, 2016, https://www.stlmag.com/news
/rev-traci-blackmon-on-ferguson-hillary-clinton-and-the-pope/.

57 Blackmon, phone interview.

58 Traci Blackmon, Facebook video, August 11, 2017, https://www.facebook
.com/traci.blackmon/videos/10213136595310876/.

59 Paul Duggan, "Militiamen came to Charlottesville as neutral First Amendment protectors, commander says," *The Washington Post*, August 13, 2017,
https://www.washingtonpost.com/local/trafficandcommuting/militiamen
-came-to-charlottesville-as-neutral-first-amendment-protectors-commander
-says/2017/08/13/d3928794-8055-11e7-ab27-1a21a8e006ab_story.html.

60 Joshua Eaton, "Before the torches and after: The activists fighting white supremacy in Charlottesville," *ThinkProgress*, October 31, 2017, https://think
progress.org/cville-fighting-right-9e82a5d4b768/.

61 Heather Wilson, "Charlottesville, Virginia Photo Essay," HW Creative at
https://www.heatherwilsoncreative.com/charlottesville.

62 Jack Jenkins, "Meet the clergy who stared down white supremacists in Charlottesville," *ThinkProgress*, August 16, 2017, https://thinkprogress.org/clergy
-in-charlottesville-e95752415c3e/.

63 Jenkins, "Meet the clergy."

64 Jenkins, "Meet the clergy."

65 West, phone interview.

66 West, phone interview.

67 "What do Christians think of the Alt right?," *Bitcoin Uncensored*, accessed on YouTube, August 28, 2017, https://www.youtube.com/watch?v=Ou8670ZuuLg.

68 Blackmon, phone interview.

SIX Welcoming the Stranger

1 "Church Trends: One SITE for Your PCUSA Data" at https://church-trends .pcusa.org/church/67/overview/.

2 Caitlin Dickson, "This Church Is Reviving the Sanctuary Movement to Shelter Undocumented Immigrants from Deportation," *The Daily Beast*, June 11, 2014, https://www.thedailybeast.com/this-church-is-reviving-the-sanctuary -movement-to-shelter-undocumented-immigrants-from-deportation.

3 Dickson, "Reviving the Sanctuary Movement."

4 Alison Harrington, "The Rev. Alison Harrington: Neyoy Ruiz is staying with us until his immigration case is closed," *Arizona Daily Star*, May 18, 2014, https://tucson.com/news/opinion/column/guest/the-rev-alison-harrington -neyoy-ruiz-is-staying-with-us/article_adf5428a-473b-5749-88bc-d22b17 5bd963.html.

5 Susan Gzesh, "Central Americans and Asylum Policy in the Reagan Era," *Migration Policy Institute*, April 1, 2006, https://www.migrationpolicy.org/article /central-americans-and-asylum-policy-reagan-era.

6 Judith McDaniel, "The Sanctuary Movement, Then and Now," *Religion & Politics*, February 21, 2017, https://religionandpolitics.org/2017/02/21/the -sanctuary-movement-then-and-now/.

7 Linda Rabben, *Sanctuary and Asylum: A Social and Political History* (Seattle and London: Univ. of Washington Press, 2016), 135–36.

8 Minerva G. Carcaño (United Methodist Bishop), interview by author, March 28, 2019.

9 Carcaño, interview.

10 Jay Mathews, "Five in Sanctuary Movement Given Probation," *The Washington Post*, July 2, 1986, https://www.washingtonpost.com/archive/politics /1986/07/02/five-in-sanctuary-movement-given-probation/902ffcad-b350 –4367-a2d9–35ec857e5190/.

11 "American Baptist Churches v. Thornburgh (ABC) Settlement Agreement," US Citizen and Immigration Services website, https://www.uscis.gov/laws/legal -settlement-notices/american-baptist-churches-v-thornburgh-abc-settlement -agreement.

12 Peter Mancina, "In the Spirit of Sanctuary: Sanctuary-City Policy Advocacy and the Production of Sanctuary-Power in San Francisco, California" (PhD diss., Vanderbilt Univ., 2016), https://etd.library.vanderbilt.edu/available/etd -07112016-193322/unrestricted/Mancina.pdf.pdf.

13 Donald Trump, Twitter, April 18, 2018, 5:59 a.m., https://twitter.com/real DonaldTrump/status/986544648477868032.

14 Ted Hesson, "7th Circuit gives Trump temporary win on 'sanctuary' policy," *Politico*, June 26, 2018, https://www.politico.com/story/2018/06/26/trump-sanctuary-cities-grants-678721.

15 Serena Marshall, "Obama Has Deported More People Than Any Other President," ABC News, August 29, 2016, https://abcnews.go.com/Politics/obamas-deportation-policy-numbers/story?id=41715661.

16 Mirren Gidda, "Obama vs. Trump: Who has deported more immigrants?," *Newsweek*, April 18, 2017, https://www.newsweek.com/illegal-immigration-undocumented-migrants-obama-trump-585726.

17 John Morton, memorandum to Field Office Directors, Special Agents in Charge, Chief Counsel, October 24, 2011, US Immigration and Customs Enforcement, https://www.ice.gov/doclib/ero-outreach/pdf/10029.2-policy.pdf.

18 John Morton, memorandum to All Field Office Directors, All Special Agents in Charge, All Chief Counsel, June 17, 2011, US Immigration and Customs Enforcement, https://www.ice.gov/doclib/secure-communities/pdf/prosecutorial-discretion-memo.pdf.

19 Randal C. Archibold, "Illegal Immigrant Advocate for Families Is Deported, *New York Times*, August 21, 2007, https://www.nytimes.com/2007/08/21/us/21immigrant.html.

20 Margo Cowan (attorney and activist), interview by the author, May 16, 2019.

21 Paul Bedard, "200,000 deportation cases quietly 'closed' under Obama," *Washington Examiner*, August 28, 2017, https://www.washingtonexaminer.com/200-000-deportation-cases-quietly-closed-under-obama.

22 Noel Anderson (grassroots coordinator for immigrants' rights, Church World Service), interview by the author, March 22, 2019.

23 Dickson, "Reviving the Sanctuary Movement."

24 Dickson, "Reviving the Sanctuary Movement."

25 Ted Robbins, "Home of Sanctuary Movement Revives Strategy to Stop Deportation," NPR, May 14, 2014, https://www.npr.org/2014/05/14/312523840/home-of-sanctuary-movement-revives-strategy-to-stop-deportation.

26 Dickson, "Reviving the Sanctuary Movement."

27 "Church gives sanctuary to undocumented man," *MSNBC.com*, June 1, 2014, http://www.msnbc.com/melissa-harris-perry/watch/church-gives-sanctuary-to-undocumented-man-271640643715.

28 Erik Wemple, "The ugliness of Melissa Harris-Perry's departure from MSNBC," *The Washington Post*, March 2, 2016, https://www.washingtonpost.com/blogs/erik-wemple/wp/2016/03/02/the-ugliness-of-melissa-harris-perrys-departure-from-msnbc/.

29 Luis F. Carrasco, "Illegal immigrant sheltered at church gets deportation stay," *Arizona Daily Star*, June 10, 2014, https://tucson.com/news/local/border/illegal-immigrant-sheltered-at-church-gets-deportation-stay/article_03bdb28b-4fe9-5848-a98a-eb6ecbb281a7.html.

30 Carrasco, "Illegal immigrant sheltered."

31 Emily Mullins, "Arizona UCC to provide sanctuary to immigrant family facing

deportation," United Church of Christ, June 25, 2014, http://www.ucc.org /arizona-ucc-to-provide-sanctuary-06252014.

32 "CWS Joins Nationwide Sanctuary Movement for Immigrants Facing Deportation," Church World Service, September 24, 2014, https://cwsglobal.org/cws -joins-nationwide-sanctuary-movement-for-immigrants-facing-deportation/.

33 María Inés Taracena, "Rosa Robles Loreto Leaves Sanctuary at Tucson Church After 15 Months," *Tucson Weekly*, November 11, 2015, https://www.tucson weekly.com/TheRange/archives/2015/11/11/after-15-months-in-sanctuary -undocumented-mom-rosa-robles-loreto-moving-out-of-tucson-church.

34 Curt Prendergast, "Rosa Robles Loreto leaves sanctuary of Tucson church," *Arizona Daily Star*, November 11, 2015, https://tucson.com/news/local/rosa -robles-loreto-leaves-sanctuary-of-tucson-church/article_2e0ae3c4-8891 -11e5-b998-173e7444fbbf.html.

35 Rev. Alison Harrington (pastor, Southside Presbyterian Church, Tucson), interview by author, April 30, 2019.

36 Martin Luther King Jr. and James Melvin Washington, ed., *A Testament of Hope: The Essential Writings and Speeches of Martin Luther King Jr.* (San Francisco: HarperSanFrancisco, 1991), 127.

37 Washington, ed., *A Testament of Hope*, 127.

38 Washington, ed., *A Testament of Hope*, 60.

39 Nate Silver, "Police Clashes Spur Coverage of Wall Street Protests-NYTimes .com." *FiveThirtyEight (blog), NYTimes.com,* October 7, 2011, http://fivethirty eight.com/2011/10/07/police-clashes-spur-coverage-of-wall-street-protests/.

40 Daniel Cox, E. J. Dionne Jr., Robert P. Jones, PhD, William A. Galston, "What Americans Want from Immigration Reform in 2014," *PRRI,* June, 10, 2014, https://www.prri.org/research/immigration-reform-06-2014/.

41 Matthew 25: 31–40 (NRSV translation).

42 Exodus 23:9 (JPS TANAKH translation), accessed via Safaria at https://www .sefaria.org/Exodus.23.9?lang=bi&with=Versions&lang2=en.

43 Kimberly Winston, "Ohio Mosque Is First to Join Sanctuary Movement," *Religion News Service,* January 23, 2017, https://religionnews.com/2017/01/23 /ohio-mosque-is-first-to-join-sanctuary-movement/.

44 Bhikkhu Bodhi, Myokei Caine-Barrett, Norman Fischer, Joan Halifax, Mushim Patricia Ikeda, Jack Kornfield, Ethan Nichtern, Roshi Pat Enkyo O'Hara, Lama Rod Owens, Greg Snyder, Gina Sharpe, Rev. angel Kyodo williams, and Jan Willis, "Stand Against Suffering: A Call to Action by Buddhist Teachers," *Lion's Roar,* August 21, 2017, https://www.lionsroar.com/stand-against-suffering/.

45 Kimberly Gross and John Sides, "No wonder there's a shutdown: New poll shows how much Republicans and Democrats really disagree on immigration," *Washington Post,* January 15, 2019, https://www.washingtonpost.com /news/monkey-cage/wp/2019/01/15/no-wonder-theres-a-shutdown-new-poll -shows-republicans-and-democrats-disagree-profoundly-on-immigration/.

46 Grace Yukich, *One Family Under God: Immigration Politics and Progressive Religion in America.* (New York: Oxford Univ. Press, 2013), 9.

47 Harrington, interview.

48 Tina Vasquez, "Exclusive: Five Immigrants Briefly Leave Sanctuary to Learn How to Organize," *Rewire.News*, August 23, 2018, https://rewire.news/article /2018/08/23/exclusive-five-immigrants-briefly-leave-sanctuary-to-learn-how -to-organize/.

49 Hilda Ramirez, interview by the author via phone, December 17, 2019.

50 Jennifer Hawks, "Churches and the 'New Sanctuary Movement," *Baptist Joint Committee for Religious Liberty*, June 15, 2017, https://bjconline.org /churches-and-the-new-sanctuary-movement/.

51 Jack Jenkins, "Arizona Church Defies Immigration Officials, Shelters Undoc- umented Immigrant," *ThinkProgress*, August 6, 2014, https://thinkprogress .org/arizona-church-defies-immigration-officials-shelters-undocumented -immigrant-6aaa74ed377d/.

52 "Accompaniment," New Sanctuary Movement New York, https://www.new sanctuarynyc.org/accompaniment_training.

53 Jack Jenkins, "Faith Groups Create Emergency Hotline for Immigrants to Call During a Deportation Raid," *ThinkProgress*, May 25, 2016, https://think progress.org/faith-groups-create-emergency-hotline-for-immigrants-to-call -during-a-deportation-raid-2a8eab6a97a2/.

54 Jack Jenkins, "As Federal Government Launches New Deportation Raids, Churches Vow to Take in Immigrants," *ThinkProgress*, January 15, 2016, https:// thinkprogress.org/as-federal-government-launches-new-deportation-raids -churches-vow-to-take-in-immigrants-5a68b78d9ecb/.

55 Jeff Gammage, "New Sanctuary Movement has been on a dead run since Trump's election," *Philadelphia Inquirer,* December 14, 2017, https://www.philly .com/philly/news/new-sanctuary-movement-immigration-ice-trump-deportation -20171214.html.

56 Michelle Ye Hee Lee, "Donald Trump's false comments connecting Mex- ican immigrants and crime," *Washington Post*, July 8, 2015, https://www .washingtonpost.com/news/fact-checker/wp/2015/07/08/donald-trumps -false-comments-connecting-mexican-immigrants-and-crime/?utm_term= .fb451930d47c.

57 Gregory Korte and Alan Gomez, "Trump ramps up rhetoric on undocumented immigrants: 'These aren't people. These are animals,'" *USA Today*, May 16, 2018, https://www.usatoday.com/story/news/politics/2018/05/16/trump -immigrants-animals-mexico-democrats-sanctuary-cities/617252002/.

58 "Sanctuary Movement," *Religion & Ethics Newsweekly*, February 3, 2017, http://www.pbs.org/wnet/religionandethics/2017/02/03/sanctuary-movement /34422/.

59 "Second Trump Immigration Protest Held at PHL," Power, January 30, 2017, https://powerinterfaith.org/second-trump-immigration-protest-held-at-phl/.

60 Jack Jenkins, "Inside the battle for immigrant rights at Dulles airport," *Think- Progress*, January 30, 2017, https://thinkprogress.org/inside-the-battle-for -immigrant-rights-at-dulles-airport-d052b97ddf39/.

61 Danielle Corcione, "Demonstrators Occupy ICE Building in Philadelphia Amid Police Brutality," *Rewire.News*, July 6, 2018, https://rewire.news/article /2018/07/06/demonstrators-occupy-ice-building-philadelphia-amid-police -brutality/.

62 David Pastor, "What I Learned from Trying to Make My Campus a Sanctuary," *The Nation*, September 6, 2017, https://www.thenation.com/article /what-i-learned-from-trying-to-make-my-campus-a-sanctuary/.

63 Alan Gomez, "ICE sets record for arrests of undocumented immigrants with no criminal record," *USA Today*, March 21, 2019, https://www.usatoday.com /story/news/politics/2019/03/21/ice-sets-record-arrests-undocumented -immigrants-no-criminal-record/3232476002/.

64 Esther Yu Hsi Lee and Jack Jenkins, "A family mulls risking it all in the name of justice by sheltering the undocumented in their home," *ThinkProgress*, June 5, 2017, https://thinkprogress.org/virginia-home-sanctuary-1b45647a14d/.

65 Anderson, interview.

66 Myrna Orozco and Rev. Noel Andersen, "Sanctuary in the age of Trump: The rise of the movement a year into the Trump administration," January 2018, https:// www.sanctuarynotdeportation.org/uploads/7/6/9/1/76912017/sanctuary _in_the_age_of_trump_january_2018.pdf.

67 Kanyakrit Vongkiatkajorn, "Here Are the Churches Fighting Back Against Trump's Immigration Crackdown," *Mother Jones*, February 21, 2017, https:// www.motherjones.com/politics/2017/02/sanctuary-church-movement -trump-deportation/.

68 Sarah Jones, "What's Next for Evangelicalism?," *New Republic*, June 7, 2018, https://newrepublic.com/article/148779/whats-next-evangelicalism.

69 Sarah Ruiz-Grossman, "Why This Church Is Providing 'Sanctuary' to Undocumented Immigrants," *HuffPost*, October 20, 2017, https://www.huffington post.com/entry/southside-presbyterian-church-sanctuary-movement_us _59b722dfe4b027c149e1be39.

70 "CO church offering sanctuary to undocumented mother," *MSNBC*, February 15, 2017, https://www.msnbc.com/kate-snow/watch/co-church-offering -sanctuary-to-undocumented-mother-878076483548.

71 "Special series: Finding Sanctuary," *The Nation*, https://www.thenation.com /special/sanctuary/.

72 Kyung Lah and Alberto Moya, "Inside a Safe House, Hiding from ICE," CNN, March 14, 2018, https://www.cnn.com/2018/03/14/us/california-immigrant -safe-house/index.html.

73 Gregory S. Schneider, "As politics of immigration heat up, Virginia churches join growing sanctuary movement," *Washington Post*, July 5, 2018, https:// www.washingtonpost.com/local/virginia-politics/as-politics-of-immigration -heat-up-virginia-churches-join-growing-sanctuary-movement/2018/07/05 /3d6cccc6–7a45–11e8–80be-6d32e182a3bc_story.html.

74 Liz Robbins and Jonathan Wolfe, "Told to Go Back to Guatemala, She Sought Sanctuary Instead," *New York Times*, August 18, 2017, https://www.nytimes

.com/2017/08/18/nyregion/told-to-go-back-to-guatemala-she-sought-sanctuary
-instead.html.

75 Dave Eggers, "No one is safer. No one is served: An immigrant family hides
from Donald Trump in a Connecticut Church," *The New Yorker*, August 24,
2018, https://www.newyorker.com/news/daily-comment/no-one-is-safer-no
-one-is-served.

76 Anna Palmer, "Immigration's latest ally: Christian right," *Politico*, February 6,
2013, https://www.politico.com/story/2013/02/immigrations-new-ally-the
-christian-right-087241. See also: William McKenzie, "William McKenzie:
Evangelicals press GOP in House on immigration," *The Dallas Morning News*,
July 22, 2013, https://www.dallasnews.com/opinion/opinion/2013/07/22
/william-mckenzie-evangelicals-press-gop-in-house-on-immigration.

77 Alan Rappeport, "Donald Trump Criticizes Pope Francis as 'Very Political'
for Mexico Trip," *FirstDraft (blog), New York Times*, February 11, 2016,
https://www.nytimes.com/politics/first-draft/2016/02/11/donald-trump
-criticizes-pope-francis-as-very-political-for-mexico-trip.

78 Gerard O'Connell, "Pope responding to questions on Trump: 'A person who
only thinks of building walls, and not building bridges, is not Christian,'" *America*, February 18, 2016, https://www.americamagazine.org/content/dispatches
/aboard-plane-home-mexico-pope-francis-responds-questions-donald-trump.

79 "Take Action: Tell Congress to Stop Separating Families and Protect Family
Unity," *Church World Service*, May 30, 2018, https://greateras1.org/take-action
-tell-congress-to-stop-separating-families-protect-family-unity/.

80 Jack Jenkins, "Catholic bishops rebuke Trump's asylum changes, suggest 'canonical penalties,'" *Religion News Service*, June 13, 2018, https://religion
news.com/2018/06/13/catholic-bishops-rebuke-trumps-asylum-changes-
suggest-policy-is-a-life-issue/.

81 Colleen Long, "Sessions cites Bible to defend separating immigrant families,"
Associated Press, June 14, 2018, https://www.apnews.com/0bcc5d5d07724
7769da065864d215d1b.

82 Long, "Sessions cites Bible."

83 FCNL (Friends Committee on National Legislation), Twitter, June 15, 2018,
10:40 a.m., https://twitter.com/FCNL/status/1007633844713984005.

84 Sikh Coalition, Twitter, June 18, 2018 5:21 p.m., https://twitter.com/sikh
_coalition/status/1008822083885981696.

85 "Faith leaders' statement on family separation" United Methodist Church,
June 7, 2018, https://web.archive.org/web/20190620063911/http://www.umc
.org/who-we-are/faith-leaders-statement-on-family-separation.

86 "Over 2,500 Women of Faith Demand Department of Homeland Security
Keep Families Together," Faith in Public Life, June 6, 2018, https://www.faith
inpubliclife.org/families-belong-together.

87 Jack Jenkins, Twitter, June 15, 2018 6:49 p.m., https://twitter.com/jackm
jenkins/status/1007756888983916544.

88 Eliza Rockefeller and Matthew Abrahams, *Tricycle Magazine*, "Buddhist

Leaders Condemn Child Separation at US-Mexico Border," June 20, 2018, https://tricycle.org/trikedaily/buddhist-border/.

89 Church of the Nazarene, Twitter, June 16, 2018 10:39 p.m., https://twitter.com/Nazarene/status/1008177226406416390.

90 "Southern Baptist Convention reaffirms support for immigrants," Evangelical Immigration Table, June 13, 2018, http://evangelicalimmigrationtable.com/southern-baptist-convention-reaffirms-support-for-immigrants/.

91 Jack Jenkins, Twitter, June 18, 2018 4:42 p.m., https://twitter.com/jackmjenkins/status/1008812232996769792.

92 Willa Frej, "Franklin Graham Blasts Trump's Immigrant Family Separations at Border," *HuffPost*, June 14, 2018, https://www.huffpost.com/entry/franklin-graham-blasts-trump-border_n_5b223db7e4b09d7a3d7a7c16.

93 Michelle Boorstein, Twitter, June 15, 2018 10:32 a.m., https://twitter.com/mboorstein/status/1007631966697598978.

94 Samuel Smith, "Evangelical Leaders Condemn Trump for Separating Immigrant Children From Families at Border," *Christian Post*, June 5, 2018, https://www.christianpost.com/news/evangelical-leaders-condemn-trump-separating-immigrant-children-from-families-border-224629/.

95 Jack Jenkins and Emily McFarlan Miller, "More than 600 United Methodists file formal church complaint against Jeff Sessions," *Religion News Service*, June 19, 2018, https://religionnews.com/2018/06/19/more-than-600-united-methodists-sign-on-to-formal-church-complaint-against-jeff-sessions/.

96 There remains a curious bit of mystery regarding why the case was dismissed, with many Methodist leaders expressing confusion as to why an Alabama-based bishop threw out the case by arguing there is a distinction between personal behavior and the actions of public officials. The rationale mystified Rev. William B. Lawrence, a former president of the UMC's Judicial Council, who described the Bishop's logic as "problematic." For more, see: Jack Jenkins, "Jeff Sessions cleared in church complaint, perplexing some top Methodists," *Religion News Service*, August 9, 2018, https://religionnews.com/2018/08/09/jeff-sessions-cleared-in-church-complaint-perplexing-some-top-methodists/.

97 MCAN, Twitter, October 29, 2018, 2:13 p.m., https://twitter.com/mcanfia/status/1056972283716210689.

98 Jack Jenkins, "Jeff Sessions speech interrupted by Methodist, Baptist clergy," *Religion News Service*, October 29, 2018, https://religionnews.com/2018/10/29/jeff-sessions-speech-interrupted-by-methodist-baptist-clergy/.

99 "Jeff Sessions Farewell Cold Open-SNL," *Saturday Night Live* video, accessed on YouTube, November 10, 2018, https://www.youtube.com/watch?v=EGy-xpK-1mw.

100 Jack Jenkins, "At least 30 faith leaders arrested in border protest," *Religion News Service*, December 11, 2018, https://religionnews.com/2018/12/11/at-least-30-faith-leaders-arrested-in-border-protest/.

101 Yonat Shimron, "After arrest of protected immigrant, sanctuary church members cry out for justice," *Religion News Service*, November 26, 2018, https://

religionnews.com/2018/11/26/after-arrest-of-protected-immigrant-sanctuary -church-members-cry-out-for-justice/.

102 Travis Long, "Man who left sanctuary is now in Georgia detention center. His supporters rally in Raleigh," *The News & Observer*, November 26, 2018, https://www.newsobserver.com/news/local/article222214765.html.

103 Cowan, interview.

104 Craig Smith, "Protestors stage "play date" at McSally's office," 9KGUN ABC, June 13, 2018, https://www.kgun9.com/news/local-news/protestors-stage-play -date-at-mcsallys-office.

105 Chelsea Bailey, "Protest Fatigue: Have Weeks of Protests Made an Impact?," NBC News, May 13, 2017, https://www.nbcnews.com/news/us-news/protest -fatigue-have-weeks-protests-made-impact-n759091.

106 Harrington, interview.

107 John Abraham, "Study finds that global warming exacerbates refugee crises," *The Guardian*, January 15, 2018, https://www.theguardian.com/environment /climate-consensus-97-per-cent/2018/jan/15/study-finds-that-global-warming -exacerbates-refugee-crises. See also: Oliver Milman, Emily Holden, and David Agren, "The unseen driver behind the migrant caravan: climate change," *The Guardian,* October 30, 2018, https://www.theguardian.com/world/2018 /oct/30/migrant-caravan-causes-climate-change-central-america.

SEVEN Creation Care

1 Jack Jenkins, "The growing indigenous spiritual movement that could save the planet," *ThinkProgress*, September 30, 2016, https://thinkprogress.org /indigenous-spiritual-movement-8f873348a2f5/.

2 Chase Iron Eyes (head, Lakota People's Law Project), interview by the author, April 25, 2019.

3 Sue Skalicky and Monica Davey, "Tension Between Police and Standing Rock Protesters Reaches Boiling Point," *New York Times,* October 28, 2016, https:// www.nytimes.com/2016/10/29/us/dakota-access-pipeline-protest.html.

4 Saul Elbein, "These Are the Defiant 'Water Protectors' of Standing Rock," *National Geographic,* January 26, 2017, https://news.nationalgeographic.com /2017/01/tribes-standing-rock-dakota-access-pipeline-advancement/.

5 Karen Pauls, "'We must kill the black snake': Prophecy and prayer motivate Standing Rock movement," CBC News, December 11, 2016, https://www.cbc .ca/news/canada/manitoba/dakota-access-pipeline-prayer-1.3887441.

6 LaDonna Brave Bull Allard, phone interview by the author, September 12, 2019.

7 Iron Eyes, phone interview.

8 Mikki Halpin, "Standing Rock Sioux Tribe Historian LaDonna Brave Bull Allard on DAPL Protests and Seventh Generation Activists," *Teen Vogue,* April 26, 2017, https://www.teenvogue.com/story/standing-rock-sioux-tribe -ladonna-brave-bull-allard-interview-dapl-protests.

9 Dave Archambault II (chief consulting officer, FirstNation HealthCare), interview by the author, April 29, 2019.

10 "Standing Rock Special: Unlicensed #DAPL Guards Attacked Water Protectors with Dogs & Pepper Spray," *Democracy Now!*, November 24, 2016, https://www.democracynow.org/2016/11/24/standing_rock_special_unlicensed_dapl_guards.

11 "Guards accused of unleashing dogs, pepper-spraying oil pipeline protesters," CBS News, September 5, 2016, https://www.cbsnews.com/news/dakota-access-pipeline-protest-turns-violent-in-north-dakota/.

12 Daniel A. Medina, "Dakota Pipeline Company Buys Ranch Near Sioux Protest Site, Records Show," NBC News, September 23, 2016, https://www.nbcnews.com/news/us-news/dakota-pipeline-company-buys-ranch-near-sioux-protest-site-records-n653051.

13 Gyorgy Toth, "The radical story of the Native American liberation movement, 50 years on," *The Conversation*, June 22, 2018, http://theconversation.com/the-radical-story-of-the-native-american-liberation-movement-50-years-on-97824.

14 Jenkins, "The growing indigenous movement."

15 Saul Elbein, "The Youth Group That Launched a Movement at Standing Rock," *New York Times Magazine*, January 31, 2017, https://www.nytimes.com/2017/01/31/magazine/the-youth-group-that-launched-a-movement-at-standing-rock.html.

16 Robert Boos, "Native American tribes unite to fight the Keystone pipeline and government 'disrespect,'" PRI, February 19, 2015, https://www.pri.org/stories/2015-02-19/native-american-tribes-unite-fight-keystone-pipeline-and-government-disrespect. See also: Archambault II, phone interview.

17 Jack Jenkins, "Citing Religious Freedom, Native Americans Fight to Take Back Sacred Land from Mining Companies," *ThinkProgress*, July 24, 2015, https://thinkprogress.org/citing-religious-freedom-native-americans-fight-to-take-back-sacred-land-from-mining-companies-446fb032f611/.

18 Jenkins, "The growing indigenous movement."

19 Iron Eyes, phone interview.

20 Lyng v. Northwest Indian Cemetery Protective Association, 485 US 439 (1988).

21 Employment Division v. Smith, 494 US 872 (1990).

22 Ian Milhiser, *Injustices: The Supreme Court's History of Comforting the Comfortable and Afflicting the Afflicted*, (New York: Nation Books, 2015), 252.

23 Iron Eyes, phone interview.

24 Pope Francis, "Mass, imposition of the pallium and bestowal of the Fisherman's Ring for the beginning of the Petrine ministry of the Bishop of Rome: Homily of Pope Francis," *Vatican Media*, March 19, 2013, http://w2.vatican.va/content/francesco/en/homilies/2013/documents/papa-francesco_20130319_omelia-inizio-pontificato.html.

25 Jason Horowitz, "Catholic Church inaugurates Pope Francis in huge, open-air Mass," *Washington Post*, March 19, 2013, https://www.washingtonpost.com

/world/catholic-church-inaugurates-pope-francis-in-huge-open-air-mass
/2013/03/19/72a80ff2-9064-11e2-9cfd-36d6c9b5d7ad_story.html.

26 Jack Jenkins, "Pope Francis Makes Biblical Case for Addressing Climate Change: 'If We Destroy Creation, Creation Will Destroy Us,'" *ThinkProgress*, May 21, 2014, https://thinkprogress.org/pope-francis-makes-biblical-case-for-addressing-climate-change-if-we-destroy-creation-creation-will-61737d78418d/.

27 Daniel Cox, Juhem Navarro-Rivera, and Robert P. Jones, "Believers, Sympathizers, and Skeptics: Why Americans Are Conflicted about Climate Change, Environmental Policy, and Science," *PRRI*, November 21, 2014, https://www.prri.org/research/believers-sympathizers-skeptics-americans-conflicted-climate-change-environmental-policy-science/.

28 Cox, et al., "Believers, Sympathizers, and Skeptics."

29 Pope John Paul II, "Message of his holiness Pope John Paul II, For the celebration of the World Day of Peace," *Vatican News*, January 1, 1990, http://w2.vatican.va/content/john-paul-ii/en/messages/peace/documents/hf_jp-ii_mes_19891208_xxiii-world-day-for-peace.html.

30 Daniel Stone, "How Green Was the 'Green Pope'?," *National Geographic*, February 28, 2013, https://news.nationalgeographic.com/news/2013/2/130228-environmental-pope-green-efficiency-vatican-city/.

31 Natasha Geiling, "Santorum Wants the Pope to Back Off Talking About Climate Science," *ThinkProgress*, June 3, 2015, https://thinkprogress.org/santorum-wants-the-pope-to-back-off-talking-about-climate-science-7b4263a00e88/.

32 Amanda Terkel, "Rick Santorum Tries to Explain Why He Can Weigh In on Climate Change But Pope Shouldn't," *The Huffington Post*, June 7, 2015, https://www.huffpost.com/entry/rick-santorum-pope_n_7529166.

33 Emily Atkin, "What Did Actual Scientists Think of the Pope's Climate Encyclical?," *ThinkProgress*, June 18, 2015, https://thinkprogress.org/what-did-actual-scientists-think-of-the-popes-climate-encyclical-59f0848bafb9/.

34 "Evangelical Declaration on Global Warming," Cornwall Alliance, accessed April 7, 2019, https://cornwallalliance.org/landmark-documents/evangelical-declaration-on-global-warming-2/.

35 Igor Bobic, "GOP Congressman: God Will 'Take Care of' Climate Change If It Exists," *HuffPost*, May 31, 2017, https://www.huffpost.com/entry/tim-walberg-climate-change_n_592edc73e4b0540ffc837acf.

36 Emily Atkin and Jack Jenkins, "In Leaked Encyclical, Pope Francis Deconstructs Conservative Talking Points on Climate and Fossil Fuels," *ThinkProgress*, June 15, 2015, https://thinkprogress.org/in-leaked-encyclical-pope-francis-deconstructs-conservative-talking-points-on-climate-and-fossil-878fbdc11838/.

37 "Interfaith Power & Light: 2016 annual report," Interfaith Power and Light, https://www.interfaithpowerandlight.org/wp-content/uploads/2017/06/IPL-AR-16-FINAL.pdf.

38 "Interfaith Power & Light: 2009 annual report," Interfaith Power and Light,

https://www.interfaithpowerandlight.org/wp-content/uploads/2009/08/2009-annual-report-web.pdf.

39 Interfaith Power & Light, "2016 annual report."

40 Lyndsay Joyner and Anna Jane Joyner, "Faith in Action: Communities of Faith Bring Hope for the Planet," *Sierra Club*, June 2008.

41 Qur'an 6:165, *The Study Quran*, (New York: HarperOne, 2015), 405.

42 "Pope Francis' Encyclical Kit: Faith Climate Action Kit," Interfaith Power and Light, 2014, https://www.interfaithpowerandlight.org/wp-content/uploads/2015/07/PopeFrancisActionKitFINALJulysm.pdf.

43 "Buddhist Climate Change Statement to World Leaders 2015," *Global Buddhist Climate Change Collective*, October 29, 2015, http://gbccc.org/.

44 Hozan Alan Senauke, "Buddhists Go to the White House," *Lion's Roar*, May 15, 2015, https://www.lionsroar.com/white-house-buddhist-leadership-conference-hozan-allan-senauke/.

45 "The Green Bible," *Sierra Club* (blog), October 28, 2008, https://blogs.sierraclub.org/greenlife/2008/10/green-bible.html.

46 Bill McKibben, "What Religion Can Teach Climate Scientists," *The Boston Globe*, July 26, 2015, https://www.bostonglobe.com/magazine/2015/07/25/what-religion-can-teach-climate-scientists/LAZYZ6DBVHr1THqvWFXffO/story.html.

47 Newsweek Staff, "Al Gore's Climate-Change Revolution," *Newsweek*, October 30, 2009, https://www.newsweek.com/al-gores-climate-change-evolution-80935.

48 "Pope Francis speaks from White House lawn," WJBK, FOX 2 News Detroit video, September 23, 2015, accessed on YouTube, https://www.youtube.com/watch?v=w00Q0LllR4Q.

49 Daily Press Briefing by the Press Secretary, June 23, 2015, Obama White House, https://obamawhitehouse.archives.gov/the-press-office/2015/09/24/daily-press-briefing-press-secretary-9232015-0.

50 Clare Foran, "Tom Steyer Sends Hillary Clinton a Message, Via Pope Francis and Martin O'Malley," *The Atlantic*, June 18, 2015, https://www.theatlantic.com/politics/archive/2015/06/tom-steyer-sends-hillary-clinton-a-message-via-pope-francis-and-martin-omalley/445020/.

51 Jason Horowitz and Yamiche Alcindor, "Bernie Sanders Meets with Pope Francis," *New York Times*, April 16, 2016, https://www.nytimes.com/2016/04/17/us/politics/bernie-sanders-pope-francis-vatican.html.

52 Hillary Clinton, "Heed Francis' message: be good stewards of the earth," *National Catholic Reporter*, September 25, 2015, https://www.ncronline.org/blogs/ncr-today/heed-francis-message-be-good-stewards-earth.

53 Paul Gosar, "Why I Am Boycotting Pope Francis' Address to Congress," *Townhall*, September 17, 2015, https://townhall.com/columnists/congressmanpaulgosar/2015/09/17/why-i-am-boycotting-pope-francis-address-to-congress-n2053596.

54 "Chief Arvol Looking Horse Calls on Religious Leaders to Come to Standing

Rock," United Religions Initiative-North America video, October 26, 2016, accessed on YouTube, https://www.youtube.com/watch?v=SjsZFJHcOL0.

55 Lynette Wilson, "Image Gallery: 500 interfaith clergy and laity answered the call to stand with Standing Rock," Episcopal News Service, November 3, 2016, https://www.episcopalnewsservice.org/2016/11/03/image-gallery-500 -interfaith-clergy-and-laity-answered-the-call-to-stand-with-standing-rock/.

56 "Churches denounce Doctrine of Discovery," Native Momma, November 3, 2016, accessed on YouTube, https://www.youtube.com/watch?v=q1x6zuY p0g0&list=PLhbakolSUzZx5o0JYE8tMuvpV5eSFTxqQ&index=8&t=0s.

57 "Clergy Protest Against N.D. Pipeline," AP Archive, November 8, 2016, accessed on YouTube, https://www.youtube.com/watch?v=UBturARyTFQ.

58 Mark Charles, "Doctrine of Discovery: Part II," *Red Letter Christians* (blog), April 12, 2016, https://www.redletterchristians.org/doctrine-discovery-part-ii/.

59 Paul Barnsley, "Church considering request to rescind doctrine of discovery," APTN News, June 1, 2016, https://aptnnews.ca/2016/06/01/church-conside ring-request-to-rescind-doctrine-of-discovery/.

60 Jack Jenkins, "Native Americans Say This Man Enslaved Them. Pope Francis Wants to Call Him a Saint," *ThinkProgress*, May 7, 2015, https://think progress.org/native-americans-say-this-man-enslaved-them-pope-francis -wants-to-call-him-a-saint-bb569d85107b/.

61 Archambault II, phone interview.

62 John Thavis, "Standing Rock activists see Pope Francis as spiritual ally," *Religion News Service*, December 2, 2016, https://religionnews.com/2016/12/02 /standing-rock-activists-see-pope-francis-as-spiritual-ally/.

63 Thavis, "Standing Rock activists see Pope Francis as spiritual ally."

64 Pope Francis, "The Pope greets representatives of Indigenous Peoples participating in the Third Forum held by the International Fund for Agricultural Development (IFAD), 15.02.2017," *Vatican Press*, February 15, 2017, https://press.vatican.va/content/salastampa/en/bollettino/pubblico/2017/02 /15/170215a.html.

65 Juliet Eilperin and Brady Dennis, "Trump administration to approve final permit for Dakota Access pipeline," *Washington Post*, February 7, 2017, https://www.washingtonpost.com/news/energy-environment/wp/2017/02/07 /trump-administration-to-approve-final-permit-for-dakota-access-pipeline/.

66 "Cheyenne Lose Emergency Bid to Halt Dakota Access Drilling," *Law360*, February 13, 2017, https://www.law360.com/articles/891222/cheyenne-lose -emergency-bid-to-halt-dakota-access-drilling.

67 Ben Walker, "In a Surprising Move, the Anti-Pipeline Movement Is Taking a Page from Hobby Lobby," *In These Times*, January 11, 2018, http://inthese times.com/article/20832/pipeline-protest-hobby-lobby-standing-rock.

68 Jack Jenkins, "How religious conservatives unwittingly laid the groundwork to help Native Americans save their land," *ThinkProgress*, December 8, 2016, https://thinkprogress.org/standing-rock-religious-liberty-d0a6aacef81c/.

69 Robinson Meyer, "Oil Is Flowing Through the Dakota Access Pipeline,"

Atlantic, June 9, 2017, https://www.theatlantic.com/science/archive/2017/06/oil-is-flowing-through-the-dakota-access-pipeline/529707/.

70 Timothy Cama, "Trump admin rejects environmental concerns over Dakota Access pipeline," *Hill*, August 31, 2018, https://thehill.com/policy/energy-environment/404633-trump-admin-rejects-environmental-concerns-over-dakota-access.

71 *Adorers of the Blood of Christ, United States Province, et al., Petitioners v. Federal Energy Regulatory Commission, et al.*, 8, (2018) (cert. denied, https://www.supremecourt.gov/DocketPDF/18/18-548/73252/20181126161016037_18-548%20Amicus%20Brief%20The%20Rutherford%20Institute.pdf.

72 Ad Crable, "US Supreme Court will not hear Columbia nuns' claim that gas pipeline violated their religious beliefs," *LancasterOnline*, February 21, 2019, https://lancasteronline.com/news/local/u-s-supreme-court-will-not-hear-columbia-nuns-claim/article_d72394c0-35e9-11e9-8b7f-034e9c58ea3c.html.

73 Dan Zak, "Al Gore is near the end of his quest to save the Earth. Nina Barrett just got started," *Washington Post,* April 1, 2019, https://www.washingtonpost.com/lifestyle/style/al-gore-is-near-the-end-of-his-quest-to-save-the-earth-nina-barrett-just-got-started/2019/03/29/cba0ec48-4989-11e9-9663-00ac73f49662_story.html.

74 Rev. Dr. William J. Barber II, "Why Is No One Talking About the Land Battle in Oak Flat, AZ?," posted on Medium, April 2, 2019, https://medium.com/brepairers/why-is-no-one-talking-about-the-land-battle-in-oak-flat-az-38c7f625e365.

75 Jack Jenkins, "Presidential candidate and former pastor Mark Charles confronts American history," *Religion News Service*, September 11, 2019, https://religionnews.com/2019/09/11/presidential-candidate-and-former-pastor-mark-charles-confronts-american-history/.

76 Mark Charles and Soong-Chan Rah, *Unsettling Truths: The Ongoing, Dehumanizing Legacy of the Doctrine of Discovery*, (Downers Grove, Illinois: IVP Books, 2019).

77 Lynda V. Mapes, "The violent Dakota Access Pipeline protest raged for hours — until this tribal elder stepped in," *The Seattle Times*, October 29, 2016, https://www.seattletimes.com/seattle-news/environment/tribal-members-dig-in-for-long-fight-at-north-dakota-pipeline-site/.

78 "Final Environmental Impact Statement, Volume 1: Thirty Meter Telescope, Island of Hawaiʻi," S-8, http://www.malamamaunakea.org/uploads/management/plans/TMT_FEIS_vol1.pdf.

79 Kaʻiulani Milham, "How Lanakila Mangauil came to Mauna Kea," *The Hawaii Independent*, August 18, 2015, http://www.thehawaiiindependent.com/story/how-lanakila-mangauil-came-to-mauna-kea.

80 Elizabeth Warren, Twitter, July 22, 2019, 11:03 p.m., https://twitter.com/ewarren/status/1153500734006185985?s=20.

81 Marianne Williamson, Twitter, (July 24, 2019, 11:42 p.m., https://twitter.com/marwilliamson/status/1154054332444225536?lang=en.

82 Deirdre Fulton, 'Silence Is Not Acceptable': Indigenous Youth Demand Clinton Take Stand on DAPL," *Common Dreams,* October 27, 2016, https://www.commondreams.org/news/2016/10/27/silence-not-acceptable-indigenous-youth-demand-clinton-take-stand-dapl.

83 Bernie Sanders, "Sanders Opposes Dakota Access Pipeline," Bernie Sanders Senate Website, August 25, 2016, https://www.sanders.senate.gov/newsroom/press-releases/sanders-opposes-dakota-access-pipeline.

84 Evelyn Nieves, "Hillary Clinton's Silence on Standing Rock Is a Moral Mistake—and a Political One," *The Nation,* November 6, 2016, https://www.thenation.com/article/hillary-clintons-silence-on-standing-rock-is-a-moral-mistake-and-a-political-one/.

85 Diane S. W. Lee, "Bruno Mars joins Jason Momoa and Dwayne 'The Rock' Johnson to voice support for TMT opponents," *Star Advertiser*, July 31, 2019, https://www.staradvertiser.com/2019/07/31/breaking-news/bruno-mars-joins-jason-momoa-and-dwayne-the-rock-johnson-to-voice-support-for-tmt-opponents/.

86 Jack Jenkins, "In Hawaii, 'protectors' fight telescope project with prayer," *Religion News Service*, September 5, 2019, https://religionnews.com/2019/09/05/in-hawaii-protectors-fight-telescope-project-with-prayer/.

87 Anita Hofschneider, Twitter, July 17, 2019, 3:37 p.m., https://twitter.com/ahofschneider/status/1151576570399617024?s=20.

88 Latino Rebels, "Alexandria Ocasio-Cortez: The 'In the Thick' Interview," *Latino Rebels,* July 27, 2018, https://www.latinorebels.com/2018/07/27/alexandriaocasiocortez/.

89 A joint resolution recognizing the duty of the Federal Government to create a Green New Deal. 116th Cong. 1st sess. S.J.Res.8, https://www.congress.gov/bill/116th-congress/senate-joint-resolution/8/text.

90 Sarah K. Burris, "White House patronizes 'freshman' AOC to FOX News—and tells her to leave climate change up to God," *RawStory,* January 22, 2019, https://www.rawstory.com/2019/01/white-house-patronizes-freshman-aoc-to-fox-news-and-tells-her-to-leave-climate-change-up-to-god/.

91 Alexandria Ocasio-Cortez, Twitter, January 23, 2019 5:21 p.m., https://twitter.com/AOC/status/1088200188089565184.

92 Kyle Meyaard-Schaap, *Relevant magazine,* January 2018, https://relevantmagazine.com/current/stopping-climate-change-is-a-part-of-following-jesus/.

93 Alexandria Ocasio-Cortez, Twitter, January 23, 2019 5:21 p.m., https://twitter.com/AOC/status/1088200189524017157.

94 "Our Meeting With AOC," Lakota Peoples Law Project, June 6, 2019, accessed on YouTube, https://www.youtube.com/watch?v=olLjEgVy8UU.

95 Alexandria Ocasio-Cortez, Twitter, July 19, 2019, 6:59 p.m., https://twitter.com/AOC/status/1152352267309334528?s=20.

EIGHT Prophets over Profits

1 Jack Jenkins, "'Protest chaplains' shepherd movement's spiritual side," *Religion News Service,* October 10, 2001, https://religionnews.com/2011/10/10/protest-chaplains-shepherd-movements-spiritual-side/. Additional quotes pulled from my interview notes.

2 Gary Dorrien (professor, Union Theological Seminary), interview by the author, April 15, 2019.

3 Jenkins, "'Protest chaplains.'"

4 Walter Rauschenbusch, *A Theology for the Social Gospel* (New York: The MacMillian Company, 1918), 26, 184.

5 Maurice Isserman, *The Other American: The Life of Michael Harrington* (New York: PublicAffairs), 25.

6 "History," About Us, *Forward,* accessed May 11, 2019, https://forward.com/about-us/history/.

7 James Cone, *Martin & Malcolm & America: A Dream or a Nightmare,* (Ossining, NY: Orbis Books, reprint edition, June 7, 2012), Kindle edition, location number 5583.

8 Kevin Kruse, *One Nation Under God: How Corporate America Invented Christian America* (New York: Basic Books, 2015).

9 Martin Luther King Jr., "Preaching Ministry," The Martin Luther King Jr. Research and Education Institute, https://kinginstitute.stanford.edu/king-papers/documents/preaching-ministry.

10 Martin Luther King Jr., "To Coretta Scott," The Martin Luther King Jr. Research and Education Institute, https://kinginstitute.stanford.edu/king-papers/documents/coretta-scott.

11 Martin Luther King, Jr., "Address by Martin Luther King, Jr.," at the Southern Christian Leadership Conference staff retreat, November 14, 1966, accessed in the King Center archives.

12 Jeff Spross, "Stockton's Awesome Public Experiment," *Democracy Journal,* March 14, 2018, https://democracyjournal.org/arguments/stocktons-awesome-public-experiment/.

13 Martin Luther King Jr., *Where Do We Go from Here: Chaos or Community?* (Boston: Beacon Press, King Legacy Series, Book 2, January 1, 2010), Kindle, locations numbers 159, 2719.

14 Liz Theoharis (co-chair, Poor People's Campaign), interview by the author, January 25, 2019.

15 Jack Jenkins, "The strange origins of the GOP ideology that rejects caring for the poor," *ThinkProgress,* June 9, 2017, https://thinkprogress.org/bad-theology-conservative-benefits-1d42ef90b387/.

16 Theoharis, interview.

17 Holly Meyer and Natalie Allison, "Poor People's Campaign protesters stall downtown Nashville traffic during rush hour," *The Tennessean,* May 14, 2018, https://www.tennessean.com/story/news/religion/2018/05/14/poor-peoples

-campaign-protesters-block-crosswalk-tennessee-state-capitol-charlotte /607972002/.

18 Adelle M. Banks, "Poor People's Campaign rally ends with vows to keep organizing and protesting," *Religion News Service*, June 25, 2018, https:// religionnews.com/2018/06/25/poor-peoples-campaign-ends-with-vows-to -keep-organizing-and-protesting/.

19 "Announcing PCUSA Commitments in the Poor Peoples Campaign—A National Call for a Moral Revival," Presbyterian Mission, December 4, 2017, https://www.presbyterianmission.org/opw/2017/12/04/announcing-pcusa -commitments-poor-peoples-campaign-national-call-moral-revival/.

20 "Poor People's Campaign: A National Call for Moral Revival," Facebook Live video, June 12, 2018, https://www.facebook.com/anewppc/videos/us-con gressional-hearing-in-response-to-the-poor-peoples-campaign-a-national-cal /1719442051485296/.

21 Sarah Ngu (host of *Religious Socialism* podcast), interview by the author, May 3, 2019.

22 Dean Dettloff (cofounder, Christians for Socialism), interview by the author, May 13, 2019.

23 "FAQs," the website of the Friendly Fire Collective, accessed May 13, 2019, https://friendlyfirecollective.wordpress.com/about-us//.

24 Hye Sung (member, Friendly Fire Collective), interview by the author, May 7, 2019.

25 FOX News, "DNC speaker claims Bible promotes socialism," FOX News, August 24, 2019, https://video.foxnews.com/v/6076642580001/#sp=show -clips.

26 Alyana Alfaro, "In New Jersey, Arab Americans Rally for Bernie Sanders," *Observer*, June 3, 2016, https://observer.com/2016/06/in-new-jersey-arab -americans-rally-for-bernie-sanders/.

27 Linda Sarsour, Twitter, June 20, 2018, 1:34 a.m., https://twitter.com/lsarsour/ status/1009308534658490368.

28 Bernie Sanders, "Cornel West Introduces Bernie Sanders in South Carolina," YouTube video, September 12, 2015, https://www.youtube.com/watch?v=W 8cex4VTrwg.

29 Sister Simone Campbell, "Good Friday: The Only Way to Easter," *Ignatian Solidarity Network*, April 19, 2019, https://ignatiansolidarity.net/blog /2019/04/19/good-friday-the-only-way-to-easter/.

30 Sister Simone Campbell, (head, Network), interview by the author, April 18, 2019.

31 "About Us," the website of Network Lobby, https://networklobby.org/about/.

32 Pope Francis, *Evangelii Gaudium*, http://w2.vatican.va/content/francesco/en/ apost_exhortations/documents/papa-francesco_esortazione-ap_20131124_ evangelii-gaudium.html#CHAPTER_FOUR.

33 Daniel Burke, "Pope: Marxist ideology is 'wrong,'" *Belief* (blog), CNN, December 14, 2013, http://religion.blogs.cnn.com/2013/12/14/pope-im-not-a -marxist/.

34 Bill Glauber, "Paul Ryan signals support for Kenosha casino," *Milwaukee Journal-Sentinel*, December 19, 2013, http://archive.jsonline.com/news/state politics/paul-ryan-signals-support-for-kenosha-casino-b99167734z1-236 595381.html/.

35 Addy Baird and Jack Jenkins, "The Catholic nun who asked Paul Ryan about caring for the poor didn't like his answer," *ThinkProgress*, August 23, 2017, https://thinkprogress.org/nun-paul-ryan-interview-2d28106d76af/.

36 Jack Jenkins, "A nun called out Paul Ryan on health care. His response was awkward," *ThinkProgress*, August 22, 2017, https://thinkprogress.org/nun -challenge-paul-ryan-health-care-3661cf5d8cc0/.

37 Jack Jenkins, "The strange origins of the GOP ideology that rejects caring for the poor," *ThinkProgress*, June 9, 2017, https://thinkprogress.org/bad-theology -conservative-benefits-1d42ef90b387/.

38 Michael B. Katz, *The Undeserving Poor: America's Enduring Confrontation with Poverty*, (New York: Oxford Univ. Press, 2013, Second Edition), 165.

39 David Gibson, "Paul Ryan's subsidiarity," *Commonweal*, April 10, 2012, https://www.commonwealmagazine.org/paul-ryans-subsidiarity.

40 Christopher Warshaw and David Broockman, "G.O.P. Senators Might Not Realize It, but Not One State Supports the Republican Health Bill," *New York Times*, June 14, 2017, https://www.nytimes.com/2017/06/14/upshot/gop -senators-might-not-realize-it-but-not-one-state-supports-the-ahca.html.

41 Dan Merica, Jim Acosta, Lauren Fox and Phil Mattingly, "Trump calls House health care bill 'mean,'" CNN, June 14, 2017, https://www.cnn.com/2017/06/13 /politics/trump-senators-health-care-white-house-meeting/index.html.

42 "Letter to the president-elect," Circle of Protection, January 18, 2017, http:// circleofprotection.us/wp-content/uploads/2017/01/circle-of-protection-letter -to-president-elect-january-2017.pdf.

43 Jay Willis, "Paul Ryan Releases Six-Part Documentary Celebrating His His- torically Unpopular Tax Reform Bill," *GQ*, December 18, 2018, https://www .gq.com/story/paul-ryan-tax-bill-documentary.

44 "Paul Raushenbush: Occupying the Gospel," *On Being with Krista Tippett*, *podcast*, November 17, 2011, https://onbeing.org/programs/paul-raushenbush -occupying-the-gospel/.

45 Paul Raushenbush, "We Have a Love Crisis in our Country," *HuffPost*, June 13, 2016, https://www.huffpost.com/entry/we-have-a-love-crisis-in-our-country _b_10440392.

NINE The Hard Work of Transformation

1 Bishop Gene Robinson, interview by the author, March 18, 2019.

2 Laurie Goodstein, "Openly Gay Man Is Made Bishop," *New York Times*, No- vember 2, 2003, https://www.nytimes.com/2003/11/03/us/openly-gay-man-is -made-a-bishop.html.

3 Jonathan Finer, "Episcopalians Consecrate First Openly Gay Bishop," *Washington*

Post, November 3, 2003, https://www.washingtonpost.com/archive/politics /2003/11/03/episcopalians-consecrate-first-openly-gay-bishop/5e64c11e-34 6a-49d1-84d0-80e13a698cb2/?utm_term=.d81e89b05ed2.

4   Kenneth A. Briggs, "Bishop Moore Ordains a Lesbian as Priest in the Episcopal Church," *New York Times*, January 11, 1977, https://www.nytimes.com /1977/01/11/archives/bishop-moore-ordains-a-lesbian-as-priest-in-the-episcopal -church.html.

5   Mireya Navarro, "Openly Gay Priest Ordained in Jersey," *New York Times*, December 17, 1989, https://www.nytimes.com/1989/12/17/nyregion/openly -gay-priest-ordained-in-jersey.html.

6   "About our LGBT Ministries," the website of the United Church of Christ, accessed May 19, 2019, http://www.ucc.org/lgbt_about.

7   Anthony Weiss, "As Acceptance Grows, Gay Synagogues Torn Between the Straight and Narrow," *The Forward*, March 20, 2008, https://forward.com /news/12994/as-acceptance-grows-gay-synagogues-torn-between-t-01523/.

8   Rebecca Nagle, "The Healing History of Two-Spirit, A Term That Gives LGBTQ Natives a Voice," *HuffPost*, June 30, 2018, https://www.huffpost.com /entry/two-spirit-identity_n_5b37cfbce4b007aa2f809af1.

9   Bayard Rustin, *Time on Two Crosses: The Collected Writings of Bayard Rustin* (Jersey City, NJ: Cleis Press, Paperback, July 10, 2003), 275.

10   Alex Vandermaas-Peeler, Daniel Cox, Molly Fisch-Friedman, Rob Griffin, and Robert P. Jones, "Emerging Consensus on LGBT Issues: Findings from the 2017 American Values Atlas," *PRRI*, May 1, 2018, https://www.prri.org /research/emerging-consensus-on-lgbt-issues-findings-from-the-2017-american -values-atlas/.

11   "Who We Are," the website of *ReconcilingWorks*, accessed May 18, 2019, https:// www.reconcilingworks.org/about/.

12   "Our Story," the website of *More Light Presbyterians,* accessed May 18, 2019, https://mlp.org/our-story/.

13   "The History of the Movement," the website of *Reconciling Ministries Network*, accessed May 18, 2019, https://rmnetwork.org/who-we-are/history/.

14   Patrick S. Cheng, *Radical Love: An Introduction to Queer Theology* (New York: Seabury Books, 2011), Kindle edition, location numbers 319–336.

15   Gregg Drinkwater, Joshua Lesser, and David Shneer, *Torah Queeries: Weekly Commentaries on the Hebrew Bible* (New York: New York Univ. Press, 2009).

16   John Rivera, "Presbyterian blessing of gay union upheld," *The Baltimore Sun*, March 15, 2001, https://www.baltimoresun.com/news/bs-xpm-2001-03-15-01 03150250-story.html.

17   Hillary Goodridge & others vs. Department of Public Health & another, *Mass Cases*, accessed May 19, 2019, http://masscases.com/cases/sjc/440 /440mass309.html.

18   Lory Hough, "Holding Court," *Ed.: Harvard Ed. Magazine*, Winter 2013, https://www.gse.harvard.edu/news/ed/13/01/holding-court.

19 Spencer Buell, "On its 350th Birthday, 10 Things You Didn't Know about Boston's Old South Church," *Boston magazine*, May 10, 2019, https://www .bostonmagazine.com/news/2019/05/10/old-south-church-350/.

20 Adelle Banks, "Lutherans lift ban on gay clergy," *Religion News Service*, August 21, 2009, https://religionnews.com/2009/08/21/lutherans-debate-gay -clergy1/.

21 Jack Jenkins, "Presbyterians to officially allow gay clergy," *Religion News Service*, July 9, 2011, https://religionnews.com/2011/07/09/presbyterians-to -officially-allow-gay-clergy/.

22 Eileen Flynn, "Episcopal convention approves a 'pastoral solution' on same-sex marriage," *Religion News Service*, July 13, 2018, https://religionnews.com /2018/07/13/episcopal-convention-approves-a-pastoral-solution-on-same-sex -marriage/.

23 Jack Jenkins, "Top Methodist Court Officially Reinstates Pastor Defrocked for Officiating Son's Gay Wedding," *ThinkProgress*, October 27, 2014, https:// thinkprogress.org/top-methodist-court-officially-reinstates-pastor-defrocked -for-officiating-sons-gay-wedding-a65428c88a6d/.

24 "History," the website of Foundry United Methodist Church, accessed May 18, 2019, https://www.foundryumc.org/about/history.

25 "Believe Out Loud Power Summit, Oct. 9–11, Orlando, Fla.," National LGBTQ Task Force video, accessed on YouTube, October 6, 2010, https://www.you tube.com/watch?v=CJV-PaFt_9o.

26 "Believe Out Loud Power Summit to Draw Hundreds of Protestants," *GLAAD*, September 17, 2010, https://www.glaad.org/2010/09/17/believe-out-loud-power -summit-to-draw-hundreds-of-protestants/.

27 "Rev. Debra Peevey Speaks at Believe Out Loud Power Summit (Part 3)," National LGBTQ Task Force video, accessed on YouTube, October 10, 2010, https://www.youtube.com/watch?v=UKTMJ3bx3_M.

28 Dan Merica, "After gay marriage successes, activists look to build on new faith outreach techniques," *Belief (blog)*, CNN, November 30, 2012, http:// religion.blogs.cnn.com/2012/11/30/after-gay-marriage-successes-gay-activists -look-to-build-on-new-faith-outreach-techniques/comment-page-6/.

29 "Maine Gay Marriage Ads Promote Shared Values Between LGBT and Straight Couples," *HuffPost*, November 1, 2011, https://www.huffpost.com/entry /maine-gay-marriage-ads_n_1106314.

30 Ross Murray, "Faith Front and Center in Marriage Equality Ads," *GLAAD*, October 2, 2012, https://www.glaad.org/blog/faith-front-and-center-marriage -equality-ads.

31 "A unique argument for marriage equality," *MSNBC.com*, May 1, 2014, http:// www.msnbc.com/the-last-word/watch/a-unique-argument-for-marriage -equality-243508291555.

32 "The Briefing 04-30-14," *AlbertMohler.com*, April 30, 2014, https://albert mohler.com/2014/04/30/the-briefing-04-30-14/.

33 Judge Max Cogburn, Memorandum of decision and order, General Synod of the United Church of Christ, et al. v. Drew Resinger, Register of Deeds for Buncombe County, et al., October 10, 2014, accessed online, https://southern equality.org/wp-content/uploads/2018/11/Cogburn-Order_2014.pdf.

34 Jack Jenkins, "The Unlikely Story of How Religion Helped Bring Same-Sex Marriage to North Carolina," *ThinkProgress*, November 18, 2014, https:// thinkprogress.org/the-unlikely-story-of-how-religion-helped-bring-same-sex -marriage-to-north-carolina-c3884a574dc3/.

35 Able Allen and Virginia Daffron, "Making history: Jasmine Beach-Ferrara to become first openly gay Buncombe County Commissioner," *Mountain XPress*, March 16, 2016, https://mountainx.com/news/making-history-jasmine-beach-ferrara-to-become-first-openly-gay-buncombe-county-commissioner/.

36 Laurie Goodstein, "Gay Bishop Is Asked to Say Prayer at Inaugural Event," *New York Times*, January 12, 2009, https://www.nytimes.com/2009/01/13/us /13prayer.html.

37 Auburn Seminary, "Bishop Gene Robinson asked to deliver the Easter Prayer by President Obama," *Vimeo video*, 2014, https://vimeo.com/92052690.

38 "Hillary Clinton for HRC's Americans for Marriage Equality," Human Rights Campaign video, March 18, 2013, accessed on YouTube, https://www.youtube. com/watch?v=6RP9pbKMJ7c.

39 Diana Reese, "Sen. Claire McCaskill announces support for same-sex mar-riage," *The Washington Post*, March 25, 2013, https://www.washingtonpost .com/blogs/she-the-people/wp/2013/03/25/sen-claire-mccaskill-announces -support-for-same-sex-marriage/?utm_term=.dcd63323d6e0.

40 "Robin Roberts ABC News Interview with President Obama," ABC News transcript, May 9, 2012, https://abcnews.go.com/Politics/transcript-robin -roberts-abc-news-interview-president-obama/story?id=16316043.

41 Michael Wear, *Reclaiming Hope: Lessons Learned in the Obama White House About the Future of Faith in America* (Nashville, TN: Thomas Nelson), 147.

42 Derrick Harkins, (Faith Outreach Director, Democratic National Commit-tee), interview by the author, April 24, 2019."

43 Cheryl Corley, "After NAACP Marriage Stance, Discord and Discussion," *Morn-ing Edition*, NPR, June 8, 2012, https://www.npr.org/2012/06/08/1545222 87/after-naacp-marriage-stance-discord-and-discussion.

44 Ian Duncan, "NAACP leaders urge yes vote on same-sex marriage," *The Balti-more Sun*, October 15, 2012, https://www.baltimoresun.com/news/maryland /politics/bs-md-naacp-same-sex-20121015-story.html.

45 Vandermaas-Peeler, et al., "Emerging Consensus."

46 Vandermaas-Peeler, et al., "Emerging Consensus."

47 Tim Hains, "Trump: We Need to Tell the Truth; Radical Islam Is Anti-Woman, Anti-Gay, Anti-Jewish," *RealClearPolitics*, June 13, 2016, https://www.real clearpolitics.com/video/2016/06/13/trump_we_need_to_tell_the_truth_radical _islam_is_anti-woman_anti-gay_anti-jewish.html.

48 Jack Jenkins, "The Other Group Mourning the Orlando Massacre: LGBT Muslims," *ThinkProgress*, June 13, 2016, https://thinkprogress.org/the-other-group-mourning-the-orlando-massacre-lgbt-muslims-3919d9f2fbe/.

49 "US Catholics more likely now to support same-sex marriage; abortion attitudes comparatively stable," Pew Research Center, February 28, 2018, https://www.pewforum.org/2018/03/06/pope-francis-still-highly-regarded-in-u-s-but-signs-of-disenchantment-emerge/pf_03-06-18-pope-00-15/.

50 Rachel Donadio, "On Gay Priests, Pope Francis Asks, 'Who Am I to Judge?'" *New York Times*, July 29, 2013, https://www.nytimes.com/2013/07/30/world/europe/pope-francis-gay-priests.html.

51 "Chastity and homosexuality," *Catechism of the Catholic Church*, accessed May 21, 2019, http://www.vatican.va/archive/ccc_css/archive/catechism/p3s2c2a6.htm.

52 James Martin, *Building a Bridge: How the Catholic Church and the LGBT Community Can Enter into a Relationship of Respect, Compassion, and Sensitivity*, (New York: HarperOne, 2017).

53 Jack Jenkins, "Pope Francis meets with priest to discuss LGBTQ Catholics," *Religion News Service*, September 30, 2019, https://religionnews.com/2019/09/30/pope-francis-meets-with-priest-to-discuss-lgbt-catholics/.

54 Jack Jenkins, "'Alt-right Catholics' are getting faith leaders disinvited from speaking at colleges," *ThinkProgress*, September 23, 2017, https://thinkprogress.org/alt-right-catholics-targeting-lgbtq-8802b5ed1729/.

55 Vandermaas-Peeler, et al., "Emerging Consensus."

56 "The Gay Debate: The Bible and Homosexuality," Matthew Vines video, March 10, 2012, accessed on YouTube, https://www.youtube.com/watch?v=ezQjNJUSraY.

57 Mathew Vines, *God and the Gay Christian: The Biblical Case in Support of Same-Sex Relationships*, (New York: Convergent Books, 2014).

58 Tim Keller, "The Bible and same-sex relationships: A review article," Redeemer Churches and Ministries, June 2015, https://www.redeemer.com/redeemer-report/article/the_bible_and_same_sex_relationships_a_review_article.

59 Albert Mohler, "God, the Gospel, and the Gay Challenge—A Response to Matthew Vines," *AlbertMohler.com*, April 22, 2014, https://albertmohler.com/2014/04/22/god-the-gospel-and-the-gay-challenge-a-response-to-matthew-vines/.

60 Jack Jenkins, "At 'Red Letter Revival,' leaders give voice to evangelicals on the margins," *Religion News Service*, April 9, 2018, https://religionnews.com/2018/04/09/at-red-letter-revival-leaders-give-voice-to-evangelicals-on-the-margins/.

61 Shae Washington, Reed Lively, Myles Markham, Sara Renn, Marshaé Sylvester, and Lauren Gray, "Reformation continues," *Reformation Continues*, May 29, 2019, https://web.archive.org/web/20190529183117/https://www.reformationcontinues.com/.

62 Matthew Vines, "A Statement from Matthew Vines About the Reformation Project," *The Reformation Project*, May 30, 2019, http://www.matthewvines.com/a-statement-from-matthew-vines-about-the-reformation-project/.

63 Sarah Pulliam Bailey, "Evangelicals helped get Trump into the White House. Pete Buttigieg believes the religious left will get him out," *The Washington Post*, March 29, 2019, https://www.washingtonpost.com/religion/2019/03/29/evangelicals-helped-get-trump-into-white-house-pete-buttigieg-believes-religious-left-will-get-him-out/.

64 "2019 Thomas A. Dooley and LGBTQ Leadership Awards," Gay and Lesbian Alumni of Notre Dame and Saint Mary's, accessed May 21, 2019, http://www.galandsmc.org/2019-thomas-a-dooley-award/.

65 Gene Robison, "Transgender Welcome: A Bishop Makes the Case for Affirmation," Center for American Progress, January 2016, https://cdn.americanprogress.org/wp-content/uploads/2016/01/15125721/TransFaith-report.pdf.

66 Sarah McBride, telephone interview by the author, August 21, 2019.

TEN Troubled Waters

1 Linda Sarsour (co-chair, the Women's March), interview by the author, March 10, 2019.

2 Beatrice Dupuy, "Muslim children twice as likely to be bullied, new report finds," *Newsweek,* October 31, 2017, https://www.newsweek.com/more-half-muslim-students-are-bullied-new-report-finds-698023.

3 Jack Jenkins, "Using Islamophobia to Win Elections Doesn't Work," *ThinkProgress,* February 11, 2015, https://thinkprogress.org/using-islamophobia-to-win-elections-doesnt-work-1f5079289b2/.

4 Didi Martinez, Ron Mott, and Jareen Imam, "Alleged Kroger Gunman Uttered, 'Whites Don't Kill Whites,' Witness Says," NBC News, October 25, 2018, https://www.nbcnews.com/news/us-news/alleged-kroger-gunman-uttered-whites-don-t-kill-whites-witness-n924641.

5 Eboo Patel, "MLK Was an Interfaith Visionary, Too," *HuffPost,* January 17, 2011, https://www.huffpost.com/entry/mlk-was-a-religious-visio_b_809874.

6 Martin Luther King Jr., *"In a Single Garment of Destiny": A Global Vision of Justice*, ed. Lewis V. Baldwin, (Boston: Beacon Press, 2013) Kindle edition, location numbers 3239–3250, 3354–3381, 3389.

7 Jack Jenkins, "What *The Atlantic* Left Out About ISIS According to Their Own Expert," *ThinkProgress,* February 20, 2015, https://thinkprogress.org/what-the-atlantic-left-out-about-isis-according-to-their-own-expert-afd98cf1c134/.

8 2017 Hate Crime Statistics, Federal Bureau of Investigations, https://ucr.fbi.gov/hate-crime/2017/topic-pages/tables/table-1.xls.

9 Yanqi Xu, "Explaining the numbers behind the rise in reported hate crimes," PolitiFact, April 3, 2019, https://www.politifact.com/truth-o-meter/article/2019/apr/03/hate-crimes-are-increasingly-reported-us/.

10 Jack Jenkins, "ThinkProgress has been tracking hate since Trump's election. Here's what we found," *ThinkProgress,* February 10, 2017, https://thinkprogress.org/thinkprogress-has-been-tracking-hate-since-trumps-election-here-s-what-we-found-e0288ed69869/.

11   Jack Jenkins, "There have been more than 300 reported hate incidents since Election Day," *ThinkProgress*, November 14, 2016, https://thinkprogress.org /300-hate-incidents-since-election-day-bf9fd91edbd6/.

12   "Religious Landscape Survey," Pew Research Center, 2014, https://www.pew forum.org/religious-landscape-study/.

13   Matt Stevens and Matt Hamilton, "Man stabs worshiper near Simi Valley mosque in hate crime, police allege," *Los Angeles Times*, December 12, 2016, https://www.latimes.com/local/lanow/la-me-ln-simi-valley-mosque-stabbing -20161211-story.html.

14   Simran Jeet Singh, Twitter, November 13, 2016, 6:47 p.m., https://twitter. com/SikhProf/status/797949139115974656.

15   Cleve R. Wootson Jr., "'We've never had anything like this': Racist, threatening message left on door of black church," *Washington Post*, November 28, 2016, https://www.washingtonpost.com/news/acts-of-faith/wp/2016/11/28/weve -never-had-anything-like-this-racist-threatening-message-left-on-door-of- black-church/.

16   Joe Rosemeyer, "Hebrew Union College sign vandalized with swastika," WCPO Cincinnati, January 4, 2017, https://www.wcpo.com/news/local-news /hamilton-county/cincinnati/clifton/hebrew-union-college-sign-vandalized -with-swastika.

17   Sarah Hollenbeck, "LGBT Church vandalized with chalk swastikas," 10News WTSP, St. Petersburg, FL, November 16, 2016, https://www.wtsp.com/article /news/local/lgbt-church-vandalized-with-chalk-swastikas/352806518.

18   Jack Jenkins, "Progressive faith communities face their own wave of hate," *ThinkProgress*, March 15, 2017, https://thinkprogress.org/progressive-faith -communities-face-their-own-wave-of-hate-e26294d22861/.

19   Jack Jenkins, "What religious solidarity looks like in Trump's America," *Think-Progress*, March 3, 2017, https://thinkprogress.org/what-religious-solidarity -looks-like-in-trumps-america-fab755128248/.

20   David Paulsen, "Immigrants' fears fuel outreach at Maryland church targeted by post-election racist graffiti," Episcopal News Service, February 16, 2017, https://www.episcopalnewsservice.org/2017/02/16/immigrants-fears-fuel -outreach-at-maryland-church-targeted-by-post-election-racist-graffiti-2/.

21   Colby Itkowitz, "A church was defaced with 'Trump Nation, Whites Only.' The community had a different message," *The Washington Post*, November 23, 2016, https://www.washingtonpost.com/news/inspired-life/wp/2016/11/23/a -church-was-defaced-with-trump-nation-whites-only-the-community-had-a -different-message/.

22   Muslim leaders at the center would later explain to me that they were inspired to act after a different church in the region had sent them letters from Sunday school children following the rise in Islamophobia in 2016.

23   Muslim Community Center, Silver Spring, Maryland, Facebook post, March 17, 2019, https://www.facebook.com/muslimcommunitycentermd/posts/2038 329132932767.

24 Aysha Kahn, "Interfaith leaders urge political parties to reject Islamophobia," *Religion News Service,* April 14, 2016, https://religionnews.com/2016/04/14/interfaith-leaders-urge-political-parties-to-reject-islamophobia/.

25 Judy Maltz, "Trump Effect: Jewish and Muslim Organizations Form New Alliance," Haaretz, November 14, 2016, https://www.haaretz.com/world-news/trump-effect-jewish-and-muslim-organizations-form-new-alliance-1.5461573.

26 "Muslims Unite for Pittsburgh Synagogue," a campaign on LaunchGood, https://www.launchgood.com/campaign/muslims_unite_for_pittsburgh_synagogue#!/. See also the *Snopes* debunking of inaccurate claims that the centers kept the money for themselves: Dan MacGuill, "Did Muslim Groups Keep Money Intended for Victims of the Pittsburgh Synagogue Shooting?," *Snopes,* November 29, 2018, https://www.snopes.com/fact-check/tree-of-life-muslim-groups-donations-mosque/.

27 "Standing with Our Muslim Neighbors," an update from the Jewish Federation of Greater Pittsburgh, March 21, 2019, https://jewishpgh.org/update-standing-with-our-muslim-neighbors/.

28 "Donald Trump: 'I Would Certainly Implement' Database for Muslims,'" MSNBC video, November 20, 2015, accessed on YouTube, https://www.youtube.com/watch?v=8Q4SDWMnjak.

29 Bruce Leshan, "Faith leaders push back against 'Muslim Registry,'" *WUSA9,* Washington, DC, November 18, 2016, https://www.wusa9.com/article/news/local/dc/faith-leaders-push-back-against-muslim-registry/353922486.

30 Nadia Khomami and Mazin Sidahmed, "Jonathan Greenblatt: 'This proud Jew would register as a Muslim' in database," *The Guardian,* November 18, 2016, https://www.theguardian.com/us-news/2016/nov/18/jonathan-greenblatt-muslim-registry-database-trump.

31 Madeleine Albright, Twitter, January 25, 2017, 1:18 p.m., https://twitter.com/madeleine/status/824320652278693892.

32 Rabia Chaudry, Twitter, January 24, 2017, 11:35 p.m., https://twitter.com/rabiasquared/status/824113413777424385.

33 Jack Jenkins, "Cory Booker could be a candidate for the 'religious left,'" *Religion News Service,* October 24, 2018, https://religionnews.com/2018/10/24/cory-booker-fashions-himself-as-a-candidate-for-the-religious-left/.

34 "Muslim Registry," Cory Booker video posted on Facebook, January 5, 2017, https://www.facebook.com/corybooker/videos/muslim-registry/10156423253722228/. (Confirmed to be a Bible and a Tanakh by Booker's staff.)

35 Daniel Burke and Madeleine Stix, "Imam Omar Suleiman: The rising star," CNN.com, https://www.cnn.com/interactive/2018/05/us/influential-muslims/#suleiman.

36 Zac Crain, "The Preacher," *D Magazine,* July 2017, https://www.dmagazine.com/publications/d-magazine/2017/july/the-preacher-imam-omar-suleiman/.

37 Crain, "The Preacher."

38 Jack Jenkins, "Inside the battle for immigrant rights at Dulles airport," *ThinkProgress,* January 30, 2017, https://thinkprogress.org/inside-the-battle-for-immigrant-rights-at-dulles-airport-d052b97ddf39/.

39 Talia Richman, "Silver Spring group, citizens, and attorney general join suits against travel order," *Takoma Voice*, February 8, 2017, https://takomavoice.com /2017/02/08/silver-spring-group-citizens-and-attorney-general-join-suits -against-travel-order/.

40 Rev. Katharine R. Henderson (president, Auburn Seminary), interview by the author, April 15, 2019.

41 Henderson, interview.

42 Valarie Kaur (founder, Revolutionary Love Project), interview by the author, June 13, 2019.

43 Valarie Kaur, "Announcing Groundswell," September 4, 2011, https://valariekaur .com/2011/09/announcing-groundswell/.

44 For more campaigns, see the Groundswell webpage here: https://action.ground swell-mvmt.org/.

45 Jack Jenkins, "How Trump is paving the way for a revival of the 'religious left.'" *The Washington Post*, December 14, 2016, https://www.washingtonpost .com/news/acts-of-faith/wp/2016/12/14/how-trump-is-paving-the-way-for-a -revival-of-the-religious-left/.

46 Amy Brittain and Michelle Boorstein, "Divestment vote by Presbyterian Church strains long ties with Jewish community," *The Washington Post*, June 21, 2014, https://www.washingtonpost.com/local/2014/06/21/932cb71a-f976-11e3 -8aa9-dad2ec039789_story.html.

47 John W. Vest, "The Things That Make for Peace," John W. Vest (blog), June 13, 2014, https://johnvest.com/2014/06/13/the-things-that-make-for-peace/.

48 Jack Jenkins, "Presbyterian Church Divests from Companies That Provide Equipment for Occupied Territories," *ThinkProgress*, June 21, 2014, https:// thinkprogress.org/presbyterian-church-divests-from-companies-that-provide -equipment-for-occupied-territories-552471ab36d0/.

49 Leah McSweeney and Jacob Siegel, "Is the Women's March Melting Down?," *Tablet*, December 10, 2018, https://www.tabletmag.com/jewish -news-and-politics/276694/is-the-womens-march-melting-down.

50 Sarsour, interview.

51 Aiden Pink, "3 Jewish Groups Work with Women's March on Anti-Semitism," *The Forward*, December 20, 2018, https://forward.com/news/national/416396 /these-jewish-organizations-have-been-teaching-the-womens-march-about -anti/.

52 Bend the Arc Jewish Action, Facebook Live video, October 28, 2018, https:// www.facebook.com/jewishaction.us/videos/267458627308065/.

53 Linda Sarsour, "A Letter on Loyalty, Agency, Unity, and the Farrakhan Contro-versy," November 18, 2018, https://mavenroundtable.io/lindasarsour/politics /a-letter-on-loyalty-agency-unity-and-the-farrakhan-controversy-EqyktSghwk ywYL1jKsADdQ/.

54 Aiden Pink, "Women's March Adds 3 Jews to Steering Committee," *The For-ward*, January 14, 2019, https://forward.com/fast-forward/417553/womens -march-adds-3-jews-to-steering-committee/.

55 William Barber, Twitter, November 19, 2018, 10:57 a.m., https://twitter.com /RevDrBarber/status/1064548181126582272.

56 Valarie Kaur, "A Sikh Sermon at the Pentagon: 'Seva: The Call of Our Times,'" *HuffPost,* May 4, 2015, https://www.huffpost.com/entry/a-sikh-sermon-at-the -pent_b_7201434.

57 "Sister Simone Speaking at Womens March, DC," Network Lobby video, January 23, 2017, accessed on YouTube, https://www.youtube.com/watch?v=wcr bgSKF80U.

58 Julie Zauzmer, "People are looking for a 'Religious Left.' This little-known network of clergy has been organizing it," *The Washington Post,* April 26, 2017, https:// www.washingtonpost.com/news/acts-of-faith/wp/2017/04/26/people-are-looking -for-a-religious-left-this-little-known-network-of-clergy-has-been-organizing-it/.

59 Jack Jenkins, personal recording of 2017 health care protest, June 30, 2017.

60 "Leaders Support Congresswoman Ilhan Omar," *MPower Change: Muslim Grassroots Movement,* March 5, 2019, https://mpowerchange.org/westand withilhan/.

61 A Resolution Condemning Hateful Expressions of Intolerance, House Resolution 183, 116th Cong. (2019).

62 Farah Stockman, "Three Leaders of Women's March Group Step Down After Controversies," *New York Times,* September 18, 2019, https://www.nytimes .com/2019/09/16/us/womens-march-anti-semitism.html.

63 Simran Jeet Singh, (professor, Union Theological Seminary), interview by the author, May 10, 2019.

ELEVEN The New God Gap

1 Matea Gold and Christi Parsons, "Democrats stumble on party platform language," *Los Angeles Times,* September 6, 2012, https://www.latimes.com/politics/la-xpm-2012-sep-06-la-na-dnc-platform-20120906-story.html.

2 Kevin Liptak, "Ryan hits 'tragic' Democratic platform changes," CNN, September 5, 2012, http://politicalticker.blogs.cnn.com/2012/09/05/ryan-hits-tragic -democratic-platform-changes/.

3 Jaweed Kaleem, "Democratic Faith Rep. Responds to Anti-God Accusations About DNC Platform," *HuffPost,* September 5, 2012, https://www.huffpost .com/entry/dnc-platform-god_n_1858891.

4 Derrick Harkins, (Faith Outreach Director, Democratic National Committee), interview by the author, April 24, 2019.

5 "Bishop Vashti Murphy McKenzie," C-SPAN video, September 5, 2012, https://www.c-span.org/video/?c3872873/bishop-vashti-murphy-mckenzie.

6 "Julian Castro's DNC Keynote Address," NPR, September 4, 2012, https://www .npr.org/2012/09/04/160574895/transcript-julian-castros-dnc-keynote-address.

7 David Gibson, "Sister Simone Campbell, 'Nun from the Bus,' calls GOP budget 'immoral,'" *Religion News Service,* September 6, 2012, http://religion. blogs.cnn.com/2012/09/03/first-on-cnn-whos-delivering-prayers-at-the-dnc.

8 Sister Simone Campbell, (head, Network), interview by the author, April 18, 2019.

9 "Convention floor erupts as Dems restore references to God, Jerusalem in platform," FOX News, September 5, 2012, https://www.foxnews.com/politics /convention-floor-erupts-as-dems-restore-references-to-god-jerusalem-in -platform.

10 Mara Vanderslice Kelly (former progressive faith operative), interview by the author, May 31, 2019.

11 Joseph Williams, "Obama vows $500m in faith-based aid," *Boston.com*, July 2, 2008, http://archive.boston.com/news/nation/articles/2008/07/02/obama _vows_500m_in_faith_based_aid/.

12 Joshua DuBois, phone interview by the author, May 10, 2019.

13 "About the President's Advisory Council on Faith-based and Neighborhood Partnerships," the website of the White House of President Barack Obama, https://obamawhitehouse.archives.gov/administration/eop/ofbnp/about /council and "Inaugural Advisory Council" at https://obamawhitehouse.archives .gov/administration/eop/ofbnp/about/2009-2010 and "President's Advisory Council 2012–2013," at https://obamawhitehouse.archives.gov/administra tion/eop/ofbnp/about/2012-2013.

14 Mark Silk, "Obama campaign taps young adviser, Michael Wear, for faith outreach," *Religion News Service*, May 14, 2012, https://religionnews.com /2012/05/14/obama-campaign-taps-young-adviser-for-faith-outreach/.

15 Michael Wear, *Reclaiming Hope: Lessons Learned in the Obama White House About the Future of Faith in America*, (Nashville, TN: Thomas Nelson, 2017), Kindle edition, 168–169.

16 Josh Israel, "Inaugural Benediction to Be Delivered by Pastor Who Gave Vehemently Anti-Gay Sermon," *ThinkProgress*, January 9, 2013, https://think progress.org/inaugural-benediction-to-be-delivered-by-pastor-who-gave -vehemently-anti-gay-sermon-e58c9362c949/.

17 Wear, *Reclaiming Hope,* 183.

18 Jaweed Kaleem, "Luis León, Episcopal Priest, Will Deliver Obama's Inauguration Benediction, Replacing Louie Giglio," *HuffPost*, January 15, 2013, https://www.huffpost.com/entry/luis-leon-benediction-obama-inauguration -louie-giglio_n_2468824.

19 Laurie Goodstein, "White House Director of Faith-Based Office Is Leaving His Post," *New York Times*, February 7, 2013, https://www.nytimes.com/2013 /02/08/us/politics/white-house-director-of-faith-based-initiatives-will-step -down.html.

20 Melissa Rogers (former head of the White House Office of Faith-Based and Neighborhood Partnerships), interview by the author, May 31, 2019.

21 Rhina Guidos, "Panel: Democrats face challenges engaging faith voters," Catholic News Service, via Crux, June 21, 2018, https://cruxnow.com/church-in -the-usa/2018/06/21/panel-democrats-face-challenges-engaging-faith-voters/.

22 Elizabeth Bruenig, "Talk of a rising religious left is unfounded. It already

exists," *Washington Post*, April 11, 2019, https://www.washingtonpost.com/
opinions/the-religious-left-is-always-just-about-to-happen-will-it-ever-arrive
/2019/04/11/f4500bc6-5c83-11e9-9625-01d48d50ef75_story.html.

23 Guthrie Graves-Fitzsimmons, "Is This the Religious Left's Kairos Moment?,"
Religion & Politics, May 14, 2019, https://religionandpolitics.org/2019/05/14
/is-this-the-religious-lefts-kairos-moment/.

24 John McCarthy (former faith outreach director for Hillary Clinton's 2016
presidential campaign), interview by the author, May 30, 2019.

25 Ryan Teague Beckwith, "Read Hillary Clinton's Super Tuesday Victory
Speech," *TIME.com*, March 2, 2016, http://time.com/4244178/super-tuesday
-hillary-clinton-victory-speech-transcript-full-text/.

26 Amy Chozick, "Hillary Clinton Gets Personal on Christ and Her Faith," *New
York Times*, January 25, 2016, https://www.nytimes.com/politics/first-draft
/2016/01/25/hillary-clinton-gets-personal-on-christ-and-her-faith/.

27 "Presidential Candidate Hillary Clinton at the National Baptist Convention,"
C-SPAN video, September 8, 2016, https://www.c-span.org/video/?414956-1
/hillary-clinton-addresses-national-baptist-convention.

28 "Special Event with Hillary Clinton at the AME 2016 General Conference,"
African Methodist Episcopal Church video, August 3, 2016, accessed on You-
Tube, https://www.youtube.com/watch?v=W3PPiV5bT2s.

29 "Presidential Candidate Hillary Clinton Community Meeting in Florissant,
Missouri," C-SPAN video, June 23, 2015, https://www.c-span.org/video/?32
6745-1/hillary-clinton-community-meeting-florissant-missouri.

30 Jack Jenkins, "Inside Donald Trump's 'tremendous problem' in Utah," *Think-
Progress*, September 8, 2016, https://thinkprogress.org/inside-donald-trumps
-tremendous-problem-in-utah-25087b54968c/.

31 "American Values Atlas," Public Religion Research Institute, http://ava.prri.
org/#religious/2018/States/religion/m/US-UT.

32 Jana Riess, "Mormons now most Republican religious group in America," *Religion News Service*, February 23, 2016, https://religionnews.com/2016/02/23
/mormons-now-republican-religious-group-america/.

33 CSPAN, Twitter, August 11, 2016, 3:45 p.m., https://twitter.com/cspan/status
/763823585299345408.

34 Jack Jenkins, "How Donald Trump Could End the Republican Lock on the
Mormon Vote," *The Atlantic*, March 22, 2016, https://www.theatlantic.com
/politics/archive/2016/03/donald-trump-gop-mormon-vote-utah/474819/.

35 Jack Jenkins, "What a 19th Century Campaign to Declare Mormons 'Non-White'
Tells Us About Modern Islamophobia," *ThinkProgress*, February 12, 2016,
https://thinkprogress.org/what-a-19th-century-campaign-to-declare-mormons
-non-white-tells-us-about-modern-islamophobia-231556790c58/.

36 "Church Points to Joseph Smith's Statements on Religious Freedom, Pluralism," *The Church of Jesus Christ of Latter-day Saints*, December 8, 2015,
https://newsroom.churchofjesuschrist.org/article/church-statement-religious
-freedom-pluralism.

37 Liz Halloran, "Mormon Democrats Battling Romney—and What Would Be Church History," NPR, September 4, 2012, https://www.npr.org/sections /itsallpolitics/2012/09/04/160570257/mormon-democrats-battling-romney -and-what-would-be-church-history.

38 Jenkins, "Inside Donald Trump's problem."

39 Annette Harris, interview by the author.

40 Robert Gehrke, "While Mormons nationally stuck with Trump, in Utah he lagged," *Salt Lake Tribune*, November 18, 2016, https://archive.sltrib.com/article .php?id=4573783&itype=CMSID&fullpage=1.

41 Gehrke, "While Mormons nationally stuck."

42 2016 General Election Results, Utah State Board of Canvassers, https://elections .utah.gov/Media/Default/2016%20Election/2016%20General%20Election %20-%20Statewide%20Canvass%203.pdf.

43 Jana Riess with Benjamin Knoll, "Most Mormons planned NOT to vote for Trump. What the heck happened?," *Religion News Service*, November 15, 2016, https://religionnews.com/2016/11/15/most-mormons-planned-not-to-vote -for-trump-what-the-heck-happened/.

44 Asma Khalid, "Black Voters Need More Convincing from Democrats In 2018," NPR, March 17, 2018, https://www.npr.org/2018/03/17/593643801 /black-voters-need-more-convincing-from-democrats-in-2018.

45 Ruby Cramer, "Hillary Clinton Let Him Stay. Women Say His Harassment Continued," *BuzzFeed*, January 27, 2018, https://www.buzzfeednews.com/. article/rubycramer/hillary-clinton-let-him-stay-women-say-his-harassment.

46 Maggie Haberman and Amy Chozick, "Hillary Clinton Chose to Shield a Top Adviser Accused of Harassment in 2008," *New York Times*, January 26, 2018, https://www.nytimes.com/2018/01/26/us/politics/hillary-clinton-chose -to-shield-a-top-adviser-accused-of-harassment-in-2008.html.

47 Vann R. Newkirk II, "North Carolina's New Rainbow Coalition," *Atlantic*, November 30, 2016, https://www.theatlantic.com/politics/archive/2016/11 /identity-politics-north-carolina-governor/509153/.

48 Emily Todd VanDerWerff, "The Democratic convention's most surprising argument: Christianity is a liberal religion," *Vox*, July 29, 2016, https://www .vox.com/2016/7/29/12320252/democrats-christian-religion-dnc-convention.

TWELVE The Future of Faith

1 Jesse Remedios, "Festival builds community through 'Spirit, Justice, Music and Art,'" *National Catholic Reporter*, July 6, 2019, https://www.ncronline .org/news/justice/festival-builds-community-through-spirit-justice-music-and -art.

2 Jack Jenkins, "In remote Appalachia, liberal Christians gather at Wild Goose to pray—and plan," *Religion News Service*, July 15, 2019, https://religionnews .com/2019/07/15/in-remote-appalachia-liberal-christians-gather-at-wild -goose-to-pray-and-plan/.

3   "Voices of the Emerging Church-The Wild Goose Festival 2011," Odyssey Impact video, July 20, 2011, accessed on YouTube, https://www.youtube.com /watch?v=VGFW_4V04RI.

4   Brian McLaren, "Letter from Brian McLaren," *Matthew 25 Network*, archived on August 10, 2008 at https://web.archive.org/web/20080913232503/http:// www.matthew25.org/mclaren.htm.

5   Brian McLaren (author and activist), interview by the author, July 25, 2019.

6   Jonathan Merritt, "Best-selling author Eugene Peterson changes his mind on gay marriage," *Religion News Service*, July 12, 2017, https://religionnews .com/2017/07/12/best-selling-author-eugene-peterson-changes-his-mind-on -gay-marriage/.

7   Kate Shellnutt, "LifeWay Prepared to Stop Selling the Message Over Eugene Peterson's LGBT Comments," *Christianity Today*, July 12, 2017, https://www .christianitytoday.com/news/2017/july/lifeway-prepared-to-stop-selling-message -over-eugene-peters.html.

8   Albert Mohler, "We Have Seen All This Before: Rob Bell and the (Re)Emergence of Liberal Theology," *AlbertMohler.com*, March 16, 2011, https://albert mohler.com/2011/03/16/we-have-seen-all-this-before-rob-bell-and-the -reemergence-of-liberal-theology/.

9   Brian D. McLaren, "Will 'Love Wins' Win? We're Early in the First Inning . . . ," *HuffPost*, May 25, 2011, https://www.huffpost.com/entry/will-love-wins-win -were-e_b_839164.

10   "Rob Bell responds to Universalism in 'Love Wins' debate," Premier On Demand video, April 27, 2011, accessed on YouTube, https://www.youtube.com /watch?v=2m49jau2gOM.

11   McLaren, interview.

12   "Trevor McLaren and Owen Ryan," *New York Times*, September 23, 2012, https://www.nytimes.com/2012/09/23/fashion/weddings/trevor-mclaren-ow en-ryan-weddings.html.

13   Diana Butler Bass, Twitter, May 2, 2019, at 3:19 p.m., https://twitter.com/diana butlerbass/status/1124030584387514368.

14   Jack Jenkins, "Faith groups mount election turnout efforts that could help both parties," *Religion News Service*, November 5, 2018, https://religionnews .com/2018/11/05/faith-groups-mount-election-turnout-efforts-that-could -help-both-parties/.

15   Vote Common Good, Facebook Live video, October 11, 2018, https://www.face book.com/votecommongood/videos/vb.189285628396655/51794410533 5267/?type=2&theater.

16   Jack Jenkins, "Bishop Michael Curry walks a fine line in the political fray," *Religion News Service*, May 31, 2018, https://religionnews.com/2018/05/31 /curry-fray/.

17   Michael Clawson, *Crossing Boundaries, Redefining Faith: Interdisciplinary Perspectives on the Emerging Church Movement* (Eugene, OR: Pickwick Publications, an Imprint of Wipf and Stock Publishers), 34, Kindle Edition.

18 Erin Williams, "Faith Leaders Gather to Craft Strategies to Counter 'White Supremacy, Structural Racism,'" *PICO National Network*, October 24, 2017, http://piconetwork.faithinaction.org/news-media/releases/faith-leaders-gather-to-craft-strategies-to-counter-white-supremacy-structural-racism.

19 Faith in Action, Facebook Live video, October 24, 2017, https://www.facebook.com/FIAnational/videos/vb.54580146753/10156456346621754/?type=2&theater.

20 Lisa Sharon Harper (activist and author), Skype interview by the author, May 8, 2019.

21 "Racial and ethnic composition," Pew Research Religious Landscape Study, https://www.pewforum.org/religious-landscape-study/racial-and-ethnic-composition/.

22 Jack Jenkins, "'We're not the "nice" faith people!': Faith leaders are battling white supremacy, Trump," *ThinkProgress*, October 31, 2017, https://thinkprogress.org/prophets-resistance-undermine-trump-8cfdda05ab1a/.

23 Michael-Ray Mathews, "Will you be a chaplain to the Empire or prophet of the resistance?" *Sojourners*, February 16, 2017 at https://sojo.net/articles/faith-action/will-you-be-chaplain-empire-or-prophet-resistance.

24 Sharon Brous, "I Need You To Breathe," prepared remarks for sermon delivered at the Prophetic Resistance Summit on October 24, 2017, http://ikar-la.org/wp-content/uploads/PICO-Prophetic-Resistance-Keynote.pdf.

25 Party affiliation among Jews, Pew Research Center, https://www.pewforum.org/religious-landscape-study/religious-tradition/jewish/party-affiliation/.

26 Sarah Price Brown, "Emergent Jews," *Jewish Journal*, January 26, 2006, https://jewishjournal.com/news/nation/12585/.

27 Aysha Khan, "In Chicago, one mosque charts its own path," *Religion News Service*, March 26, 2019, https://religionnews.com/2019/03/26/in-chicago-one-mosque-charts-its-own-path/.

28 "The Courage to Change," Alexandria Ocasio-Cortez video, May 30, 2018, accessed on YouTube, https://www.youtube.com/watch?v=rq3QXIVR0bs.

29 Simran Jeet Singh, (professor, Union Theological Seminary), interview by the author, May 10, 2019.

30 "Our endorsing partners include," the website of the Poor People's Campaign, accessed Aug 4, 2019, https://web.archive.org/web/20191203204319/https://www.poorpeoplescampaign.org/partners/.

31 Jenkins, "In remote Appalachia."

32 Rose White, "Democratic pastor launching congressional campaign against Huizenga," *WZZM13.com*, July 21, 2019, https://www.wzzm13.com/article/news/democratic-pastor-launching-congressional-campaign-against-huizenga/69-9e336e68-ae12-44d2-8631-092a060f07aa.

EPILOGUE

1   Jack Jenkins, "At victimized Charleston church, Booker condemns gun vio-
    lence, racism," *Religion News Service*, August 7, 2019, https://religionnews
    .com/2019/08/07/at-victimized-charleston-church-booker-condemns-gun
    -violence-racism/.

2   Jack Jenkins, "Julián Castro opens his presidential bid with a Catholicism
    aimed at Latino vote," *Religion News Service*, February 14, 2019, https://
    religionnews.com/2019/02/14/julian-castro-opens-his-presidential-bid-with
    -a-catholicism-aimed-at-latino-vote/.

3   Kevin Sullivan, "'I am who I am': Kamala Harris, daughter of Indian and
    Jamaican immigrants, defines herself simply as 'American,'" *Washington
    Post*, February 2, 2019, https://www.washingtonpost.com/politics/i-am-who
    -i-am-kamala-harris-daughter-of-indian-and-jamaican-immigrants-defines
    -herself-simply-as-american/2019/02/02/0b278536-24b7-11e9-ad53-824
    486280311_story.html.

4   "2020 candidate asked if Pence would be better than Trump," CNN, March
    11, 2019, accessed on YouTube, https://www.youtube.com/watch?v=gSY6A
    qyBrYA.

5   Maggie Astor, "Pete Buttigieg Calls Climate Change 'a Kind of Sin,'" *New York
    Times*, September 4, 2019, https://www.nytimes.com/live/2019/democrats
    -climate-town-hall/pete-buttigieg-climate-change.

6   "Buttigieg: The kind of person to take WH next is what's important," *MSNBC.
    com*, March 20, 2019, https://www.msnbc.com/morning-joe/watch/buttigieg
    -the-kind-of-person-to-take-wh-next-is-what-s-important-1461532739696.

7   "Mayor Pete Buttigieg," Real Time video, *Real Time with Bill Maher*, HBO,
    accessed on YouTube, March 29, 2019, https://www.youtube.com/watch?v=
    rJCwUwziRvY.

8   Linh Ta, "Kirsten Gillibrand at Iowa Baptist church preaches that Trump is
    'contrary to the gospel,'" *Des Moines Register*, May 26, 2019, https://www.
    desmoinesregister.com/story/news/elections/presidential/caucus/2019/05/26
    /donald-trump-baptist-christian-iowa-caucus-2020-kirsten-gillibrand-says
    -contrary-gospel-waterloo/1246688001/.

9   Jack Jenkins, "In remote Appalachia, liberal Christians gather at Wild Goose
    to pray—and plan," *Religion News Service*, July 15, 2019, https://religionnews
    .com/2019/07/15/in-remote-appalachia-liberal-christians-gather-at-wild-goose
    -to-pray-and-plan/.

10 Jack Jenkins, "Democrats' new faith outreach director launches 'listening ses-
    sions,'" *Religion News Service*, June 25, 2019, https://religionnews.com/2019
    /06/25/democrats-new-faith-outreach-director-launches-listening-sessions
    -with-religious-leaders/.

11 Jack Jenkins, "Boisterous faith leaders and a silent Pete Buttigieg rally against
    Trump at White House," *Religion News Service*, June 12, 2019, https://religion

news.com/2019/06/12/boisterous-faith-leaders-and-a-silent-pete-buttigieg
-rally-against-trump-at-white-house/.

12 Jack Jenkins, "Joe Biden and other candidates speak to diverse faith leaders,
activists," *Religion News Service*, June 17, 2019, https://religionnews.com
/2019/06/17/joe-biden-and-other-candidates-speak-to-diverse-faith-leaders
-activists/.

13 Salvador Rizzo, "Joe Biden's claim that 'almost half' of Americans live in
poverty," *The Washington Post*, June 20, 2019, https://www.washingtonpost
.com/politics/2019/06/20/joe-bidens-claim-that-almost-half-americans-live
-poverty/.

14 Conveyed through confidential sources familiar with the matter.

15 Aysha Kahn, "Sanders, Castro to Attend Muslim-led Presidential Forum in
Texas," *Religion News Service*, August 6, 2019, https://religionnews.com/2019
/08/06/sanders-castro-to-attend-muslim-led-presidential-forum-in-texas/.

16 Kolby KickingWoman, "Senators Warren and Klobuchar Join Native American Presidential Forum," *Indian Country Today*, August 5, 2019, https://news
maven.io/indiancountrytoday/news/senators-warren-and-klobuchar-join-native
-american-presidential-forum-0IX3zMW8Ik-hp3G-ciAscQ/.

17 Emily McFarlan Miller, "Warren, Williamson among candidates at historic Native American presidential forum," *Religion News Service*, August 19, 2019,
https://religionnews.com/2019/08/19/warren-williamson-among-candidates
-at-historic-native-american-presidential-forum/.

18 Jack Jenkins, "Truck drives into line of Jewish demonstrators protesting ICE
in Rhode Island," *Religion News Service*, August 15, 2019, https://religion
news.com/2019/08/15/truck-drives-into-line-of-jewish-demonstrators-protesting
-ice-in-rhode-island/.

19 Tara Culp-Ressler, "'God Loves Women Who Have Abortions': The Religious
Abortion Advocates That History Forgot," *ThinkProgress*, December 16, 2014,
https://thinkprogress.org/god-loves-women-who-have-abortions-the-religious
-abortion-advocates-that-history-forgot-8e28030230f1/.

20 Brian Lyman, "At rally against abortion ban, Barber denounces 'immoral hypocrisy,'" *Montgomery Advertiser*, May 28, 2019, https://www.montgomery
advertiser.com/story/news/2019/05/28/rally-against-abortion-ban-barber
-denounces-immoral-hypocrisy/1257820001/.

21 Emily McFarlan Miller, "Independent report finds allegations against Willow
Creek founder Bill Hybels credible," *Religion News Service*, February 28, 2019,
https://religionnews.com/2019/02/28/independent-report-finds-allegations
-against-willow-creek-founder-bill-hybels-credible/.

22 Robert Downen, Lise Olsen, John Tedesco, and Jon Shapley, "Abuse of Faith,"
Houston Chronicle, February 10, 2019, https://www.houstonchronicle.com
/news/investigations/article/Southern-Baptist-sexual-abuse-spreads-as-leaders
-13588038.php.

23 Rick Rojas, "Pastor's Exit Exposes Cultural Rifts at a Leading Liberal Church,"

New York Times, July 11, 2019, https://www.nytimes.com/2019/07/11/ny region/riverside-church-nyc-sexual-harassment.html.

24 Ruth Graham, "Why Did a Progressive Pastor at an Important New York Church Get Fired?," *Slate*, July 12, 2019, https://slate.com/human-interest /2019/07/amy-butler-firing-riverside-church-harassment.html.

25 The website of Faithful Internet, at https://faithfulinternet.org/.

26 Mark Oppenheimer, "Scholars Explore Christian Perspectives on Animal Rights," *New York Times*, December 6, 2013, https://www.nytimes.com/2013 /12/07/us/exploring-christian-perspectives-on-animal-rights.html.

27 Sarah Pulliam Bailey, "Princeton Seminary students are asking for repara-tions for school's role in slavery," *Washington Post*, March 22, 2019, https:// www.washingtonpost.com/religion/2019/03/22/princeton-seminary-students -are-asking-reparations-schools-role-slavery/.

28 Jack Jenkins, "Episcopal Bishops March On Washington to Demand an End to Gun Violence," *ThinkProgress*, March 26, 2013, https://thinkprogress.org /episcopal-bishops-march-on-washington-to-demand-an-end-to-gun-violence -3ea654d01bb5/.

29 Jack Jenkins, "Urged by their youth, faith groups flocked to the March for Our Lives," *Religion News Service*, March 24, 2018, https://religionnews .com/2018/03/24/urged-by-their-youth-faith-groups-flock-to-the-march-for -our-lives/.

30 "FCNL Joins Faiths United To Prevent Gun Violence in Supporting H.R. 8," Friends Committee on National Legislation, March 14, 2019, https://www .fcnl.org/updates/fcnl-joins-faiths-united-to-prevent-gun-violence-in-supporting -h-r-8-2011.

31 Adeel Hassan, "'Thoughts and Prayers' Aren't Enough, America's First Gun Violence Minister Says," *New York Times*, July 28, 2019, https://www.nytimes .com/2019/07/28/us/minister-gun-violence-church.html.

32 Shane Claiborne, Twitter, July 15, 2019, 11:52 p.m., https://twitter.com/Shane Claiborne/status/1150976449794519041.

33 Melvin Graham (member, Emanuel AME Church), telephone interview by the author, October 7, 2019.